Buddhist Women Across Cultures

Bibliotheca Indo-Buddhica Series No.203

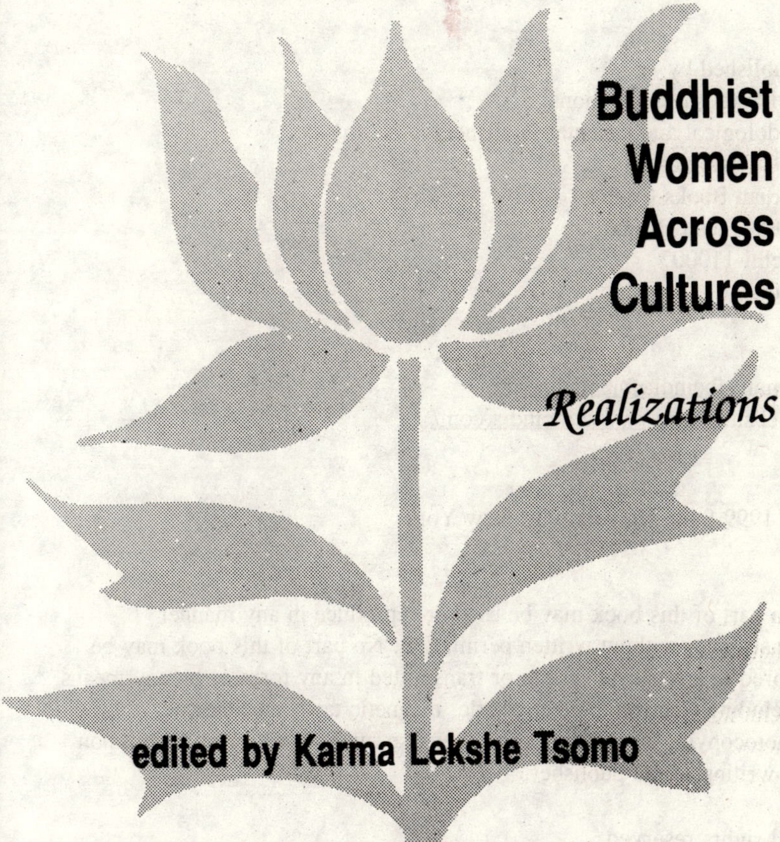

Buddhist Women Across Cultures

Realizations

edited by Karma Lekshe Tsomo

Sri Satguru Publications
A Division of
Indian Books Centre
Delhi, India

Published by
Sri Satguru Publications,
Indological and Oriental Publishers
A Division of
Indian Books Centre
40/5, Shakti Nagar,
Delhi-110007
India

Email: ibcindia@ibcindia.com
Website: http://www.ibcindia.com/

First Indian Edition; Delhi, 2000

ISBN 81-7030-660-4

The publication of this book in India is made by permission of State University of New York Press

Published by Sunil Gupta for Sri Satguru Publications, a division of Indian Books Centre, 40/5, Shakti Nagar, Delhi-110007, India and printed at Chawla Offset Press, Delhi 110 052

Contents

Part II: Contemporary Buddhist Women

Forging Identity

Shaping New Traditions: Unity and Diversity

Preface

The creation of this book has spanned many years and represents the dedication of hundreds of women, and men, from many cultures. The initial impetus grew from a dream spun by Ayya Khema, Chatsumarn Kabilsingh, and myself, in 1986. Over the years the dream has become tangible through the efforts of the women who worked to inspire and organize the Sakyadhita conferences throughout Asia, particularly Bhikṣuṇī Ayya Khema; Chatsumarn Kabilsingh of Sakyadhita Thailand; Ranjani de Silva and Bhikṣuṇī Kusuma Devendra of Sakyadhita Sri Lanka; Wendy Barzetovic of Sakyadhita U.K.; Rani Sarla Chhewang, Eshey Angmo, and Tashi Yangskit of Sakyadhita Ladakh; and Ok-sun An, Margaret Coberly, Karla Kral, and Bhikṣuṇī Tian Chang (Meihuang Lee) of Sakyadhita Hawai'i.

For their valuable editorial suggestions while compiling this diverse collection of ideas, I am deeply grateful to Donna Marie Anderson, Nancy Branch, Margaret Coberly, Donnë Florence, Ephrosine Danggelis, Rebecca French (for literally cutting and pasting my introduction onto twenty-six sheets of paper on the floor), Ramdas Lamb (my computer guru, for tirelessly illuminating the mysteries of technology), my daughter, Emily Mariko, Patricia Masters, Śrāmaṇerikā Nyuyet Thanh Minh (Lorena Cassady), Nikko Odiseos, Sharon Rowe, Śrāmaṇerikā Damcho Thinley (Jackie Minari, for also cheerfully retyping the Sakyadhita mailing list in Bodhgaya), and Alison Williams. For administrative assistance far beyond the call of duty, I sincerely thank Betty Chinn, Sandy Ozaki, June Sakaba, Hanna Santos, and Anna Tanaka of the East-West Center in Honolulu. For their research on Vinaya and the vital issue of full ordination for Buddhist women, I appreciate the pioneering scholarship of Kusuma Devendra, Friedgard Lotermoser, Geshe Thubten Ngawang, and Bhikṣuṇī Jampa Tsedroen. For being crucial catalysts for ideas and inspiration, I am indebted to many spiritual sisters, including Bhīkṣuṇī Thubten Chodron, Sierra Crawford, Bhikṣuṇī Sungak, Emila Heller, Gabriele Küstermann, Bhikṣuṇī Tenzin Palmo, and Yvonne Vaucher, without whose kindhearted support and encouragement, I would have been tempted to go meditate in a cave.

An earlier edition of Elizabeth Harris' article appeared in Aloysius Pieris, S.J., "Special Issue on Woman and Man in Buddhism and Christianity," *Dialogue new series*, 19–20 (Colombo: The Ecumenical Institute for Study and Dialogue, 1992–93). I gratefully acknowledge the Institute's kind cooperation.

KARMA LEKSHE TSOMO

Karma Lekshe Tsomo

Mahāprajāpatī's Legacy: The Buddhist Women's Movement

An Introduction

Buddhist women first began networking globally in 1987, providing a forum for the special meeting of Buddhist and feminist ideas. In that year, along with Ven. Ayya Khema, Dr. Chatsumarn Kabilsingh, and others, I organized the first International Conference on Buddhist Nuns in Bodhgaya, India, the first Buddhist conference ever to address the problems faced by Buddhist women.[1] The inaugural address by H. H. Dalai Lama, which emphasized the equal spiritual potential of women and men, was attended by over fifteen hundred people. Women from twenty-seven countries—and also a few monks and laymen—gathered to discuss the potentialities and actual conditions of women in Buddhist countries. For one week, issues such as education for Buddhist women, the role of Buddhist women in social welfare, living by the Vinaya (monastic codes) in the present day, creating opportunities for full ordination for women, livelihood for Saṅgha (the monastic community), and living as a nun in the West were discussed. Participants sought to understand not only how Buddhist societies have traditionally viewed women and how Buddhist women view themselves, but also what role women have traditionally played in the secular and religious life of Buddhist societies, and how that role might be expanded or changed. The articles presented here, first enthusiastically shared in oral form at these conferences, grew out of the research and experiences of women who are both scholars and practitioners of Buddhism. The book's methodology is to document Buddhist women's actual involvement, including their self-reflection, interactions, and interpretations of the tradition. The book is therefore itself part of the ongoing process of women transforming, and being transformed by, the tradition.

At the conclusion of this gathering, an International Association of Buddhist Women called Sakyadhita, "Daughters of the Buddha," was established. Sakyadhita's focus is fourfold: (1) to create a network of communications among the Buddhist women of the world, (2) to educate women as teachers of Buddhism, (3) to conduct research on women in Buddhism, and (4) to work for the establishment of the Bhikṣuṇī Sangha (order of fully ordained nuns) where it does not currently exist. In November 1991, Dr. Chatsumarn Kabilsingh, Professor of Philosophy at Thammasat University, organized the second International Conference on Buddhist Women in Bangkok. Since the Bhikṣuṇī Saṅgha does not exist in Southeast Asia, and there is considerable opposition to its establishment, locating this conference on Buddhist women in Thailand was a significant indication that changes are afoot. The presence of highly educated and respected *bhikṣuṇīs* from Taiwan, Korea, Vietnam, and the West eroded the common Thai misconception that "There are no *bhikṣuṇīs*." By bringing into the open the subordinate status of women in Buddhism and particularly the ambiguous status of nuns in Thailand, the conference stimulated efforts to improve religious education and to develop meditation-training centers for women.

In 1993, a third Sakyadhita conference, on the theme "Buddhist Women in Modern Society," was held in Colombo. Although the Ministry for Buddhist Affairs had warned the organizers against discussing the issue of *bhikṣuṇī* ordination, the topic could not be suppressed. A significant number of Sri Lankan women are determined to reestablish the Bhikṣuṇī Saṅgha in Sri Lanka, not only to recover a lost part of their Buddhist heritage but also to affirm their personal heritage as women. Ayya Khema, an internationally recognized meditation teacher of German Jewish descent, was a significant force in encouraging Buddhist women's practice in Sri Lanka and founded Parapaduwa Nuns' Island in Dodanaduwa. Although she was unable to attend the Conference in Colombo, her presence was strongly felt as the English-educated Sri Lankan elite and their humble forest-dwelling renunciant sisters began forging alliances to work toward reinstituting the Bhikṣuṇī Saṅgha in their country. Many Sri Lankans view the eventual reestablishment of an order of fully ordained nuns as inevitable and have begun eliciting support from young, educated Sri Lankan *bhikṣus* to make it happen.

The fourth international conference, "Women and the Power of Compassion: Survival in the 21st Century," took place in Ladakh, northern India, in August 1995. Over 108 delegates from abroad formed bonds of solidarity with hundreds of Buddhist women from Ladakh, Tibet, Bhutan, Nepal, and other Himalayan areas, women who have otherwise had little contact with contemporary women's movements. Despite their disparate lifestyles, these women found their practical needs and spiritual aspirations to be remarkably in tune. Global networking of people who are actively concerned about the role of women in both the past and future of Buddhism is ending centuries of Buddhist women's isolation. By uniting and offering mutual support, Buddhist women have begun taking leadership roles in new fields: health, education, communications, ecology, and cultural preservation. Inspired by these exchanges, Buddhist women have initiated projects to research their own social and religious history and to publish biographies of eminent Buddhist women.

Each Sakyadhita conference has been a landmark in galvanizing the energies of the world's Buddhist women. Each gathering is truly international in character, highlighting a wide range of Buddhist cultural expressions, but each also has the distinctive flavor of the host country, whose women usually benefit the most. Lay and ordained, young and old, women and men, dressed in saffron, maroon, pink, brown, white, gray, black, and flowered prints, all mingle, meditate, chant, chat, envision their future, and enjoy the moment in harmony and friendship. Without windy speeches or fatuous pomp and ceremony, they cut directly to their core concerns, integrating academic research, spiritual practice, and social action without hesitation or disjunction. Working on the principle that Asian and Western women have much to learn from one another, Sakyadhita promotes unity among diverse schools of Buddhist thought and practice.

The fifth Sakyadhita conference in Cambodia at the end of 1997 took the discussion in new directions, using diversity—of views, practices, lifestyles, and experiences—as a theme. More than 150 people from twenty-four countries gathered at Wat Onnalom, Cambodia's most sacred temple in Phnom Penh, a temple that is normally reserved for the bi-monthly *upoṣadha* ritual of Cambodia's leading monks. Discussions covered a wide range of topics: rediscovering Cambodian Buddhist women's past, Buddhism and human rights, Buddhist laywomen in the New World, women and celibacy, inaccuracies in Buddhist women's history, Buddhist women and the media, women's role in creating a culture of nonviolence, growing up as a Buddhist woman, nunneries in contemporary China, engaged Buddhism, the revival of the Bhikṣuṇī Saṅgha in Sri Lanka, sexual conduct and misconduct, and inner transformation for world peace. Incorporating panel discussions, meditations, group discussions, videos, stories, and movement, the conference was a lively and creative forum for diverse views, spiritual practices, and approaches to social action.

In June, 1997, a North American Conference on Buddhist Women in Claremont, California, was sponsored jointly by Sakyadhita and the Claremont Colleges. The aim was to bring together scholars and practitioners in North America to encourage dialogue on issues of social, cultural, and personal concern to Buddhist women. Meditation was a primary focus, with opportunities to learn from Buddhist women teachers from three different traditions each day. In the process of discussions, it became clear that the issues for Buddhist women in North America are quite different than in Asia. In North America, the prominent issues seem to be sexualities, environment, race, sexual exploitation, and social engagement, whether through the performing arts, writing, or direct action. In Asia, by contrast, the major issues are survival, education, training, and ordination. It emerged that the task of creating bridges of understanding—among Buddhists and non-Buddhists of many races, cultures, and sexualities, women and men, advantaged and disadvantaged—is just beginning. By foregrounding rather than stashing issues that many find uncomfortable, and exploring methodologies for processing those issues both individually and in groups, the gathering proved that Buddhist women and their friends are willing to take practical and constructive steps toward social reconciliation.

The dialogue is continuing and the circle is growing. The sixth Sakyadhita conference in Lumbini, Nepal, in 2000 will move discussions ahead in important directions. One direction is pushing forward the frontiers of research on Buddhist women—compiling individual and collective histories, and encouraging cooperative research projects. Another direction is direct, compassionate social action at the grassroots level that will implement changes for women in specific constructive and culturally appropriate ways, particularly education and training in leadership, meditation, languages, counselling, and human rights. As the circle grows and the vision expands, it is obvious that institutional structures and economic resources need to expand, not as ends in themselves, but as a means to make it all possible. In this, Sakyadhita is playing a crucial role in bringing together people and ideas to accomplish goals, both spiritual and mundane. The colorful Sakyadhita gatherings of cultures and traditions have accented women's innovative role in revitalizing and reenvisioning Buddhism toward the goal of personal and global transformation.

Buddhist Women Face Their History

Several centuries before the Christian era began, an aristocratic woman by the name of Mahāprajāpatī began a spiritual and social revolution in northern India. After trudging several hundred miles barefoot across the dusty plains to make her point, she lobbied Śākyamuni Buddha, who was both her nephew and stepson, for an order of women renunciants.[2] Due to her courageous agitation for equal opportunity, the Buddha affirmed the equal potential of women to achieve spiritual enlightenment and recognized their right to wear the robes of a Buddhist mendicant. The Buddha was unable to ensure the total reformation of patriarchal Indian society, however. After the Buddha's death, earlier modes of gender relations gradually reasserted themselves. The positive attitude toward women evident among the early Buddhists seems to have declined sharply around the time written Buddhist literature began to appear. These texts contain contradictory statements on women, who are portrayed as capable of enlightenment on par with men and also as sirens luring men from the spiritual path. These ambivalent attitudes toward women persist today in the minds and institutions of Buddhist Asia.

As we read through studies on the interrelationship between Buddhism and political power in Asia over the past two and a half millennia, we are struck by the conspicuous lack of information on women. We encounter a few scattered references to prostitutes or beggars in the garb of nuns, yet women are rarely mentioned as playing a role in either religion or politics, two of society's most important spheres of activity. Ample attention is given to the monks' order, the Bhikṣu Saṅgha, and its role in religion and politics. Clearly this sector of society is a force to be reckoned with in any analysis of the region. Throughout history, the support of the Saṅgha has been actively sought as a means of legitimation by those wishing to gain and maintain positions of political power in Buddhist countries.[3] When we look closely, however, we find that in certain Buddhist countries—Burma, Cambodia, Laos, Sri Lanka, and Thailand—women are categorically denied admission to the Saṅgha, Buddhism's most fundamental institution.

However egalitarian the Buddha's original teachings may have been, today preconceptions about the inferiority of women prevail in Buddhist cultures. Although these attitudes may trace to patriarchal social mores with no verifiable connection to Buddhist tenets, women have consistently been excluded from religious structures. They certainly are not barred from commerce or agriculture—where there is profit to be gained from her endeavors, a woman is given free rein. In many cultures, she is in control of affairs within the family, such as the keys, the finances, the children, and decisions of major importance. In the realm of the unseen or transcendent, however, she is thwarted, as if the spiritual potential within and among women posed a threat greater than financial control. This suggests that the issue of gender in religion is an issue of power politics at a very fundamental level.

The history of women in Buddhism dates to even before the Buddha's enlightenment.[4] After realizing that physical austerities do not lead to liberation, Siddhartha Gautama is said to have accepted an offering of rice pudding from a village woman named Sujātā and regained strength to become enlightened. Thus, since the very earliest days, women have been credited as nurturers and supporters of the tradition, symbolized by Sujātā reviving Siddhartha's physical strength at a juncture critical to his ultimate achievement. Although his cohorts mocked him for this perceived weakness, the Buddha continued to instruct and counsel women throughout his fifty-year-long teaching career. With Siddhartha's stepmother Mahāprajāpatī in the vanguard, women began to create their own communities and the order of women renunciants, the Bhikṣuṇī Saṅgha, has continued to thrive up to the present day. Women throughout India and later abroad became renowned for their spiritual achievements—the depth of their realizations, their talent as teachers, and their miraculous powers. This spiritual legacy has inspired women for centuries.

The Buddha allegedly hesitated to admit women to the Saṅgha, and several theories have been put forward to explain why. First, it is obvious that close proximity between an order of celibate women and an order of celibate men could lead to sexual temptations. There are statements attributed to the Buddha warning monks to be wary of contact with women as a distraction from spiritual pursuits. There are no records to prove it, but the Buddha may have similarly warned nuns against close contact with men. Human beings do not necessarily eradicate desire by living a celibate lifestyle; close relations between ordained men and women can easily lead to infatuations and eventually to disrobing. A second theory about the Buddha's hesitation to admit women to the Saṅgha attributes it to the Indian cultural context. In ancient Indian society, women's ideal role was in the family. Allowing a woman to leave her family and roam about unprotected was considered both dangerous for women and a threat to family life, the bedrock of society.

A third theory about the Buddha's hesitation to admit women to the Saṅgha concerns the organizational difficulties that might arise in monastic institutions that include members of both genders. The *bhikṣus* and *bhikṣuṇīs* had to develop systems for effectively organizing practical matters, such as housing, seating, ritual activities, and communications. The systems that evolved are evident in the regulatory monastic codes of the two orders. With parallel orders of women and men, the Saṅgha could potentially double in size. The difficulty of ensuring the smooth functioning of such a large monastic institution may have been another consideration in the Buddha's hesitation.

A fourth theory, which is whispered but rarely articulated, claims that monks saw nuns as unwanted competition, both for limited material resources and for spiritual achievement. The two are interrelated, since spiritual prowess attracts donations from the laity. If nuns were perceived as competition and a threat to the material welfare of the monks, and it was monks who transcribed the scriptures, this could explain certain misogynist statements that appear in the texts, including certain discriminatory statements attributed to the Buddha.

In some cases, negative stereotypes of women prevalent in Buddhist societies actually derive from Brahmanical, Confucian, or other sources, yet some are also found in both Theravāda and Mahāyāna texts. Whether these passages are the authentic words of the Buddha and his disciples or not, they are often used to legitimize negative typecasting of women. Interpretations of these passages vary, but they are difficult to justify or ignore. To repudiate the canonical texts altogether is problematic for Buddhists. Not only is it an affront to the sensibilities of orthodox adherents, but it also calls into question the validity of the texts as a whole. Even a revisionist view ruffles feathers among the orthodox, yet a reevaluation of the texts is essential if women in Buddhism are to meaningfully apply and actualize the teachings the texts contain.

In the earliest stratum of *sūtras,* the Buddha affirms women's capacity to achieve liberation and, from among the thousands of women who achieved *nirvāṇa* at that time, names many individually for their exceptional qualities. The Mahāyāna *sūtras,* which appeared several hundred years later, symbolize wisdom as female and inclusively address the "sons and daughters of good family." Along with accounts of the virtuous lives and spiritual achievements of women, however, we encounter repeated warnings against the temptations of women and a prophecy (as yet unfulfilled) warning that women's admission to the order would shorten the life of the Dharma.[5] The images of women are thus equivocal and often confusing.[6] An extreme example occurs in the *Upāyakauśalya Sūtra,* where the girl Dakṣiṇottarā sets herself on fire out of frustrated desire for the bodhisattva Priyaṃkara and achieves the fortunate result of birth as a male in paradise surrounded by fourteen thousand celestial females.[7] Even though the girl compounds lust with a horrifying suicide, her meritorious act of generosity to a (male) bodhisattva results in a heavenly (male) rebirth. Another perplexing example is the *Tathāgataguhya Sūtra,* where innumerable beings are cured of all diseases and afflictions by consummating union with the bodhisattva Vaidyarāja manifesting the form of a girl.[8] In the early Mahāyāna *sūtras,* a woman transforms herself into a male body upon enlightenment; in others, she achieves enlightenment in a female body. All these conflicting images make the study of women in Buddhism complex and intriguing; there are problems both in authenticating allusions to women in the texts and in discounting the texts altogether.

Throughout most of Buddhist history, the socially approved roles available to women were those of wife and mother. In these roles, laywomen accumulated merit by tending to the family shrine, making offerings to the Saṅgha, giving charity to the needy, transmitting the Buddhist teachings to children, keeping precepts, promoting ethical principles in the household, chanting the *sūtras*, and meditating. The most famous laywoman in the Buddha's day was Visākhā, who regularly fed two thousand monks at her home and was often called upon to mediate disputes.[9] The spiritual achievements of laywomen are described in a number of texts, such as the *Saddharma Ratnāvaliya*, where Subhadra and her younger sister achieve the state of a Stream-enterer (*sotāpanna*) and Sumanā attains the stage of a Once-Returner (*sakadāgāmī*).[10] Laywomen are portrayed as having more flexibility in Buddhist societies than previously; women had the right to divorce, remarry, inherit, and the freedom to practice religion without depending on men. Women gain inspiration from the Buddhist teachings on loving kindness and compassion, which use as their primary example the tremendous kindness and compassion that mothers have for their children. The central role of the mother in ensuring the happiness and harmony of the family is a common theme.

To exploit physical beauty and lead the life of a courtesan was one alternative lifestyle for women, and to renounce physical beauty and lead the life of a nun was another. For a woman, to renounce the pleasures of worldly life and become a nun represented the most radical departure from social expectations. In the *Therīgāthā*, we have the stories of dozens of women who achieved the final stage of liberation and became *arhats*. A number of these women, such as Kisāgotamī[11] and Vāsiṭṭī,[12] turned to intensive spiritual practice due to intense grief at the loss of a child. The story of Paṭācārā,[13] who became deranged after her husband died of snake bite and her two children were carried off by wild animals, is particularly poignant. After recovering her sanity, she became an *arhat* and, by explaining the sufferings of birth and death, became a source of consolation and inspiration to other women. Bhaddā Kuṇḍalakesā rejected lay life after being duped and almost killed by a lover she saved from execution, then went on to become the *bhikṣuṇī* most skilled in philosophical debate. The decision to shave the head and don shapeless robes powerfully symbolized a rejection of the expected reproductive and familial roles, and asserted a new, independent identity as a full-time religious practitioner.

Religious leadership in Buddhist countries is traditionally in the hands of fully ordained monks (Sanskrit: *bhikṣu*, Pāli: *bhikkhu*).[14] The monks are revered as the ideal model for human development and are financially supported by devout members of the lay community, primarily women. Around the eleventh century, the Bhikṣuṇī Saṅgha died out in India and Sri Lanka,[15] and as far as is known, was never officially established in Cambodia, Japan, Laos, Mongolia, Thailand, or Tibet. In the fifth century C.E., the lineage of fully ordained nuns was transmitted from Sri Lanka to China[16] and subsequently to Korea and Vietnam. The lineage of full ordination for women has flourished in these countries uninterruptedly to the present day.

The status of nuns within the Buddhist traditions seems to correlate with ordination status. Coincidentally or not, where full ordination as a *bhikṣuṇī* is available, the nuns' level of education and status within the society also tend to be high. Where novice ordination as a *śrāmaṇerikā* is available to nuns, women are recognized as members of the Saṅgha (the monastic order), even though they are not afforded equal treatment. Without access to full ordination or even novice ordination, women in such Theravādin countries as Burma, Cambodia, Laos, Sri Lanka, and Thailand are in a secondary and often subservient role, relative to the monks, in the religious sphere. The subordinate position of women in Buddhism does not derive solely from the lack of higher ordination, however, for even those women who have access to some level of ordination are sometimes marginalized and their needs ignored. For example, although women in the Chinese, Korean, and Vietnamese traditions enjoy parity in being fully ordained, they hold a clearly subordinate position in the religious power structures of their traditions. Certain wealthy women have exerted influence from behind the scenes, but most women over the centuries have typically lacked both a voice and power in Buddhist institutions. Today they are gaining courage and beginning to speak out. The following sections provide a brief glance at the current conditions of Buddhist women in Asian and Western cultures.

Meditation Allowed: Buddhist Women of Burma (Myanmar)

In the Theravāda countries of South and Southeast Asia at present, conditions for religious practice among Burmese women are relatively favorable. Educational standards have improved considerably since Marie Byles, a barrister resident in Burma in 1962, observed: "The village boys still go to the monastery schools and learn to read and write. The girls have no school and do not learn to read and write."[17]

Yet even today, there is evidence of gender discrimination, particularly in the sphere of religion. Rites of passage clearly indicate the different expectations of the sexes: at the same age that little boys become novice monks, little girls have their ears pierced. Although women retain their own names after marriage, supervise their husbands' earnings, and excel in business management, often heading large trading enterprises, a pollution stigma still attaches to them. Menstrual taboos underlie prohibitions that prevent women from entering many Buddhist shrines in Burma.[18] The desire to be reborn as a man is pervasive among women.[19]

Men are reluctant to seek women as teachers and most monks strongly oppose any change in the system of nuns' ordination. There is evidence that women has opportunities to become fully ordained *bhikṣuṇīs* in the Pyu kingdom in southern Burma in the eleventh century,[20] but today nuns who take ten precepts are not accorded recognition as *śrāmaṇerikās* (novices); instead they are known as *tila shin* (possessors of morality).[21] As in Sri Lanka and Thailand, the estimated sixty thousand nuns in Burma are not considered full-fledged members of the monastic community.

Burmese women have access to meditation facilities and Buddhist education, and most are content with their lot, but they are barred from the Saṅgha, considered the highest calling in Buddhist societies, and do not enjoy equal status or opportunities. As an educated (male) merchant informed an Australian (female) attorney during her stay in Burma in 1962, it is common to hear discriminatory statements such as "Of course men are superior to women because only men can don the yellow robe, and that is the most superior of all![22] The yellow robe, thought to be imbued with power and protective magic,[23] is revered as a symbol of moral purity and is worn only by the Bhikṣu Saṅgha. In contradistinction to the monks, nuns wear pale pink garments,[24] including a blouse with an uncomfortably high neck and tight sleeves. Whereas a deceased monk will be embalmed and left undisturbed for several days, a nun must be buried the same day of her death.[25] Even in death, there is discrimination.

From one point of view, the eight- and ten-precept nuns of the Theravāda tradition enjoy greater freedom than monks, since they are not formally constrained by as many Prātimokṣa[26] precepts as monks. Although the full ordination (*upasampadā*) and precepts of a *bhikṣuṇī* are not currently available to them, these nuns generally follow the discipline of a fully ordained nun strictly anyway. One visible difference is that nuns must prepare their own food, since by custom they are offered only uncooked rice and foodstuffs. Those who do not receive support from family members must go to neighboring villages for alms twice a week or travel long distance twice a year to their home villages to collect donations of rice, which they carry in huge bundles on their heads. Most telling of all, when monetary donations are distributed, nuns generally receive only a fraction of what the monks are offered: "Ten kyats are given to a monk when only one will be given to a nun. It is our Burmese custom."[27] Since it is supposed that not much merit derives from offering to nuns, there is a noticeable difference in their standards of living.[28] Although the nuns do not seem to resent it, their humble dwellings stand in marked contrast to the monks' palatial quarters. In religious terms, the humility of Burmese women is a virtue, yet in political terms, it keeps them consigned to a second-rate religious status.

The Ordination Crisis: Buddhist Women in Sri Lanka

From the eleventh century, when the bhikṣuṇī order died out in Sri Lanka, until a young Sinhalese woman named Catherine de Alvis returned from a trip to Burma in 1905, there were few opportunities for Singhalese women to live a celibate religious life.[29] For nearly nine hundred years, monastic life had been the purview of *bhikṣus* alone; the only women in robes were reportedly some ragged old beggars in white. Even after Catherine returned as Sister Sudharmācari and established Lady Blake's Ārāma in 1907, it took many years before the idea of women as renunciants became acceptable; in fact, the struggle for equal recognition continues to this day.

Many of the wealthy urban women who have supported the nuns (called *dasasilmātās*, or "ten-precept mothers")[30] in recent times have envisioned a social service role for them. But the majority of the *dasasilmātās* themselves, typically from poor rural backgrounds, are interested only in spiritual pursuits and have thwarted attempts to shunt them into activities such as hospital work and handicrafts. They feel that their objective is Dharma practice, not spinning and weaving, and if they had wanted to do hospital work, they need not have become nuns. With the advent of more frequent, open communications, their supporters are coming to more fully appreciate the sincere religious orientation of the nuns, and the nuns are coming to more fully appreciate the value of social service activities.

Another shift in perspectives is occurring among the nuns themselves. As the laity begin to develop greater respect for the religious practice of almswomen, the nuns are beginning to develop greater respect for themselves and each other. Fortuitously, an upsurge of interest in meditation practice, particularly the technique imported from Burma known as *vipassana*, has resulted in the construction all over Sri Lanka of new meditation centers that are enthusiastically patronized by women. This phenomenon has resulted in strong bonds between serious meditators, both lay and ordained. The spiritual communication and mutual encouragement that take place at these centers are advantageous to both groups—an overall positive development for women. It is widely believed that eventually, from among these meditators, more highly educated women will begin to take robes, which will lead to a revival of the *bhikṣuṇī* order, despite the widespread opposition of conservative monks.

The controversy over full ordination for women in Sri Lanka is heated. There is increasingly strong support for the idea, particularly among the English-educated elite, and there is equally strong opposition among conservative monks. The conservatives include some of the highest ecclesiastical officials in the land, such as Madihee Paññasīha Mahāthero, head of Amarapura Nikāya, one of the three major monastic orders in Sri Lanka. Instead of lending support to the first international Buddhist women's gathering ever held in Sri Lanka, he asked the conveners of the third Sakyadhita conference in Colombo to pledge in writing that the *bhikṣuṇī* issue would not be discussed at the conference. Progressives and conservatives spar vociferously over the issue and controversy flares recurrently in the press.

Ironically, those least affected by this media controversy are the nuns it most concerns. In predominantly Buddhist Sri Lanka, many of the nuns are poor, untrained, uneducated, and neglected, living with a companion or two in tiny rooms without adequate sanitation. For most of them, there are more pressing matters to attend to than demands for higher ordination. Disempowered as they are, their primary energies are directed toward spiritual practices designed to liberate them from the cycle of rebirth. Even some of the most respected female meditation masters, such as Sudharma Māniyo, disavow interest in receiving higher ordination, possibly for fear of alienating conservatives among the monks. They tend to accept the opinion of conservative monks that the Bhikṣuṇī Saṅgha cannot be revived until the coming of Maitreya Buddha thousands of years hence and that the ordinations received by nuns in Mahāyāna countries are not authentic from a Theravāda point of view, despite the fact that the *bhikṣuṇī* lineage in China traces its roots to Sri Lanka.

Nevertheless, a delegation of ten Sri Lankan nuns traveled to the United States in 1988 to receive *bhikṣuṇī* ordination in the Chinese tradition at Hsi Lai Temple, a mammoth Taiwan-funded monastery in Hacienda Heights, California. Unable to adjust to the climate and the rigorous discipline, five of the group left without receiving the precepts and the remaining five who received the full ordination have kept a low profile since returning to Sri Lanka. In December 1996, another delegation of ten nuns traveled to Sarnath, India, site of the first ordination of monks during the Buddha's time, to receive a *bhikṣuṇī* ordination in the Korean tradition organized by monks associated with the Mahabodhi Society in India. Kusuma Devendra, a well-known Pāli scholar, teacher of Buddhism, and one of the founders of Sakyadhita, took the lead in what is considered a daring step. The ordination of such a highly educated and widely respected woman as a *bhikṣuṇī* in the face of widespread opposition is important in gaining support for the restoration of the *Bhikṣuṇī Saṅgha.* The Sarnath *bhikṣuṇī* ordination has been denounced by many leading monks in Sri Lanka and the ten newly ordained *bhikṣuṇīs* plan to stay in India for three years until the controversy, hopefully, cools down.

Meanwhile another event transpired that took the *bhikṣuṇī* movement further than anyone dared imagine during the first Sakyadhita conference just eleven years before. This was an International Full Ordination Ceremony held in Bodhgaya in February, 1998, sponsored and organized by Fo Kuang Shan, Taiwan's largest monastery. At this weeklong ceremony 132 nuns were fully ordained as *bhikṣuṇīs,* including fifty nuns from the Theravāda tradition. Among them were twenty candidates from Sri Lanka who had been carefully selected by a group of prominent Sri Lankan monks at the request of *bhikṣuṇīs* from Fo Kuang Shan. Prior to receiving *bhikṣuṇī* ordination, the candidates, most of them well-educated heads of temples, had received the *śrāmaṇerikā* precepts from *bhikṣus* in Sri Lanka, a pioneering step in itself, and special training in preparation for the rigorous discipline to be expected at the ceremony. Because a few vocal opponents to the full ordination of women remain, the new *bhikṣuṇīs* felt somewhat apprehensive about their future. But when they returned to Sri Lanka, they were greeted by joyful crowds of supporters and led from the airport in procession. Not only did this historical event evoke the image of Sanghamitra arriving from India to transmit the *bhikṣuṇī* lineage to Sri Lanka in the third century B.C.E., it represented a triumphant culmination of efforts to restore the lineage from China. Sri Lanka *bhikṣus* lost no time in taking matters one step further. On March 12, 1998, along with the Sri Lankan *bhikṣuṇīs* just ordained in Bodhgaya, they conferred the higher ordination on twenty-two nuns at Dambulla. After a lapse of some nine centuries, the Bhikṣuṇī Saṅgha had returned to Sri Lankan soil.

Seen but Not Heard: Buddhist Women of Thailand

Women have been an important force in the recent economic development of Thailand. They make up approximately one half of the total workforce, participating in agriculture, commerce, manufacturing, education, and health services. Their participation cannot be said to be on an equal footing with men, however, since they have few opportunities for government or management positions. Women's largest roles are in agricultural production, fishing, petty trade, domestic labor, food services, and manufacturing—all lower-paid jobs, if they are paid at all. The most respected profession, the Saṅgha, is off-limits. When a woman does elect a religious vocation, she usually observes five or eight precepts and becomes a *maeji* ("mother ascetic").[31] The estimated ten thousand *maejis* in Thailand currently wear the white robes of a layperson, receive little support, and enjoy little prestige.[32] Among the several alternative movements of nuns that exist are the *sikkhamats* of Santi Asoke, who are vegetarian and strictly observe the ten precepts under the guidance of Bodhirak.[33]

One of the most common reasons a Thai woman becomes a nun is to fulfill a vow. She vows to become a nun for some specified period of time if her wish, such as recovery from an illness or respite from some personal difficulty, is fulfilled.[34] Many of these women do not stay in robes for long, nor do they necessarily exhibit a strong interest in Dharma practice. This is not surprising; since opportunities for women to study Buddhism are limited and the status of nuns is low, the vocation generally does not attract Thailand's most talented, educated women. Furthermore, there is little or no material support for women in robes, so once their savings are exhausted, nuns often have no choice but to revert to lay life.

Lest we imagine that women enjoy great opportunities in the worldly sphere, however, we are reminded that between seven hundred thousand and one million women support themselves as prostitutes in Thailand, more than double the number of monks.[35] This would indicate a certain lack of other lucrative career opportunities for women. Frustrated in their attempts at worldly success as well as their spiritual aspirations, women until now have had few viable alternatives. A woman's best hope and highest meaning is thought to be bearing children and enhancing the family income through productive activities. Her most acceptable religious role is one of nurturing: conscientiously supporting the male Saṅgha and mothering a son who will become a monk. Despite their best efforts, women continue to be excluded from positions of power both in worldly life and in religious life.

Lands in Turmoil: Buddhist Women of Cambodia, Laos, and Vietnam

Buddhism in Cambodia, Laos, and Vietnam has been seriously threatened and very nearly obliterated by war and political unrest in recent years. Not only have indigenous Buddhist institutions been severely disrupted, but the survival of Buddhist culture itself has been uncertain. By 1978, sixty-five thousand monks had been killed in Cambodia as the result of war and political purges, and the Buddhist fabric of Cambodian society had been torn asunder. Amidst this ten-year debacle, women struggled against all odds to maintain their families and their mental health. A few hundred nuns escaped or became ordained after migrating to camps on the Thai border, and nunhood became regarded as a sage refuge for older women. Like other refugees, many of these nuns have been traumatized by their wartime experiences.

Most Cambodian nuns hold eight precepts and become nuns after raising families, but as Buddhism revives, some younger women are becoming nuns and receiving ten precepts. Like Thai nuns, Cambodian and Laotian nuns[36] occupy a subordinate, ambiguous status in society. Since domestic violence, suicide, rape, and severe depression are common consequences of war and refugee life, women often turn to these nuns with their problems. Yet the nuns, trained only in the devotional aspects of Buddhism, are ill-equipped to handle psychological disorders, family crisis, and other problems of this dimension. Their religious status is marginal; without full ordination, they are ineligible to engage in many aspects of religious life, yet their shaven heads and robes disengage them from worldly life. Neither Saṅgha nor lay, lacking education and financial support themselves, they have little consolation to offer their sisters.

Buddhism in Vietnam has endured, miraculously, despite the massive destruction of war and the oppression suffered under both Christian and communist governments. Although the early history of the *bhikṣuṇī* order in Vietnam remains shrouded in uncertainty,[37] nuns have worked enthusiastically to promote the Dharma in Vietnam, building temples, teaching, and establishing the *bhikṣuṇī* order. Laboring always under the patriarchal legacy of Confucian social structures and values, women did not gain positions in either the religious or secular spheres, but nevertheless played an important role in inculcating Buddhist values and transmitting devotional practices.

Many Vietnamese women are convinced that it is through the women that Buddhism is transmitted from generation to generation. A Vietnamese refugee, who is now a lay leader of a temple in the United States, told me that everything she knows about Buddhism she learned from her grandmother. Although most Vietnamese women were previously illiterate (in the vernacular, not to mention the classical Chinese of the Buddhist scriptures), they had a good grasp of basic Buddhist principles, and it was they who imparted these principles to the younger generation, especially through the medium of stories. The men of the village, she said, worshipped at the small temple where Confucius and other deities were enshrined, while the women all went to the pagoda, located at the respected "head" direction of the village, to worship the Buddha. When questioned, "Why, then, do men hold the top Buddhist positions?" she responded that it is due to Confucian attitudes toward gender, which dictate a quiet, unobtrusive role for wives and daughters. Women are never to put themselves forward or hold public positions, since it is considered inappropriate behavior for them; instead, they voice their ideas through their husbands. The informant's husband confirmed this, venturing that ninety percent of the real power was in women's hands.

Religion has begun to flourish in Vietnam in the last few years, with women as powerful participants in the process. Of the thousands of nuns that existed prior to 1962, many were killed during the war or disrobed in its aftermath. The decade following the fall of Saigon was one of dislocation and deprivation; the future of Buddhism appeared very uncertain. Recently, however, there has been a resurgence of interest in religious life, with women entering the order in far greater numbers than men. Unlike the precommunist era, nuns and monks now depend primarily on their own agricultural production for a livelihood. With limited time and few opportunities for religious instruction, it is unclear exactly what institutional role nuns will play in future, yet numbers alone indicate that they will be a force in Vietnamese Buddhism that will lead to a change in the status of women within the religious order.

Quiet Voices: Buddhist Women in Japan

Even if they have rarely captured the limelight, Buddhist women have contributed significantly to the history of Japanese Buddhism. According to the Genkoji chronicles, the first persons to become fully ordained in Japan were three nuns named Zenshin, Zenzo, and Kenzen.[38]

They traveled by ship to Korea and received the *bhikṣuṇī* ordination in the kingdom of Paekche in 590 C.E., considerably earlier than the Chinese master Chien-chen (Jpn: Ganjin) who reached Japan in 754 by invitation of the imperial court at Nara to initiate an authentic lineage of ordination for monks. The three nuns failed to establish a Bhikṣuṇī Saṅgha in Japan, however, since five or more *bhikṣuṇīs* are needed to preside over a valid ordination procedure. We have no way of knowing why more nuns did not go to Paekche to receive the ordination or why Korean *bhikṣuṇīs* were not invited to Japan.

It is also unclear whether women after this time received the ten precepts of a novice nun, the bodhisattva precepts, or were self-ordained,[39] but in any case, nuns figure prominently in the early literature of Japan. Their renunciation follows a standard scenario: an abandoned lady at court, realizing the transience of life and the futility of worldly involvements through her disappointment in love, cuts her hair and retires to a secluded hermitage for the rest of her life. Some, as related in the *Genji Monogatari* and other works of the Heian period, managed to exert considerable influence at court despite their seclusion.

Although in Japanese Buddhism the monastic model of practice has largely been superseded by lay models, communities of well-disciplined nuns continue their ancient traditions even today and many are also innovators[40] in their own way. Whereas male religious specialists in Japan typically marry and raise families, passing their temples to a son (or occasionally a daughter), most nuns live a celibate, reclusive, and traditional lifestyle. A few Japanese masters, notably Dogen (1200–1253) and Nichiren (1222–1282), publicly affirmed women's enlightenment potential, but women in Japan have typically assumed a subservient position in the sphere of religion.

No doubt the most well-known nun in Japan today is Setouchi Jakucho, an extremely popular novelist who was ordained on Mt. Tendai after a full and cosmopolitan life. In a private conversation with her in Kyoto in 1990, she related to me that, while women can receive ordination equally with men and be assigned to take charge of temples, they do not receive sufficient support from the laity to adequately maintain the temples and many are therefore forced to abandon the religious life. This lack of support for women results from a belief found lurking in many Buddhist cultures— that women's spiritual practice is somehow less potent or creates less karmic benefit than that of men. Such beliefs permeate the culture, often in subtle ways, and make it difficult for women to improve their status or even survive as female religious specialists. Economic factors and the onslaught of modern materialist values seem to be responsible for a declining number of female religious specialists in Japan.

The largest community of nuns in Japan today is the Aichi Semmon Nisodo, a convent in Nagoya.[41] This convent belongs to the Sōtō Zen school, which is said to have about a thousand nuns altogether, and provides thorough training in meditation and the traditional arts such as tea and flower arrangement (*ikebana*). Another well-known convent is Jakko-in, located in Kyoto and headed by Chikō Komatsu.[42] In recent decades, there has also been a move to ordain the wives of priests after a short period of religious training, according them a status parallel to that of noncelibate male priests. In some cases, these women are known as nuns (*nisō*) and included in nuns' associations. Although they may shave their heads once during their training, they ordinarily do not shave them afterwards or wear robes, except perhaps on ceremonial occasions. They serve primarily in a supportive role to their husbands, making arrangements for ceremonies, offering words of advice to parishioners, and fulfilling all the duties necessary for maintaining a temple, in addition to their own personal family responsibilities. Though their efforts are essential for the smooth functioning of the temple, such women are often overworked and underacknowledged, and one may question whether their accommodation to the status quo will significantly improve conditions for women in religion.

Powerfully Isolated: Buddhist Women of Korea

Buddhism was integral to Korean national identity and culture, flourishing in both the cities and countryside until the Choson dynasty (1392–1910), when it suffered persecution due to the government's preference for Neo-Confucian ideology. Then, under Japanese colonization (1910–45), Korea was subjected to intensive missionary activities by mostly lay Japanese Buddhist denominations, which challenged the celibate monastic orientation of the traditional Korean schools. Although politics and human frailty swayed some male religious specialists away from their celibate lifestyle, most nuns managed to preserve their commitment to monastic celibacy throughout this period of hardship. Unable to adequately voice their concerns within the established, male-dominated Chogye monastic order, Bhikṣuṇī Eunyeong Sunim founded Pumun-Jong, an independent order of nuns.[43] Even though this movement is no longer a force in Korea today, there are several thousand *bhikṣuṇīs* united through the Korean Bhikṣuṇī Association begun under the leadership of Bhikṣuṇī Hyechun

Sunim, as well as several thousand female novices (*śrāmaṇerikā*) in training for full ordination.[44]

Seeing Buddhism as a political threat, successive regimes have attempted to isolate it in the countryside, which has suited the meditation-minded monastics. Yet recently Buddhism has begun losing large numbers of followers both to Christianity and secular pursuits. To reverse this trend, efforts are now being made to reach out and serve the needs of increasingly urban Korean society. In response to improved standards of secular education, greater opportunities for religious education are becoming available to both women and men. Efforts are also being made to instill Buddhist values in the younger generation through activities such as Sunday school classes and other programs along the lines of the Christian model. Korean women, especially the nuns, are taking an active role in efforts to disseminate Buddhism in urban centers, particularly among the youth.[45]

Partially in response to limited options in the political sphere, large numbers of young people today continue to be attracted to monastic life. Several hundred take vows annually. Women in recent years, sparked by religious aims and a concern for the social good, have begun seeking ordination in even greater numbers than men. Although positions of power and responsibility in the Buddhist world are almost totally controlled by men, Korean nuns have gained the respect of the laity through their moral integrity, hard work, and dedicated social service. Some have opted out of the existing religious orders and created independent organizational structures, an interesting model for women in general to explore.

The Success Story: Buddhist Women of Taiwan

In all of East Asia, no place can boast a resurgence of Buddhism equal to that of Taiwan, nor a Bhikṣuṇī Saṅgha as strong. Chinese Buddhist women have as role models the female saints who figure prominently in the *sūtras,* such as the laywoman Queen Śrīmālā, whose depth of realization is attested by the Buddha who predicts her perfect enlightenment in the form of the Buddha Universal Light.[46] The Chinese also have several prominent female cultural heroes, such as the legendary Miao-shan, the devout Buddhist princess who was almost martyred for her chastity, and Kuan Yin, the bodhisattva of compassion, who in China typically appears in female form. Laywomen throughout generations have organized Buddhist vegetarian societies and sponsored innumerable Dharma activities (*fa-hui*).[47] Many among them have chosen a life of renunciation, most commonly as a *bhikṣuṇī*, but also sometimes as a laywomen with bodhisattva precepts living and helping in a temple. It is estimated that at certain times during the T'ang dynasty Chinese *bhikṣuṇīs* numbered five hundred thousand.[48] Today, in Taiwan alone, there are an estimated five thousand Chinese nuns engaged in studies, teaching, meditation, and social service.

When refugee monks fled mainland China after the Communist victory in the early 1950s, a hardworking core of dedicated Taiwanese nuns helped them establish temples, schools, and a foundation of lay support that made possible a spirited revival of Buddhist thought and practice in the Republic of China. Quietly and relentlessly challenging Confucian preconceptions of the servile wife and daughter, Chinese women in Taiwan have proved their strength in business, government, education, and religion. Although still underrepresented in the male-dominated bastions of ecclesiastical power, Buddhist women in Taiwan exert their influence through material generosity and sheer numbers. A significant number have rejected marriage in favor of ordination as Buddhist nuns. Women entering monastic life outnumber men more than five to one; on the whole they are better educated, more active, and younger than male candidates, entering the order as a first option, rather than after another career.

In addition to traditional temple activities, nuns have gained fame in education, the arts, activism, and social service. Bhikṣuṇī Shig Hiu Wan, an artist, educator, and meditation master from Guangzhou Province who taught for many years at the Chinese Cultural University in Taipei, established a monastic training center for nuns, and at the age of seventy-six established Hua Fan University, where she hopes to create a meditation hall for four hundred.[49] As the present generation of male Buddhist scholars passes away, women teachers will hopefully take leadership roles, despite the prevalent tendency to place men in positions of power. Bhikṣuṇī Heng-ching Shih, trained at the University of Wisconsin and now professor of philosophy at National Taiwan University, became the first ordained practitioner to teach at the university level in Taiwan. Young nuns and laywomen currently taking advanced degrees in Japanese, American, and British universities in preparation for scholarly careers will bring fresh perspectives to Buddhist theory and practice. Presumably, through demonstrating their academic and personal merit, these women will gradually help correct the gender imbalance in the upper echelons of Chinese Buddhism.

Perhaps the most remarkable example of Buddhist social service in the world is Ciji, the Buddhist Compassion Relief Foundation, founded by Bhikṣuṇī Zhengyan after she saw a young woman refused medical care because she was unable to pay.[50] Since 1966, Ciji has evolved into the largest civic organization in Taiwan, distributing 20 million dollars annually to relieve sufferings caused by poverty and natural disasters.[51] Ciji's four million members, 80 percent of them women, are motivated by the bodhisattva ideal to extend the values of loving kindness and compassion beyond home and family to the world at large. Emphasizing social service activities more than meditation or ritual practices, and fully acknowledging women's leadership capabilities, Ciji offers a new model of women's participation in Buddhist organizations.

Minority Buddhist Women: Indonesia, Malaysia, and the Philippines

Indonesia, Malaysia, the Phillipines, Singapore, and Thailand have significant ethnic Chinese populations engaged primarily in business, including a significant proportion of Buddhists. Within these cultural enclaves, ethnic Chinese nuns have established temples and conscientiously devote themselves to chanting *sūtras,* performing rituals for lay devotees, and supervising the upkeep of the temples. Some of these nuns have traveled abroad, primarily to Taiwan and Hong Kong, for Buddhist studies and training in monastic discipline. Those who are highly motivated and have the financial means aspire to participate in a monthlong Triple Platform Ordination,[52] held annually in Taiwan, with its exemplary standards of discipline and quality instruction.

As members of a frequently persecuted minority, sometimes even denied citizenship on the basis of race, these Chinese nuns keep a very low profile. Confucian societal mores and politics conspire to keep them silent and in the shadows. Many of these nuns have no formal schooling; they may be unable to speak the national or regional language, or even Mandarin, serving their temple's following entirely in their own Chinese dialect. Disenfranchised, extremely isolated, and generally unaware of any larger role they might play, these nuns typify a cultural pattern for women's behavior that appears antiquated when viewed from a Western perspective, yet serves the valuable purpose of maintaining cultural cohesion and providing female spiritual leadership within the local Chinese community.

A Tragic Case: Tibet

Throughout centuries of Tibetan Buddhist history, women have distinguished themselves in spiritual practice time and again. The Vajrayāna or Secret Mantra teachings, which thrive in the Tibetan milieu, guarantee women the possibility of enlightenment "in this very life, in this very body."[53] Although the lineage of full ordination for women apparently was not transmitted from India to Tibet, both laywomen and nuns became famous for their spiritual achievements.[54] Among those who availed themselves of this precious opportunity, perhaps the most famous is Machig Labdronma (1055–1149 C.E.), whose heroic example has inspired generations of Tibetan women. The twentieth century has also produced exemplars, such as Samding Dorje Palmo and Shungseb Jetsun Lochen Rinpoche, both of whom are said to have reached high levels of spiritual realization.[55]

Unfortunately, social and political factors have intruded and perforce compromised many ordinary women's spiritual potential. Mundane realities have mitigated against large numbers of women being recognized for their religious attainments: for example, societal expectations of women's roles, the time-consuming duties of family life, and in recent years, the takeover of the Tibetan homeland by an uncompromising Communist regime. The potential to manifest enlightened female meditational deities such as Tārā, Vajrayoginī, Saraswatī, and Prajñāpāramitā is ever present; the mystique of legendary female spiritual masters such as Gelongma Palmo, Yeshe Tsogyal, Mandarava, Niguma, and others, remains to inspire women on the path. In actual fact, however, most Tibetan women see their chances for immanent enlightenment as somewhat remote. Many are content to simply pray to be reborn as a male and indeed, for most, Buddhist practice consists of doing their best in everyday life situations.

Still, there are improvements that would enhance Tibetan women's spiritual well-being. Fundamental ones are greater literacy, greater educational opportunities at all levels, both secular and religious, and better facilities for religious study and practice for both lay and ordained women. Most crucial to the process of improving women's spiritual well-being is an improved image of the feminine—a bridging of the gap between theoretical possibilities and limited everyday realities.

An Order of Nuns Is Born: Mangolia

After its introduction in Tibet, Buddhism naturally spread north to Mongolia, in the form of the Gelugpa tradition pioneered by the

Tibetan reformer and scholar Tsongkhapa (1357–1419). Tsongkhapa's emphasis on monastic discipline and moral purity nurtured within the Gelugpa tradition what was probably the world's largest monastic order prior to 1950, with one-fifth of the male population of Tibet becoming monks. The Mūlasarvāstivādin lineage of *bhikṣu* ordination, transmitted to Tibet from India, was subsequently transmitted to Mongolia, and the steppes beyond. But since the *bhikṣuṇī* lineage had not been transmitted from India to Tibet, there was nothing to pass on to Mongolia. Apparently the Tibetan custom of ordaining nuns with the ten novice precepts did not take hold in Mongolia; consequently, until recently Mongolia was bereft of nuns.

This is not to say that Mongolian women were not ardent supporters of the faith; as in all Buddhist countries, they have been enthusiastic and generous devotees for centuries. Despite this, as in other Buddhist countries without a *bhikṣuṇī* order, they have been considered ineligible for admission to the Saṅgha. Rumors of devout women who wished to practice as nuns began circulating soon after the dissolution of the Soviet Union and in 1992 eight Mongolian women received the *śrāmaṇerikā* precepts from Ven. Bakula Rinpoche, a respected Ladakhi lama who have been instrumental in reviving monastic discipline during his tenure as Indian Ambassador to Mongolia (1989–99).[56] Most of these nuns are now studying in India and Nepal.[57]

There are currently four communities of female practitioners in Mongolia, with a core of ten to thirty-five women at each, situated in and around the capital, Ulaan Bataar. Their members are principally laywomen with the five lay precepts (*upāsikā*)[58] who live at home and gather daily to recite or support the recitation of texts. Although some have received private tutoring in Buddhist doctrine, there is as yet no formal study program available for women in Mongolia. It is hoped that the nuns now studying in India and Nepal will gain the expertise needed to become leaders and teachers in Mongolian Buddhist women's communities. The Mongolia Buddhist Women's Association, located near Ganden Thekchokling, the largest monk's monastery, is headed by a laywoman named Natsagdorjiin Gantumur who is actively promoting women's religious welfare. Another nearby women's community, well known for performing rituals of Vajrayoginī, is headed by a young laywoman named Basup who established a pilot Buddhist studies program for women in 1997. A third community, situated just outside of Ulaan Bataar and led by a laywoman named Batan Han, specializes in practices of the female bodhisattva Tārā. The fourth, a residential community housed in two small tents in Chingoltei, a half-hour drive from the capitol, is the only one headed by a nun. The members of these communities are girls and young women, all of whom are receiving a secondary education in public schools. Many would like to become nuns, but are unable to get their parents' permission. Lacking historical precedents for such matters as dress and education, these communities are influenced both by egalitarian socialist ideology as well as by ancient Mongolian Buddhist traditions very similar in style to the Tibetan traditions from which they derive.

The resurgence of interest in Buddhism in Mongolia is strongly linked with national and cultural identity. After seventy years of Communist rule, a sense of both spiritual and political urgency is apparent in attempts to revive it. Since 1989, Christian evangelists have been flooding in with Bibles to fill the spiritual vacuum created by the collapse of the Soviet Union and the long stretch of religious repression. Economically strapped, distressed by rapid social changes, and bereft of Buddhist literature in the vernacular, many Mongolians have been converted to Christianity. The Buddhist tradition has survived in Mongolia in monasteries where rituals are performed in Tibetan and are thus incomprehensible to all but learned scholars and religious specialists. Elements of the Buddhist teachings are embedded in popular folk beliefs and practices, but due to a dearth of accessible teachers and texts, the tradition remains somewhat distant from many people's everyday lives and has thus failed to meet their immediate psychological needs. As women gain opportunities for study and practice, they are beginning to play vital roles in the resuscitation of a culture.

Buddhism Moves West

The importation of Buddhist traditions to Western countries has occasioned a ripening of feminist awareness by bringing traditional Asian patterns of patriarchy to the attention of Western Buddhist practitioners who have then questioned these patterns and attitudes within their own cultures.[59] Not only are most Buddhist teachers male, and the leaders of most Buddhist institutions male, but the authority for all Buddhist rites of passage—becoming a Buddhist by going for refuge, becoming a Buddhist lay follower by receiving five precepts, becoming a nun or a monk, receiving instructions and empowerments for practice—rests almost entirely in male hands.

In the modern world, especially in Western countries, the Buddhist tradition has come under scrutiny in the light of various feminist ideas. Four major issues are being examined: (1) the inferior status of women in Buddhist societies, (2) sexist interpretations of Buddhist texts and tenets, (3) male domination of Buddhist institutions, and

(4) the authoritarian role of religious teachers. The growth of feminist awareness globally has been simultaneous with a general increase of awareness of Buddhist techniques for personal and spiritual growth. The intellectual coincidence of Buddhist and feminist ideas constitutes a fertile matrix for thought, not only in North America, but across cultures. For the first time in history, Buddhists in different cultures—from Japan to Peru, from Norway to Cambodia—are exchanging ideas on a daily basis. For the first time in history, women can be equal players in this philosophical exchange.

The social and cultural factors that affect the future of Western Buddhist women are quite different from those that affect Asian women, however. As Anne Klein has pointed out, "Western feminism and Buddhism are starting from very different cultural and philosophical understandings of personhood."[60] Although Western women comprise only a small minority of the world's Buddhist women—perhaps one percent of an estimated 300 million—the factors that affect both their assimilation and their practice of Buddhism warrant consideration. The same cultural assumptions Western people bring to Buddhism will increasingly apply to Asian societies influence by Western values: feminist ideologies, individualism, scientific rationalism, egalitarianism, Western psychological theories, anti-authoritarianism, consumerism, changes in attitudes toward family and gender, and certainly not least, materialism. Buddhists and contemporary feminists are similar in their concern for constructions of personal identity, issues of social justice, and awareness of both the rational and affective dimensions of human experience. At the same time, there are great differences in the assumptions underlying Buddhist and feminist systems of thought. For example, in contrast to the traditional Buddhist emphasis on suffering, impermanence, enlightenment, and happiness in future lives, popular American culture stresses sense pleasures, worldly achievements, immediate gratification, and happiness in this life. American culture encourages self-esteem, self-fulfillment, and self-worth, whereas most Buddhists view an essentialist concept of self as the root of innumerable problems. As Buddhism gains popularity in the West, an exploration of the tensions between Buddhist and Western cultural assumptions becomes crucial for Western practitioners. The process by which Buddhist women evaluate these various viewpoints—rejecting, reshaping, or assimilating them—will be both a struggle and an opportunity for meaningful and creative crosscultural dialogue.[61]

Applying feminist analysis to religious studies presupposes an attitude of respect for woman's spiritual potential, recognizes the worth of women's spiritual endeavors, demands equal opportunities for ordination and religious leadership, promotes equal participation and the use of inclusive language in liturgical practice, and encourages the exploration of topics such as sexuality, family life, intuition, and emotion. Applying this type of analysis to Buddhism gives women an unprecedented opportunity to influence the direction the Buddhist tradition(s) will take, especially in Western countries.[62] Many of the most devoted, capable, and committed students in Western Buddhist centers are women. The spiritual teachers are generally Asian men and, because they are usually kind and generous in providing teachings and spiritual guidance, women students serve these male teachers as cooks, secretaries, translators, publicists, drivers, administrative assistants, personal assistants, janitors, editors, cultural interpreters, and confidants. Since the teachers are often totally dependent on them, these women have the power to influence their thinking on gender issues enormously. On the other hand, if women become emotionally dependent or simply perpetuate the myth of male superiority, the relationship may become a lost opportunity or an emotional liability on both sides.

Patriarchy or Social Equality?

Although some writers have argued to the contrary, historical records paint a fairly dismal picture of Indian women's lot prior to the advent of the Buddha.[63] When the Buddha recognized the equal spiritual potential of women, it represented a significant departure from prevailing views that defined women almost entirely in terms of their biological function and their capacity for productive labor. Significant as it was, this recognition alone was not sufficient to transform the gender stereotypes of entire cultures. Despite the fact that the Buddha established a female mendicant order, along with regulations to ensure its continuous, harmonious, functioning, the male order has remained dominant throughout history. Male dominance in institutional structures persisted as Buddhism spread abroad, along with a pattern of affirming the equal enlightenment potential of women in theory, while assuming that they are less capable of actualizing that potential in actuality. The assumption of women's spiritual inferiority and the neglect it engenders characterize most of Buddhist history.

A glance at Buddhist history reveals that Asian males have dominated Buddhist traditions for two and a half millennia. Until now, despite theoretical equality, the two genders have been trained differently in the Buddhist traditions: men are educated to become scholars and teachers: women are trained to nurture and support them.

Although realized women have emerged and some have been recognized by the traditions, ecclesiastical power and transmission of the teachings remains firmly in the hands of men. Philosophically, the Buddhist traditions propound the equal spiritual potential of all human beings, regardless of caste, class, or gender, but the Buddhist institutions that later evolved in Asia clearly favor men. Poor boys from the countryside gain access to valuable educational opportunities—opportunities not similarly available to women—when they join the Saṅgha. By joining the order, males automatically gain status, receive a good education, and become eligible for positions within the elite and powerful ecclesiastical hierarchy. In Thailand, for example, any boy can hypothetically climb the clerical ladder, which culminates in the post of Saṅgharāja, Supreme Patriarch, appointed by the king. Men who disrobe, having gained a high-quality education free of charge, are eligible to apply for administrative posts in the secular sphere, and may assume positions of considerable influence in politics and government—opportunities remote for women. Although the temples in these countries are thronged with women and supported primarily by them, women play no significant role in Buddhist religious hierarchies.

The superior position that monks occupy in Buddhist religious institutions requires explanation. It is said that because the Bhikṣu Saṅgha was established five or six years earlier than the Bhikṣuṇī Saṅgha, it occupies a position of seniority. This reasoning seems inadequate to explain why monks have held superior positions and commanded greater authority than women not only in Buddhist monasteries, but in all echelons of society, ever since. Furthermore, the chronological seniority of the Bhikṣu Saṅgha does not explain the ranking of junior monks as higher in status than even senior nuns, a ranking institutionalized in the eight special rules (*gurudharma*) pertaining to nuns.[64] The ordination of Mahāprajāpatī, the first *bhikṣuṇī* (fully ordained nun), is said to have been conferred by the Buddha only upon the nuns' acceptance of the eight special rules—rules that ensure the subordination of nuns to monks.[65]

Although the eight special rules are clearly discriminatory, they are held in abeyance much of the time. Moreover, the authenticity of the eight rules is suspect for a number of reasons, both logical and philological. For example, the requirement that a *bhikṣuṇī* be ordained by both Bhikṣu and Bhikṣuṇī Saṅghas could not possibly have been imposed on Mahāprajāptī by the Buddha because the Bhikṣuṇī Sangha did not yet exist at the time; it was only with the ordination of Mahāprajāpatī that the order began. Similarly, one of the eight special rules imposes a two-year training period for women (*śikṣamaṇa*) to ensure that a female candidate for full ordination is not pregnant. This rule could not have been imposed upon Mahāprajāpatī then either, since the precedent involving a pregnant candidate, upon which the rule was formulated, did not arise until after the Bhikṣuṇī Saṅgha was fully functioning. Textual analysis reveals that these discriminatory passages have been artificially embedded in earlier texts.[66] It is unlikely that these are the only examples of textual interpolation related to women.[67]

Even if the deprecating remarks about women in the texts are discounted as later sexist incursions, they remain a hindrance to Buddhist women's advancement up to today. Whenever the issue of full ordination for nuns in Sri Lanka is raised, unfounded claims and distorted interpretations of scripture are advanced to lobby against reinstating the Bhikṣuṇī Saṅgha. Some claim that women wish to take over the Saṅgha and push the monks out, others that nuns seeking full ordination are causing a schism in the order.[68] Some claim that proponents are promoting a heretical tradition (Mahāyāna), even though lineage of monastic discipline being advanced (Dharmagupta) is orthodox and unrelated to Mahāyāna. Opposition to the full ordination of women cannot properly be based on scriptural authority, certainly; the Buddha declared the Bhikṣuṇī Saṅgha an essential element in a balanced Buddhist society, and provided clear statutes for its establishment and governance. Opposition is most likely based on more mundane matters: reluctance to share power and financial support, hesitation to accommodate a new tradition, fear of change, and the blunt weight of top-heavy tradition. As nuns grow in numbers and become more visible, there is an increasing uneasiness among monks about having to share resources. Even when the standards of conduct and practice among women are exemplary, they may not be fully appreciated.[69]

Reflecting on Buddhist history, we see the recurrent paradigm of populist renewal in response to elitist domination and stagnation. Because the ascetic ideals of the Theravāda and the transcendent ideals of the Mahāyāna often seem beyond the reach of ordinary mortals, Buddhism undergoes periodic declines and renewals to redeclare its relevance to everyday life. A natural process of synthesis and transformation occurs continuously through the reevaluation and reinterpretation of cultural values, resulting in an ongoing symbiosis of imported and indigenous systems of thought. This socially and culturally transformative process, illustrating Buddhism's remarkable tolerance for indigenous beliefs and practices, is strikingly evident today, as Buddhism accommodates to changes in Asia and begins to take root in the West. Once again Buddhism must demonstrate its relevance and effectiveness on a practical level—synthesizing Asian and Western insights and values, ancient and modern. A revaluation of women's place in the tradition and forum for voicing women's concerns are key elements in the personal and intellectual dynamics of this process.

As patriarchal as Buddhist institutions may be, the boundaries imposed by gender are not as rigid as may be assumed. For example, there are no statutes in Buddhism that discriminate laywomen from laymen. Whatever can be practiced by men can be practiced by women and whatever can be achieved by men can be achieved by women. It is in the statutes related to monastics that discrimination occurs, but the authenticity of the textual sources for that discrimination is now being seriously questioned. The Buddha reportedly required that the monks instruct the nuns once every fortnight and participate in *bhikṣuṇī* ordinations. Although the monks' duties in relation to nuns were supposedly established to ensure the protection and adequate instruction of the nuns, they reflect patriarchal attitudes, and obligations that are not reciprocal. What is sometimes forgotten is that, on an everyday level, monastic institutions for women functioned entirely independent of male control. The presence of monks in the lives of nuns was required only on certain occasions, and the authenticity of the texts that stipulate such participation is under review. A total feminist reevaluation of the tradition—historical, philosophical, and sociological—is now underway.

Buddhism's dialogue with feminism has already caused some major shifts within Buddhism, and the dialogue has been all the richer for the multiplicity of feminist perspectives and Buddhist traditions that inform it. The goal of Buddhist practice is spiritual enlightenment, not simply as an abstraction, but as a concrete possibility available to all human beings, women included. The issue of women in Buddhism, therefore, is primarily the issue of women's full participation, both in the practice and interpretation of the tradition.

A glass ceiling definitely exists for women in Buddhism institutions today, and some women are questioning whether the ceiling exists in places they really wish to go. Buddhism's history of male dominance has not prevented women from achieving spiritual realizations, nor has it prevented them from working independently to create monasteries, publications, art exhibits, orphanages, radio programs, hospitals, hospices, and universities. The key to women's achievements in recent years has been education, so education has naturally become the emphasis of the current Buddhist women's movement.

In Buddhist societies, the monasteries have traditionally provided a conducive setting for nurturing teachers, providing thorough education and training, primarily for men. In Asian Buddhist countries men continue to enjoy the status, privileges, and access to education that full ordination brings, and to develop as recognized masters of these ancient traditions. The tradition recognizes women's spiritual potential, but to develop as teachers women must have opportunities to study. Therefore, for women to emerge as recognized Buddhist teachers in numbers equal to men, they must have equal access to ordination and to facilities for education and training that are equal in quality.

Facilities for education and training require financial support, so the development of quality facilities for women requires Buddhists to examine the choices they make and the institutions they support. The majority of donors to Buddhist institutions are women, especially in Asia.[70] If women assume that men's potential is greater than women's, and support the development of men's potential over women's, they are themselves creating inequalities, in a self-fulfilling prophecy. But there is no philosophical basis in Buddhism for claiming that men have greater potential than women. Therefore, through increased awareness and equitable support, women have the power to correct whatever imbalances or injustices currently exist in Buddhist institutions. The tradition itself invites inquiry and critique, to "test the teachings as one would test gold." This dictum is apt for a feminist analysis of Buddhist texts and traditional practices. As Thich Nhat Hahn has said, "If a teaching is not in accord with the needs of the people and the realities of society, it is not truly Buddhist."[71]

Buddhist Women as Leaders in Social Transformation

The Buddhist women's movement is a vital aspect of the current cross-fertilization of cultures that is occurring as Buddhism assumes global significance. Another is the new emphasis on social action projects, in what is known as "socially engaged Buddhism." These two developments are integrally linked. Although Buddhist organizations in Asia have been slow to see women as logical beneficiaries of their efforts, individual women working independently, such as Bhikṣuṇī Zhengyan in Taiwan and Maeji Khunying Kanitha Wichiencharoen in Thailand, have been exemplary agents of social change.[72] Social welfare programs directed by Buddhist women are having immediate constructive results for women in developing countries, including institutions for educating and training women, refugee relief projects, women's shelters, health care projects, counseling centers, economic development projects, and meditation retreat centers. As important as compassionate social service is, however, it would be unfair to promote the idea that women do social work while men meditate—it is not necessary to make a choice between mediation and service to humanity.

The Buddhist women's movement emphasizes women's social problems along with the traditional agenda of spiritual liberation. It is inspired by both the awakening social awareness of practicing Buddhists and the awakening spiritual consciousness of women discovering, individually and collectively, their own history of neglect and oppression, a history that must be reversed in order to ensure that women are optimally engaged in the continually challenging process of social renewal. Women's increasingly active engagement in social and spiritual renewal may yield quite a revolutionary outcome.

The Buddhist worldview recognizers change as intrinsic to human experience and essential for transforming both our inner life and the outer world. Buddhist agents of social change in recent history include B. R. Ambedkar in India,[73] Aung San Suu Kyi in Burma, Bhikṣu Mahagoshananda in Cambodia, A. T. Ariyaratne in Sri Lanka, Bhikṣu Buddhadasa in Thailand, Bhikṣu Thich Nhat Hahn in Vietnam, Bhikṣuṇī Zhengyan in Taiwan, and Bhikṣu Tenzin Gyatso, the fourteenth Dalai Lama of Tibet. The term "engaged Buddhism," coined by Thich Nhat Hahn,[74] describes the active application of Buddhist principles toward social transformation. The concept which has spawned an entire literature.[75]

Socially engaged Buddhists need to recognize that Buddhist women are among the poorest, least educated, and most neglected sectors of society, often concentrating on religious practice at the expense of their own social welfare. It is common the hear both nuns and laywomen state: "I don't care about equality. I only care about *nirvāṇa,*" or "What is the point of my getting an education? It is enough for me just to recite prayers." Lacking confidence in their own abilities, many women concentrate on merit-making through reciting prayers and making offerings to monks. It is common for Buddhist women to denigrate their own potential and abdicate responsibility for their spiritual life to men, praying for rebirth as a man in the next life. A major revaluing of women in the tradition is crucial—both a renewed affirmation of women's spiritual worth and an increased appreciation of women's spiritual practice.

In the Buddhist worldview, spiritual practice and helping living beings are accorded the highest value, but it is unrealistic to expect women to serve others if their own basic needs are not being met. While literacy is not essential to human happiness, for many women literacy is a major step toward empowerment, allowing women access to improved livelihood, to information on health and hygiene, to upward social mobility, to personal development and greater self-confidence, to greater educational options for their children, and to the texts that encode their spiritual heritage. It does not take vast resources or government initiatives to set up adult literacy programs: once one generation is literate, women can continue these programs themselves.

Progressive Buddhists may place their hopes in a future generation of socially enlightened young monks, but this is still only a dream. Even if open-minded monks gain access to positions of power, this does not ensure changes that would benefit women. Those in positions of power rarely relinquish their privileged positions with grace. Therefore, Buddhist women must work for their won social and spiritual liberation. Once women fully acknowledge their own spiritual potential and support women's spiritual practice, a profound social and spiritual transformation is possible. The effective mobilization of some 300 million Buddhist women for the good of the world is not to be underestimated.

The dialogue between Buddhism and feminism is a confluence of rich narratives. Just as Buddhist perspectives on personal development, nonviolence, and ethics can contribute toward social regeneration in Western countries, feminist perspectives can contribute to social renewal in Buddhist countries. Women's experiences are being articulated and analyzed in ways that may contribute to a rethinking and revitalization of Buddhist thought and culture. Rather than investing in gold statues and temples, for example, women are interested in creating more childcare programs, literacy programs, meditation courses, leadership programs, health care training, Buddhist hospice programs, rehabilitation centers, disaster relief programs, and creative expressions of spiritual practice. As the marginalized enter the stream, they inevitably change the stream. Women can move freely across sectarian and ethnic boundaries and pool their energies as never before. New dimensions of understanding and benefit will surely open up as women in the Dharma find their own unique and individual voices, for virtually the first time in 2,500 years of Buddhist history.

Many Women, Many Voices

The focus of the present volume is to illuminate the lives and thinking of women in Buddhist cultures through a multiplicity of voices and experiences. To more fully understand the socioreligious heritage that Buddhism brings to contemporary discussions of women and religion, the authors who have contributed to this volume examine women's roles in different Buddhist cultures and time periods, integrating various philosophical, social, and political perspectives.

The essays included in Buddhist women in Asian Traditions present portraits of women in different places and periods of Buddhist history. As these essays sketch women's history against a backdrop of widely variant cultural adaptations, the patterns of lost opportunity and benign neglect distinctly emerge. In the section titled South Asian Traditions, Elizabeth J. Harris investigates the roots of this history through early Buddhist philosophical literature in "The Female in Buddhism," to discern whether the rejection of women can be linked with a rejection of sexuality in general. Tracing the history of pioneering women in early history in "Buddhist Women in India and Precolonial Sri Lanka," Lorna Dewaraja contends that women were not as oppressed as ordinarily assumed, particularly against the background of earlier cultural norms. In "Restoring the Order of Nuns to the Theravādin Tradition," Senarat Wijayasundara explores the complex issue of full ordination, which is critical for gaining institutional equality for Buddhist women and is at the heart of a heated controversy in Sri Lanka.

Historically the lineage of full ordination for women was transmitted from Sri Lanka to China, where it has been preserved for centuries. In the first essay on East Asian Traditions, "The Red Cord Untied: Buddhist Nuns in Eighteenth-Century China," Beata Grant analyzes the meaning that particular aspects of Buddhist thought have held for Chinese women and how this has been expressed in women's voices in literature. In "Japanese Buddhist Nuns: Innovators for the Sake of Tradition," Paula K. R. Arai illuminates the history of Zen Buddhist women through the challenges and successes of one of the foremost communities of female practitioners today. Hae-ju Sunim (Ho- Ryeon Jeon) investigates the spiritual potential of women in the Mahāyāna tradition in her study, "Can Women Acheive Enlightenment? A Critique of Sexual Transformation for Enlightenment" and disputes the notion of gender transformation as necessary for women's enlightenment. In the section on the Tibetan Tradition, Janice D. Willis illustrates women's spiritual achievements in "Tibetan Buddhist Women Practitioners, Past and Present: A Garland to Delight Those Wishing Inspiration," and constructs her own personal lineage of spiritual exemplars. In "Pregnancy and Childbirth in Tibetan Culture," Sarah Pinto discusses some of the myths and pollution taboos that surround childbearing, and attempts to trace their history in the context of Buddhist belief systems. And in "Change in Consciousness: Women's Religious Identity in Himalayan Buddhist Cultures," I discuss the impact of Buddhist ideology on women's everyday lives in the Himalayan region and the transformation of attitudes presently occurring in the Tibetan Buddhist diaspora in India. In juxtaposing the histories of women from a wide range of cultures, a central theme emerges: the paradox and apparent conflict between women's theoretical spiritual equality and their everyday realities.

The fortuitous meeting of feminism and Buddhism is an unprecedented opportunity for a cross-cultural exploration of issues vital to women, including those related to the spiritual dimension of feminist awareness and the social dimension of Buddhist awareness. Following this descriptive background on women's struggle for spiritual identity in Asian cultures, the section on Contemporary Buddhist Women explores Buddhist women's expressions of their spirituality in modern world cultures. The essays in Forging Identity investigate, from a variety of angles, definitions of personhood implied and made possible by this mutual infusion of values. Cait Collins begins at the beginning by discussing the philosophical implications of reproductive issues from both medical scientific and Buddhist perspectives in "Conception and the Energy of Consciousness: When Does a Life Begin?" Next, in her essay "East, West, Women, and Self," Anne C. Klein looks at the cultural assumptions pertaining to subjectivity and personhood that underlie Western Buddhists' commitment to social engagement. Sara Shneiderman then explores facets of the Western assimilation of Asian Buddhist traditions from a feminist perspective in, "Appropriate Treasure? Reflections on Women, Buddhism, and Cross-Cultural Exchange."

The section on Shaping New Traditions: Unity and Diversity explores the relevance of Buddhist philosophical views and lifestyles for women creating meaning in today's changing societies. It begins with a discussion of women's spirituality from an ecumenical perspective in my article, "Comparing Buddhist and Christian Women's Experiences." Next, in "Aung San Suu Kyi: A Woman of Conscience in Burma," Theja Gunawardhana examines the ramifications of Buddhist pacifist ideology in the creation of political identity through the life experience of this eminent Buddhist democracy activist. The last two articles deal with different styles of integrating Buddhist practice in Western women's everyday lives. Dharmacharini Sanghadevi presents one contemporary alternative to Buddhist women's traditional roles in, "A Model for Laywomen in Buddhism: The Western Buddhist Order." Rita M. Gross discusses other possible models for serious lay practitioners and straightfowardly tackles such practical issues as how to juggle diapers and meditation in "Feminism, Lay Buddhism, and the Future of Buddhism."

The aim of this book is to examine Buddhist philosophical tenets and their expression in diverse Buddhist cultures from women's unique vantage points. In their own voices, women share their experiences, their research, and their hopes for recovering Buddhism's original egalitarian approach to enlightenment. The essays here place the voices of women from different Buddhist cultures side by side with women from non-Buddhist cultures to examine a pivotal question: In what ways is Buddhism a constraint for women and in which ways is it liberative? As Buddhism acculturates in the West and Buddhist cultures in Asia modernize, the tradition's benefit and utility are being carefully weighed. It is my hope that this book makes a contribution toward this reevaluation.

Notes

1. The edited proceedings of this conference have been published in Karma Lekshe Tsomo, *Sakyadhita: Daughters of the Buddha* (Ithaca, N.Y.: Snow Lion Publications, 1989).

2. Her story is recounted in C. A. F. Rhys Davids' *Poems of Early Buddhist Nuns (Therīgāthā)* (Oxford: Pali Text Society, 1989), pp. 4–5, 71–73.

3. See, for example, E. Michael Mendelson, *Sangha and State in Burma: A Study of Monastic Sectarianism and Leadership* (Ithaca, N.Y.: Cornell University Press, 1975), and four books edited by Bardwell L. Smith: *Religion and Legitimation of Power in South Asia* (Leiden: Brill, 1978), *Religion and Legitimation of Power in Sri Lanka* (Chambersburg, Pa.: Anima Books, 1978), *Religion and Legitimation of Power in Thailand, Laos, and Burma* (Chambersburg, Pa.: Anima Books, 1978), and *The Two Wheels of Dhamma: Essays on the Theravada Tradition in India and Ceylon* (Chambersburg, Pa.: American Academy of Religion, 1972).

4. The best overall treatment of this history is probably still I. B. Horner's *Women under Primitive Buddhism: Laywomen and Almswomen* (Delhi: Motilal Banarsidass, 1930).

5. This story appears in several places in the Pāli canon and also in the literature of other early schools. See Jan Nattier, *Once upon a Future Time: Studies in a Buddhist Prophecy of Decline* (Berkeley: Asian Humanities Press, 1991), pp. 28–33. She notes that the *Mahāvibhāṣā* offers a second interpretation: "According to other teachers, what the Buddha meant was that if women were allowed to enter the monastic order but did not obey the eight additional rules (*gurudharma*) imposed upon them—rules clearly designed to keep them in subordinate positions with respect to men—the *saddharma* [pure Dharma] would have lasted for only five hundred years. Since these rules were implemented, however, the *saddharma* will remain in the world for a full 1,000 years." Ibid., p. 44.

6. A compendium of unflattering portrayals of women in Buddhist literature appears in Liz Wilson's book, *Charming Cadavers: Horrific Figurations of*

the Feminine in Indian Buddhist Hagiographic Literature (Chicago: University of Chicago Press, 1996).

7. Mark Tatz, *The Skill in Means (Upāyakauśalya) Sūtra* (Delhi: Motilal Banarsidass, 1994), pp. 39–45.

8. Related in Cecil Bendall and W. H. D. Rouse's tradition of Śāntideva's *Śikṣāsamuccaya: A Compendium of Buddhist Doctrine* (Delhi: Motilal Banarsidass, 1990), pp. 157–58.

9. Bimala Churn Law, *Women in Buddhist Literature* (Varanasi: Indological Book House, 1981), pp. 93–97.

10. Dharmasēna Thera (trans. Ranjini Obeyesekere), *Jewels of the Doctrine: Stories of the Saddharma Ratnāvaliya* (Albany: State University of New York Press, 1991), pp. 224–25. In this text, the Buddha describes Sumanā, the youngest daughter, as senior in goodness to her father, because of her superior spiritual attainment.

11. Rhys Davids, *Poems*, pp. 88–91.

12. Ibid., pp. 64–66.

13. Ibid., pp. 55–59.

14. See note 3.

15. See Nancy Falk, "The Case of the Vanishing Nuns: The Fruits of Ambivalence in Ancient Indian Buddhism," *Unspoken Worlds: Women's Religious Lives in Non-Western Culture*, ed. Nancy Falk and Rita Gross (San Francisco: Harper & Row, 1979), pp. 207–24.

16. See Kathryn Ann Tsai, *Lives of the Nuns: Biographies of Chinese Buddhist Nuns from the Fourth to Sixth Centuries* (Honolulu: University of Hawaii Press, 1994), pp. 37–38, 53–54, 62–63.

17. Marie B. Byles, *Journey into Burmese Silence* (London: George Allen & Unwin, 1962), p. 102.

18. Byles relates that, "At one stall, gold leaf was being sold for affixing to a giant Buddha statue and a man was standing on the folded arms of the Blessed One while he did so. I rather fancied a photo of myself fixing gold leaf, but was told women were unclean and might not stand on Buddha statues; they must get a man to fix the gold leaf for them. . . . The uncleanness of my sex was becoming depressing." Ibid., p. 91.

19. Melford Spiro comments on the Burmese expression: "A male dog is superior to a human female," in *Buddhism and Society: A Great Tradition and Its Burmese Vicissitudes* (New York: Harper and Row, 1970), pp. 82–83.

20. See Mi Mi Khiang's *The World of Burmese Women* (London: Zed Books, 1984), p. 1.

21. The ten precepts of a novice nun or monk are to abstain from: (1) taking life; (2) taking what is not given; (3) engaging in sexual activities; (4) telling lies; (5) taking intoxicants; (6) taking untimely food; (7) singing, dancing, and watching entertainments; (8) wearing garlands, jewelry, and cosmetics; (9) sitting on high seats and beds; and (10) handling gold or silver. The eight precepts are : (1) to (6), (7), and (8) combined into one, and (9). The difference, then, between one who holds eight precepts and one who holds ten precepts is that the latter refrains from handling gold and silver, ordinarily interpreted as money. This is significant because it means that ten-precept holders depend on the generosity of the laity to provide them with food.

22. Byles, *Journey*, p. 72.

23. Spiro, *Buddhism and Society*, p. 263.

24. "The more serious nuns wore dark russet red." Byles, *Journey*, p. 119.

25. Ibid., p. 124.

26. These are the regulations of monastic discipline contained in the Vinaya. In the Theravāda tradition preserved in Pāli translation there are 227 precepts for *bhikṣus* and 311 precepts for *bhikṣuṇīs*, in the Dharmagupta tradition preserved in Chinese translation there are 250 for *bhikṣus* and 348 for *bhikṣuṇīs*, and in the Mūlasarvāstivādin tradition preserved in Tibetan translation there are 253 for *bhikṣus* and 364 for *bhikṣuṇīs*. See Karma Lekshe Tsomo, *Sisters in Solitude: Two Traditions of Buddhist Monastic Ethics for Women: A Comparative Analysis of the Dharmagupta and Mūlasarvāstivāda Bhikṣuṇī Prātimokṣa Sūtras* (Albany: State University of New York Press, 1996).

27. Byles, *Journey*, p. 86.

28. Ibid., p. 167. Ms. Byles was told that the nuns had to leave the Leper Meditation Center for lack of support: "There is little merit in giving to healthy nuns, let alone diseased ones, so the nuns could get no food."

29. Richard F. Gombrich states, "When Vihaya-Bahu I reconquered the throne in 1065 it was no longer possible to hold a higher ordination ceremony, as there were not five monks left to form a quorum, so he had to send to Burma for some monks to establish a new line of succession. The Order of nuns had died out completely, and this could not be reinstated, as there were no Theravadin nuns elsewhere, so that Order became extinct in Ceylon." (*Precept and Practice: Traditional Buddhism in the Rural Highlands of Ceylon* [Oxford: Clarendon Press, 1971], p. 32.) However, Tessa Bartholomeusz, citing Mi Mi Khiang, contends that "Burmese inscriptions attest that the order of Buddhist nuns continued to thrive there until at least the thirteenth century." (*Women under the Bō Tree.* [Cambridge: Cambridge University Press, 1994], p. 40.)

Other references to the history of nuns in Sri Lanka are found in Abhaya Weerakoon's "Nuns of Sri Lanka," in Tsomo, *Sakyadhita*, pp. 140–44; Kusuma

Devendra's unpublished manuscript, "The Dasasil Nun: A Study of Women's Buddhist Religious Movement in Sri Lanka" (Colombo: Department of Pali and Buddhist Studies, 1987); Lowell Bloss, "The Female Renunciants of Sri Lanka: The *Dasasil mattawa*," *Journal of the International Association of Buddhist Studies* 10.1 (1987): 7–32; R. A. L. H. Gunawardena's "Subtle Silks of Ferreous Firmness: Buddhist Nuns in Ancient and Early Medieval Sri Lanka and Their Role in the Propagation of Buddhism," (*Sri Lankan Journal of the Humanities* 14.1–2 (1988): 1–59; Tessa Bartholomeusz' article, "The Female Mendicant in Buddhist Sri Lanka," in José Cabezón, ed., *Buddhism, Sexuality, and Gender* (Albany: State University of New York Press, 1992), pp. 37–61, and her book, *Women under the Bō Tree* (New York, N.Y.: Cambridge University Press, 1994).

30. Because the nuns typically receive ten precepts, I do not feel that it is accurate to refer to them as *upāsikās*, a term referring to laywomen with five precepts, or as lay nuns, a term that does not appear in Buddhist texts and is an oxymoron in the Buddhist context. The nuns are generally referred to as *dasasilmātā*, but the suffix *-mātā* meaning "mother" is not really appropriate to describe a celibate woman; instead, the term *sil māniyo* is increasingly being used. It seems to me unjustifiable that, although the ten precepts received by the nuns of Sri Lanka are the same as the ten precepts of the *śrāmaṇera* (novice monk) and also the same as the ten precepts that *śrāmaṇerikās* (novice nuns) received in ancient times, the Sri Lankan nuns are not recognized as *śrāmaṇerikās* or as members of the Saṅgha.

Some monks justify this discrimination by saying that the nuns' precepts are taken singly, not as a group, or that their precepts are taken daily, not for life. However, it is a matter of history, recorded in both the *Mahāvaṃsa* and the *Dīpavaṃsa*, that Queen Anulā and several hundred noblewomen received ten precepts and wore the yellow robe for six months prior to the arrival of King Aśoka's daughter, Bhikṣuṇī Saṅghamitra. Because there were no nuns in Sri Lanka at that time, these women could only have received the precepts from monks. And because the *śrāmaṇerikā* precepts were a prerequisite for receiving the *bhikṣuṇī* precepts, which Saṅghamitra conferred immediately upon her arrival, it may be assumed that the ten precepts the noblewomen received from the *bhikṣus* were recognized as being *śrāmaṇerikā* precepts. Such is the case today in China, Korea, Vietnam, and Tibet. By contrast, most Sinhalese *bhikṣus* maintain that only *bhikṣuṇīs* can legitimately confer these precepts. Because they do not recognize the ordination of contemporary *bhikṣuṇīs* as legitimate, referring to them as "Mahāyāna *bhikṣuṇīs*," they contend that there is no way to revive an authentic Bhikṣuṇī Saṅgha.

For a fuller discussion of this matter, see chapter 8, "The Bhikṣuṇī Issue," in Tsomo, *Sakyadhita*, pp. 215–76.

31. This term is also sometimes romanized as *mai-chee*.

32. Chatsumarn Kabilsingh, *Thai Women in Buddhism* (Berkeley, Calif.: Parallax Press, 1991), p. 38.

33. On December 29, 1995, several of these nuns received a suspended sentence of two years for alleged political involvement and were prohibited from traveling abroad.

34. This custom is similar to the custom of *rowzeh,* popular among urban Muslim women in Iran. There, women make a request through God as an intermediary and vow to sponsor a particular religious ceremony if the boon is granted. These ceremonies have become popular social occasions, so the practice is often criticized. See Anne H. Betteridge's article, "The Controversial Vows of Urban Muslim Women in Iran," *Unspoken Worlds,* ed. Falk and Gross, (San Francisco: Harper & Row, 1980), pp. 141–55.

35. Pasuk Phongpaichit, *From Peasant Girls to Bangkok Masseuses* (Geneva: International Labour Office, 1982), p. 7.

36. Older nuns are known as *yay chee,* while younger nuns are called *mai chee.*

37. One historical source, *Dai Nam Thien Uyen Truyen Dang Tap Luc,* states that a princess of the Ly dynasty, Dieu Nhan (d. 1113 C.E.), became the first Vietnamese *bhikṣuṇī.* Other sources, cited by Ven. Thich Man Giac in his article, "Establishment of the Bhikṣuṇī Order in Vietnam," assert that the first *bhikṣuṇī* in Vietnam, named Pho Minh, was ordained seven centuries earlier, in 429 C.E. The latter chronology coincides with the arrival of the first mission of *bhikṣuṇīs* to China (from Ceylon) in 429 C.E. Thich Man Giac states that Bhikṣuṇī Pho Minh was ordained by a *bhikṣu,* Truc Phap Do. The orthodox procedure for the *bhikṣuṇī* ordination requires *bhikṣuṇī* as well as *bhikṣu* preceptors.

38. This history is recounted in Akira Hirakawa, "The History of Buddhist Nuns in Japan," *Buddhist Christian Studies* 12 (1992): 143–58.

39. A Buddhist layperson receives five Prātimokṣa precepts, a novice nun or monk receives ten, and a fully ordained nun or monk receives more. See note 26. A person who resolves to become a fully enlightened Buddha for the sake of other living beings may also choose to receive bodhisattva vows. For a description of the differences between these two types of precepts, see my article, "Buddhist Ethics in Japan and Tibet: A Comparative Study of the Adoption of Bodhisattva and Prātimokṣa Precepts," *Buddhist Behavioral Codes and the Modern World,* ed. Charles Wei-hsun Fu and Sandra A. Wawrytko (Greenwood Press, 1994), pp. 123–38. Ordinarily, both types of precepts are received in a formal ordination ceremony. A person who assumes the precepts without formally receiving them, as occurred in early Chinese and Japanese Buddhist history, for example, may be termed self-ordained.

40. See Paula Arai's "Japanese Buddhist Nuns: Innovators for the Sake of Tradition," in this volume.

41. See Shundo Aoyama, *Zen Seeds: Reflections of a Female Priest* (Tokyo: Kosei Publishing Company, 1990), and Paula Arai, "Sōtō Zen Nuns in Modern

Japan: Keeping and Creating Tradition," *Bulletin of the Nanzen Institute for Religion and Culture* 14 (Summer 1990): 38–51.

42. A short autobiography appears in the preface of her book, *The Way to Peace: The Life and Teachings of the Buddha* (Kyoto: Hōzōkan Publishing Company, 1989), pp. xix–xxvi.

43. See Samu Sunim, "Eunyeong Sunim and the Founding of Pomum-Jong, the First Independent Bhikshuni Order," *Women & Buddhism* (Toronto: Zen Lotus Society, 1986), pp. 129–62.

44. Myongsong Sunim describes the training of Korean nuns in "The Water and the Wave," in *Walking on Lotus Flowers: Buddhist Women Living, Loving and Meditating,* ed. Martine Batchelor (London: Thorsons, 1996), pp. 75–83.

45. See, for example, Hi Kyun Kim, "Children's Culture and Popular Buddhism in Korea: The Work of Jebeom Sunim," *Sakyadhita: International Association of Buddhist Women* 8.1 (1997): 3–6.

46. See Diana Paul, *The Buddhist Feminine Ideal: Queen Śrīmālā and the Tathāgatagarbha* (Missoula: Scholars Press, 1980) and Alex and Hideko Wayman, *The Lion's Roar of Queen Srīmālā* (Delhi: Motilal Banarsidass, 1974).

47. Kenneth K. S. Ch'en comments on the existence of a Buddhist women's society in Tun-huang as early as the year 959 C.E., a society that encouraged religious practice and friendships among women, be it with rather rigidly imposed discipline. *Buddhism in China: A Historical Survey* (Princeton: Princeton University Press, 1964), p. 293.

48. Ch'en also notes that statistics on the clergy in the Chinese chronicles routinely include nuns, although they record a decrease in the numbers of nuns relative to the numbers of monks over time. For example, in the K'ai-yuan era (713–741) there were said to be 50,576 nuns and 75,524 monks, but by the time of K'ang-hsi (1662–1721) during the Ch'ing dynasty, there were a mere 8,651 nuns to 110,292 monks. It is not clear whether this decrease reflects a decline in the social status of women or whether some other factor is accountable.

49. She tells her story in "Enlightened Education," in *Walking on Lotus Flowers: Buddhist Women Living, Loving and Meditating,* ed. Martine Batchelor (London: Thorsons, 1996), pp. 84–94.

50. William Hu, "Glorious Honor for a Humble Nun," *Sakyadhita: International Association of Buddhist Women* 5.2 (1994): 12–13.

51. Chien-yu Julia Huang and Robert P. Wellner, "Merit and Mothering: Women and Social Welfare in Taiwanese Buddhism," *Journal of Asian Studies* 57.2 (May 1998): 379–96.

52. The Triple Platform Ordination refers to a ceremony that includes receiving the novice precepts, the precepts of a fully-ordained *bhikṣuṇī* or *bhikṣu,* and the bodhisattva precepts.

53. Miranda Shaw presents a thorough study of women in Tantric Buddhism in *Passionate Enlightenment: Women in Tantric Buddhism* (Princeton: Princeton University Press, 1994). A feminist critique of women's role within this tradition is found in June Campbell, *Traveller in Space: In Search of Female Identity in Tibetan Buddhism* (New York: George Braziller, 1996).

54. See Reginald Ray's "Accomplished Womei in Tantric Buddhism of Medieval India and Tibet," in *Unspoken Worlds: Women's Religious Lives in Non-Western Cultures,* ed. Nancy Falk and Rita Gross (San Francisco: Harper and Row, 1979), pp. 227–42.

55. See Janice D. Willis, *Feminine Ground: Essays on Women and Tibet* (Ithaca: Snow Lion Publication, 1989).

56. A report by D. Batsukh, President of the Asian Buddhist Conference for Peace, Ulaan Bataar, that thirty women had received the ten precepts of a *śrāmaṇerikā* from Mongolian *bhikṣus* in April 1991 proved unfounded. In fact, these women received the five precepts of a laywoman (*upāsikā*).

57. Four Mongolian nuns—Thubten Chodron, Thubten Dechen, Thubten Dolma, Thubten Kunze—studied Buddhist philosophy, Tibetan grammar, meditation, and English for three years at Jamyang Choling Institute in Dharmasala, India. Three more Mongolian nuns are currently studying at Ganden Choling Nunnery in Dharamsala and two are at Khachoe Ghakhyil Nunnery in Kathmandu, Nepal.

58. The five precepts of a laywoman (*upāsikā*) or a layman (*upāsaka*) are to refrain from: (1) killing, (2) stealing, (3) lying (especially about one's spiritual achievements), (4) sexual misconduct (principally adultery), and (5) taking intoxicants.

59. Resources on the transmission of Buddhism to the West include Steven Batchelor, *Awakening of the West: The Encounter of Buddhism and Western Culture* (Berkeley: Parallax Press, 1994); Rick Fields, *How the Swans Come to the Lake: A Narrative History of Buddhism in America* (Boston: Shambhala Publications, 1992); Emma Layman, *Buddhism in America* (Chicago: Nelson-Hall Publishers, 1976); Helen Tworkov, *Zen in America; Five Teachers and the Search for an American Buddhism* (Tokyo and New York, Kodansha International, 1994); Christmas Humphreys, *Zen Comes West: The Present and Future of Zen Buddhism in Western Society* (London: Curzon Press, 1997).

60. Anne C. Klein, *Meeting the Great Bliss Queen: Buddhists, Feminists, and the Art of the Self* (Boston: Beacon Press, 1994), p. xvii.

61. Additional resources on Western women in Buddhism include Sandy Boucher, *Turning the Wheel: American Women Creating the New Buddhism* (Boston: Beacon Press, 1993); June Campbell, *Traveller in Space: In Search of Female Identity in Tibetan Buddhism* (New York: George Braziller, 1996); Marianne Dresser, *Buddhist Women on the Edge: Contemporary Perspectives from the Western Frontier;* Lenore Friedman, *Meetings with Remarkable Women: Buddhist Teachers in America* (Boston: Shambhala, 1987); Rita Gross, *Buddhism after Patriarchy: A*

Feminist History, Analysis, and Reconstruction of Buddhism (Albany: State University of New York Press, 1993); and Karma Lekshe Tsomo, *Buddhism through American Women's Eyes* (Ithaca, N.Y.: Snow Lion Publications, 1995).

62. For instance, the term for the Buddha's spiritual offspring, a phrase that occurs frequently in Mahāyāna *sūtras* and prayers, was originally translated as "the Buddha's sons," but is now widely being translated as "the Buddha's children." Again, in the '70s and '80s, the leadership of most Western Buddhist centers was in the hands of men, while the bulk of the work was done by women, but in the '90s women began to assume visible leadership roles. Previously, almost all visiting teachers from Asia were male, but in the '90s this began to change. For example, in the early phases of the Tibetan/Benedictine Monastic Exchange Program all the Tibetan participants were monks, but since 1987 nuns have regularly been included in the delegations. The Beastie Boys specifically requested, through the Milarepa Foundation, that nuns as well as monks be invited to chant at the huge Tibet Concert held in Golden Gate Park in San Francisco in June 1996; as a result, eight nuns were invited from Dharamsala. The event, which attracted 200,000 people, began and ended everyday with chanting by both nuns and monks, and a special tent was erected where Buddhist chanting was performed continuously by the nuns and monks, alternately and together. Subsequent Tibet events held in New York in 1997 and Washington, D.C., in 1998 routinely included nuns.

63. See, for example, S. R. Goyal, *A History of Indian Buddhism* (Meerut, India: Kusumanjali Prakashan, 1987), pp. 292–98. Goyal tries to argue that the large numbers of educated women identified with early Buddhism were actually the product of Brahmanical society, and contends, fancifully enough, that women of the day received equal training in the Vedas.

64. The eight special rules for *bhikṣuṇīs* are discussed in Tsomo, *Sakyadhita*, pp. 223–24; in Yong Chung's M.A. thesis, *"A Buddhist View of Women: A Comparative Study of the Rules for* Bhikṣuṇīs *and* Bhikṣus *Based on the Chinese* Prātimokṣa" (Berkeley: Graduate Theological Union, 1995), pp. 87–97; and Akira Hirakawa's *Monastic Discipline for the Buddhist Nuns: An English Translation of the Chinese Text of the Mahāsāṃghika-Bhikṣuṇī-Vinaya* (Patna, India: K. P. Jayaswal Research Institute, 1982), pp. 35–37.

65. Nancy Schuster Barnes notes that although the Buddhist monks and nuns are alike in appearance and lifestyle, "by imposing rules on nuns which would place them in a permanently inferior position in all their interactions with monks, the monks reserved for themselves the control and leadership of the entire saṃgha." See "Buddhism," in *Women in World Religions*, ed. Arvind Sharma (Albany: State University of New York Press, 1987), p. 108.

66. I am indebted to Kusuma Devendra and Friedgard Lotermoser, whose ongoing Vinaya research has uncovered textual evidence to support these findings.

67. In her article, "An Image of Women in Old Buddhist Literature: The Daughters of Māra," Nancy Falk notes that the positive view toward women

evident among the early Buddhists declines sharply around the time written Buddhist literature began to appear. *Women and Religion,* ed. Judith Plaskow and June Arnold (Missoula, Mont.: Scholars Press, 1974), p. 105.

68. The charge of creating a schism in the Saṅgha is commonly leveled against those who advocate a restoration of full ordination for women, even though the Buddhist texts clearly state that one nun (or monk) alone is incapable of creating a schism. The charge is serious, because creating a schism in the Saṅgha is categorized as one of the five heinous crimes that result in a rebirth in the lowest hell, Avici. The other four heinous crimes are patricide, matricide, killing an *arhat,* and shedding the blood of a Buddha.

69. For example, when a delegation of sixteen *bhikṣuṇīs* from the Sino-Indian Institute of Buddhist Studies in Taiwan attended the International Buddhist Studies Conference held in Tokyo in 1983, a Japanese speaker stated, from the podium: "The presence of so many nuns is evidence of the decline of the Dharma."

70. For example, informants in Burma report that whereas monks may receive an offering of 10,000 *kyats* for participating in a ceremony, nuns at the same ceremony may receive only ten. Although the differential varies by country and situation, the privileged status of monks is evident in the far greater material support they and their monasteries receive. Paradoxically, this support is offered primarily by women donors.

71. From Thich Nhat Hahn, *Innerbeing: Commentaries on the Tiep Hien Precepts* (Berkeley, Calif.: Parallax Press, 1987), p. 17.

72. Bhikṣuṇī Zhengyan, founder of Ciji Foundation, received the Magasasay Award in 1992. (See *Sakyadhita: International Association of Buddhist Women* 5.2, [Summer 1994]: 12–13.) Maeji Khunying Kanitha Wichiencharoen, director of the Thai government's Commission for the Promotion of the Status of Women, has founded a shelter which serves as a haven for battered women, unwed mothers, and pregnant women who are HIV positive. She was ordained as an eight-precept nun following the Third Sakyadhita Conference in Sri Lanka in 1993.

73. The life of Dr. Ambedkar and the movement he inspired are described in two recent articles: Christopher S. Queen's "Dr. Ambedkar and the Hermeneutics of Buddhist Liberation" and Alan Sponberg's "TMBSG: A Dhamma Revolution in Contemporary India," in *Engaged Buddhism: Buddhist Liberation Movements in Asia,* ed. Christopher S. Queen and Sallie B. King (Albany: State University of New York Press, 1996), pp. 45–71, 73–120. Also see Hilary Blakiston's book, *But Little Dust: Life amongst the Ex-Untouchables of Maharashtra* (Cambridge, U.K.: Allborough Press, 1990).

74. Queen and King, *Engaged Buddhism,* pp. 2, 34n.

75. For example, see Fred Eppsteiner, *The Path of Compassion: Writings on Socially Engaged Buddhism* (Berkeley, Calif.: Parallax Publications, 1988); Ken Jones, *The Social Face of Buddhism: An Approach to Political and Social Activism*

(London: Wisdom Publications, 1989); Dhananjay Keer, *Dr. Ambedkar: Life and Mission* (Bombay: Popular Prakashan, 1990); Sulak Sivaraksa, *Seeds of Peace: A Buddhist Vision for Renewing Society* (Berkeley, Calif.: Parallax Press, 1992); Chan Khong, *Learning True Love: How I Learned and Practiced Social Change in Vietnam* (Berkeley, Calif.: Parallax Press, 1993); Ken Jones, *Beyond Optimism: A Buddhist Political Ecology* (Oxford: Jon Carpenter, 1993); Thich Nhat Hahn, *Love in Action: Writings on Nonviolent Social Change* (Berkeley, Calif.: Parallax Press, 1993); Christopher Queen and Sallie B. King, *Buddhist Liberation Movements in Asia* (Albany: State University of New York Press, 1996).

Part I

Buddhist Women in Asian Traditions

South Asian Traditions

Elizabeth J. Harris

1. The Female in Buddhism

Antithetical positions seem to be present in Buddhism's attitude to women. Some observers insist that Buddhism is a male-dominated, patriarchal religion, unwilling to accept women into its hierarchy and therefore is a force keeping women subordinate and exploited. On the other side, it has been argued that women in Buddhist societies of Asia are actually more independent and self-confident than women in other Asian societies and that this is due to a Buddhism that stresses the rights of women and supports their spiritual aspirations. Still others maintain that the male/female distinction is irrelevant to the core of Buddhism. They argue that Buddhism transcends this duality and that women and men who are concerned with this issue are deviating from the true spiritual path.

The subject is a vast one that encompasses over two and a half thousand years, across varying countries in Asia and Europe, and the different schools of Buddhism. Here I will restrict my discussion to Theravāda Buddhism and to an assessment of the attitudes found in the five *nikāyas* of the Pāli canon. I will ask what evidence in these texts justifies any or all the above polarized views, examining the material in the spirit of free enquiry advocated by the Buddha himself in his advice to the Kalamas.[1] I have been influenced by two main factors: a feminist perspective concerned with the place of women in society and the roles forced upon her, and my belief that religion should provide resources for the human journey and the human struggle in the context of the world's political, social, and economic realities.

Two levels of material about women emerge from the Buddhist texts. The first is the level of symbol and image, in which the female represents something larger than herself, embodying forces central to life and death. The second level is the flesh-and-blood reality, the reality of individual women living within the constraints and contradictions of society. Each will be dealt with in the following discussion.

Examining the religions of the world, certain images of women arise again and again. First, there is the image of woman as temptress, the incarnation of evil. Here, the woman appears as the witch, the serpent, and the siren. She is a danger to man's spiritual progress—a force that can lure a man with false promises of fulfillment, only to bring him to destruction. Second, there is image of woman as mother. Here, woman is the symbol of birth, regeneration, and mature, self-giving love—that to which men often yearn to return. In both these images, temptress and mother, the female is surrounded by mystery. The first image is dangerous, while the second is life-giving. There is also a third category, of woman as the mystic, the goddess, as one who has transcended the material and, perhaps, the sexual to gain mystical knowledge and wisdom. Here, the feminine is linked with ultimate spiritual reality. It becomes part of a godhead or, in some religious groups, the truest expression of the Absolute.

Woman as Temptress

Passages can be extracted from the texts to build up a seemingly impressive case. The argument could begin with words which question a woman's ability to become a respected member of society and present her as morally reprehensible. For example, when Ānanda asks why women never sit in court, embark on business, or reach the "essence of the deed," the Buddha is said to reply:

> Womenfolk are uncontrolled, Ānanda. Womenfolk are envious, Ānanda. Womenfolk are greedy, Ānanda. Womenfolk are weak in wisdom, Ānanda.[2]

In addition, an uncontrolled sexual appetite is attributed to women in certain texts of the Pāli canon. The following passages, taken from different texts, are attributed to the Buddha:

> Monks, I know of no single form, sound, smell, savor and touch by which a woman's heart is so enslaved as it is by the form, sound, scent, savor and touch of a man. Monks, a woman's heart is obsessed by these things.[3]
>
> Monks, womenfolk end their life unsated and unreplete with two things. What two? Sexual intercourse and childbirth. These are the two things.[4]

Such words allude to an inherent licentiousness in woman. Thus, she becomes an obstacle to the spiritual progress of man, and, in addition, the embodiment of evil:

> Monks, I see no other single form so enticing, so desirable, so intoxicating, so binding, so distracting, such a hindrance to winning the unsurpassed peace from effort, that is to say, monks, as a woman's form. Monks, whosoever clings to a woman's form—infatuated, greedy, fettered, enslaved, enthralled—for many a long day shall he grieve, snared by the charms of a woman's form.[5]
>
> Monks, if ever one would rightly say: it is wholly a snare of Māra—verily, speaking rightly, one may say of womanhood: it is wholly a snare of Māra.[6]

A quote from *Mahāparinibbāna Sutta* illustrates how members of the Saṅgha are advised to respond in the face of this snare. When Ānanda asks how men should conduct themselves with women, the Buddha's reply is:

> "As not seeing them, Ānanda."
> "But, if we should see them, what are we to do?"
> "No talking, Ānanda."
> "But, if they should talk to us, Lord, what are we to do?"
> "Keep wide awake, Ānanda."[7]

These quotes appear to make a strong case for misogynist attitudes. Yet, of course, there is danger in selecting passages at random. Without context and comparison, the analysis is not complete. For one thing, it is unreasonable to believe that all parts of the Buddhist scriptures bear equal weight. Furthermore, the texts were first committed to memory and it is not impossible that additions were made by the disciples, who succumbed to the prejudices of the wider society. Passages that raise such suspicions must be compared with a spectrum of texts and analyzed in sociohistorical context.

Sexuality within Buddhism

A larger doctrinal context is needed for this and can be found in the Buddhist treatment of sexuality as a whole. An important text here is the *Aggañña Sutta,* a mythological story of the development of human society. According to this story, self-luminous beings descend to earth from a world of radiance. Gradually concepts of private property, the division of labor, and an elected ruler evolve. Each stage in this evolutionary process is presented as a deterioration due to ever-increasing craving (*taṇhā*). Beings gradually lose their luminosity and take on the grossness of the earth. Sexual differentiation is a significant part of this "fall." At first, the beings are described as neither male nor female but, as they begin to eat solid food, cravings develop, gender distinctions arise and, with them, sexual attraction.

> Then truly did woman contemplate man too closely, and man, woman. In them contemplating over much the one the other, passion arose and burning entered the body. They in consequence thereof followed their lusts. And beings seeing them so doing threw some sand, some ashes, some cow dung, crying: Perish, foul one! Perish foul one! How can a being treat a being so.[8]

When sexuality emerges in this myth, it is treated with revulsion. Sexual differentiation is viewed as an integral part of *saṃsāra*, as part of the unsatisfactoriness (*dukkha*) of existence and a cause of suffering. Since it is motivated by craving, it is also regarded as a potential cause for anarchy in society. This is apparent in a text that records the Buddha as saying that the world is protected from anarchy by a sense of shame and the fear of blame. The text continues:

> Monks, if these two states did not protect the world, then there would be seen no mother or mother's sister, no uncle's wife nor teacher's wife, nor wife of honorable men; but the world would come to confusion—promiscuity such as exists among goats and sheep, fowls and swine, dogs and jackals.[9]

In the context of the *Aggañña Sutta*, sexuality becomes part of *saṃsāra* because it is linked with the craving for sensual pleasure that binds humans to rebirth. Here and in other texts, danger in relationships between men and women is highlighted because of the potential for such things as possessiveness, jealousy, and violence. Hence, the early monks were taught to view the sexual and the sensual with revulsion, as a manifestation of craving and the ego-notion. In one *sutta*, the *arahant* Bakkula is asked by another ascetic, "And how many times have you, revered Bakkula, indulged in sexual intercourse?" Bakkula, eighty years old, replies that the question is wrongly formed. It should have been, "How many times have perceptions of sense pleasures arisen in you?" Bakkula asserts that he has not been aware of any time when they had.[10] This was the ideal to be emulated. The world of sensual pleasure was fraught with evil, so it was taught. It was but a short step from this premise to projecting the blame onto woman—a stereotyped image of woman as dangerous, beautiful, and the cause of sexual feelings in man. Since we do not have records of the Buddha giving discourses specifically designed for nuns, evidence is not available to prove that he would have reversed the argument when speaking to them. The scriptures as passed down to us are dominated by males speaking to males.

Woman as Mother

The second image of woman mentioned at the beginning of our discussion was as mother. It must be asked whether this concept is idealized in Buddhism as in some other religions. Although Buddhism recognizes a mother's love as something good and worthy, evidence suggests it is not idealized. A striking image of its positive aspect is presented in the *Saccavibhaṅga Sutta* when the Buddha describes his two main disciples:

> Monks, like a mother, so is Sāriputta;
> Like a child's foster mother, so is Moggallāna.[11]

Here, the loving care of a mother becomes an image of holiness. In the *Hiri Sutta* in the Sutta Nipāta—a section of the canon that makes scant mention of women—the maternal bond is a powerful symbol:

> He is not a friend who always eagerly suspects a breach and looks out for faults; but he with whom he dwells as a son at the breast (of his mother), he is indeed a friend that cannot be severed by others.[12]

A mother's love is recognized and elevated in these similes. In fact, the love of both mother and father is exalted in Buddhism:

> Even if one should carry about his mother on one shoulder and his father on the other, and so doing should live a hundred years; and if he should support them, anointing them with unguents, kneading, bathing and rubbing their limbs . . . even so he could not repay his parents. . . . Monks, parents do much for their children; they bring them up, they nourish them, they introduce them to this world.[13]

The *Karanīya Metta Sutta* is another example. At its heart is the image of a mother's love and her wish to protect her child.

> Just as a mother protects her only child as if he were her own life, (he should) extend thoughts of unbounded kindness to all living beings.[14]

The centrality of this *sutta* within the religiosity of Theravāda Buddhism indicates the significant role of woman's image as mother.

This is not the only presentation of motherhood within Buddhism, however. A verse in the *Dhammapada,* for instance, uses a maternal simile in a totally different context:

> Insofar as one has not cut down the last little sapling of the jungle of the lust of man for woman, insofar his mind is in bondage, like a sucking calf to his mother.[15]

Here, sexual love for a woman is seen as bondage, but what is noteworthy is that maternal love and filial love are placed in the same category. Motherhood is not glorified, but is seen as part of *saṃsāra*. Other texts describe the pain involved in the loving nurture of a child,[16] a pain that is a barrier to spiritual attainment.[17]

There is, in fact, a consistent strand within the Buddhist texts that presents a woman's role in society in unglamorous terms, particularly child-bearing. Kisāgotamī, a woman who lost her child and eventually renounced the world to become a nun, attributed the following view to the Buddha:

> Woeful is a woman's lot, hath he declared,
> Tamer and driver of the hearts of men:
> Woeful when sharing home with hostile wives,
> Woeful when giving birth in bitter pain
> Some seeking death or e'er they suffer twice,
> Piercing the throat, the delicate poison take
> Woe too when mother-murdering embryo
> Comes not to birth and both alike find death.[18]

A *Saṃyutta Nikāya* passage echoes these sentiments. The Buddha is recorded as saying that the special woes of women are "leaving relatives behind to go to a husband, menses, pregnancy, giving birth and having to wait upon a man."[19] Many a twentieth-century feminist would welcome the realism in these words. Within Buddhism, they gain added impact due to the concept of numerous lives within *saṃsāra*.

The story of Ubbiri illustrates this. Ubbiri was a queen who, upon losing her daughter, was thrown into deep mourning. Enlightenment came when the Buddha asked her which daughter she was weeping for, saying that eighty-four thousand of her daughters had been buried in the same cemetery.[20] Then, in another text, a mother's milk becomes a symbol for explaining the immensity of *saṃsāra:* "As to that, what think ye brethren? Which is greater: the mother's milk that ye have drunk as ye have fared on, run on the long while, or the water in the four seas?" The answer: mother's milk.[21]

Impermanence (*anicca*) is another aspect of *saṃsāra* that is illustrated with reference to womanhood. The fleeting quality of feminine beauty is repeatedly noted. A girl is at the height of her loveliness at fifteen or sixteen, but imagine the same woman at ninety, says the *Mahādukkhakhanda Sutta:* "Crooked as a rafter, bent, leaning on a stick, going along palsied, miserable, youth gone, teeth broken, hair thinned, skin wrinkled, stumbling along, the limbs discolored." We are then asked to imagine the same woman ill, lying in her own excrement, or dead: "swollen, discolored, decomposing."[22] The lesson to be learned is that suffering is inherent in craving for impermanent objects. The danger of using the image of woman to illustrate this is apparent to anyone concerned with the position of women. If the feminine is equated with external beauty and its impermanent nature inevitably leads to suffering, then woman is seen only in this light.

Therefore, I argue, when woman or the feminine is used in a symbolic or metaphoric way, it is more often linked with *dukkha* and *saṃsāra* than with the holy or mystical.[23] As a symbol, the female is used to illustrate sensuality, suffering, and impermanence. She is also seen as an obstruction to a world renouncer.

What, then, of real flesh and blood women? How did the Buddha advise them? Did women find liberation within his teachings?

Woman as Lay Follower

It is often said that the Buddha rejected the view of his contemporaries that the birth of a daughter was bad news. He is recorded as having said these words to King Pasenadi after the king's wife gave birth to a daughter:

> A woman child, O lord of men, may prove
> Even better offspring than a male
> For she may grow up wise and virtuous
> Her husband's mother reverencing, true wife
> The boy that she might bear may do great deeds
> And rule great realms, yea, such a son
> Of noble wife becomes his country's guide.[24]

These words were radical in the sixth century B.C.E., but feminists would question them now. A woman is praised as a bearer of sons and as a virtuous and devoted wife. A certain role is imposed upon her as soon as she breathes air in this world and her worth is defined accordingly.

In the following exchange, the Buddha is seen to affirm the complete subordination of a wife to her husband's wishes. Giving advice to the daughters of a lay follower, he says,

> Wherefore, girls, train yourself in this way:
> To whatsoever husband our parents shall give us . . .
> For him we will rise up early, be the last to retire,
> Be willing workers, order all things sweetly and be gentlevoiced.[25]

He further advises them to revere relations, to learn their husband's craft, and to look after slaves and workers. This is the picture we find in works considered later than the main body of doctrine as well. The *Vimānavatthu* of the *Khuddaka Nikāya*, for instance, tells of wives rewarded with mansions due to their good deeds. The words spoken by these exemplary wives are:

> When I was human, young and innocent
> Serene in heart I delighted my Lord
> So by day and by night I acted to please
> A virtuous woman in days of old was I
> Utterly chaste in body, I lived in purity.[26]
>
> When I was human, living among men
> A faithful wife with heart for no other was I
> I sheltered my Lord as a mother her child
> Even though angry I spoke no rough word.[27]

Late twentieth-century norms lead us to view the wifely model suggested here as exploitative of women, yet there are other voices within the Pāli canon.

The *Sigālovāda Sutta* presents one. It mentions six relationships in society, stressing that each involves both rights and duties. These include the employer/employee, teacher/pupil, and wife/husband relationships. A wife is advised to show her love by duties well-performed (though not specified), hospitality to family members, watching over the goods of her husband, faithfulness, and industry in all matters. In return, she has a right to receive from her husband respect, courtesy, faithfulness, a certain amount of authority in the home, and gifts for her adornment.[28] This is an advance over social norms that demand complete submissiveness, in that the wife has rights and is considered worthy of respect.

The Fourfold Society

The early Buddhist concept of a balanced society included four divisions: monks, nuns, laymen, and laywomen. Each of these is seen as essential for the well-being of the religion:

> Monks, these four are accomplished in wisdom, disciplined, confident, deeply learned, Dhamma-bearers, who live according to Dhamma—these four illuminate the Order.[29]

Woman is described here as on equal terms with man regarding the contribution she can make to society and religion. Although there is a hierarchy in the ordering of the four categories, they are described in exactly the same terms: all four are said to illuminate the order.

On the basis of this evidence, it would be unjust to declare that Buddhism favors the subordination of women. The *Sigālovāda Sutta* does delineate clear roles for women and men: the wife manages the household and hospitality, and the husband procures the goods. Yet while the traditional division of labor within the family is reinforced, it is within the context of respect rather than submission. By affirming the centrality of mutual care and concern in the institution of marriage and setting forth guidelines for its implementation, this model lays the foundation for more self-confidence and fulfillment for women within the fourfold society.

In this connection, the commentarial story for verse 18 of the Dhammapada is worth mention.[30] Sumana, the youngest daughter of Anāthapiṇḍika, lying on her death-bed, addresses her father as "younger brother" and dies. Anāthapiṇḍika is horrified at such irreverence and mentions the incident to the Buddha. The Buddha tells him that her address was correct because she has reached a higher spiritual stage than her father. The process of religious and social change is clearly shown here. Buddhism challenges traditional patterns of subordination through suggesting new criteria for social relationships. It is through those who joined the Bhikkhunī Order, however, that the question of women and religious attainment is most poignantly brought into focus.

Woman as Renunciant

The story of the founding of the Bhikkunī Order has been taken as evidence that the Buddha was not a supporter of the spiritual aspirations of women. It portrays the Buddha as agreeing only reluctantly to the admission of women and laying down extra rules to ensure their subservience to men. It is said that he also forecast the decline of Buddhism due to the entry of women into its ranks.[31] For instance, one of the eight extra rules for the nuns enjoins them to honor a monk, however junior in age or experience. This meant that a nun of forty years standing had to bow down to a monk ordained but a day. Yet as humiliating as this is seen to be, it must be viewed within the context of social change. It does not necessarily mean that the Bhikkhunī Order was in a patriarchal stranglehold.

The Buddha was critical of many aspects of contemporary brahminical society, drawing opposition as well as praise.[32] Patterns of social behavior were changing in the growing urban centers. Nevertheless, there was reason for him to be circumspect in a culture with many patriarchal elements.

More reliable indicators of the situation in early Buddhism are contained in the words of the nuns and in dialogues between nuns and laypeople. In contrast to texts describing women as snares on a man's spiritual path, we find texts with women teaching men. The nun Dhammadinna teaches her former husband, a lay person, and is in every way the spiritual director, not a wife. Addressing her former husband, the Buddha declares, "Clever, Visākhā, is the nun Dhammadinna, of great wisdom, about this matter. I too would have answered exactly as the nun Dhammadinna argued."[33] Nor is this an isolated incident, for the Buddha commends Sister Khema and others in the same way.[34]

A text in the *Aṅguttara Nikāya* lists prominent people within the four sections of society, including forty monks and thirteen nuns. It is significant that the qualities for which nuns are known are wisdom, meditational power, Dhamma teaching, energetic striving, and supernormal powers. No case can be made to support the view that the nuns are allocated inferior qualities. The principle virtues and achievements are all found equally among the nuns and the monks.[35]

The *Therīgāthā* comes down to us as a collection of verses ascribed to nuns. At the beginning are words by the Buddha addressed to individual nuns. If only as a counterbalance to words predicting the downfall of Buddhism because of the admission of women to the order, they are worth quoting. Strong, sensitive, and full of respect, these verses exhort and encourage women to reach the highest goals. And the verses make it obvious that some have succeeded in doing so. For instance, Mutta is told:

> Get thee free, Liberta, free e'en as the Moon
> From out the Dragon's jaws sails clear on high.
> Wipe off the debts that hinder thee, and so,
> With heart at liberty, break thou thy fast.[36]

Dhirā is exhorted thus:

> Come, O Dhirā, reach up and touch the goal
> Where all distractions cease, where sense is stilled
> Where dwelleth bliss; win thou *Nibbāna*, win
> That sure Salvation (*yogakkhema*), which hath no beyond.[37]

And another Dhirā:

> Dhirā, brave Sister, who hath valiantly
> Thy faculties in noblest culture trained,
> Bear to this end thy last incarnate frame
> For thou has conquered Māra and his host.[38]

The words ascribed to the nuns reveal women who have been liberated and it is clear from what they have been freed. The tensions surrounding a woman's place in society are openly voiced. The bondage experience takes many forms, including the chains of marriage, the pressures of suitors, the bondage of being seen only as a sex object, and the grief of bereavement after the loss of a husband or child. Mutta, for instance, is married to a hunchback and later becomes a renunciant:

> O free, indeed! O gloriously free
> Am I in freedom from three crooked things:
> From quern, from mortar, from my crookback Lord
> Ay, but I'm free from rebirth and from death
> And all that dragged me back is hurled away.[39]

And there is Sumaṅgala's mother who was unhappily married to a mat weaver before leaving lay life:

> O woman well set free! how free am I
> How thoroughly free from kitchen drudgery
> Me stained and squalid 'mong my cooking pots
> My brutal husband ranked as even less
> Than the sunshades he sits and weaves alway[s].[40]

Isidāsi, thrown out of her home by three successive husbands, says of one of them:

> And as a mother on her only child
> So did I minister to my good man.
> For me, who with toil infinite thus worked,
> And rendered service with a humble mind,
> Rose early, ever diligent and good
> For me he nothing felt save sore dislike.[41]

The wish to renounce often comes when the reality of *dukkha*, unsatisfactoriness, is seen for what it is. The verses of the nuns are a comment on the pressures placed upon females in society, which could lead to this insight. Some of the nuns leave apparently happy and comfortable marriages, but others are aware of the peculiar chains placed around laywomen. Subha, for instance, is the beautiful daughter of a goldsmith. Her verses vehemently reject wealth and sense pleasures. It is as though she addresses the world of men when her verses say:

> Ruthless and murderous are sense desires
> Foemen of cruel spear and prison bonds
> Why herewithal, my kinsmen—nay my foes—
> Why yoke me in your minds with sense desires?
> Know me as her who has fled the life of sense,
> Shorn of her hair, wrapt in her yellow robe.[42]

Subha challenges a stereotype of women beloved of androcentrism The same pattern can be seen in the *Bhikkhunī Saṃyutta* of the *Saṃyutta Nikāya* when Māra attempts to dissuade some nuns from their chosen path. One of the stereotypes he uses is that of sexual uncontrollability To a nun, named the Ālavite, he says:

> Ne'er shall you find escape while in the world.
> What profits you then your loneliness?
> Take you your fill of sense desires and love.[43]

And Gotamī is asked:

> You who have plunged into the woods alone
> Is it a man that you have come to find?[44]

Both nuns strip Māra's words of power. They are *arahants* and Māra's caricatures become meaningless—even ludicrous.

Women and Liberation

All of the *therīs* in the *Therīgāthā* reach the highest goal of enlightenment or arahantship. Their verses speak of the death of ignorance, the bliss of knowledge, and the destruction of craving. Concerns usually linked with the female, such as clothes, ornaments, and beauty, no longer have meaning for them. There is a rejection of the stereotypical role that male-dominated society projects on a woman. Subha rejects the male tendency to see her only as a sex object, as a manifestation of external beauty. Others reject the kind of marital exploitation that demands continual work and continual willingness from a woman The fact that the nuns find liberation in the order is not only a comment on the truth of the Buddha's teaching, but also upon the restricted nature of the female's role in Indian society at the time Significantly, part of the nuns' sense of liberation comes from being in a situation where the male/female distinction loses importance.

In the *Bhikkhunī Saṃyutta* of the *Saṃyutta Nikāya,* when Māra, the evil one, tries to tempt the nun Soma away from meditation, saying that a woman can never hope to achieve progress, she replies:

> What should a woman's nature signify
> When consciousness is tense and firmly set. . .
> To one for whom the question doth arise:
> Am I a woman, (in these matters) or
> Am I a man, or what not am I then?
> To such a one is Māra fit to talk.[45]

Here she is saying that one who distinguishes between male and female regarding spiritual abilities is under the sway of evil. Such an insight accords with the *Aggañña Sutta* and its stress on sexual distinction as an aspect of deterioration. The implication is that true spiritual progress leads to a point where beings are beyond male and female. Thus, the nuns claim equality with men. Bhadda claims equality with Kassapa, one of the foremost monks, in this verse:

> We both have seen, both he and I, the woe,
> And pity of the world, and have gone forth
> We both are arahants with selves well tamed
> Cool are we both, ours is *Nibbāna* now![46]

In this context, the woman as *arahant* finds herself worthy of respect because what she now embodies—wisdom and knowledge—is beyond the sexual sphere. She is respected not because she is a woman, but because she is enlightened. The verses of the *Therīgāthā* present us with strong, determined, spiritual women. Renunciation provided these women with answers to their questions about existence and to the unsatisfactory position of women in society, either as wife and mother or as a young woman courted for her beauty. It gave them the opportunity to leave behind the craving (*taṇhā*) inherent in a male-dominated society and move toward acceptance as spiritual seekers.

The Bhikkunī Order cannot be found in Theravāda countries today. Nuns exist and women are inevitably drawn to the renunciant life, but higher ordination is denied them. The religious hierarchy is male, which goes against the thrust of early Buddhism. In the eyes of women seeking new patterns of relationships between women and men, this reinforces the impression that Theravāda Buddhism is male chauvinist and sexist. Male dominance in the hierarchy shows how far Buddhism has traveled from its origins and how much it has succumbed to the older, more tenacious stereotypes through which male power has become entrenched.

Conclusion

At the beginning, I outlined three positions concerning the female in Buddhism: that Buddhism is male-dominated and blocks a woman's path to fulfillment; that Buddhism has advanced the status of women and helped them become more self-confident; and that the male/female distinction is irrelevant to the true message of Buddhism. All three of these positions can be supported by textual material. They are all, in particular contexts, true in relation to different levels of experience within Theravāda Buddhism. Thus, a unified, clearly defined position is difficult to reach.

In Theravāda countries today, it is hard to deny that there are obstacles in the path of women who wish to renounce lay life and follow the complete Vinaya rules. In addition to the vicissitudes of history, these difficulties seem rooted in the attitudes expressed in the texts, which present women as sexually uncontrollable, lacking in wisdom, and a snare to men. I do not feel that these attitudes are true to the core of early Buddhism, yet they seem to have entered Buddhism at an early stage. Since such attitudes exist in most cultures of the world, it is not remarkable that Buddhism and most of the religions of the world have succumbed to them.

The position that Buddhism has advanced the status of women is supported by the importance given to women in the fourfold society of early Buddhism. Buddhism also attempted to protect women from exploitation in marriage by stressing that a husband has duties to his wife. On one hand, the difficulties a woman faces in leaving her childhood home to look after a husband and giving birth are not denied; yet on the other, there are images of genuine marital happiness, as when the parents of the monk Nakula come to the Buddha and ask whether they will be together in a future life. The husband says:

> Lord, ever since the housewife Nakula's mother was brought home to me when a mere lad, she being a mere girl, I am not conscious of having transgressed against her even in thought, much less in person. Lord, we do desire to behold one another not only in this very life but also in the life to come.[47]

The Buddha's responds that they will, since they are matched in virtue.

Although the Buddhist texts hold that marriage is central to lay life, Buddhism demythologizes human existence. Human dreams are stripped bare to reveal impermanence and the deep-seated unsatisfactoriness behind what seems desirable. In this light, marriage, childbirth, and even affection are seen as flawed and painful. While feminists today may see this suffering as due to the role imposed upon women and a reason to struggle for change in society, the Buddha's answer was to renounce lay life, lead the spiritual life of a nun, and work for the elimination of suffering, leaving the male/female differentiation behind.

In terms of the ultimate spiritual goal of Buddhism, liberation (*nibbāna*), the Theravāda tradition rejects the woman/man differentiation. It holds that the potential for spiritual growth through mind-training and effort is present in all beings. It sees the enlightened one, or *arahant,* as having transcended sexuality to reach a stage where gender is irrelevant. The verses of the nuns confirm this. They seem to have discovered that fullness in life is possible only through a renunciation of that which distinguishes woman from man in society. Liberation involves transcending their femaleness.

An important question that follows from this is whether Buddhism's assertion that in spiritual terms we are neither male nor female can accommodate the view that there is a distinctive worth in womanhood. Many women today feel that the distinctively feminine must be reasserted if the world is to avoid a steady drift toward self-destruction through war, ecological abuse, and injustice. They resist a transcending of sexual division, urging positive valuation of the feminine. Theravāda Buddhism seems to answer that those qualities often regarded as distinctively feminine—nonaggression, nurturing of life, and compassion—must be reasserted. However, these qualities can and should be the possession of both male and female. These wholesome qualities are not restricted by gender, but are potential attributes for beings in general. Both male and female need to shed the stereotypical roles imposed upon them, as well as the craving and selfish defense of the feminine or masculine ego. This is perhaps one of the greatest challenges presented by the study of gender in Buddhism.

One final question remains for me, as a woman. Sumedha in her poem describes the body as "foul, unclean, emitting odors . . . a repulsive carcass, plastered over with flesh." Her words express a violent denial of the material and an aversion toward what is distinctively human. This forms a significant strand within Theravāda Buddhism. Yet later, in tantric Buddhism, sexuality and the sacred mystically mingle. Some Buddhist monuments, such as Temple No. 45 at Sanchi, contain sculpture with potentially erotic elements. Is it possible to maintain a rejection of sexuality? I do not deny that the traditional roles imposed on men and women by society have been a cause of suffering and the exploitation of women. I sympathize with the early nuns and find the way Buddhism frees women from idealization refreshing. Yet, I also believe that sexuality can be positive. What is needed is a transformation of our attitudes rather than a rejection with revulsion. Buddhism assists this process by teaching the futility of assessing our sexuality through externals such as physical beauty. The affirmation of our gender seems more than just this. Should Buddhism perhaps address the relation of sexuality and spirituality anew?

Notes

All quotes and references are taken from the volumes of the Pāli Text Society, Oxford.

AN	*Aṅguttara Nikāya*
Dhpda	*Dhammapada*
DN	*Dīgha Nikāya*
MN	*Majjihima Nikāya*
SN	*Saṃyutta Nikāya*
Sn	*Sutta Nipāta*
Therī	*Therīgāthā*
Vimāna	*Vimānavatthu*

1. AN, I.188.
2. AN, II.81.
3. AN, I.2.
4. AN, I.77.
5. AN, III.67.
6. AN, III.67.
7. D, II.141.
8. D, III.88–89.
9. AN, I.50.
10. MN, III.125.
11. MN, III.248.
12. Sn, v. 255.
13. AN, I.61.
14. Sn, v. 143ff.
15. Dhpda, v. 284.
16. See, for example, verses such as AN, I.177 and AN, III.62, which describe the disasters, such as fire, flood, and old age, which separate mother and child, and cause pain.
17. Reference can be made to such texts as AN, IV.159 and the *Khaggavisāṇa Sutta* of the Sutta Nipāta (Sn, v. 35ff.), which imply that spiritual progress is hindered by familial affection and the sexual drives connected with it.
18. Therī, vv. 215–16.
19. SN, IV.239.

20. Therī, v. 51ff.

21. SN, II.181.

22. SN, II.181.

23. See also Diana Paul, *Women in Buddhism: Images of the Feminine in the Mahayana Tradition* (Berkeley: Asian Humanities Press, 1979), which deals in detail with different images of the female in the Mahāyāna tradition.

24. SN, I.85.

25. AN, III.36–37.

26. Vimāna, 31.

27. Vimāna, 11.

28. DN, III.190.

29. AN, II.8.

30. "Here he is happy, hereafter he is happy. In both states the well-doer is happy. Thinking 'Good have I done,' he is happy. Furthermore, he is happy having gone to a blissful state."

31. *The Book of the Discipline,* Vol. 5, X.253ff. (*Vinaya Pitaka, Cullavagga*).

32. For example, the Buddha was critical of the caste system (See MN, II.83ff.; MN, II.125ff.), oppressive systems of service (See MN, II.177ff.), unquestioning acceptance of tradition (See MN, II.164ff.), sacrifice and ritual (See D, I.127ff.; D, III.180ff.).

33. MN, I.304–5.

34. See SN, IV.373ff., where Bhikkhunī Khema teaches King Pasenadi.

35. AN, I.23ff.

36. Therī, v. 2.

37. Therī, v. 6.

38. Therī, v. 7.

39. Therī, v. 11.

40. Therī, v. 23.

41. Therī, vv. 412–13.

42. Therī, vv. 347–48.

43. SN, I.128.

44. SN, I.129.

45. SN, I.129.

46. Therī, v. 66.

47. AN, I.61.

Lorna Dewaraja

2. Buddhist Women in India and Precolonial Sri Lanka

How should the women's nature hinder us?
Whose hearts are firmly set, who ever move
With growing knowledge onward in the Path?
What can that signify to one in whom
Insight doth truly comprehend the Norm?[1]

These words were uttered twenty-five centuries ago by a Buddhist nun named Soma, when Mara, the "Evil One," sneered and jeered at her while she was mediating: "How could you women with your 'two-finger wisdom' ever hope to attain a higher mental state which even the sages find hard to reach?" There was a popular notion in India that, although women cook rice daily throughout their lives, they can never learn how long it takes for the rice to cook; they need to take some grains in a spoon and press them with two fingers to test whether it is done. With her dignified retort to Mara's abusive words, Soma challenged the notion of women's inherent inferiority and their incapacity to attain higher mental or spiritual states. Here we have an example of a woman who defied the notion of sexual inequality 2,500 years before the women's liberation movement appeared in the West.

Sri Lanka attracted international attention in 1960 when Sirimavo Bandaranaike, a woman, was elected the country's first woman prime minister. Sri Lankans, however, did not regard this as outrageous. It was no revolutionary deviation from tradition for a woman to rise to a position of importance and responsibility and no violation of social-cultural norms for a woman to step into the male-dominated world of politics.

Of course, it cannot be argued that in Buddhist societies the position of women was equal to that of men, for the myth of male superiority is universal. Nevertheless, it can be demonstrated that women in Buddhist societies were relatively free from the extreme forms of discrimination and harassment that were characteristic of other major Asian cultures. In the present work I will examine the fundamental tenets of Buddhism to see whether there is a fundamental difference in attitudes toward men and women. Then I will discuss how Buddhist ideology influenced the position and status of women in India and Sri Lanka before the impact of the West was felt.

Examining the position of women in pre-Buddhist India on the basis of evidence in the earliest literature of the Indo-Aryans, the Ṛgveda, it is clear that women held an honorable place in early Indian society. Women had access to the highest knowledge and could participate in all religious ceremonies. There were also a few hymns composed by women. Later, when the priestly Brahmin caste began to dominate society, it is apparent that religion lost its spontaneity and became a complex system of rituals. At this point, a downward trend in the position of women began.

The most relentless of Brahmin law-givers was Manu, considered the founder of social and moral order. From the outset, Manu deprived women of their religious rights and access to the spiritual life. As with people born into the lower castes, women were prohibited from reading the sacred texts, and could neither worship nor perform sacrifices on their own. A woman could not attain heaven through any merit of her own, but only through obedience to her husband. She was taught that a husband, even one devoid of good qualities, should be worshipped incessantly as a god.[2] Despite this humiliating subordination of women in the religious domain, there was always in India a parallel line of thought that glorified motherhood and idealized the concept of the feminine. In actual practice, however, Manu's Code of Laws adversely influenced social attitudes toward women, especially in the higher rungs of society.

It is against this background that we must view the emergence of Buddhism in northern India in the sixth century B.C.E. There are records of long conversations the Buddha had with his female disciples. The devout benefactress Visākhā frequented the monastery decked out in all her finery. Accompanied by a maidservant, she attended to the needs of the celibate monks. The Buddha's liberal attitude toward women has had a great impact on the behavior of both men and women in Buddhist societies. This is not to suggest that the Buddha inaugurated a campaign for the liberation of Indian womanhood, but he did create a minor stir by speaking out against prevailing dogma and superstition. He condemned the caste structure dominated by Brahmins and denounced excessive ritual and sacrifice. Denying the existence of a creator God, he emphasized emancipation through individual effort.

The Buddhist doctrine of salvation through an individual's own efforts presupposes the spiritual equality of all beings, male and female. This assertion of women's spiritual equality, explicitly enunciated in the texts, has had a significant impact on social structures and how women are viewed in the world. Women and men alike are able to attain the Buddhist goal by following the prescribed path; no external assistance in the form of a priestly intermediary or veneration of a husband is necessary. In domestic life in ancient India, religious observances and sacrifices were performed jointly by husband and wife. In Buddhism, however, all religious activities, whether meditation or worship, are acts of self-discipline created by individuals, independent of one's partner or outside assistance.

In patriarchal societies, the desire for male offspring for the continuation of the patrilineage is very strong. And in Indian society, the importance attached to ritual led to an even stronger desire to beget sons, for only a son could perform the funeral rites and thus ensure the future happiness of the deceased. Indeed, a father was believed to achieve immortality through a son's intercession. This custom was so widespread that a wife without sons could be legally superseded by a second or even a third wife, or even be turned out of the house.[3] By contrast, a Buddhist funeral ceremony is a very simple rite that can be performed by the widow, the daughter, or anyone else. Future happiness does not depend on funeral rites, but on an individual's actions while living.

The birth of a daughter was a cause for lamentation in society at that time, but the Buddha did not concur with this view. It is a well known that when King Pasenadi of Kosala came grieving that his queen Mallika had given birth to a daughter, the Buddha said: "A female offspring, O king, may prove even nobler than a male."[4] Even today, the birth of girl children may be mourned. A report prepared to mark South Asia's Year of the Girl Child says that, although girls are born biologically stronger, three hundred thousand more girls than boys die each year.[5] Many are aborted after sex detection tests. A study conducted in 1984 mentions that 7,999 of 8,000 aborted fetuses tested at a Bombay clinic were female. Although it is rampant in India today, the custom of female infanticide seems to have been extremely rare in Buddhist times.

In Buddhism, unlike in Christianity and Hinduism, marriage is not a sacrament. It is a purely secular contract and Buddhist monks do not participate in it. In Sri Lankan, Thai, and Burmese society, there is much ceremony and merrymaking connected with weddings, but these are not of a religious nature. Nevertheless, in the *Sigālovāda Sutta* the Buddha gives advice of a very practical nature to a young layman on how spouses should treat one another. The marital union is approached in a spirit of warm fellowship and is not raised to an exalted spiritual level. These instructions can be summarized as follows: Husbands should respect their wives and comply as far as possible with their requests. They should not commit adultery. They should give their wives full charge of the home and supply them with fine clothes and jewelry, as far as their means permit. Wives should be thorough in their duties, gentle and kind to the whole household, chaste, careful in housekeeping duties, and should carry out their work with skill and enthusiasm.

The significant point is that the Buddha's injunctions are applicable to both parties. The marital relationship is a reciprocal one with mutual rights and obligations, which was a momentous departure from ideas prevailing at his time. For instance, Manu says, "Offspring, the due performance of religious rites, faithful service, highest conjugal happiness and heavenly bliss for one's ancestors and oneself depend on one's wife alone."[6] Similarly, Confucian codes detailed the duties of son to father, wife to husband, and daughter-in-law to mother-in-law, but never vice versa.[7] Wives had only duties and obligations, while husbands had only rights and privileges. In the Buddha's injunctions, by contrast, domestic duties and relationships were reciprocal, whether between husband and wife, parent and child, or master and servant. Theoretically, therefore, a Buddhist marriage is a contract between equals, even if social practice does not necessarily conform to the ideal.

European authors describing Buddhist societies have commented favorably on the position of women. For instance, a British visitor in the late eighteenth century says, "The Cingalese women are not merely the slaves and mistresses but in many respects the companions and friends of their husbands. . . . The Cingalese neither keep their women in confinement nor impose on them any humiliating constraints."[8] Commenting on the situation in Burma in 1878, Lieutenant General Albert Fytche, wrote that "woman holds among them a position of perfect freedom and independence. She is with them not a mere slave of passion, but has equal rights and is the recognized and duly honored helpmate of man, and in fact bears a more prominent share in the transactions of the more ordinary affairs of life than is the case perhaps with any other people either eastern or western."[9] These and other references by European writers to women in the Buddhist societies of Sri Lanka, Thailand, Burma, Sikkim, Bhutan, and Tibet make it clear that, long before the impact of Westernization was felt, women held an honorable place within the institution of marriage.

Marriage and family are basic to all societies and the position of women in a given society is reflected in the status she holds within these institutions. Marriage contracts, in particular—whether a woman has the same rights as her husband to dissolve the marriage bond and to remarry—are primary indicators of women's rights. In many Asian cultures, a woman is irrevocably bound by the chains of matrimony, whereas a man can dissolve the contract with ease. In Sri Lankan Buddhist society, however, marriages receive no religious sanction and Sinhala law provides for the dissolution of marriage contracts and the remarriage of both partners. This is indicated as early as 1769 in a document presenting the orthodox and official view on the subject at the time. The Dutch, who were ruling the maritime provinces of Sri Lanka, wished to codify the laws and customs of the island. The Dutch Governor Iman Willem Falck (1765–83) sent a questionnaire to the eminent Buddhist monks in Kandy and recorded their answers in a document called the *Lakraja lo sirita.*[10] According to this document, both husband and wife are allowed to initiate action for dissolving a marriage contract by proving the improper conduct of a spouse before a court of law. After divorce, both husband and wife were free to remarry and the wife was treated very liberally. There are records of the remarriage of many divorced women, among the royalty, nobility, and common folk. Robert Knox, a British sailor who was shipwrecked and spent nineteen years in the Kandyan kingdom, from 1660 to 1679, left a fascinating account of the socioeconomic conditions of the time. With regard to marriage customs, he writes, "But if they chance to mislike one another and part asunder . . . then she is fit for another man, being as they account never the worse for wearing."[11]

In ancient India a widow was expected to lead a life of strict celibacy and severe austerity upon the demise of her husband, for she was thought to be bound to him beyond death. Furthermore, she lost her social and religious status and was considered a most unfortunate person. In Buddhism, by contrast, death is considered a natural and inevitable end for all beings. As a result, a woman suffers no moral degradation on account of widowhood, nor is her social status altered in any way. In Sri Lankan society, a widow does not have to proclaim her widowhood in any tangible way, such as relinquishing her ornaments, shaving her head, or practicing self-mortification. Robert Knox observes, "These women are of a very strong courageous spirit, taking nothing very much to heart, mourning more for fashion than affection, never overwhelmed neither with grief or love. And when their husbands are dead, all they care is where to get others, which they cannot long be without."[12] The remarriage of widows was prevalent even in the royal family, with no stigma attached. As one example, when Vimala Dharma Suriya I (1594–1605) of Kandy died, his successor Senarat (1605–1635) married his widow.

In many societies, wives are regarded as the personal property of their husbands. The custom of slaying, sacrificing, or burying a woman alive with her deceased husband's other possessions, has been found in lands as far removed as Africa, America, and India. The best known example is the *sati* ritual, self-immolation of high-caste Hindu widows, a custom unknown in the Ṛgveda. Although the custom was never widespread, isolated instances continue in India even today, and it is questionable whether all cases are voluntary. The *sati* ritual is unknown in Sri Lanka or any other Buddhist society.

The social freedom enjoyed by women in Buddhist societies has evoked comment from many Western observers. Although women were not equal in status, a complete lack of segregation of the sexes has distinguished Buddhist societies from those of the Middle East, the Far East, and the Indian subcontinent, where segregation has often lead to the seclusion and confinement of women behind walls and veils. In contradistinction to the Confucian code, which sets forth detailed rules on etiquette between women and men, early Buddhist literature describes the free intermingling of the sexes. Even celibate monks and nuns mingled freely with the rest of society.

The free social intercourse between men and women in Sri Lanka in the seventeenth century surprised Robert Knox: "The men are not jealous of their wives for the greatest ladies of the land will frequently talk and discourse with any men they please although their husbands be in presence." In 1928, Sir Charles Bell, British political representative in Tibet, Bhutan, and Sikkim, wrote about Tibetan women: "They are not kept in seclusion as are Indian women. Accustomed to mix with the other sex throughout their lives they are at ease with men and can hold their own as well as any women in the world." He continues, "And the solid fact remains that in Buddhist countries women hold a remarkably good position. Burma, Ceylon and Tibet exhibit the same picture."

The Bhikkhuṇī Saṅgha, or Order of Buddhist Nuns

There are certain sections of the Pāli canon that are devoted entirely to nuns. For instance, the *Therīgāthā*, or *Psalms of the Sisters*, consisting entirely of verses attributed to seventy-three women who became spiritually realized *therī*s (nun elders), is unique in any literature. There is also the *Apadana*, or biographies in verse of forty nuns who were the Buddha's contemporaries. During the life of the Buddha, his aunt and foster mother, Mahāpajāpatī, was the leader of a movement clamoring for the admission of women to the Saṅgha. When the Buddha showed reluctance to allow this, Mahāpajāpatī and hundreds of other women shaved their heads, donned the yellow robe like the monks, walked barefoot to the monastery where the Buddha lived, and rallied outside. This constitutes the first time in recorded history that women marched in procession demanding equal rights.

Ānanda, the Buddha's faithful disciple, seeing these aristocratic women with swollen, bleeding feet, pleaded on their behalf. He approached the Buddha, asking whether women were as capable as men in leading a life of contemplation and attaining the goal of final emancipation, or *nibbāna*. The Buddha's reply was affirmative. If so, Ānanda argued, then it is proper that women be allowed to leave the household life, join the Saṅgha, and strive toward their salvation. Though the Buddha finally consented to the admission of women to the order, it was on rather humiliating terms. The price of admission was their unequivocal acceptance of eight rules (*aṭṭha garudhamma*), all of which upheld the superiority of the monks.

The first rule is that, even if she has been ordained for a century, a *bhikkhunī*, or fully ordained nun, must rise up from her seat, greet respectfully, and salute a monk who had been ordained even that very day. The implications of these rules are perfectly compatible with the assumptions of other religions, namely, that all men, by virtue of their maleness, are spiritually superior to all women. However, it has been argued that these discriminatory rules were intended, in the context of the sixth century B.C.E., to maintain women's status in society within the Saṅgha and protect them from becoming completely dislocated from traditional mores and behavior.

In all probability, the real reason for the Buddha's reluctance to found an order of nuns was his desire to retain the approval of the laity. No religious or political leader, however broad his vision, can succeed if he forges far ahead of the masses, completely ignoring public opinion. Though not entirely without precedent (since the first order of nuns had already been established by the Jainas, a sect founded by the Buddha's contemporary, Mahāvīra), the presence of single, independent women following religious careers of their own was still a very daring innovation.

Once the doors were flung open, however, there was an immediate impact, for women of all strata of society flocked to the cloister, where they could follow a culturally accepted lifestyle free from irksome masculine dominance. From many verses in the *Therīgāthā*, it is clear how much the nuns relished their newly found independence, released from the shackles of patriarchal society and relieved from unpleasant domestic drudgery. For instance, Sister Mutta exulted, saying:

> O free indeed! O gloriously free am I,
> Free from three crooked things:
> From quern, from mortar, from my crooked lord!
> Ay, but I am free from rebirth and death
> And all that dragged me back is hurled away.

The Order of Nuns in Sri Lanka

The order of nuns begun by Mahāpajāpatī was introduced to Sri Lanka soon after the introduction of Buddhism. According to the Sri Lankan chronicle, the *Mahāvaṃsa,* the famous Emperor Aśoka of India sent his daughter, the nun Sanghamitta, to Sri Lanka in the third century B.C.E. At the express request of the king of Sri Lanka Devanampiya Tissa (250–210 B.C.E.), whose kinswoman Anula wished to enter the order together with many women of the palace, Sanghamitta founded the Bhikkhunī Saṅgha.

As is clear from literary and archaeological evidence, women were the most enthusiastic supporters of the new faith from its very inception. The first to attain spiritual fulfillment were also women. A large number of inscriptions dating from the third to the first century B.C.E., written in the early Brahmi script, testify to the patronage extended by women to Buddhism during the early stages of its spread in Sri Lanka. Paranavitana, writing in 1970 and basing his conclusion on evidence from the inscriptions he examined, says that the names of 91 male lay devotees (*upāsaka*) and 105 female lay devotees (*upāsikā*) have been preserved. However, there are only ten *bhikkhunis* or nuns among them, as opposed to nearly three hundred *bhikkhus,* or monks.

Compared with an abundance of architectural remains from the monks' monasteries at ancient sites in Sri Lanka, there are few remains that can be identified as nunneries. This evidence indicates that nuns were not as numerous as monks. Nevertheless, it can be proven that there were learned, active, and adventurous women among them. The *Dīpavaṃsa,* written in the forth century C.E., is the first redaction in Pāli verse of the historical and ecclesiastical literature found in different monasteries in Sri Lanka in slightly varying recensions. While the author of the *Mahāvaṃsa* is known to be a monk named Mahānāma, the author of the *Dīpavaṃsa,* which predates it, is unknown. Chapter 18 of the *Dīpavaṃsa* highlights the activities of the *therīs,* or nun elders, who were the spiritual descendants of Mahāpajāpatī.

It is clear from the *Dīpavaṃsa* account that soon after its inception the Bhikkhunī Saṅgha spread throughout the island. The order consisted of women of all ages and from all levels of society, and at least those whose names are mentioned were well versed in the scriptures and imparted their knowledge to others. There was a strong tradition of learning and teaching among the nuns, and their forte was the study and exposition of the Vinaya, or rules of discipline.

In chapter 18 of the *Dīpavaṃsa*, in five places the nuns are described as learned in religious history. The numerous references to *therīs* found in the *Dīpavaṃsa* have led scholars to believe that the work was written by nuns. The *Mahāvaṃsa*, which was written by a monk over a century later, elaborates and expands on the information given in the *Dīpavaṃsa*. Other than the arrival of Sanghamitta, however, there is little information about nunṣ. It is suspected that this may have been an attempt on the part of Mahānāma to soft-pedal the achievements of women.

The nineteenth-century antiquarian Hugh Nevill draws attention to the "unique consequence given to nuns" in the *Dīpavaṃsa* and feels that it affords a clue as to the text's authorship. Malalasekere supports the view that this chronicle was the work of the community of nuns and R. A. L. H. Gunawardana concurs, based on the attitude adopted by the *Dīpavaṃsa* toward the past history of the Saṅgha. If this is the case, Gunawardana concludes, "It would appear that nuns not only excelled in their study of the Buddhist canon but were also among the pioneers in historiography in the island." He adds, "The emphasis laid in the chronicle on the intellectual accomplishments of nuns probably represents an attempt to counter the tendency among some monks to underestimate their capabilities."

Sri Lankan nuns seem to have emulated their founder Saṅghamittā when they led delegations to foreign lands to spread the faith and establish the Bhikkhunī Saṅgha. The Chinese work *Pi-chiu-ni-chuan*, or *The Biographies of Nuns*, written in the sixth century, mentions that in the years 429 and 432 C.E. two groups of nuns arrived in China from Sinhala in a foreign merchant vessel belonging to a person named Nandi. They were housed in a nunnery in the Sung capital, learned the Chinese language, and ordained three hundred Chinese nuns. Although this event was considered important enough to be mentioned in Chinese histories, the Sri Lankan records are strangely silent about the achievements of these courageous women who braved a hazardous voyage across the seas to spread the order of nuns.

Another renowned nun who ventured abroad was the Sinhala nun Candramāli, a scholar of the Tantric sect. Unhonored and unsung in her motherland, she undertook the rigorous journey across the Himalayas to Tibet in the eleventh century. From the Tibetan and Mongolian versions of the Tripitaka, we learn that Candramāli translated Buddhist Tantric texts in collaboration with a Tibetan monk named Ye Ses. It is likely that she is the author of a text that bears her name, the *Śrī Candramālā-tantrarājā.*

Surveying the position of women in India in pre-Vedic times, it is apparent that women enjoyed religious freedoms that became curtailed under Brahmin dominance. Subsequently, with the spread of Buddhism, there is evidence of a positive correlation between Buddhist tenets of spiritual equality and social freedoms for women, as evident in marriage and funeral customs. Although a preference for male offspring in Buddhist societies is evident, sons are not indispensable at funerals and extreme forms of discrimination are not found. Women had equal rights in religious practice and could practice the life of a renunciant as a member of the Bhikkhunī Saṅgha.

Likewise in precolonial Sri Lanka, whether as wives, workers, widows, spinsters, or nuns, women were respected members of society and performed duties other than childbearing. They participated in the main economic activity—paddy culture—and were preeminent in religious activities, a feature that is still evident today. Nuns not only led lives of seclusion, but as evident in various texts in the Pāli canon, also made significant contributions as scholars. They excelled as teaches of religious doctrine and religious history and, as missionaries, undertook long voyages over land and sea to spread their faith. Despite the loss of the Bhikkhunī Saṅgha, this tradition of independence has continued for more than two thousand years, allowing women to play important roles in religion and government. In recent times, also, it has helped Sri Lankan women face the challenges of modernization without a violent disjunction from cultural norms.

Notes

1. C. A. F. Rhys Davids, *The Psalms of the Sisters* (London: Pali Text Society, 1980), p. 45.

2. *Laws of Manu*, trans. Georg Buhler, *Sacred Books of the East*, vol. 25 (Oxford, 1866), IX.10.

3. Ibid., IX.81.

4. Quoted by I. B. Horner in *Women in Early Buddhist Literature,* Wheel Publication no. 30 (Colombo, 1961), pp. 8–9.

5. Government of India, *The Lesser Child: The Girl in India,* 1990.

6. *Laws of Manu*, IX.28.

7. *The Sacred Books of China: The Texts of Confucianism*, trans. James Legge, *Sacred Books of the East*, vol. 28 (Oxford, 1879), p. 431.

8. L. D. Campbell, *The Miscellaneous Works of Hugh Boyd, with an Account of His Life and Writings* (London, 1800), pp. 54–6. In 1782, Boyd was sent as an envoy to the Kandyan court by the British governor at Madras.

9. Lt. General Albert Fytche, *Burma Past and Present*, vol. 2 (London, 1878).

10. Bishop Edmund Pieris, ed. and trans., *Lakraja lo Sirita* (Colombo: Ceylon Historic Manuscripts Commission, 1769), pp. 10–11. An English translation appears in an appendix to Anthony Bertolacci's *A View of the Agricultural, Commercial and Financial Interests of Sri Lanka* (London, 1817).

11. Robert Knox, *An Historical Relation of Ceylon* (Dehiwala: Tisara Prakasakaya, 1966), p. 149.

12. Ibid.

Senarat Wijayasundara

3. Restoring the Order of Nuns to the Theravādin Tradition

Followers of the Buddha's teachings consist of four components: monks, nuns, laymen, and laywomen. Of the two major Buddhist traditions, Mahāyāna and Theravāda, Mahāyāna alone has all four of these components extant. For a number of reasons, including a series of invasions in Sri Lanka, the Theravādin tradition lost its order of nuns sometime after the 10th century. This puts women in Theravādin societies at a spiritual disadvantage through no fault of their own. One may legitimately question why steps have not been taken over the last nine hundred years to restore the order to its rightful place.

The origin of the Bhikkhunī Saṅgha is documented in the Pāli canon.[1] Permission to enter the order for nuns was won with much difficulty thanks to the skilful diplomacy of the monk Ānanda who appealed to the Buddha on behalf of Mahāpajāpatī[2] and her companions. The position of the Buddha in this matter requires investigation. In her book, *Women under Primitive Buddhism*, I. B. Horner states, "I hope to show that [the Buddha] did not, as is usually said of him, grudge women entry into the order, but his compassion for the many folk included, from the beginning, women as well as men and animals. He saw the potentially good, the potentially spiritual in them as clearly as he saw it in man. Hence, were their life spent in the world or in the religious community, he spared himself no trouble to show them the way to happiness, to salvation—a way which they might train themselves to follow by self-mastery."[3]

Ānanda was later criticized for having prevailed upon the Buddha for the establishment of the Bhikkhunī Saṅgha,[4] although the order appears to have functioned successfully. At the Third Buddhist Council held in India in the third century B.C.E., it was decided to dispatch nine missions abroad to spread Buddhism.[5] One mission, headed by

Mahinda, son of Emperor Aśoka of India, reached Sri Lanka. The tremendous success it achieved was such that within a short time there was a request from a group of five hundred women, led by Anula, to join the order. Mahinda's sister Saṅghamittā was invited to Sri Lanka to initiate the Bhikkhunī Saṅgha. Both Bhikkhu and Bhikkhunī Saṅghas grew quickly in strength and popularity.

By the turn of the tenth century, however, Buddhism in Sri Lanka was being seriously affected by internal political conflicts and foreign invasions, during which the monastic orders disappeared. Eventually a king named Vijayabahu was able to establish law and order in the country and became keen to revive Buddhism from the pathetic state to which it had fallen. Realizing that no members of the Bhikkhu Saṅgha remained, he sought assistance from Burma to restore the order of monks,[6] but there is no mention of reviving the order of nuns.[7] If monks suffered so extensively that their order became extinct, there can be little doubt about the plight of the order of nuns. There is no record that the king tried to revive it.

Even though the Bhikkhunī Saṅgha disappeared in Sri Lanka, Buddhist women remained earnest in their quest for spiritual awakening. Rather unusual steps have been taken by women in Thailand[8] and Sri Lanka.[9] In Thailand several groups of women have come forward who wish to practice religion with an earnestness beyond that common among laywomen. The status of one group, the *maejis*, is far from satisfactory. Another group of women, known as *silacarinis*, began in 1957 with the ordination of five women who observe ten precepts. They have a nunnery centered in Bangkok and wear brown robes. Another group wearing dark brown robes live under the guidance of a self-ordained monk, Bodhiraksa, who initiated the ordination lineage himself. Yet another group is headed by Bhikkhunī Voramai Kabilsingh who began as a *maeji*, but later received full ordination in Taiwan. Members of this group wear light yellow robes. I believe that this group will have the best opportunity of meeting the needs of Buddhist women who choose to lead a life of renunciation.

In Sri Lanka a movement known as *dasasilmātā* can be traced to the pioneering efforts of Sudhammacari (1885–1937). Born into a Christian family in Bentota, Catherine de Alwis Gunatilaka became interested in Buddhism and wished to become a nun. As there were no nuns in Sri Lanka and no monk would administer the ten precepts, she went to Burma (Myanmar) where she underwent training and was given ordination by Daw Ni Chari. She received the name Sudhammacari at ordination and founded the Lady Blake Nunnery at Katukele (Kandy) when she returned to Sri Lanka in 1903. Many women from various parts of the country came to her to receive the precepts.

From there the number of *dasasilmātās* grew. These women now command respect from the lay community and receive assistance from the Buddha Sasana Ministry of the Government of Sri Lanka for their educational and material needs. Some of them are satisfied with the traditional ten precepts, but many are hopeful of becoming fully ordained nuns, either within or outside of the Theravādin tradition.

Many heads of the *nikāyas* (monastic orders) in Sri Lanka oppose ordination for nuns and maintain that it cannot be granted within the Theravādin tradition of Vinaya. Moreover, they oppose nuns receiving ordination from any other Buddhist tradition. Fortunately some other leading members of the Saṅgha are of the opinion that Sri Lankan women may legitimately receive ordination from countries like China, Korea, or Taiwan where the lineage has been maintained without a break.[10] Considerable numbers of laymen and laywomen also favor such a step and support this cause.

Opposition to the revival of an order of Buddhist nuns seems to run counter to the spirit as well as the religious aims of Buddhism. Two significant statements found in two authoritative *suttas* indicate how important the presence of nuns is in Buddhism and how much is lost in their absence. The first statement occurs in a relevant discussion between the Buddha and a wanderer, Vacchagotta.[11] In this discussion the Buddha affirms that all six components of Buddhist society named by Vacchagotta are expected to realize their ideals. These six components are: monks, nuns, celibate laymen, celibate laywomen, ordinary laymen, and ordinary laywomen. In another text, in a discussion with Māra, the Buddha is reminded of his commitment not to pass away until the four components of a Buddhist society, namely monks, nuns, laymen and laywomen, became eligible for *nibbāna* by cultivating the necessary qualities.[12]

Although in the Theravāda tradition women who aspire to be nuns are prevented by historical circumstances from receiving ordination, their counterparts in the Mahāyāna tradition fortunately are not. Therefore it is possible to overcome these obstacles by turning to the nuns of the Mahāyāna countries.

Historians believe that Buddhism reached China around the first century C.E.[13] Pao-Chang gives an account of the early beginnings of the order of nuns in China.[14] Given the extreme hardships of travel either over the Himalayas or through the deserts of Central Asia, it was difficult for an order of monks to become established in China; how much more difficult it would have been for nuns to survive the journey and establish an order there. Eventually, it was by the sea route from Sri Lanka that the Bhikkhunī Saṅgha reached China in the fifth century.

Soon after Buddhism's arrival in China, a number of Chinese women became interested in becoming nuns. There appear to have been many discussions on the ordination of women among the Buddhists in China prior to the establishment of a *bhikkhunī* order. Some maintained that the establishment of an order was not possible without the participation of nuns in the ordination ceremony. Others were of the opinion that it was possible for Chinese women to receive only the initial, novice (*sāmaṇerī*) ordination. Others believed that the Vinaya rules for full ordination could be interpreted to permit monks to grant ordination to women in spite of the absence of ordained nuns.[15] This seemingly unresolvable problem was vexing to unimaginative minds.

Finally, the problem of full ordination for women was referred to Gunavarman of Kashmir by Hui Kuo, the woman who was to become the first Chinese *bhikkhunī*, herself an expert in Vinaya.[16] When she asked him whether it was legitimate for women to receive full ordination without the participation of nuns, Gunavarman responded by saying that there would be nothing wrong with such an ordination. When she asked whether it would be wrong for monks to grant *bhikkhunī* ordination to women without the participation of nuns, he replied that there would be no fault on the part of the monks if they did so. He explained that monks would be deemed at fault only if they gave *bhikkhunī* ordination without nuns when nuns were available to participate. Since there were no nuns in China at the time, there would be nothing wrong with such an ordination. This was a wise solution that was within the limits of Vinaya.

But Gunavarman, an intelligent and ardent propagator of Buddhism, did not stop there. He worked to get a sufficient number of nuns to perform the full ordination. In 429 C.E., eight nuns from Sri Lanka arrived in China, but were deemed insufficient in number to perform an ideal dual ordination.[17] Therefore another group of nuns, eleven in number and headed by Devasara, was brought from Sri Lanka and reached China in 432 C.E.[18] Prior to his death, Gunavarman thoughtfully left instructions for performing the dual ordination with a Sinhala monk, Saṅghavarman, who completely fulfilled the instructions.[19] The two groups of nuns who had arrived in China from Sri Lanka conferred the dual ordination of nuns for the first time in China. It is said that at that time, "more than 300 Chinese nuns received full ordination from Sinhala Bhikkhunīs."[20] Strangely enough, no Sri Lankan chronicle mentions this important event. It comes to us only from Chinese sources.

The Bhikkhunī Siṅgha became firmly rooted in China and gradually spread through neighboring countries, such as Korea and Vietnam. In 1992, at a well-attended ceremony held to bid farewell to a group of five Chinese monks who had completed their education in Sri Lanka, Prof. W. Rahula referred to the regrettable lack of fully ordained Theravādin nuns. He suggested that Sri Lankan *dasasilmātās* could receive their full ordination from one of these countries.[21]

The two *suttas* discussed earlier show that the disappearance of the nuns' component disables the Theravādin tradition. Dr. Senarat Paranavitana has asserted that without the Bhikkhunī Saṅgha, the present-day Bhikkhu Saṅgha in Sri Lanka cannot be called a Mahāsaṅgha (great order). In addition, the inability of the Theravādin tradition to meet the legitimate demands of women to practice Buddhism equally makes it vulnerable to criticism. Therefore, it is imperative for the Theravādin tradition to meet this serious challenge and open its doors to nuns.

The following are possible ways to achieve this aim. The first three possibilities were presented by Prof. G. P. M. Malalasekara, founder of the World Fellowship of Buddhists (WFB), when he called for the restoration of the order of Buddhist nuns. His contributions to this effort have appeared as far back as 1934 in the *Ceylon Daily News*.[22] He put forth six recommendations.

First, according to the *Mahāparinibbāna Sutta*, the Buddha, when lying on his death bed, is said to have told his attendant Ānanda that the Saṅgha was permitted to abolish lesser and minor rules.[23] Malalasekara says, "That, then, is the first possibility—a decision by a representative assembly of the Saṅgha to dispense with the traditional ceremonial in the ordination of nuns."[24] Making use of the Buddha's final concession, it is within the power of the Bhikkhu Saṅgha to make the necessary amendments to restore the Bhikkhunī Saṅgha by performing an ordination without the participation of nuns. If any monk believes that the rules pertaining to the ordination of nuns are of major concern and do not fall within the category of "lesser and minor rules," he would be invited to come forth and justify his position.

Second, it is possible to make use of an injunction issued by the Buddha that stipulates, "I permit you monks, to confer full ordination on nuns."[25] There are references in the texts that show that some regulations were amended, altered, or abrogated by the Buddha himself on various occasions under special circumstances. The absence of *bhikkhunīs* in Theravāda clearly being a special circumstance, these textual references should be sufficient cause for granting monks the authority to ordain nuns with a clear conscience that no transgression of the Vinaya rules has been committed. Those who oppose the restoration of the Bhikkhunī Saṅgha on the grounds of Vinaya technicalities seem to ignore this relevant injunction.

Third, certain special procedures have been performed in Buddhist history, such as when Mahāpajāpatī Gotamī and her companions took the precepts before the Bhikkhunī Saṅgha had been instituted. The ordination of Buddhist monks or nuns essentially consists of followers taking upon themselves voluntarily the observance of certain precepts. Ordination is not something that is transmitted from one person to another; rather, it is certain precepts that one undertakes to keep and observe in accordance with one's own motivation. Buddhist ordination is essentially different from the ordination of priests found in other religions, where priests are regarded as intercessors between human beings and a divine power. In the Buddhist context, there is no delegation of authority, no question of acting on earth as a divine ministrant. Just as Buddhist laypeople in Sri Lanka undertake to observe the eight or ten precepts on *poya* days by reciting the precepts at a shrine, there is nothing to prevent women from observing the precepts of novice or full ordination. There cannot be any serious objection to this type of self-ordination.[26]

If any one of the above suggestions by Prof. Malalasekera is accepted, it would be possible to restore the Bhikkhunī Saṅgha within the Theravādin tradition. What is required is an understanding of the spirit, rather than the letter, of the Vinaya regulations. There are three further options available for the restoration the Bhikkhunī Saṅgha which have come to light because of the public discussions and debates that have taken place on this issue in Sri Lanka, particularly in the past ten years.[27]

Fourth, due to improved relations and closer contact with China, Korea, and Taiwan, in recent years, it became known that the Bhikkhunī Saṅgha transmitted to China by Sinhalese nuns continues in these countries in an unbroken succession. Therefore it is possible to reintroduce the Bhikkhunī Saṅgha to Sri Lanka from one of these three countries (or Vietnam), either by bringing a chapter of nuns to Sri Lanka or by sending a group of applicants to those countries to be ordained. Sending applicants to one of these countries is a better approach, since they would have the opportunity to undergo training there. This proposed step is not as drastic as some would make it out to be. It is merely the receiving back of the Bhikkhunī Saṅgha that was earlier sent from Sri Lanka to China. It would be like accepting back the great gift that was given in earlier times.

There are precedents for this proposed reintroduction. In the latter part of the eighteenth century, a delegation from Thailand was invited to Sri Lanka to reestablish the Bhikkhu Saṅgha and began the Siam Nikāya.[28] In the nineteenth century, two separate groups of monks went to monasteries in Amarapura and Ramanna in Burma and received full ordination there. On their return, they founded the Amarapura sect in 1803[29] and the Ramanna sect in 1864.[30] It is also well known that Sri Lanka has been instrumental at times in reviving and reorganizing Buddhism in Thailand and Burma. Therefore, there can be no legitimate objection to seeking the assistance of Chinese or Korean nuns in restoring the Bhikkhunī Saṅgha to Sri Lanka.

Fifth, if the venerable Mahānayakas, the leading *bhikkhus* of the Theravādin tradition in Sri Lanka, are not prepared to accept the authenticity of the Bhikkhunī Saṅghas in China and other Mahāyāna countries, Sri Lankan Buddhist women are still free to seek ordination in any Buddhist tradition they like.[31] Nuns fully ordained in other traditions should be recognized as *bhikkhunīs* without any discrimination. Theravādin leaders in Sri Lanka should not be hasty to oppose such a move.

The choice to renounce worldly life and practice "the holy life" is the inalienable right of all Buddhist women. No Buddhist can legitimately deny women this right. Those who oppose women's right to obtain ordination within the Theravādin tradition cannot oppose their right to become *bhikkhunīs* in another tradition. Gunapala Dharmasiri has stated that, since the tradition of Vinaya ordination is fundamentally the same in Mahāyāna and Theravāda, if an ordination lineage has been lost in one tradition, it can be reinstated by borrowing from those countries where it has been preserved.[32] The respected scholar Ananda Wellawatte Thera holds a similar view.[33] For tradition to question the validity of an ordination given by another established Buddhist tradition is not reasonable or justified.

Sixth, a meeting may be convened of a special body comprised of leading members of the international Saṅgha community, representing several Buddhist traditions from all over the world. Sri Lankan candidates can be given *sāmaṇerī* and full *bhikkhunī* ordination by this representative body. At present there are several international Buddhist organizations of this type, including one recently established in Colombo. Therefore, the convening of an international body of monks and nuns would not be a difficult task.

❧

The *dasasilmātās* of Sri Lanka have dedicated their lives to the Buddhist path as nuns in an age when few are committed to spiritual values. Helping to promote their aspirations would encourage them and would promote the welfare of Buddhism as a whole. As Prof. Jotiya Dhirasekera has stated, Buddhism has contributed much to the emancipation of women.[34] This contribution has been impaired by the opposition of Theravādin leaders in Sri Lanka to the revival of the

Bhikkhunī Saṅgha. Some Buddhist leaders proudly assert that from its inception Buddhism has stood for the liberty of womankind. Their words are rendered idle boasts in the face of their opposition to the revival of the Bhikkhunī Saṅgha. Revival of the traditional order of nuns can no longer be delayed, for it constitutes a rejection of the fundamental principles of the Universal Declaration of Human Rights.

Notes

1. *Cullavagga,* part 2, Buddha Jayanti Tripitaka Granthamala (BJE), (Colombo: Janarajaya, 1977), p. 472.

2. Pāli equivalent of the Sanskrit name Mahāprajāpatī.

3. I. B. Horner, *Women under Primitive Buddhism* (Delhi: Motilal Banarsidass, 1975), p. xxiv.

4. *Cullavagga,* part 2, p. 289.

5. *Mahāvaṃsa,* XII.1ff.

6. *University History of Ceylon,* vol. 1, part 2, p. 563.

7. R. A. L. H. Gunawardana has given evidence to prove the existence of Buddhist nuns in Burma at the time when the Sri Lankan king was seeking the assistance of Burmese monks for the revival of the Bhikkhu Saṅgha in Sri Lanka. He says, "Owing to the inadequacy of information bearing on this problem it is not possible to give a satisfactory explanation of their surprising lack of clerical or lay interest in reviving the order of nuns." *Robe and Plough: Monasticism and Economic Interest in Early Medieval Sri Lanka* (Tucson: University of Arizona Press, 1979), p. 39.

8. Chatsumarn Kabilsingh, "The Role of Woman in Buddhism," in *Sakyadhita: Daughters of the Buddha* (Ithaca, N.Y.: Snow Lion Publications, 1989), pp. 225–35; "The Future of the Bhikkhuni Sangha in Thailand," in Diana Eck, ed., *Speaking of Faith: Global Perspectives on Women, Religion, and Social Change* (Philadelphia, Pa.: New Society Publishers, 1987), pp. 139–48; "Mae-Ji: A Religious Minority in Contemporary Thailand," *Sri Lanka Journal of Buddhist Studies,* 11(1988):141–47.

9. Hema Goonatilake "The Dasa Sil-Mata Movement in Sri Lanka," *Sri Lanka Journal of Buddhist Studies,* 11(1988):124–40; Pānadure Vajirā Silmāthā, *Bhikkhunī Vamsaya* (in Sinhala, Colombo 1992), pp. 370–76.

10. *Ceylon Daily News,* February 6, 1992.

11. *Mahāvacchagotta Sutta, Majjhima Nikāya,* part 2 (Colombo: BJE, 1973), pp. 270–74.

12. *Mahāparinibbāna Sutta, Digha Nikāya,* part 2 (Peradeniya, Sri Lanka: BJE, 1967), pp. 162–66.

13. K. W. Morgan, *The Path of the Buddha* (Delhi: Motilal Banarsidass, 1986), pp. 184–85.

14. Pao Chang, *Biographies of Buddhist Nuns,* trans. Li Jung-hsi (Osaka: Tohokai, 1981).

15. Morgan, *Path of the Buddha,* p. 63.

16. Pao Chang, *Biographies,* pp. 36–38.

17. Ibid., p. 53–54.

18. Ibid., p. 54.

19. Ibid., pp. 62–63.

20. Ibid., p. 54.

21. *Ceylon Daily News,* February 6, 1992.

22. Reproduced in *The Buddhist Vesak Annual,* Colombo, 1989, pp. 24–28.

23. *Mahāparinibbāna Sutta, Digha Nikāya,* part 2 (Oxford: Pali Text Society [PTS]), p. 154.

24. *The Buddhist Vesak Annual.*

25. *Mahāparinibbāna Sutta, Digha Nikāya,* part 2, p. 257.

26. *The Buddhist Vesak Annual.*

27. "Ven. Sanghamitta and the Order of Nuns," *Daham Ama Mahinda Commemorative Volume* (in Sinhala) (Colombo: Department of Buddhist Cultural Affairs, 1993), pp. 21–26.

28. K. L. Hazra, *History of Theravada Buddhism in Southeast Asia* (New Delhi: Munshiram Manoharlal Publishers, 1982), pp. 166–74.

29. Ibid., pp. 86–87.

30. "On Restoration of the Bhikkhunī Order" (in Sinhala), paper presented at the 2nd Saṅgha Seminar, Maharagama, Sri Lanka, 1988.

31. Ibid.

32. "Buddhist Monks in the 20th Century," Vimutti Symposium of the Ramana Sect Annual Ordination Ceremony (Kalutara, Sri Lanka: 1991).

33. Ananda Wellawatte, "The Life of the Mahāyāna Bhikṣu," Prajnasara Felicitation Volume (in Sinhala), pp. 250–57.

34. Jotiya Dhirasekera, *Buddhist Monastic Discipline* (Colombo: Ministry of Higher Education Research Publication Series, 1982), p. 141.

East Asian Traditions

Beata Grant

4. The Red Cord Untied

Buddhist Nuns in Eighteenth-Century China

Women in late imperial China faced what was in many ways a unique and contradictory set of social and historical circumstances. On the one hand, there was the widespread practice of footbinding, concubinage, female infanticide, and the infamous widow chastity cult; on the other, more women then ever before benefited from the general growth of literacy during this period. In fact, there were more educated women painting, writing, and publishing in late imperial China than anywhere in the world at the time, so much so that scholars like Dorothy Ko speak of the emergence of a clearly defined "women's culture."[1] This did not lead, however, to rebellion and transgression. Rather, from what we can reconstruct of their lives it would seem that in this time of combined oppression and opportunity, most women struggled, with varying degrees of success, to negotiate a middle way between self-expression and self-effacement.

It is in this context that a study of women's religious life becomes particularly interesting, for here, also, traditional (largely Confucian) views of women primarily as submissive wives and mothers come into tension with religious (largely Buddhist and Taoist) promises of an individual salvation that transcends both familial ties and gender restraints. Here, too, women attempt to find ways to negotiate a middle way between the two. The general male, Confucian literati concern (sometimes misogynist, but more often simply anxious) with reminding women of their proper place within the home is reflected, if only indirectly, in the increasingly domestic Buddhism of the period. An example of this is a collection entitled *Biographies of Pious Women* compiled by the famous Confucian–turned-lay Buddhist, Peng Shaosheng (1740–96).[2] Peng's "biographies" consist of brief accounts of devout women through the ages (including his own wife and niece), who during their lifetimes were models of proper Confucian womanly behavior and yet, at the point of death, were able to detach themselves from family concerns and focus their minds completely on the recitation of the Buddha's name, thus winning birth in the Pure Land. In this way, Peng's biographical constructions, although supportive of women's spiritual needs, resulted in portraits of women able to successfully fulfill both their Confucian familial and filial obligations and satisfy their yearning for personal salvation.

These portraits bore some resemblance to their Confucian prototypes, but only some. For Buddhist piety is not exactly the same as Confucian filial piety, something the male literati who concerned themselves with these issues fully realized. The main problem, as they saw it, was that Buddhist belief and practice tended to lure pious women from their homes to visit temples or participate in pilgrimages, and, in more extreme cases, from their proper and "natural" place as mothers and wives to a life of cloistered celibacy. Thus even such protofeminist literati as Zhang Xuecheng (1738–1801) and Chen Hongmou (1696–1771), both of whom advocated female literacy, had little sympathy for women who left home to enter the religious life. Nor were they alone: Buddhist nuns, along with other socially marginal women such as instructresses, diviners, go-betweens, and peddlers were commonly referred to in the literature of the period as "hags," and warnings against the pernicious influence of these women sounded, as Susan Mann notes, "throughout the lexicon of [Qing] writings on the domestic realm."[3]

There was some basis for these concerns: there is no question that by the late seventeenth and eighteenth century, the Chinese Buddhist monastic institution had fallen into a state of moral and religious disrepair, as evidenced by the fact that the eminent religious figures of this period devoted most of their considerable energies to restoring a sense of moral and spiritual discipline among their monastic followers. This state of disrepair only served to reinforce and confirm a long-standing popular resistance to the idea of women leaving the home. The male Confucian literati were reluctant to acknowledge that the religious life offered women more than mere physical or economic refuge, and the male Buddhist literati often failed to acknowledge that, for many women, the religious life might represent a serious alternative to domestic life, not simply a supplement or something to be engaged in toward the end of one's life. What is missing from both these perspectives, of course, are the voices of religious women themselves.

Identifying what these women's perspectives might have been is not easy given the scarcity of primary materials related to Buddhist nuns. However, a significant number of these eighteenth-century women were from educated families, and many wrote poetry, some of which fortunately is extant today. These poems, together with scattered fragments of biographical and anecdotal information, are really all we have to go by. Although they cannot provide as full a picture of these nun's lives as we might wish, they do provide us with a tantalizing glimpse into the inner worlds of these religious women. They serve as a reminder that we can no longer speak of a *homo religiosus* defined exclusively in terms of the experiences of men. They also remind us that it will not do to try to create an equivalent feminized version of this *homo religiosus;* we must realize that women's experience often differs not only from that of men, but also from that of other women.

This essay represents a brief exploration of the varieties of female religious experience among a small and rather circumscribed group of educated Buddhist nuns, most of whom came from Jiangsu Province, the economic, cultural and intellectual heart of eighteenth-century China. Although all of these women were both literate and literary, their backgrounds and their motivations for entering the religious life were quite different. Some sought economic and psychological refuge from an unhappy marriage, the loss of a husband, or a general feeling of disillusionment with their lives; others entered out of more clearly defined religious motivations. Some found a measure of the comfort and solace they sought, while others appear to have attained a deep level of spiritual fulfillment and insight. Overall, these women's religious lives were far more varied and interesting than official accounts, whether Buddhist or Confucian, would lead us to imagine.

Whether in China or the West, the most conventional explanation of why a woman would enter the religious life has always been: "She had no other choice" or "She's given up on life; she simply can't handle it." And there is no question that for many women in traditional China, entering the convent was a last resort. An example of this is the nun Wugou, *née* Chen, a highly educated woman who even as young girl was known for her prodigious poetic talents. She later married a student from a wealthy family who doted on her and with whom she appears to have been very happy. However, because she failed to bear him a son, a concubine was brought in and she was sent away. We are not told why Wugou became a nun instead of returning to her natal family, but it is quite possible that they had fallen on hard times, as had many of the traditional elite, and were unwilling to take her back. The rest of Wugou's life was filled with poverty and illness, and her biographers tell us she fell to her death as she tried to rise from her sickbed to look out the window. It would seem that she was sustained through her suffering, not so much by her Buddhist faith and religious devotion, as by her writing of poetry. The following poem reveals an emptiness distinct from its more Buddhist definition, although sorrow and silence would have certainly have deepened her awareness of the natural world—the fragrant grasses and the fallen blossoms of the *wutong* (pawlonia) tree.

Inner Chamber Lament

Kingfisher-blue filters through the blinds:
All day I have kept to the hidden chambers.
Sunk in sorrow: I smell the fragrance of the grasses,
Lost in silence; I realize the *wutong* flowers have fallen
Toilet case and mirror: a spot for a spider web.
The courtyard *wutong* tree: a nest for magpies,
The dream over, the sorrow does not cease.
The evening falls, my heart naturally resentful.
All alone I sit and write in the emptiness,
As a light rain deepens the desolation.[4]

Wugou was sent away for failing to bear a child, traditionally a legitimate cause for divorce. Less traditional is the case of Deri (whose secular name was Jiang Kui) from Taizhou, who apparently was divorced by her husband for being too aggressively intelligent. A precocious young girl—her biographers relate that she had a photographic memory—even after her marriage to Chen, she would stay up late at night reading. When not engaged in solitary study, she would arrange for gatherings of women in the inner chambers, complete with wine, in which she would preside, reciting poetry and making speeches. Although her family members affectionately called her "female student" and her biographers note that she had the "the air of a great scholar,"[5] it would appear that her husband did not appreciate this type of behavior. In any case, their marriage was not a happy one, and Deri left—it may well be that her husband divorced her or perhaps she left of her own accord. Because her natal family had fallen into economic straits, which was not an unusual occurrence during this period of rapid social and economic change, Deri took up residence at the Qinglian chapel in Taizhou.[6] Not long after, she was joined by her younger sister, Jiang Hui; presumably the family was so poor they could not afford to marry her off. Jiang Hui took the name of Deyue (Virtue Moon) to complement that of her sister, Deri (Virtue Sun), and the two spent their lives together, engaged in religious devotions, studying, writing poetry, and struggling to survive periodic bouts of hunger, deprivation, and illness.

Wugou, Deri, and Deyue all had unhappy marriages. Most eighteenth-century Chinese nuns, however, entered the religious life as widows. A significant number of these women were widowed even before marriage, due to the early deaths of the men to whom they were betrothed. Traditionally, such women would remain with the family of their deceased husband or fiancé for the rest of their lives, providing the services of a filial, if childless, daughter-in-law. Not surprisingly, a significant number of widows, concubines, and courtesans found in the convent a source of solace and support after the loss of their husbands, consorts, or companions. In many of these cases, however, widowhood did not so much compel as free a woman to enter the religious life. An example is Miaocheng (d. 1814) from Gucheng, Huzhou, who "from birth had a wise disposition and as a young girl was very serious-looking and upright, not like other children her age."[7] Moreover, she would imitate her mother when her mother was making offerings to the Buddha, putting her palms together with a happy smile on her face. Despite these signs of early piety, Miaocheng was married at the age of twenty-one to a young scholar who died after less than a year. Miaocheng remained in her husband's family and took up sewing and embroidery in order to help support them. Despite her many domestic duties, she would recite the *Avataṃsaka Sūtra* at dawn and at dusk, and remain mindful of the name of Buddha. After ten years, her mother-in-law died and her father-in-law became a monk, finally leaving Miaocheng free to become a nun.

Miaocheng was able to stay amicably with her in-laws until that time, but other widows were looked upon less as a source of filial support than as an additional burden. This is what happened to the nun Wanxian (*née* Shi) from Changzhou, after the death of her fiancé. Unwilling to become a burden for her destitute natal family, she took up residence in a modest hermitage on Dongting East Mountain, in the middle of scenic Lake Taihu. A poem she wrote gives us a glimpse of how she felt about her new life, a life very different from the life of wife and mother for which she had prepared. In her new live she would not be bound, or secured, by the "red cord" of marriage and the "threefold submission," meaning submission to father, husband, and son.

Writing of My Feelings from within the Hermitage

The Chan gates are shut the entire day, cutting off all traces of [worldly] dust.
In front, groves of fine bamboo, and in back, trees of pine.
The departure of the wild geese leaves me bereft of companions.
Where the dawn clouds rise is a brushstroke of dark mountain peak.
At this moment, I suddenly realize the shallowness of worldly roots.
On this day, who else understands the pungent flavor of the Way.
The red cord that stretches a thousand *li* is at this moment cut in two.
In this sublime setting, there is no point in speaking of the Three Submissions.[8]

The image of a red cord or rope that ties together the feet of a future husband and wife comes from a well-known folktale set in the Tang dynasty and is influenced by popular interpretations of the workings of karma. According to this tale, "Even if their families become enemies, even if their social rank diverges drastically, even if they go to the ends of the earth to serve in office, or live in different villages in Wu and Chu, this rope, once tied, can never be untied."[9] In other tales, this conjugal connection continues beyond the grave. This poem by Wanxian, however, reflects an awareness of having moved beyond such socially constructed identities.

If women like Wanxian were simply sent home, others were strongly pressured to remarry. As is well known, during the eighteenth century, the cult of widow chastity was in full swing, replete with strong social and governmental incentives and injunctions against remarriage. Thus, being pressured to remarry put many women in an impossible moral bind, one that, for some, could be resolved only through suicide. The nun Miaohui, *née* Fan, was a young widow who after being sent home to her natal family, was pressured by her own parents to remarry. In a polite but firm manifesto, she expressed her determination to remain chaste. Her literary eloquence moved her parents to relent, and Miaohui was allowed to remain at home with them. After their deaths, she entered the Bore Monastery in Fengxi Prefecture, Hunan Province. Over the next several decades, until her death at the age of eighty, she became a well-respected teacher, attracting a considerable number of disciples. The following poem provides a glimpse of a woman who was resolute in her resistance to remarriage and determined to overcome some of the obstacles and inner tensions involved in the struggle for spiritual enlightenment.

Dawn Mediation in Bore Monastery

The night rain washes the mountain cliffs,
By dawn, the blue green is soaked through.

Sitting crosslegged, I meditate on emptiness,
As a clear breeze fills the entire temple.
At the source, words are inherently empty,
And yet, I have a fondness for brush and ink.
My mind is already like ashes after the fire,
And yet, I've still to understand worldly bonds.
Bamboo window, all the mind of emptiness.
Courtyard pine, fully manifesting innate purity.
The trunk of this lofty, blue-green tree,
Inherently neither emptiness nor form.
Not to mention that between bell and fish-drum
I've still to grasp the principles of the Dharma.
After a long sitting, I catch a whiff of a wonderful fragrance,
As if I may actually be crossing on the Ship of Compassion.

There are at least two sets of inner tensions in this poem. The first is Miaohui's ongoing struggle to completely purge herself of worldly attachments and understand the nature of Buddhist emptiness, or *śunyatā*. However, the last two lines would seem to indicate that she is by no means a complete spiritual novice, but has reached a certain level of meditative self-transcendence. The emptiness Miao contemplates in Bore Temple is different from the emotional emptiness referred to by Wugou, discussed earlier. In fact, Miaohui's principle struggle is not with her attachment to worldly comforts or familial consolation—unlike Wugou, she had no memories of connubial bliss—but rather to words and language. This was an ongoing dilemma for some Buddhists, especially those from the Chan school, which took pride in a nonreliance on words and letters. The Chan school produced a very great number of words and letters, of course, but usually, conveniently rationalized as "skillful means." However, it was also true that, as William LaFleur puts it, "The writing of poetry and involvement in the world of lyrical exchange and competition constantly threatened to deflect the energies of those who had chosen a religious vocation."[10] In short, there was always the danger that too deep an immersion in the world of words would lead to an "addiction" to language for its own sake.

This apparent dilemma was shared by eighteenth-century women religious, although with considerably different implications than for Chan practitioners. As mentioned earlier, during the late Ming and Qing period, a significant number of aristocratic women, including those who later entered religious life, were afforded a classical literary education that had previously been largely denied them. These women used their new literary skills not only to read women's instruction manuals and the Confucian classics, which some of their male contemporaries thought was quite enough, but also to express themselves, usually through poetry.[11] Many educated women during this period struggled with whether or not they should give up writing poetry after marriage and focus their energies on domestic duties. Some did, even going so far as to consign their writings to flames, but many did not. Faced with this same dilemma, many educated, committed Buddhist nuns express a profound reluctance to give up their newly acquired expressive voice. This reluctance was no doubt even greater for religious women than for men, because writing was a pursuit similar to religious practice—a means by which to transcend, or at least temporarily escape, the socially imposed limitations and restrictions of their everyday lives.

A dramatic example of a woman who turned to Buddhism at the end of an eventful and rebellious life was the nun Wuqing, *née* Weng Shilian. When orphaned as a young girl, Wuqing left Jiangsu and went to Beijing to live with her elder sister Yunqin. Yunqin was the concubine of Helin, the younger brother of the notorious Heshen,[12] a highly corrupt Manchu official and personal favorite of the Qianlong emperor. Helin himself held a number of important positions, including vice-president of the Board of War, and led many military campaigns. On one of these campaigns, in 1796, Helin was killed. As befitted a faithful concubine, Yunqin committed suicide, apparently in the presence of Wuqing, who only about fifteen at the time. This traumatic event marked a turning point in Wuqing's life. Shortly after her sister's death, she is said to have observed that, "Human life, wealth, and rank are empty names. Once one is dead, everything changes. So what is the point of emulating the partiality of the sunflower, the fickleness of the willow blossom?"[13]

After the death of her sister, Wuqing returned to the southeast, where she took refuge with Luo Qilan, a young widow and noted member of the circle of female poets around the famous Qing poet Yuan Mei (1716–98). She never married and, indeed, is said to have completely rejected the arts of feminine coquetry, refusing to wear makeup; as her biographies put it, she kept her face "like that of a man" and conducted herself in a "masculine and heroic" fashion. She became famous, not only for her poetry and flute-playing, but also for her shooting and equestrian skills. It is said that, "She rode her horse as if flying in the art." She was very much the talk of the town, and counted many prominent literati and officials among her friends. It was only after the death of Luo Qilan, herself a lay Buddhist who may well have influenced Wuqing, that she formally entered the religious life. The following set of regulated verses, presumably written after Wuqing became a nun, dwells at length on the disappointments and disillusions of life, but makes an effort to end on a transcendent note.

Together these verses may be read as a kind of manifesto of a woman who believes she understands the dangers of emotion and desire. After all, her religious name Wuqing means "to realize [the true nature of] of *qing*, feelings." The title of the poem is not *wuqing*, however, but *ganhuai*, "profound emotions."

Profound Emotions

In a turn of the head, the wink of an eye, the myriad causes are empty.
I've learned how life is made of obstacles and opportunities.
I've seen how dukes and lords rise and fall in quick succession.
A pitiful fate for two sisters for whom life and death are one,
This day I am left with only the monk's robe I wear.
The embroidered silks of yesteryear forever gone.
Sitting, I wear through my meditation mat, my breath like waves,
As the observing mind crosses unperturbed, a sail in the breeze.[14]

Throughout Chinese history, there are references to women who entered religious life, not as widows or rejected wives, but rather as former courtesans, concubines, or palace ladies. The assumption was often that such women, lacking children or husbands to support them, sought economic refuge in the convent after their beauty had faded. Although this may well have been true in many instances, there were also women like Zhang Ruyu, whose attraction to religious life was as much intellectual as spiritual.[15] Like so many women in eighteenth-century Jiangsu—gentry and courtesan alike—she was highly literate. Her biographers make a point of noting that she was completely conversant with the contents of the *Wenxuan* and the gamut of Tang poetry, in addition to being skilled at *li*-style calligraphy and painting. Unfortunately, we are not told why she left her life in the pleasure quarters and became a nun, taking the religious name of Miaohui. The following poem, however, presumably written before she had entered religious life, indicates that she was of a strongly contemplative bent from the start. For Miaohui, the autumn season, with its clarity, crispness, and purity, becomes a cause, not for mourning, but for celebration.

Drinking at Rain and Flowers Terrace,
I Compose a Description of the Falling Leaves

For viewing the vista, a 1000-*chi* terrace.
For discussing the mind, a goblet of wine.
A pure frost laces the tips of the trees,
Bronze leaves flirt with the river village.
Following the wave, I float with the oars;
Following the wind, I long to be enraptured.
Glory and decay, why sigh over them?
This day, I've happily returned to the source.[16]

Much of the feeling of self-containment and pleasure of being in the present can be found in the poetry of a concubine-turned-nun named Shiyan, *née* Jiang Shunying. According to her biographers, she was a precocious young girl who not only read voraciously, but was also a gifted musician, calligrapher, painter, and poet. She became a concubine in the house of a powerful family, but later left to become a nun. Although we are not told why she entered the religious life, her poetry indicates that she was very much drawn to spiritual practice. She gained a reputation not only for her ability to preach and explain the Dharma, but also for her poetry, which deftly conveyed religious ideas without slipping into dry didacticism.[17] Of all the women discussed here, she seems, in her poetry at least, to be the one who has most fully resolved the seeming conflict between language and religion, between life in the world and life in the monastery, or in Buddhist terms, between form and emptiness.

Recalling a Dream

Sitting firmly on the plantain-leaf mat, I can meditate in peace,
Surrounded by golden lamps flickering brightly by the Dharma seat.
Wise birds emerge singing from deep within the woodlands,
A confusion of mountains soar up and into my small window.
Clouds fuse with azure-blue seas to mold this glorious day,
The dew washes the empty heavens, scattering the morning mist.
I recall that in a dream, I had a meeting with the Buddha.
Form is emptiness, emptiness is form:
Now I understand what it means.[18]

Discussions of Chan Buddhism and the mind were quite common among educated women, both monastic and lay. These discussions might take place in the inner chambers, in the convent halls, or in poetic and epistolary exchanges. In many cases, women of the gentry classes became lay disciples of an eminent nun, visiting them in their temples and maintaining close literary friendships. An example of a Buddhist nun who cultivated this type of relationship was Wuyuan, *née* Wang Jiju. Wuyuan had been born in a scholarly family, but was orphaned as a young girl and raised by an elderly nun. It seems that her parents, probably her mother, had taught her the art of writing poetry when she was young. Rather than abandoning literary pursuits, she maintained enduring friendships with other well-known literary women from Jiangsu, particularly with members of a women's group called the Qingxi Poetry Club. Among the ten or more members of this group, Wuyuan appears to have become closest to a woman named Zhang Zifan.[19] Zifan, who became a widow at a relatively young age, often visited Wuyuan at her nearby hermitage, where the two women discussed poetry and Chan Buddhism, in particular. In a poem addressed to Zhang Zifan, Wuyuan paints a very positive picture of her life, surrounded by books and her "family" of disciples and friends.

Writing a Letter of Remembrance for Literata Zifan

Flowery filigree and kingfisher sleeves long since put aside,
With *sūtra* stand and rope cot, my mind is completely at ease.
By nature lazy, I have long since left behind my arrogant ways.
From a poor family, still I long for used copies of the scriptures.
For discussing emptiness, I have disciples;
We study the principles of Chan.
For fulfilling my nature, I follow my parents;
And imitate the book-burrowing worms.
I am especially glad for this quiet solitude with a lack of worldly concerns.
Grass for clothes, roughage for food—with these I can live in peace.[20]

Another example of a woman raised in a convent is the nun Luzong (d. 1790). She lost her mother when she was only two and was taken by her grandmother to a local nunnery to live,[21] but this does not mean that she had no vocation. Her biographer relates that as a young nun, she assiduously recited the *Lotus Sūtra*, but as she grew older, she became dissatisfied with the mere repetition of words she did not fully understand. She decided to go to Hangzhou, where she spent several years studying and practicing meditation, presumably under the guidance of a recognized spiritual teacher. Upon her return, she devoted herself exclusively to Pure Land devotions and made several pilgrimages to various sacred sites. At the age of fifty-three, she fell ill and went into semi-seclusion until her death some ten years later. Toward the end, we are told, she was surrounded by a large group of disciples, both monastic and lay.

This chapter represents a brief and preliminary foray into the world of Buddhist nuns of late imperial China and much remains to be done before drawing any firm conclusions. It is clear, however, that the lives of these eighteenth-century Buddhist women varied considerably, both their reasons for becoming a nun and their experiences after entering religious life. For some women, an experience of illness, death, or loss drew them to the religious life; for others, it was a spiritual inclination evident from a very early age. Some women encountered considerable familial resistance to their desire to remain unmarried; others received familial support and even encouragement. Some women appear to have been content to stay within a cloistered environment, while others, dissatisfied with mere recitation of Buddhist texts, traveled considerable distances in search of spiritual instruction and guidance. Still others became quite influential in the outside world, acquiring land, building temples, sponsoring religious feasts and charitable events, mentoring other nuns, and preaching to large numbers of people. Most importantly, however, despite the prevailing social disapprobation of nuns, there were significant numbers of women who not only found comfort and consolation in religious life, but genuine spiritual fulfillment.

Notes

1. See Dorothy Ko, *Teachers of the Inner Chambers: Women and Culture in Seventeenth-Century China* (Stanford: Stanford University Press, 1994).

2. In *Xu zang jing* (*Supplement to the Buddhist Canon*) (Hong Kong: Xianggang Fojiao zazhi shi, vol. 109, 1977), pp. 106–26. Peng also wrote a companion collection of biographies of laymen.

3. "Grooming a Daughter for Marriage: Brides and Wives in the Mid-Ch'ing Period," in *Marriage and Inequality in Chinese Society*, Rubie Watson and Patricia B. Ebrey (Berkeley: University of California Press, 1991), p. 226n26.

4. Wanyan Yunzhu, *Guochao guixiu zhengshiji* (1831) *fulu*, pp. 9b–14b.

5. Xu Shichang, *Wanqing yishi hui*, (Beijing: Zhonghua shuju, 1929, (rpt. 1990), p. 9169.

6. Zhenhua, ed., *Xu biqiuni zhuan*, in *Biqiuni zhuan quanji* (Taipei, 1988), p. 65.

7. Ibid.

8. Wanyan Yunzu, *Guochao guixiu zhengshiji*, pp. 18b–19a.

9. Translated and quoted by Patricia B. Ebrey in her book, *The Inner Quarters: Marriage and the Lives of Chinese Women in the Sung Period* (Berkeley: University of California Press, 1993), p. 57.

10. William R. LaFleur, *The Karma of Words: Buddhism and the Literary Arts in Medieval Japan* (Berkeley: University of California Press, 1983), p. 7.

11. There are now many excellent studies on female literacy and literature of the Ming and Qing periods. The best place to begin is Dorothy Ko's *Teachers of the Inner Chambers: Women and Culture in Seventeenth-Century China*, which contains a useful bibliography for further reference.

12. Wanyan Yunzu, *Guochao guixiu zhengshiji*, p. 14b; Zhenhua, *Xu biqiuni zhuan*, p. 86.

13. Wanyan Yunzu, *Guochao guixiu zhengshiji,* p. 14a.

14, Ibid., pp. 14a–b.

15. Ibid., pp. 17b–18a.

16. Ibid., p. 19b.

17. Zhenhua, *Xu biqiuni zhuan,* p. 85.

18. Xu Shichang, *Wangqing yishi hui,* vol. 10, p. 9159.

19. Zhang Fen, also styled Zifan, was a cousin of Zhang Cilan (b. 1756) whose husband Ren Zhaolin (fl. 1781–96) in 1789 published the poetry collections of all ten members of the Qingxi Poetry Club.

20. Wanyan Yunzhu, *Guochao guixiu zhengshiji,* p. 14a.

21. Ibid., p. 202b.

Paula K. R. Arai

5. Japanese Buddhist Nuns

Innovators for the Sake of Tradition

The question to be explored here is whether there are Buddhist nuns in Japan. Despite the various perspectives and experiences of Buddhist monastic women in the modern world, all share a concern for living according to the Dharma. Sometimes this means going against a tradition that is designed to make it difficult for women to lead lives as Buddhist renunciants. In ancient Japanese history, however, we can find examples of how women did not allow external forms and secular regulations to limit their commitment to the Dharma. First, allow me to offer some explanation as to how I, a laywoman of Japanese American heritage, became interested in the lives of monastic women.

I met Kito Shunko in the autumn of 1987, when I sojourned to India as a scholar of Buddhism. She is an elderly Sōtō Zen monastic woman who was returning to India for a final pilgrimage to the Mahabodhi Temple in Bodhgaya, site of the Buddha's enlightenment. Although my Buddhist studies were focused on Japan, I was not aware of an extant order of Japanese Zen nuns. My first glimpse of her, with clean-shaven head and saffron robes—the traditional color of Indian monastics—was compelling. Moving toward her I realized that her robes were Japanese in design, though they were not in traditional Japanese black. Her aesthetic sensitivity and cultural awareness drew me to her side. In the softened light of evening, as we walked around the bodhi tree, her face glowed with the wisdom of enlightenment. Compassion emanated from her every motion as we moved through wispy clouds of incense, carrying the prayers of devotees. Among the spirited pilgrims and anxious beggars her laughter resounded with the peace of one who has soared the heights and fathomed the depths; she embodied harmony in its richest form. What teachings helped her gain such wisdom and compassion? Where was the spring of her ebullient laughter?

I knew after our first conversation under the bodhi tree that I wanted to learn as much as possible about her way of life. As we walked along the Naranjana River, where Śākyamuni Buddha once walked, a brilliantly pink sun rose into the sky. Kito Shunko wove stories of the years she spent in India, building the Japanese Temple in Bodhgaya, with poetry by Zen master Dōgen (thirteenth century), and she spoke about a training temple for monastic women in Nagoya, Japan. I had found a living treasure of Japanese Buddhism.

Now let us go back to a historic moment that has faded from memory. The time is 584 C.E. and Buddhism is a fledgling religion in the land of *kami,*[1] having been officially introduced only about three decades previously. Cultural interaction with Korea is active, bringing in fresh energy. A young woman is moved by the new teachings of the Dharma. Because she lives in a cultural climate where she is surrounded by women engaged in religious affairs, it is natural that her family consider ordination for her. But there are no native Japanese Buddhist nuns for her to emulate, for no one in this island country has ever before been ordained into this new tradition. Nonetheless, compelled by the wisdom of these new teachings, she commits her life fully to them. She makes her historic vows and becomes the first ordained Buddhist in Japan. Over a millennium later, some people still remember her Buddhist name, Zenshin-ni.[2]

Shortly after Zenshin-ni's ordination, two other women joined her. Zenzo-ni and Ezen-ni also come to devote their lives to the Dharma.[3] In March of 588 C.E., their zeal to gain a deeper understanding of the monastic regulations propelled them to make history again by becoming the first Japanese people to go abroad to study in Paekche, on the Korean peninsula.[4] They returned to Japan after receiving full *bhikṣuṇī* ordination in March of 590.[5] Upon their return, with heightened resolve and determination to establish this new religion on Japanese soil, the first Buddhist temple, an *amadera*[6] called Sakurai-ji, was built in the central location of Yamato,[7] in the year 590. Shotoku Taishi (574–622), a prince widely recognized for his contributions to establishing Buddhism in Japan, had not yet made his entrance onto the stage of Japanese government and culture.

Although their vital contributions have been obscured in the mire of androcentric historiography, women were a significant force in the introduction of Buddhism to Japan.[8] Indeed it is no quirk of historical circumstance that the first ordained Buddhists in Japan were women,[9] because women were central figures in the religious sphere of ancient Japanese culture.[10] The tradition of women playing a central role in Japanese religion is illustrated by the fact that the highest deity in the indigenous pantheon of *kami* is Amaterasu Omikami, the Sun Goddess, and is further demonstrated by the fact that a number of empresses ruled over periods of ancient Japanese history. The most famous female ruler was a shaman named Himiko. She ruled over the state of Yamatai in the first half of the third century.[11] A man succeeded her after she passed away, but the people rejected him. He was replaced by a thirteen-year-old female relative of Himiko's, named Iyo or Ichiyo.[12]

Such events make it compellingly clear that historiography, not history, is at fault in the omission of the contributions of women. Recently scholars have begun to correct the histories that have left out numerous female participants, but some of these only highlight the story of what women could *not* do. It is important to include the ways in which women have been oppressed, but it is perhaps more important to extend one's purview to include what women *have* accomplished, especially when they do so in spite of oppressive circumstances.

Documents dating back to the mid-Heian period (794–1185) record that women protested against unfair treatment. A prime example from the ninth century begins with the Tendai and Shingon sects establishing a practice that prohibited women from their mountain-top temples and their mode of Buddhist practice. Furthermore, since the government granted Tendai, and later Shingon, control over the ordination platform, they chose to prohibit women from receiving the precepts. The women of Heian Japan, however, did not let these obstacles deter their determination to seek the Dharma. In the face of political and religious institutions threatening to exclude them from monastic life, the women of Heian exercised their acumen and determination to continue practicing Buddhism by creating their own form of Buddhist monasticism. Their actions reveal their insight that no institution has the authority to dictate the Dharma.

Confidence in their abilities enabled the women of ancient Japan to prevail over the complications perpetrated by male-dominated institutions. Without sharing the advantages of governmental sponsorship that monks enjoyed, and in the face of male Buddhists not offering ordination to women, Heian Buddhist women triumphed over this blatant inequity with innovative thinking. They created a new category that they named Bosatsukai-ni that was granted to those who took the *bodhisattva* vows. In so doing they took authority into their own hands and became "*bodhisattva* nuns." Their lives were similar to their predecessors in that they maintained the practices of nuns; they shaved their heads, wore Buddhist robes, and engaged in rigorous Buddhist practice. They were highly respected in society, partly because a number of the nuns were women from the imperial family. Their perseverance is a genuine testimony to the strength of their commitment and the depth of their understanding of the Dharma. It is easy to imagine that many nuns had sentiments similar to those expressed in the following poem by the Great Kamo Priestess (964–1035):

> With the scent of just one flower as my guide,
> Won't I, too, see all the numberless Buddhas?[13]

The innovations implemented by the nuns reveal the strength of Heian period Buddhist women. They did not allow official regulations made by male authorities, nor a technical definition of the category "nun," to dissuade them from their commitment to the Dharma. In a sense, they followed the precedent set by Mahāprajāpatī, the very first Buddhist nun, who persisted in her efforts to establish the order of Buddhist monastic women—even though Śākyamuni, the enlightened founder of the tradition, initially resisted. Since the first Buddhist nuns did not have a quorum of ten monks and ten nuns present at their ordination ceremony to qualify them as official *bhikṣuṇī,* why should it be absolutely required of those who seek ordination later?

In the next historical epoch of Japanese history, I will highlight Dōgen, the founder of Sōtō Zen in Japan. He lived during a period of inclusivism during the Kamakura period (1186–1333). It was a time when Buddhism was being introduced into the lives of common people, men and women alike. Like other reforms of his time, Dōgen took a strong stand on his views of women. Borne out of frustration with the existing Buddhist institutions of his day, he wrote this impassioned text in order to extinguish the errors of those who harbored incorrect thoughts about women and the Dharma. This excerpt is from the *Raihaitokuzui.*

> There is a ridiculous custom in Japan: it is the practice that nuns and women are not allowed to enter the places called "restricted territories" or "training halls of the Mahāyāna." Such a perverted custom has been practiced for ages, without anyone realizing its wrongness in the least. Those practicing the ancient way do not reform it, and those who are learned and astute do not care about it. While some say that it is the work of the incarnated [Buddhas and *bodhisattvas*], others claim that it is a legacy from ancient worthies. Yet all fail to reason about it. Their egregious absurdity is truly hard to believe. . . . If such obsolete practices do not have to be redressed, does it mean that the cycle of birth and death need not be forsaken either?[14]

Dōgen wrote this in the spring of 1240, just three years prior to his departure from Kyoto to the mountainous and remote region of Echizen. The timing of his exodus from the capital city, occurring shortly after this unambiguous statement regarding women, suggests that the prevailing institutions may have made it difficult for him to freely practice his understanding of the Dharma.

In the *Raihaitokuzui,* however, Dōgen does not merely denounce the ways of others. He also offers positive instruction regarding his understanding of women and the Dharma. He clearly states that male and female practitioners are equal, and he clarifies the confusion surrounding female Dharma teachers. "It is irrelevant whether a guide has male or female characteristics, and the like; what counts is that the guide be a person of virtue, of thusness."[15] He continues in the *Raihaitokuzui* with advice on what is the appropriate way to express respect and gratitude to a teacher of the Dharma regardless of their form.

> Valuing the Dharma means that, whether [your guide] is a pillar, a lantern, buddhas, a fox, a demon, a man, a woman, if it upholds the great Dharma and attains the marrow, then you should offer your body-mind as its seat and service for immeasurable *kalpas* [aeons].[16]

Nevertheless, the prevailing view of Dōgen is that, while he held egalitarian ideals in his early years, he did not take them with him when he established his "serious" monastery in Echizen. This view is based upon one sentence in a text that is recognized as one of a number that were compiled a few years after Dōgen passed away. The text, *Shukke ku doku* has a single sentence that denies the possibility of attaining Buddhahood in a female body: "Female-body Buddhahood is not the true Buddahood." The fact that Dōgen had a number of female disciples until his death contradicts the superficial meaning of these words. One nun, Egi-ni, even had the highly honored position of trust to care for Dōgen, her teacher, during his illness prior to his passing away. Furthermore, texts that strongly assert positive views of women are more numerous than the one line indicating the contrary, and they are more in harmony with the Zen master's action. Moreover, his egalitarian views on women correspond to his nondualistic philosophy. Therefore, to conclude that Dōgen had a fundamental change of heart in his understanding of women implies that he was an inconsistent philosopher, for Dōgen writes with certainty that "All existences are Buddha nature."

Although there are numerous examples of women in Japanese Buddhist history overcoming obstacles to full engagement with Buddhist monastic life, one striking one dates from a few centuries later, during the feudalistic era known as the Tokugawa period (1603–1867), when the tides had shifted to a regimented society controlled by a military government. A number of *amadera* resisted society's increasingly oppressive regulation of women. A poignant example of the sincerity of these women is displayed in the story of Eshun-ni. She was the younger sister of the founder of Saiko-ji, a temple in present-day Odawara. Her brother forbade her ordination because of her peerless beauty. Unflinching in her resolve to fully commit her life to the Dharma, she responded with swift and irreversible action. The young beauty burned her face in the *hibachi* stove. Thereafter, her dedication to the Dharma was uncontested.

In the twentieth century, Japanese women are still engaged in a deliberate and active attempt to reassert their concerns. The shackles of the male-dominated and markedly regimented Tokugawa period were shed for a renewed sense of worth. Monastic women had a similar vision and acted with swift strength. Fortified with the triumphs of female religious leaders of the past, they approached their goals with confidence.

Sōtō Zen nuns began the twentieth century with deep commitment to living a monastic Buddhist life, with the knowledge that their founder, Dōgen, had given teachings affirming women's practice. Although academics are divided over the significance of Dōgen's egalitarian teachings, practicing Zen nuns are not divided in the least. Nuns embrace the positive views of women that are found in Dōgen's writings and, empowered by them, have affected the course of Sōtō Zen history in the twentieth century.

Japanese Buddhist nuns began the century encumbered by misogynous regulations that had developed like an insidious disease in a sect administration that did not acknowledge nuns' abilities, contributions, or commitments. Monastic women always wore black robes, the color of novices, because they were not able to receive higher monastic or secular education along with the men.[17] Nuns did not have official training facilities, nor were they permitted to enter the Sōtō sect university, Komazawa. Even for the lower degrees, the coursework requirements for a nun were considerably lengthier than those of their male counterparts, sometimes necessitating one, two, even three years more training. With these unfair regulations in common practice, it was easy to prevent nuns from heading temples of any size or influence. This, in turn, meant that nuns were effectively shut out of a fiscal system that had become very lucrative by the close of the century. The regulations stated that only a monastic with a certain rank could be considered for middle and high positions, but nuns were not eligible to attain those ranks, no matter how long or hard they practiced.

This section traces the three generations of Sōtō monastic women who are responsible for releasing nuns from these systematically undue restrictions. They are: the four nuns who founded Nagoya's official training monastery for nuns in 1904; Kojima Kendo (b. 1898), the founder of the Nisōdan; and Aoyama Shundo (b. 1933), who exemplifies the contemporary life of monastic women in Japan. The first generation broke through the embankment of inequity by focusing upon the fundamental problem—denial of education to female monastics. The second generation continued to blaze the trail of the true Dharma by forcing the sect administration to unify all sect regulations and make no distinction between male and female monastics. By the third generation, the fruits of the previous generations' toil were beginning to ripen. Each new generation of women continues to manifest strength of character, depth of commitment to Buddhist life, and the spirit of egalitarianism.

Monastic women led the way for women to seek education outside the home, but it was a path filled with institutionalized obstacles. At least toward the end of the Tokugawa period, nuns lived in subtemples studying and practicing together. The sect did not acknowledge their efforts, for they did not authorize the subtemples to grant degrees. Moreover, nuns were not allowed to study or practice anything outside of the subtemples. In a move to increase the quality of their education, the first monastery school for resident nuns was established by a nun in Gifu Prefecture on April 1, 1881.[18] Although nuns had yet to receive recognition from the sect administration for their efforts, shortly thereafter each region established its own school for nuns. In 1887, Aichi Prefecture became the second location, followed by Kyoto in 1888, Tokyo in 1889, and Toyama Prefecture in 1892.[19] These monastery schools trained novices in Buddhist practice and provided a general education, but were not authorized to grant degrees. Nonetheless, they were a step above the subtemples because they offered a higher level of education.

During this period, monastic women also were active in society. They were involved in nursery schools and day care for children during the farmers' busy seasons. Although they personally had renounced the householder life, nuns had insight into the needs of householders and were eager to serve their needs. Many temples also ran schools called Terakoya,[20] and though these schools were invariable at a monk's temple, the majority of those doing the actual teaching and care of the children were nuns.[21] During the Meiji years of rapid modernization and reexamination of traditional customs and values, temple education was reformed. Sōtō nuns forced the currents of change in their favor; they won the right to officially establish schools fully authorized to train women in the monastic life and offer a general education. The barriers removed, Sōtō nuns wasted no time in fulfilling their dreams of higher education. On August 10, 1902, regulations for an official degree-granting Sōtō-shū Nisō Gakurin were established.[22]

It was originally determined that there would be three locations in the country that would give instruction on various Buddhist teachings and offer classes as found in a regular secular school. But by 1907, monastery schools for nuns had already been established in Toyama, Aichi, Nagano, and Niigata prefectures. Their curriculum was designed to prepare the nuns broadly in both Buddhist studies and general academic studies. The requirements during their tenure at the monastery school included Sōtō sect teachings, teachings of other sects, ethics, practice, Japanese, classical Chinese (*kanbun*), history, geography, math, calligraphy, chanting scriptures (*shomyo*), and sewing. To receive the preparatory degree (*yoka*), one had to attend the monastery school for a year. The standard degree (*honka*) involved three years of study and practice.

These monastery schools were distinct from a pure monastery, for their aims were to train the women to be effective both in the Buddhist community and the community at large. For the women to succeed and be respected by society, the secular component of education was indispensable. Since most schools were traditionally affiliated with a temple and there were few public schools, it was not unusual to combine the two. Nuns won the authority to grant official monastic degrees recognized by the sect administration and to grant official academic degrees recognized by the Ministry of Education.

This historical achievement was fostered in large part by the efforts of the women who established the first autonomous school officially authorized to train monastic women. Four monastic women—Mizuno Jorin, Hori Mitsujo, Yamaguchi Kokan, and Ando Kokai—established the Aichi-ken Sōtō-shū Nisō Gakurin on May 8, 1903, only nine months after the regulations enabled them to do so.

These nuns were empowered by their understanding of the teachings of Dōgen and Ejo, by faith in their "original destiny," and by what they called their "natural rights," a concept that had come into currency along with a host of Western ideas in the Meiji period. Thus they did not merely claim, but *re*claimed rights that were theirs before the sect administration instituted inequality:

> We monastic women have largely been neglected by members of the sect, to say nothing of general society. The result has been that the institution of the sect has not granted us our natural rights. Due to this negligence, a great number of monastic women have endured miserable conditions, and the situation has not changed much over time. However, we will not permit the flow of history to stop and leave us in our current situation. Indeed, we have arrived at a time when the actual day is not far away when women in society will clamor with a loud voice and claim the right to participate in govern-

ment. At the next special meeting of the legislature, the government and the people from both political parties will introduce a bill for the civil rights of women. Is there a more lucid tale to see than this? Even if only one day sooner, we monastic women, too, must awaken from our deep slumber; we must free ourselves from the bonds of iron chains. Having been granted on this occasion the opportunity to participate in a National Monastic Women's meeting at the head temple, Eihei-ji, the historic seat of the great Dharma, we monastic women must become self-aware of the important destiny to which we have been assigned. Along with this, we must claim our natural rights. This will happen soon, for we have the capacity to truly believe and not doubt the spirit of the Second Patriarch Koun Ejo and the original founder, Dōgen Zenji. The majority of us are of congenial spirit; namely, we the monastic women of Japan are ever more solidifying our joint forces. We must succeed in attaining our original destiny, and in so doing let us claim the natural rights that we deserve but have not yet gained!"[23]

Resolutions

I. We monastic women are resolved to work to achieve the important mission of educating the people along with exerting ourselves to increasingly improve and advance, and cultivate belief in ourselves by looking in the mirror to see our duty and the current of the times.

II. Beyond accomplishing our duty as monastic women, we are resolved, in the name of this large association, to petition to the sect authorities and the institution of the sect to claim our rights as follows:

A. We want authorization to designate Dharma heirs.

B. We reclaim the right to participate in the governing of each aspect of the sect and to opportunities for education and the like.

C. We reclaim the capacity to have appointments in each category of teachers of the faith.

D. We resolve to hold annual seminars that focus upon the various concerns of monastic women.

E. We reclaim the right to be granted positions as heads of temples at least as high as those with the status of full-ranking temple (*hochi*).[24]

In 1937, the Third Sōtō Sect National Assembly of Monastic Women was held at Soji-ji in honor of the 600th anniversary of Emperor Godaigo (1318–39). At this assembly the nuns wrote another resolution including petitions for authorization to designate a Dharma heir, to wear different robes (nuns were only allowed to wear the color of novices, black), to have the right to participate in all aspects of the sect governing organization, and to have increased educational opportunities. Thereafter, they decided to present their resolutions annually.[25]

The nuns formally established the Sōtō Sect Nuns Organization for the Protection of the Country (Sōtō-shū Nisō Gokukudan) in 1944.[26] Their motto is: "Do not discriminate against [a person's] sex, this is the True law of the exquisite and supreme Buddhist path." The three aims they established when they formed this organization are as follows:

1. To be authorized to grant Dharma transmission.
2. To build a school for teaching nuns and to publish a history of nuns before Koun Ejo's 700th memorial [1980].
3. Social work: For example, we started the orphanage Lumbini-en when we found children who had lost their parents in the war struggling for survival in Ueno Park and the subway station in Asakusa. Taniguchi Setsudo took sole responsibility for the long-term daily care of the children.[27]

Sōtō nuns saw their aims clearly and proceeded with confidence. They developed their role as protectors of the unfortunate, institutionally cultivating and advocating a socially engaged monastic life. After the war they renamed their organization Sōtō-shū Nisōdan, the Sōtō Sect Nuns' Organization, and were given an office in the sect headquarters building in Tokyo.

Sallie King suggests that due to these historically poor conditions, "It is scarcely possible that any outstanding nuns could appear" until recent reforms.[28] It is more to the point to say that the recent reforms were won because there *were* outstanding nuns who wrought them.

The first three generations of the twentieth-century Sōtō Zen nuns went from a position of little opportunity and recognition to a position of official equality. They won parity in sect regulations regarding instructional and religious ranks, created a national organization to officially present their specific concerns to sect headquarters, and began publishing various journals written by and for nuns. One of their journals from the early 1960s features a poem written by the twentieth-century nun Toko-ni, perhaps because it reflects an awareness that nuns are acting in accordance with the Dharma as they overturn centuries of inequity.

On Becoming a Beautiful Nun

Nuns are forever praying for beautiful things.
The Buddha probably does not like a nun who does not have spirit.
A nun whose heart and body are beautiful is an incarnation of the Buddha.[29]

Continuing their march toward institutionalizing equality in the Zen sect, monastic women made unprecedented strides in terms of educational possibilities. They established three autonomous monasteries for women in different regions in Japan. This century also saw the first monastic women educated and graduated from the Sōtō-shū's prestigious Komazawa University. In short, Sōtō Zen monastic women established the first official Zen monasteries to train women exclusively to gain equal rank with male monastics. Yet in the midst of these significant advances, they maintained the genuine quality of traditional Zen Buddhist monasticism. Finally, in the twentieth century, they succeeded in institutionalizing the equality that Dōgen taught in the thirteenth century.

These women illuminate a vital stream in modern Japanese society and culture, and can serve as a model for all women who seek liberation. Triumphant over various forms of male domination, modern Japanese Zen nuns maintain a traditional monastic lifestyle, not allowing the currents of modernity to dilute their religious commitment. They have become creative innovators in order to enforce the egalitarian teachings of their founder and to reclaim the illustrious heritage of women in Japanese religion. That is to say, the Zen nuns who lead the movement for the independence and equality of women do so precisely in order to transmit ancient religious and cultural traditions. Like their predecessors, Zen monastic women in modern Japan are innovators *for the sake of tradition.*

My field research reveals that monastic Buddhist women persist in their quest to lead the monastic Buddhist life, and that the monastic institution envisioned by Dōgen can still be found today at Eihei-ji, the monastery he founded, and at other Sōtō monasteries, both large and small. The place of the monastic lifestyle in the prevailing trends of Sōtō Zen, however, has undergone notable, and in many instances radical, change. Many ordained male Buddhists do not believe that monastic Buddhism is still a strong and viable institution. It has changed so much that monks are perhaps more accurately called priests, since their activities primarily center upon liturgical, rather than mediational, practices. The majority of male monastics marry and lead household lives where they are involved with raising children, cultivating an heir to the temple, and supporting the family economically. They are commonly found indulging in the consumption of alcohol and other luxury items.[30]

Monastic women, on the other hand, typically enter a monastery and undergo rigorous training for an average of five years, in contrast to the men, who train for an average of two. The women consider five years to be the minimal amount of training necessary for the rhythm and quality of the strict monastic life to become a natural part of one's being and body, for one must cultivate habits of mind and body that are increasingly divergent from the habits of the common householder in modern Japan. The physical demands of rising before dawn, sitting in zazen posture, eating with ritual exactness and grace, cleaning with meticulous determination, and using no assistance from convenient gadgets or solutions, requires a keen mind and strong body. Furthermore, with no chairs, all activities—chanting scriptures, drinking tea, sewing, confiding with a fellow adept—are done in the formal sitting posture called *seiza* (sitting on one's legs with back perfectly straight). Since they are monastics, these women do not even allow themselves the comfort of sitting on a cushion. The nun's hands, however, hold precious tea bowls with a familiarity and ease uncommon in the highly aristocratic tea ceremony. They frequently take time to enjoy traditional tea and cakes, a time when the comings and goings of the flowers in the garden are noted with a sense of wonder. Though conversation in the women's monastery is minimal, it is musical and sublime. Words that interrupt the silence are embellished with graceful and humble turns of phrase, and subtle feelings are expressed through refined sensitivities that are ever aware of the seasons, while their vocabulary and grammar betray patterns of centuries past. Upon graduating from the monastery, the women enter a temple in which they continue the practices they learned in training. The training of Zen monastic women enables them to be self-sufficient in a temple as they become imbued with a traditional way of life. In the world of monastic women, therefore, one may still experience traditional Sōtō Zen values interwoven with traditional Japanese culture.

The value nuns place on monastic tradition is evident in the choices they make in their lives. Sōtō Sect regulations do not restrict nuns from marrying or growing their hair, yet nearly all choose to maintain strict vows and practice. Most explained that they considered these basics to be the definition of being a monastic. Interviews, survey responses, and their actions suggest that many find the practices laid down by Buddhist tradition, especially by Dōgen, meaningful. The nun's commitment to Buddhist practice is not experienced as a burden, nor as merely clinging to old-fashioned ways. Most see that living a life according to these ancient teachings is important, because they help one understand the nature of human society. There is an underlying belief that an aspirant must strive to deepen her practice in order to help others usher in the new age.

Monastic women realize their important role in society and have confidence that they can make a positive difference. Although the range of their activities and interests is broad, they are all life-affirming.

Leading lives of aesthetic refinement, nuns keep Japanese aesthetic traditions and Buddhist values alive. They express few complaints or regrets about their lives. On the contrary, in the survey, the most frequently used word in response to an inquiry reflecting on life as a nun is *gratitude.*

The gender of nuns in modern Japan does not encumber them from full devotion to Buddhist truth, for they have defined their gender as having the qualities of a plum blossom—strong enough to be gentle in the harshest conditions. They can be warm and understanding, because they have the strength to transcend ego desires. They were able to change the sect regulations in just a few short decades, because they knew their demands were in accord with Buddhist truth. They did not let the attempts of the male-dominated sect administration undermine their effectiveness nor inhibit them from acting in a constructive manner to institutionalize the principles of Dōgen's teachings in the twentieth-century practice of Zen.

Historical and anthropological data reveals that Sōtō Zen nuns have a high respect for monastic life. Women in other traditions, contexts, and time periods who have been dismissed as oppressed and unfortunate have found their lives important and meaningful as well. The Personal Narratives Group Survey found that "while . . . women might be defined as 'marginal' from the perspective of a society's dominant norms and established power relations, the women so defined did not necessarily experience themselves as marginal."[31]

Women's lives as seen through the poetry of the *Therīgathā* suggests that women even in ancient India had the resolve to take control of their lives and not let themselves be pushed by the tides of suffering. They persisted, and found liberation and joy. Many monastic women in modern Japan are similarly strong, dedicated, and determined to lead meaningful lives. As is poignantly demonstrated in the following story, most Sōtō Zen nuns lead exemplary, yet ordinary, lives devoted to Buddhist truth.

❧

In a small, inconspicuous nun's temple in Nagoya, a hardy Zen nun with pristine sincerity, Nogami Senryo, lived Dōgen's teachings with her entire being. Though hardly known beyond the temple compound walls, her daily life was plain testimony to her supreme realization of Buddhist truth. She dedicated herself to caring for this nuns' temple, Seikan-ji, meanwhile training a quiet but alert nun named Kuriki Kakujo. Kuriki, who is currently the head nun of Seikan-ji, arrived under Nogami's tutelage at the age of eight. With a sense of awe, respect, and a hint of trepidation, Kuriki remembers how Nogami raised her on the classical Zen dictum, *Zadatsu ryubo* ("Die sitting, die standing"). This is the way of a monastic.[32]

Dōgen used this classical Zen dictum in a widely chanted and studied text, *Fukan zazengi*, to stress that practice means to do all activities with steady attention to reality here and now. According to Dōgen, practice is not for the purpose of creating sages out of ordinary people, because the distinction between an ordinary person and a sage is false. All are Buddha nature. Therefore, he admonished his student, "*Zadatsu ryubo* (Die sitting, die standing)." Since ancient times, various cultures have had a fascination with the posture of a person at the moment of death, which is interpreted as an indication of the deceased's level of spiritual attainment. In Zen, although no one can verify how many people have actually succeeded in this, sitting and standing death postures are considered absolute proof of enlightenment.

Nogami Senryo repeated this like a *mantra* as she strove to live each moment with pure and relentless concentration. On a crisp afternoon, the 17th of November, 1980, Nogami's adamantine voice pierced the silence: "It's time for *zadatsu ryubo*!" Not knowing what to expect, Kuriki rushed to the dim hallway where she saw Nogami slowly walking toward the bronze sculpture of Sakyamuni Buddha sitting full-lotus posture on the altar in the Worship Hall. Arriving in time to witness the stout ninety-seven-year old nun in simple black robes take a final step to perfect her stance, Kuriki pealed, "Congratulations!" as Nogami died standing.[33]

❧

Like the story of the first ordained Buddhists in Japan, the story of Sōtō nuns in this century illuminates a vital stream in Japanese society and culture. As exemplars of traditional monastic Zen Buddhism, they serve as moral and spiritual leaders of society. Indeed, interviews, surveys, and living with the nuns enabled me to verify that they do not see themselves as powerless victims of oppression. This raises the historiographical issue that leads us to consider the self-perceptions of women historically—not just how they have been viewed by others, primarily men. The story of Sōtō nuns helps bring to the surface the lasting role of women in Japanese religion. Women have made, and continue to make, important contributions to Japanese religious life as they participate in it and create it according to their own understanding. With the nuns in focus, it is evident that Dōgen Zen is not a matter of the past, but is alive today, in the lives of nuns as they make traditional daily activities their religious discipline.

The Dharma is conducive to modifying a form in order to more genuinely maintain the living truth. Indeed, Japanese women committed to Buddhist monastic life today thrive in the Dharma, in part due to the women of ninth-century Japan who ordained themselves as bodhisattva nuns. From the perspective of Zen nuns today, living according to the True Dharma takes precedence over forms that serve as obstacles. In this way, they can say that they are daughters of the Dharma, for the Dharma is constant through time and space. All forms are impermanent, subject to change over the years as they are experienced by people of diverse cultural and historical backgrounds.

The history of women in Japanese Buddhism is filled with courageous acts and personal victories—from the first ordained Buddhist in the sixth century, to the Heian period innovators, to the inclusive spirit of the Kamakura period, to the perspicacity and determination of nuns in the Tokugawa period, to the leaders in educational and institutional reforms in the twentieth century. The events highlighted here only suggest a dim outline of the contours of a landscape that is rich with the suffering and triumphs of centuries of women devoted to the Dharma. This is only a clue to the treasures buried in Japanese Buddhist history, waiting to be discovered.

Notes

1. *Kami* are the deities of the indigenous Japanese religious tradition primarily connected with Shintō. They are commonly referred to as animistic or nature deities, for there are mountain *kami,* wind *kami,* and tree *kami* among myriad others.

2. Tajima Hakudo, *Sōtō-shū Nisō-shi* (Tokyo, 1955), pp. 112–13. This is the most comprehensive text written on Japanese Buddhist monastic women.

3. Ibid. The *Nihonshoki* and *Gankoji Garan Engi* are the historical documents that record this event. For further information, see Ienaga Saburo and Akamatsu Shunsho, eds., *Nihon Bukkyōshi,* vol. 1 (Kyoto: Hozokan, 1967), pp. 56–57; Takagi Yutaka, *Bukkyōshi no naka no Nyonin* (Tokyo: Heibonsha, 1988), pp. 28–38; Ueda Yoshie, *Chomon Nisō Monogatari* (Tokyo: Kokusho Kankokai, 1979), pp. 34–36; and Shufunotomo, *Amadera: Kazari o Otoshita Nyonintachi* (Tokyo: Dainihon Insatsu, 1989), p. 38.

4. There are a few sources in Japanese that cite this fact. See Tajima, *Nisō-shi,* p. 114. Takagi mentions the circumstances of the first three Japanese Buddhists who went to China to study the precepts on p. 28. On p. 35, he references historical documents that recorded this event: *Nihon Shoki* and *Jogu Shotoku Hoo Teisetsu.* The *Nihongi* also records this event. The Great Imperial Chieftain told envoys from Paekche to take nuns, including Zenshin, to study the precepts in 587. This passage is cited in Wm. deBary, ed., *Sources of Japanese*

Tradition, vol. 1 (New York: Columbia University Press, 1958), p. 38. Ueda also mentions this event on p. 35.

5. Akira Hirakawa, "History of Nuns in Japan," *Buddhist Christian Studies* 12 (1992): 150. It is unclear which school of Vinaya these nuns followed, but Hirakawa speculates that it might have been the Dasabhanavara Vinaya or the Caturvarga Vinaya.

6. An *amadera* is a temple headed by a woman. *Ama* means "nun" and *tera* (or *dera*) means "temple." There is no exact equivalent in English, since there is no comparable situation.

7. Tajima, *Nisō-shi*, p. 115.

8. In Dale Spender's introduction to *Men's Studies Modified: Impact of Feminism on the Academic Disciplines* (Oxford: Pergamon Press, 1981), p. 2, she reasons that women are kept out of academic treatments of issues because of a structural problem. Since men have determined the traditional parameters, "the process itself can reinforce the 'authority' of men and the deficiency of women."

9. Although the first ordained Buddhists in China and Korea were not women, according to the *Bikuniden*, the first ordained woman in China dates to the early fourth century in Ch'ang-an. At that time she took only ten precepts and shaved her head. In 357 she and three others received full ordination. The year 544 marks the date of the first nun in Korea. She lived in Eikoji, the first *amadera* in Korea.

10. Nakamura Kyoto, a pioneer scholar of the role of women in Japanese religion, stresses, "It is clear that women had a good deal of authority [in ancient Japan], especially in religious matters." Nakamura Kyoko, "Revelatory Experience in the Female Life Cycle: A Biographical Study of Women Religionists in Modern Japan," *Japanese Journal of Religious Studies* 8. 3–4 (Sept.–Dec. 1981): 189. Takagi concurs with this analysis of history, stating that the reason women were the first to become ordained Buddhists was due to the predominance of women in "Shintō" as shamans. *Bukkyōshi*, p. 40.

11. Her reign is recorded in the *History of the Kingdom of Wei*, a section of the Chinese historical texts entitled the *San-kuo-chih*. The account notes that the region of Yamatai was beset by warfare, but peace reigned once Himoko embarked upon the throne. She never married. See Tsunoda Ryusaku, trans., *Japan in Chinese Dynastic Histories*, ed. L. Carrington Goodrich (South Pasadena, Calif.: P. D. & I. Perkins, 1951), pp. 8–16.

12. The Chinese monarch proclaimed Ichiyo ruler of Yamatai. Scholars still dispute the location of this ancient state. Some say it was in Kyushu; others claim it was the precursor of Yamato, placing it in present-day Nara Prefecture.

13. Translated by E. Kamens in *The Buddhist Poetry of the Great Kamo Priestess: Daisaiin Senshi and Hosshin Wakashū* (Ann Arbor: Center for Japanese Studies, University of Michigan, 1990), p. 101.

14. From the *Himitsu Shōbōgenzō* version of the "Raihaitokuzui." Dōgen, *Dōgen Zenji Zenshū*, vol. 1, ed. Ōkubo Dōshū (Tokyo: Chikumashobō, 1969), p. 254. English translation from Hee-Jin Kim, *Flowers of Emptiness: Selections from Dōgen's Shōbōgenzō* (Lewiston, N.Y.: Edwin Mellen Press, 1985), p. 293n18.

15. *Taishō Shinshū Daizōkyō*, 85 volumes, ed. Takakusu Junjirō, Watanabe Kaigyoku, and Ono Gemmyō (Tokyo: Taishō Issaikyō Kankōkai, 1924–34), vol. 82, pp. 33–4. English translation from Hee Jin Kim, *Flowers of Emptiness: Selections from Dōgen's Shōbōgenzō* (Lewiston, N.Y.: Edwin Mellen Press, 1985), p. 287.

16. Ibid., p. 288.

17. Dōgen is famous for having refused a purple robe, the color that symbolized highest respect, because it did not coincide with his commitment to simplicity. Nonetheless, the sect institutionalized a hierarchical system with each rank symbolized by an appropriate robe color. In keeping with their founder, many monastics prefer to wear black, regardless of their rank. For male monastics, this preference was a matter of choice. Not until the middle of the twentieth century was it a choice for women.

18. In 1872 the government officially designated Sōji-ji and Eihei-ji as the head temples of the Sōtō sect. During this time of change, the male-dominated Sōtō Zen institution did not intitiate reforms to bring equality to monastic women.

19. Ueda, *Chomon Nisō Monogatari*, pp. 79–80.

20. *Terakoya* were common in the Tokugawa period and made a positive contribution to the community by offering education to young people.

21. This information was passed on to me through oral history. Many elderly nuns today recall how their teachers and teacher's teachers taught young children in their temples.

22. I have gained access to this period of their history through sources found primarily in the monastery archives. The major documents include *Sōtō-shū Nisō-shi* (*The History of Sōtō Sect Nuns*), the authoritative book on the history of the Sōtō sect of monastic women; Tanaka Dorin, Kato Shinjo, Yamaguchi Kokan, and Tajima Hakudo, eds., *Rokujunen no Ayumi* (*A Path of Sixty Years*) (Nagoya: Aichi Senmon Nisōdo, 1963), a book that explicates the history of the Aichi Senmon Nisōdo; and *Jorin* and *Otayori*, journals written by and for monastic women. These texts, written by a number of female monastics about their own history, are supplemented by secondary texts on modern Japanese history and women in modern Japan to gain a perspective of female monastics in the context of general social and cultural changes and progress. My exploration into the world of Japanese Buddhist nuns concentrates upon the Sōtō sect of Zen, for it is currently the largest and most organized sect of nuns in Japan. The Sōtō-shū has the highest number of convents; three (Aichi Senmon Nisōdo, Niigata Senmon Nisōdo, and Toyama Senmon Nisōdo), compared to Jōdo-shū, which has one (Yoshimizu Gakuen of Chion-in). The other sects do not have a special school for the sole purpose of training nuns.

23. Cited in *Sōtō-shū Nisō-shi*, p. 439.

24. Cited in *Sōtō-shū Nisō-shi*, p. 440. *Hochi* is the standard level of temple. The vast majority of temples in Japan are this rank. Monastic women could only be head of subtemples (originally *heisochi*, but renamed *junhochi*), the rank below *hochi*.

25. The total list of resolutions can be found in *Sōtō-shū Nisō-shi*, pp. 440–43.

26. The nuns' actions are typical, for Japanese Buddhist history is filled with examples of Buddhists who organized their concern for the well-being of the country, especially during times of strife.

27. Kojima, *Bikuni no Josei*, p. 155.

28. Sallie B. King, "Egalitarian Philosophies in Sexist Institutions: The Life of Satomi-san, Shinto Miko and Zen Buddhist Nun," *Journal of Feminist Studies in Religion*, 4.1 (Spring 1988): 20.

29. Zen Nihon Bukkyō Nisō Hōdan, *Hanahachisu* 1 (Spring 1961): 11.

30. In defense of male monastics who have chosen to become householder priests, it should be pointed out that it was initially a tactical decision encouraged by the government to ensure the continuation of, ironically, the monastic institution and the extensive temple system in Japan. Although there are historical precedents for monastics to marry within the Japanese Buddhist tradition, most notably the example of Shinran (1173–1262), the governmental leaders in the early years of the Meiji Restoration (late nineteenth century) were the first to officially establish the marriage of male monastics for the purpose of formally instituting a hereditary system. In the Japanese cultural context, the notion of hereditary transmission is not hard to grasp. Shinran's reason for marrying, however, was based upon his understanding of soteriology. For more information on this topic, see Alfred Bloom, *Shinran's Gospel of Pure Grace* (Tuscon: University of Arizona Press, 1965).

31. Personal Narratives Group, eds. *Interpreting Women's Lives: Feminist Theory and Personal Narratives* (Bloomington: Indiana University Press, 1989), p. 12.

32. In the Buddhist tradition, there have been a number of adepts who have proven their state of enlightenment by passing away in the full-lotus position of meditation. In Zen, the classical dictum *zadatsu ryubo* ("Die sitting, die standing") indicates what is considered the ultimate way to die. Dōgen used the phrase in his text *The Way of Zazen Recommended to Everyone* (*Fukanzazengi*), which he wrote shortly after returning from China (1227) with the intention of making the true Buddhist teachings available to all people.

33. From an interview with Kuriki Kakujo at Seikan-ji Temple in Nagoya, Japan, July 17, 1990.

Hae-ju Sunim (Ho-Ryeon Jeon)

6. Can Women Achieve Enlightenment?

A Critique of Sexual Transformation for Enlightenment

Many examples of achieving enlightenment in a woman's body are described in various Buddhist texts.[1] In the early Buddhist texts it is said that Buddhist nuns, including Mahāprajāpatī, the Buddha's aunt and stepmother, attained arhatship just as Śākyamuni Buddha did. In Mahāyāna texts, women are shown to be capable of attaining even Buddhahood. There are predictions by the Buddha of women becoming enlightened in the future and the case for the enlightenment in a woman's body is often demonstrated, both in the texts and in actuality. However, at present in the Buddhist Saṅgha, the idea of sexual transformation as necessary for attaining enlightenment is so overwhelmingly prevalent as to obviate historical or textual evidence asserting that enlightenment can also be achieved in a woman's body.

Enlightenment through sexual transformation refers to a woman achieving enlightenment in a man's body. This theory, presupposing the impossibility of attaining Buddhahood in a woman's body, requires a woman to change her female body into that of a male. Here I approach the issue of enlightenment in a woman's body through a reexamination of the idea of sexual transformation. First, I examine the context of the episode of the sea dragon's daughter presented in the *Saddharmapuṇḍarīka Sūtra*, a text that is renowned for presenting the idea of sexual transformation. Next I investigate the reasons for assuming that a woman cannot attain Buddhahood in a female body. Then I evaluate the concept of gender transformation as an example of skillful means (*upāya*), a "method" to teach all sentient begins nondiscrimination with regard to gender. Finally, to correct the misconception that sexual transformation is necessary for women, I present the theory of enlightenment in a woman's body.

The Enlightenment of the Sea Dragon's Daughter: The Story and Its Central Problem

There are many episodes in the Mahāyāna Buddhist texts describing the transformation of a female body into a male for the attainment of Buddhahood. Among them, the story of the sea dragon's daughter depicted in the *Saddharmapuṇḍarīka Sūtra* is most representative. The episode of the sea dragon's daughter is presented in the Devadatta chapter of the *Saddharmapuṇḍarīka Sūtra* thus:

> Prajñākūṭa asked Mañjuśrī, "Are there any beings who, putting this scripture [the *Saddharmapuṇḍarīka Sūtra*] into practice speedily gain Buddhahood?"
>
> Mañjuśrī said, "There is the eight-year-old daughter of the sea dragon king Sāgara. Her wisdom is sharp and she knows the faculties of beings well. She has obtained *dhāraṇī* and she is able to accept and keep the profound treasure house of secrets preached by the Buddhas. She has entered into profound meditation and arrived at an understanding of phenomena. In the space of a moment, she generated the mind of enlightenment and attained the stage of irreversibility. Her eloquence is unobstructed and she is compassionately mindful of living beings as if they were her own children. Her merits are so perfect that whatever she recollects mentally and recites verbally is subtle and extensive. She is kindhearted and compassionate, humane and modest. Her will and thought are harmonious and refined, and she is able to attain enlightenment."
>
> Then Prajñākūṭa said, "I have seen the Tathāgatha of the Śākyas throughout incalculable time tormenting himself by hard practice, piling up merit, heaping up excellence, seeking the path of the bodhisattva, and never resting. When I look throughout the whole world, there is no place, not even the size of mustard seed, where the bodhisattva did not cast away body and life for the sake of living beings. Only then did he achieve the path of enlightenment. So who can believe that she is able to realize supreme and perfect enlightenment instantly?"
>
> Just before he finished speaking, at that very moment, the daughter of the sea dragon king suddenly appeared. Śāriputra said to her, "It is hard to believe that you could attain perfect enlightenment in a short time. Because a woman's body is filthy, it is not a suitable receptacle for Dharma. How could you attain perfect enlightenment? The path of the Buddha is so remote and massive that it is attainable only by tormenting oneself, accumulating good deeds, and cultivating the perfections. A woman's body has five hindrances: it cannot become the god Brahmā, the god Śakra, the king Māra, a Cakravartin king, or a Buddha. How can the body of a woman speedily achieve Buddhahood?"

> Just then, in the space of an instant, the assembled multitude all saw the sea dragon's daughter turn into a man, perfect the conduct of a bodhisattva, go straight south to the undefiled world, sit on a jeweled lotus blossom, and achieve perfect enlightenment with thirty-two heroic marks and eighty beautiful features, setting forth the wondrous Dharma for all living beings in all ten directions.[2]

The story continues by describing how countless living beings attained the stage of irreversibility and were able to receive a prophecy of the path. Finally, Prajñākūṭa, as well as Śāriputra and all the assembled multitude, expressed approval through their silence.

I have recounted this story at length because the episode demonstrates that enlightenment was attained by the sea dragon's daughter. From the story of the sea dragon's daughter, the following five conclusions can be drawn with confidence. First, the view that women are not suitable vessels for Buddhahood already existed before the compilation of the *Saddharmapuṇḍarīka Sūtra* (about the second century C.E.). Second, Śāriputra enumerated the five hindrances of a woman as evidence for the impossibility of woman's enlightenment. Third, Prajñākūṭa was not skeptical about the possibility of enlightenment in a woman's body, but rather about the possibility of sudden enlightenment, and his doubt was removed immediately, as soon as the sea dragon's daughter proved the possibility of sudden enlightenment through her own attainment. In this regard, there is a striking contrast between the attitudes of Prajñākūṭa and Śāriputra, the definitive character advocating the *śrāvaka* ("hearer") view. Prajñākūṭa's doubt concerning the sudden achievement of enlightenment, one that does not presume ascetic practices in innumerable past lives, reflects the historical emergence of the concept of sudden enlightenment. Consequently, the *Saddharmapuṇḍarīka Sūtra* points out that, in contrast to the *śrāvaka* view that women cannot attain Buddhahood, the bodhisattva vehicle recognizes sexual equality with respect to the ultimate goal in asserting that woman also can achieve the perfect enlightenment of a Buddha. To prove this point, in the Encouragement chapter of the *Saddharmapuṇḍarīka Sūtra,* the Buddha predicts the enlightenment of the Buddhist nuns Mahāprajāpatī and Yasodhara without any allusion to the transformation of their female bodies.[3]

Fourth, as we have seen, Mañjuśrī presents the case of the sea dragon's daughter in response to the question, "It is possible to attain Buddhahood quickly by holding firmly to the teaching of the *Saddharmapuṇḍarīka Sūtra*?" He answers this by proclaiming the idea of sudden enlightenment and, in the presence of Prajñākūṭa and Śāriputra, the attainability of Buddhahood in a woman's body. Just as Śāriputra symbolizes wisdom in the *śrāvaka* tradition, so Mañjuśrī represents wisdom in the Mahāyāna tradition. In the Mahāyāna tradition to which the *Saddharmapuṇḍarīka Sūtra* belongs, Mañjuśrī is supposed to take precedence over Śāriputra. Therefore, since Mañjuśrī never alludes to the need for transformation, it may have been possible for the girl to attain enlightenment even without the gender transformation presented in the episode. Other examples of the sea dragon daughter's enlightenment without sexual transformation are presented in different texts.

Fifth, the sexual transformation described in the Devadatta chapter of the *Saddharmapuṇḍarīka Sūtra* is historically significant, reconciling the idea of sexual transformation with the Mahāyāna view of woman that allows for enlightenment in a female body. The physical transformation described in this episode is particularly significant given the historical position of the *Saddharmapuṇḍarīka Sūtra*. This will be discussed in greater detail later on.

The Sea Dragon's Daughter Attains Buddhahood in a Female Body

Another textual reference to a female attaining enlightenment is the story of the sea dragon's daughter related in the *Sāgaranāgarāja Sūtra*. The story does not depict the dragon's daughter changing her body into that of a male; instead it declares that gender is irrelevant to the achievement of enlightenment.

> One day Ratnadatta, the daughter of a sea dragon, and 10,000 sea dragon wives donated precious pearls to the Buddha. Together they generated the mind of enlightenment with unsurpassed perfect wisdom and vowed to attain Buddhahood in a future life. At that time, Mahākāśyapa said to Ratnadatta and the other women, "Unsurpassed perfect enlightenment is extremely difficult to attain. One cannot attain Buddhahood in a woman's body." And Ratnadatta replied, "Mind and intention are originally pure. One who practices the bodhisattva path will easily become a Buddha. If one generates the mind of the path of truth, one will realize enlightenment as easily as seeing into the palm of one's hand. And when the wondrous power of wisdom is awakened, all the teachings of the Buddha will also be attained." Further she said, "Buddhahood can be attained by all, because ultimately mind is neither male nor female."[4]

With various similes, Ratnadatta declares that the path of truth is neither male nor female and receives a prophecy from the Buddha that she will attain Buddhahood in the future.

The episode in the *Sāgaranāgarāja Sūtra* closely resembles that in the *Saddharmapuṇḍarīka Sūtra*, but the omission of sexual transformation in the case of the sea dragon's daughter in the former reveals that the contexts of the two scriptures are quite different. The *Sāgaranāgarāja-paripṛcchā Sūtra* was translated into Chinese in 258 C.E. by Zhu Fahu of the Western Jin dynasty. In the *Saddharmapuṇḍarīka Sūtra,* Sāgara is the name of the sea dragon king. His daughter can be regarded as the same character as the daughter of the sea dragon in the *Sāgaranāgarāja Sūtra.* Zhu Fahu rendered the *Saddharmapuṇḍarīka Sūtra* (*Zheng fahu jing*) into Chinese in 286 C.E., along with a number of other texts containing the theme of bodily transformation. From this fact, it may be assumed that the idea of sexual transformation as necessary for enlightenment and the idea of enlightenment in a woman's body already existed before Zhu Fahu began his translation work in the latter half of the third century. Yet, as the two different stories of the sea dragon's daughter related above demonstrate, the two ideas—of gender transformation as alternatively necessary or unnecessary—have different origins. Let us now turn our inquiry to the background of the two episodes concerning the sea dragon's daughter.

The Background of the Episode of the Sea Dragon's Daughter

In contrast to the episode presented in the Devadatta chapter of the *Saddharmapuṇḍarīka Sūtra,* the *Sāgaranāgarāja Sūtra* describes the prophecy regarding the enlightenment of the sea dragon's daughter without mentioning sexual transformation. In the Encouragement chapter of the *Saddharmapuṇḍarīka Sūtra,* also, we find mention of several Buddhist nuns who are said to have achieved enlightenment in female bodies. Therefore, we need to consider the relationship between these conflicting views regarding the necessity of sexual transformation for enlightenment.

The first part of the Devadatta chapter in the *Saddharmapuṇḍarīka Sūtra* reveals that Devadatta was a teacher of the Buddha in a previous life and that, due to his previous merits, Devadatta received a prediction of enlightenment from the Buddha. The story relates that when the Buddha was a king, a seer came to him and expounded the *Saddharmapuṇḍarīka Sūtra.* The king continued practicing with the seer, attaining great wisdom and eventually becoming a Buddha. The seer of that time, who caused the Buddha to complete the six perfections, achieve the thirty-two marks, and subsequently attain perfect enlightenment to save all living beings, was Devadatta. The Buddha said that all the merits he accumulated at that time could be attributed to the seer Devadatta, who would therefore be called by ten epithets: Tathāgatha, Worthy of Offerings, the Perfectly Enlightened One, One of Wisdom and Practice, Well-Gone, Knower of the World, the Unsurpassed One, Ruler of Beings, Teacher of Gods and Human Beings, the Buddha, and the World-Honored One.[5]

It is said, however, that among the twenty-eight chapters of the *Saddharmapuṇḍarīka Sūtra,* the Devadatta chapter was inserted at a later period. Devadatta was a cousin of the Buddha, son of Amitodana,[6] but as is well known, he is portrayed as a cruel and wicked person who mocked the Buddhist community. It is said that Devadatta and his followers, such as Kokalika, fell into hell due to their harmful intentions toward the Buddha.[7] It is said that during the latter period of the Buddha's teachings, just as Buddhism was expanding enormously, Devadatta established a new sect that practiced austere discipline like the Jains, and that he and his followers insulted Śākyamuni and denigrated the alms-round of the Buddhists.

In the *Saddharmapuṇḍarīka Sūtra,* however, Devadatta is highly esteemed as a master of wisdom. This recasting of Devadatta in the *Saddharmapuṇḍarīka Sūtra* hints at a confluence between the Mahāyāna sects and the group surrounding Devadatta. The story of the sea dragon's daughter also seems to derive from Devadatta's followers, to whom it was handed down.[8] The fact that the story of the sea dragon's daughter found in the latter part of the Devadatta chapter has nothing to do with Devadatta as sage contributes to the supposition that these two stories derive from a common tradition or a particular group of religious followers, namely, the tradition of Devadatta's followers. Consequently, the story of the sea dragon's daughter seems to stem from the same sect of Devadatta that attempted to maintain austere rules of conduct and ignored the community of Buddhist nuns.[9] This conclusion is supported by the fact that Devadatta killed Utpalavarṇikā, one of the two *bhikṣuṇīs* most highly renowned for miracle powers.[10] It is very plausible, therefore, that the idea of sexual transformation as necessary for enlightenment that is found in the *Saddharmapuṇḍarīka Sūtra* derives not from authentic Buddhist tradition, but from the tradition of Devadatta's sect, which was under the influence of traditional, discriminatory Indian views of women. By contrast, the inclusive view of the *Saddharmapuṇḍarīka Sūtra,* sometimes characterized even as totalistic, may have opened the door for the idea of sexual transformation for enlightenment. The adoption of the idea of sexual transformation may thus be regarded as a result of a particular historical current, in confluence with the particular bent of Devadatta's sect, whereas the acknowledgment of sexual equality in the attainment of enlightenment may be seen as a reflecting the more inclusive philosophical foundations of the *Saddharmapuṇḍarīka Sūtra.*

Women's Bodily Transformation and the Theory of the Five Hindrances

The idea that a woman needs to transform her body into that of a man to attain enlightenment is, as has already been discussed in connection with the episode of the sea dragon's daughter, based on the presupposition that a woman cannot be reborn as the king Brahmā, the god Śakra, the king Māra, as a sage king, or as a Buddha.[11] However, the episode of the sea dragon's daughter does not give any indication as to why a woman is presumed to have these "five hindrances." An argument to explain why women possess the five hindrances is, however, found in a *sūtra* called the *Suryajihmīdaraṇaprabhā.*[12] Like the *Saddharmapuṇḍarīka Sūtra,* this text, discusses the need for sexual transformation due to the limitations of being a woman. It explains these limitations as follows:

1. Because of their impure and evil nature, women cannot be reborn as the god Śakra;
2. Because of their unbridled indulgence in lust, women cannot be reborn as Brahmā, king of gods;
3. Because of their arrogance regarding the true Dharma, women cannot be reborn as the king Māra;
4. Because of being endowed with eighty-four latent bad qualities, women cannot be reborn as a universal sage king;
5. Because of their hatred, ignorance, attachment to the mundane world, and karma accumulated through actions of body, speech, and mind, women cannot be reborn as a Buddha.

A woman named Prajñādattā, having listened to all this, begins a discussion with a monk called Uttaragata. Finally, with sharp reasoning, Prajñādattā persuades him to accept the view that discrimination with respect to gender is unfounded, since gender is illusory by nature. When apprised of this discussion, the Buddha gives a prediction regarding the enlightenment of Prajñādattā, who suddenly transforms her body into that of a man. The story thus contains an internal contradiction. Although the *Suryajihmīdaraṇaprabhā Sūtra* presents the theory of the five hindrances of women in detail, the idea of the five hindrances is contradicted by the principle of nondiscrimination with respect to gender accepted by Uttaragata and, most strikingly, by Prajñādattā's attainment.

In the *Nāgadattā Sūtra,* we find an assertive refutation of the five hindrances of women:

> A householder named Xufu had a fourteen-year-old daughter named Nāgadattā. Once, after seeing the Buddha and his disciples, Nāgadattā felt very happy and said to herself heartfully, "I shall practice the

> *bodhisattva* path in order to attain enlightenment like the Buddha." Māra, having seen the girl generate the great mind of enlightenment, disguised himself as Nāgadattā's father and attempted to discourage her mental resolve saying, "Buddhahood is too difficult to attain. It takes 100,000 eons to become a Buddha. Why don't you attain arhatship instead?" Nāgadattā was unmoved by all his various attempts at dissuasion, so Māra said again, "I have not even heard that a woman can be reborn as a sage king, so how can you be reborn as a Buddha? It takes too long to attain Buddhahood. Why not seek arhatship and attain *nirvāṇa* soon?" Nāgadattā replied, "I have also heard that a woman cannot be reborn as a sage king, a Śakra, a Brahmā, or a Buddha, and yet I shall apply appropriate effort to transform my woman's body into a man's. I have heard that if one practices the deeds of a bodhisattva diligently, one can attain Buddhahood."[13]

Eventually, Nāgadattā transforms her woman's body into a man's and is given a prediction of her enlightenment by the Buddha.

In this episode, the five hindrances of a woman are utilized by Māra to discourage Nāgadattā from practicing the bodhisattva path to attain enlightenment. Her transformation into a man's body in the story not only shows her strong resolve to withstand the temptation of Māra, but also reveals the intention of the text to challenge the idea of women's hindrances. This idea of special hindrances for women can be traced back to the Nikāya and Vinaya collections of texts, including the Mahīśāsaka Vinaya;[14] the *Majjima Āgama;*[15] the *Gautamī Prophecy Sūtra,* in which Mahāprajāpatī is acknowledged for establishing the Bhikṣuṇī Saṅgha;[16] the *Aṅguttara Āgama;*[17] and the *Four-Stage Dharma Gate Sūtra.*[18] Nevertheless, the theory of five specific hindrances for women describe in subsequent texts seems to have been interpolated at some later period. Evidence for this is that the idea of five hindrances of women found in the later part of the Mahīśāsaka Vinaya does not appear in any other text that deals with the establishment of the order of Buddhist nuns.[19]

The story of Princess Munī, found in the Chinese version of the Aṅguttara Nikāya, is another example that may be cited to illustrate that the five hindrances of women are a later interpolation. The story of Munī in Chinese translation talks about the five hindrances of women, but this part of the story is missing in the Pāli version. The *Damamūka Sūtra* (*The Sūtra of the Wise Man and the Fool*)[20] contains a revised version of Munī's story, but does not include any reference to the theory of women's five hindrances. Other texts that deal with women's five hindrances reveal a similar discrepancy between the Chinese *āgamas* and the Pāli *nikāyas*. Hence it may naturally be surmised that the idea of five hindrances for women did not exist before the emergence of the different early

Buddhist schools, since they agreed in regarding arhatship as attainable by all women and men.

Following this textual analysis, we may conclude with assurance that the idea of the five hindrances of women came into existence just before the compilation of the Mahāyāna texts—sometime between the third century B.C.E. and the first century C.E., most probably during the first century B.C.E.[21] The reason for this estimate is that, instead of the five hindrances, a theory of the three subordinations of women is presented in the *Yuye nijing*, a text that seems to have been composed before the idea of the five hindrances of women was formulated in the Mahāyāna texts.[22] This would indicate that the idea of the five hindrances probably did not arise before the first century B.C.E. Although the theory of the five hindrances of women came to exist around the first century B.C.E., a movement in opposition to the idea of women's spiritual limitations was already underway.

The Theory of the Thirty-Two Marks of a Buddha

When considering the context within which the idea of the five hindrances of women emerged, we cannot ignore the list of the thirty-two marks of a Buddha, one of which is a retractable penis. The thirty-two marks originally referred to the auspicious physical marks of a sage king, but were later attributed to the Buddha to glorify him. Various texts list the thirty-two marks, citing different names and sequences. The retractable penis occurs tenth in sequence in the *Mahāprajñāpāramitā Śāstra*.[23] The retractable penis mark is variously called "retractable horse-penis mark," "horse-penis mark," "penis mark," and "penis mark of a horse's form." All of these names unquestionably refer to the sexual organ of a Buddha, an organ hidden in his body and in the shape of a horse's sexual organ. The biased view that women cannot attain enlightenment may have stemmed from the idea of the Buddha's unique sexual mark.[24] Even though his sexual organ is concealed, the mark is characterized as male.

The list of the thirty-two marks was formulated by the disciples of the Buddha to venerate their spiritual leader after the Buddha passed away. It is widely acknowledged that a Buddhist of the first century B.C.E. would never have considered the idea that the thirty-two marks ascribed to a Buddha would have a serious impact on the idea of enlightenment for women.[25] Preconceptions and prejudices concerning women's impurity gave rise to the theory of women's sexual transformation at the time of enlightenment. Similar prejudices are evident in the theory of the thirty-two marks adopted for the veneration of the

Buddha in accordance with Indian heroic legends. This seems to be a result of the fact that the *śrāvakas* acknowledged as fully enlightened only the historical Śākyamuni Buddha, a male.

According to the *Ratnatripariprccha Sūtra*, the Tathāgatha possessed the "heroic" sexual characteristic of a horse's penis because he had protected his body and renounced sexual craving in many past lives.[26] It is also recorded that the horse-penis mark, supposedly acquired as a bodhisattva through persevering in hardship, chastity, fervent generosity, giving protection, donating to the poor, and other such practices, signifies virtue, longevity, and the acquiring of many disciples.[27] Therefore, the concept of the thirty-two marks may be interpreted as emphasizing the virtuous acts that give rise to enlightenment.

The Idea of the "Original Vows"

Another major component in the formulation of the idea of sexual transformation is the idea of original vows. The term "original vows" (Skt: *pūrvapraṇidhāna*) refers to the spiritual vows expressed by Gautama Buddha during a previous lifetime as a bodhisattva. Most representative are the forty-eight vows articulated by the bodhisattva Dharmakāra, considered one of the incarnations of Amitābha Buddha. Thirty-fifth in the list of forty-eight is a vow to transform one's female body into that of a male. According to the *Sukhāvativyūha Sūtra*, the vow is expressed thus: "Even though I am supposed to attain Buddhahood, should the women who dislike their female bodies, living in incalculable, marvelous Buddha realms, having generated the mind of enlightenment by listening to my name, be reborn as females again, I will give up perfect enlightenment."[28] This spiritual aspiration is variously called "the aspiration to become a male," "the aspiration for rebirth of women," "the aspiration to change from female to male," and so on.

In the *Amitābha Sūtra*, this aspiration is the second of twenty-four vows and is expressed thus: "May no one be born as a woman or a girl in my land and may the women born in my land change their gender to male."[29] This aspiration reflects an awareness of the terrible conditions to which women are subject, but does not presuppose that women are incapable of attaining Buddhahood. This fact is clearly demonstrated in the *Amitāyurbuddha Sūtra* where a woman gives the sufferings that a woman endures as her reason for seeking rebirth in the Pure Land. The Buddha eventually prophesizes her rebirth in the Pure Land as a result of her spiritual quest.[30] Again in the *Bhaishajyaguru-tathāgata-pūrvapraṇidhana Sūtra*, the eighth among the twelve great vows of Bhaishajyaguru is: "When I attain enlightenment in a future life, if there are women driven and oppressed by all manner of evils who consequently wish to relinquish their female form, may I be able to transform their bodies into male bodies with heroic features, and may they attain perfect wisdom by just listening to my name."[31] As in the *Sukhāvatīvyūha Sūtra,* this text prefaces the vow with the phrase "If women wish to relinquish their female form. . . ." This suggests a wish to be free from the toilsome conditions under which women live. It is therefore legitimate to say that the aspiration to take rebirth in the Pure Land does not indicate that transforming one's female form is a necessary condition for enlightenment, a view supported by the original vow of Akṣobhya that describes women's lives and deeds in Akṣobhya's Pure Land. In the *Akṣobhya-tathāgata-syavyūhā Sūtra,*[32] a woman reborn in Akṣobhya's Pure Land is said to have excellent virtues, with no bad karma resulting from gossip or harsh speech. Even when pregnant or when bearing a child, such a woman feels free, safe, and tranquil. It is said that all these merits are due to the power of Akṣobhya's original vow.

In texts related to the lineage of the *Mahāprajñāpāramitā Sūtra,* however, the Pure Land of Akṣobhya is described as a paradise in which the women are expected to be reborn as men through sexual transformation. For instance, the Gaṅgādevī chapter of the *Mahāprajñāpāramitā Sūtra* says, "At that time Gaṅgādevī will take her last female body. After she finishes that life in that body, she will be reborn as a man and never as a woman again; that is to say, after she dies, she will be reborn in the Eastern Realm of the Immutable Tathāgatha and attain unsurpassed wisdom through the practice of *brahmacārya.*"[33] The Gaṅgādevī chapter of the *Daśasāhasrikā Prajñāpāramitā Sūtra*[34] states that a woman called Gaṅgādevī will attain Buddhahood in her next life, be given the epithet "Golden Flower," and subsequently be reborn as a man in Akṣobhya's Pure Land. Similar descriptions are found in other Chinese versions of the *Daśasāhasrikā Prajñāpāramitā Sūtra,* such as the *Moho-pan-zo-chao-ching,*[35] the *Aṣṭasāhasrikā Prajñā paramita Sūtra* (*Tao-hsing-pan-zo-ching*),[36] and the *Ta-min-tu-wu-ci-ching.*[37] All these texts agree that it is because of their original vows that the women who changed into male bodies possessed excellent virtues in Akṣobhya's Pure Land. It is therefore evident that transformation into a male body does not in itself serve to explain rebirth in Akṣobhya's Pure Land.

In the *Sumatidarika-paripṛccha Sūtra,* a girl named Sumati enunciates this vow: "Like Śākyamuni Buddha, I will attain Buddhahood in a future life where there are not even words for evil doing, evil intentions, and women."[38] The *Sumati Sūtra* also contains a dialogue between Mañjuśrī and Sumati in which Mañjuśrī asks Sumati, "Why don't you transform your female body?" Sumati replies, "I have no attachment, so why should I have to transform my body?" She continues, saying that if one attains complete and perfect wisdom, not even the word "woman" will exist in the land. She then changes her body into that of a monk to prove her conviction.[39] The phrase "not even the word 'woman' " in this episode signifies nonattachment to the idea of woman. In such a world, there would be no discrimination between men and women.

As noted before, the origin of the concept of vows entailing gender transformation could well be the sufferings experienced by women. The idea of gender transformation does not necessarily imply a relationship between gender and the attainability of enlightenment.

The Theory of the Ten Practices

Unquestionably related to the idea of sexual transformation is the theory of the Ten Practices which must be mastered before a woman is able to change her body into that of a male. According to the *Strīvivarta-vyākaraṇa Sūtra,*[40] Vimalarami asks what practices will allow her to be reborn as a man and generate the mind of enlightenment. To this question, the Buddha enumerates ten practices that, when mastered, will enable her to change her body into that of a male. Another list of these ten practices, with slight variations, is found in the *Bhadraśī Sūtra.*[41] It is not necessary to list them here, but these practices resemble the general standard of discipline for Buddhist novices. For example, the first practice, or *dharma,* refers to maintaining the mind of enlightenment, the second to getting rid of pride and deceit, and the third to purify the three types of deeds (namely, what has been seen, heard, and suspected). It is very explicitly stated that these practices are not necessarily required for women who vow to be reborn as a man, as is clear when we reflect on the scene in which Vimalarami transforms her body into that of a male. Vimalarami asks the Buddha whether, if it is true that phenomena are neither male and female, her body could be changed into that of a male. Immediately upon asking the question, her body becomes that of a man with magnificent marks.[42] The theory of ten practices, which explains the reasons for transforming a woman's body, is followed by an episode that sets out to prove that all phenomena are totally indifferent to the idea of the impurity of women. Thus, in our search for a conceptual foundation for the idea of the sexual transformation, all reasons cited so far are implausible grounds for insisting on the necessity of transformation for enlightenment.

Emptiness and Gender Transformation

As previously mentioned, many texts set forth the view of nondiscrimination between male and female, yet maintain that bodily transformation is necessary to attain Buddhahood. Certain texts approach the topic from the Mahāyāna view of nondualism. In the *Candrottarā-dārikā-vyākaraṇa,*[43] for example, Dhāraṇīmdhara Bodhisattva asks a girl called Candrottarā: "So, Candrottarā, since you cannot attain Buddhahood in a female body, why don't you change your female body into a male?" The girl replies, "O good man, that which is called 'emptiness' is not realized by changing the body nor by not changing the body. This is the case with all phenomena. Why do you ask me to change my female body?" In conjunction with the teaching on emptiness, which evaporates distinctions between phenomena, this episode rejects sexual discrimination and challenges prejudices regarding a woman's physical form.

Another example, the *Vimaladattā Sūtra,* reveals the same attitude. It describes a dialogue between the well-known monk Maudgalyāyana and a woman called Vimaladattā who by virtue of her vow to attain Buddhahood changes her body into a male. The Buddha, recognizing her intention, praises Vimaladattā, saying that she has already practiced bodhisattva deeds countless times in the past, attained complete and perfect wisdom, and generated the mind of enlightenment even earlier than did Mañjuśrī. At that point, Maudgalyāyana asks Vimaladattā:

> "O child of good family, since you have already generated the mind of enlightenment for such a long time, why not change your female body into a male?" And Vimaladattā says: "O great Maudgalyāyana, attaining Buddhahood does not depend on a man's body nor a woman's, because Buddhahood cannot be regarded as something subject to rebirth nor as something attainable by a mind clinging to a body." At that moment Brahmā, king of the gods, having heard these words, vows thus: "Even a woman can attain enlightenment, so I will immediately enter the true path and practice the bodhisattva deeds."[44]

Here again is evidence of the Mahāyāna view that women are under no handicap in attaining perfect enlightenment, yet the idea of sexual transformation remains.

In addition to the episodes recounted above, the theory of bodily transformation is alluded to in many other texts, such as the *Stirīvivarta-vyākaraṇa,*[45] *Sumati-dārikā-paripṛcchā,*[46] *Mahāratnakūṭa Sūtra,*[47] *Vimaladattā-paripṛcchā,*[48] and *Aśokadattā-vyākaraṇa.*[49] None of these texts, however, give evidence of sexual discrimination. The idea of sexual equality in these Mahāyāna texts, which arose in reaction to the androcentric views of the Śrāvakayāna, is beholden to the philosophical concept of emptiness that emphasizes activities in the social sphere.[50]

A Woman's Body as Skillful Means

Examples have already been given to illustrate the doctrine commonly formulated as "Phenomena (*dharma*) are neither male nor female" and "Neither man nor woman exists in all phenomena." This doctrine is usually presented in the context of sexual transformation of a woman's body into a man's. At the same time, it is not uncommon to find texts that explain birth as a woman as a skillful means (*upāya*) to serve and teach all living beings. For example, the *Mahāratnakūta Sūtra* tells the story of Aśokadattā, daughter of the king Ajātasatru:

> The Buddha said: "This girl has already generated the mind of enlightenment with nine billion Buddhas of the past, cultivated a virtuous mind under these Buddhas' guidance, and attained the supreme and perfect wisdom." Then Śāriputra said, "Can this woman change her female body?" The Buddha replied, "Śāriputra, why do you see her as a woman? You should not have to see her as such, because this Fearless Bodhisattva has manifested in the aspect of a woman to serve living beings." Then Fearless Bodhisattva suddenly changed her body into that of a man to prove that "all phenomena are neither male nor female."[51]

The content of another version of this story that appears in the *Aśokadattā-vyākaraṇa*[52] is almost the same. In it, the dictum that a woman's body should not be denigrated, by virtue of it's being a skillful means, is authorized by the "golden mouth" of the Buddha. In fact, Mahāyāna texts often take their titles from the idea of bodily transformation as a skillful means. For example, the *Upāyakauśalya Sūtra*[53] describes a discussion between Subhūti and a beautiful woman who is later recognized as a bodhisattva emanating in the form of a woman. The Buddha affirms that this "transformation bodhisattva" has enabled countless living beings to generate the supreme and perfect mind of enlightenment. Although a woman's body is accepted as a skillful means, the tendency to gender transformation, from female into male, persists.

Enlightenment in a Woman's Body

The idea of transforming a woman's body into a man's, as noted before, can be regarded as a skillful means to serve sentient beings. It puts forward the notion of a sexual integration—of transformation between male and female bodies, from a man's body to a woman's and vice versa—that is freely reciprocal. For instance, the episode of Devī in the *Vimalakīrtinirdeśa Sūtra*[54] presents the theoretical basis for reversing the emphasis on enlightenment in a male body by replacing it with the idea of nondiscrimination with regard to gender. The goddess Devī, having listened to a dialogue between Vimalakīrti and the *śrāvakas,* scatters heavenly flowers upon the great bodhisattva and the *śrāvakas.* The flowers that land on the bodies of the *śrāvakas* cling to their bodies, while those flowers that land on the bodies of the great bodhisattvas simply fall to the ground. Even when the *śrāvakas* attempt to shake the flowers off with their supernatural powers, the flowers do not fall away. When the goddess asks Śāriputra why he is shaking off the flowers, he says that flowers are not fitting for religious saints. Devī then argues that there is no need to say that flowers are not religious, because flowers are free from conceptual discrimination. It is when Śāriputra views them that conceptual discrimination arises. The goddess says that one who conceives of neither concepts nor discriminations is one who is truly religious, and flowers would not cling to such a great bodhisattva.

This episode seems to be a strategy to support a certain doctrinal position and to criticize the discriminatory attitude of institutionalized androcentrism, an attitude that, as just illustrated, was common among the *śrāvakas* and was held even by Śāriputra, who was designated "first in wisdom." In a debate with Śāriputra, Devī raises the question of gender discrimination again. When Śāriputra asks, "Devī, why not change your womanhood?" Devī answers, "For twelve years, I have sought womanhood without ever obtaining it. How, then, could I change it? For example, if a skilled magician creates an illusory woman through his magical powers, could you reasonably ask why she does not change her womanhood?" To this Śāriputra answers, "No, she would not need to change her womanhood, because illusory women do not have definite form. Again Devī asks, "Just so, all phenomena are unreal and illusory by nature. How then could you think of asking someone to change her womanhood?" Then, through her supernatural powers, Devī causes Śāriputra to appear like herself, while she, Devī, appears like Śāriputra. At this point, she retorts, "Just as you now appear as a woman, so all women appear in the form of a woman, but are not women. It is with this intention that the Blessed One said that all *dharmas* are neither male nor female." Devī then suspends her supernatural powers and Śāriputra appears as before. Devī asks Śāriputra, "Where is your female form?" and Śāriputra replies, "My female form neither exists nor does not exist." To this Devī responds, "In the same way, phenomena neither exist nor do not exist. To say that they neither exist nor do not exist—this is the word of the Buddha."

As we have seen, the androcentric ideas evident in the soteriology fade away in the *Vimalakīrti Sūtra,* which provides a rich elaboration of the nondualistic view of the *śūnyavāda.* In terms of its philosophical foundations, the gendered view that a woman must transform her body into a male to attain enlightenment undergoes a shift toward nondualistic, androgynous integration. From the beginning, the idea of transformation played a role in countering the notion that a women is incapable of becoming a Buddha. In the course of time, however, the idea of transformation came be critiqued in accordance with the Mahāyāna philosophical position that teaches emptiness and nonattachment even to gender. This position was spacious enough to allow for the idea that a woman can become enlightened in a female body. The expressions of enlightenment in a woman's body are so vivid in the later Mahāyāna texts that, especially in the *Śrīmālā Sūtra,* there is an insistence that there can be no sexual differentiation in all phenomena.[55] Śrīmālā, the daughter of King Prasenajit and Queen Mallikā, receives from the Buddha a prophecy concerning her attainment of Buddhahood. However, the necessity of transforming her female body is not alluded to at the time Śrīmālā receives the prediction. Even the list of the Great Vows do not involve any reference to gender. As the full name of this sūtra (*Śrīmālā-devī-siṃhanāda Sūtra*) indicates, even a voice like a roaring lion, one of the marks of a Buddha, is also given to the woman Śrīmālā. This fact signifies that the religious status of women may have been high at that time. The *Śrīmālā Sūtra* elaborates the theory of *tathāgatagarbha,* including the radical idea that only one who has a female nature can attain Buddhahood.

Conclusion

The Buddhist texts that deal with the idea of sexual transformation for enlightenment are vast in number. I have taken it as my task to examine them from the perspective of their content. This examination has lead me to the conclusion that the idea of enlightenment through sexual transformation does not reflect sexism with regard to the attainability of enlightenment, but rather, represents an iconoclastic position intended to correct prejudicial views toward women. The idea of sexual transformation for enlightenment appears to be a strategy that eventually led to a theory of enlightenment in a female body. These philosophical notions, which became integrated and perpetuated in the folklore in East Asia, demonstrate that Buddhist adherents were acquainted with the Buddha's teaching on equality.

Notes

1. This phenomenon is described in Miriam Levering, "The Dragon Girl and the Abbess of Mo-Shan: Gender and Status in Ch'an Buddhist Tradition," *Journal of the International Association of Buddhist Studies* 5.1 (1982): 19–35; Nancy Schuster [Barnes], "Changing the Female Body: Wise Women and the Bodhisattva Career in Some *Mahāratna-kūtasūtras*," *Journal of the International Association of Buddhist Studies* 4.1 (1981): 33–46; and Alex and Hideko Wayman, *The Lion's Roar of Queen Śrīmālā* (Delhi: Motilal Banarsidass, 1974).

2. T 4.262.35b–c. T refers to Junjiro Takakusu, *Taishō shinshū daizōkyō* (Tokyo: Daizōkyō Gakujutsu Yōgo Kenkyūkai, 1923–32).

3. T 9.262.39a–b.

4. T 15.598.149b–150c.

5. T 9.262.34b–35c.

6. For Devadatta as son of Amitodana, see T 1.24.364b and T 1.25.419b.

7. For example, in T 2.9(16).115b, 2.99(48).251b, and 1.80.893c.

8. Yu Iwamoto, *Buddhism and Women* (*Bukkyō to josei*) (Tokyo: Daisan Bunkasha, 1980), p. 52; Y. Miyasaka, *Buddhism and the Economics Perspective* (*Bukkyo to dokan*) (Tokyo: Gousei Shuppansha, Showa 44), p. 16.

9. Ibid.

10. T 24.1450.147c–148a.

11. The Chinese version of the *Lotus Sutra* (*Zeng fahua jing*) refers to five more. T 9.263.106a.

12. T 15.638.541b, translated by Nie Chengyuan of the Western Jin dynasty (290–306 C.E.).

13. T 14.557.909a.

14. T 22.1421.186a.

15. T 1.26.607b.

16. T 1.60.856a.

17. T 2.125.577c.

18. T 17.776.712b.

19. For example, the Dharmagupta Vinaya, T 22.1428.992a.

20. T 4.202.371c.

21. As is generally accepted, textual analysis for purposes of historical data based on a comparison between the Chinese Āgamas and the Pāli texts

allows scholars to ascertain the interpolation of parts of texts by noting discrepancies between variant redactions. This provides evidence to establish the divisions of early Buddhist schools from around the third century B.C.E. for the purpose of dating these interpolations. Kajiyama Yuichi, *A View of Buddhist Womanhood* (*Bukkyō no josei kan*) (Tokyo: Jinbun Shoin, 1993), p. 199.

22. Ibid., pp. 205–7.

23. T 25.1509.90b. The name and number of this mark are a little different in other *sūtras*; for example, in the *Mahāprajñāpāramitā Sūtra*, it is third; in the *Madhyamāgama Sūtra*, first; in the *Bodhisattvabhūmi Sūtra*, ninth; etc.

24. Enichi Ochō, *Lotus Philosophy* (*Hokke Shisō*) (Tokyo: Gotosha, 1969), p. 98.

25. Kajiyama, *Buddhist Womanhood*, pp. 204–10.

26. T 13.399.469a.

27. Shinko Mochizuki, *Bukkyō Daijiten* (Tokyo: Sekai seiten kankō kyōkai, 1954–71) p. 1556b.

28. T 12.360.268b.

29. T 12.362.301a.

30. T 12.365.340c–346b.

31. T 14.450.405b.

32. T 11.313.756b; 11.310(6)105b–c.

33. That is, "pure conduct," meaning celibacy. T 7.220.833b–c.

34. T 8.227.568b.

35. T 8.226.531a.

36. T 8.224.458a–b.

37. T 8.225.497a–b.

38. T 12.336.82c, 12.335.74b–78c, 11.310(30)547b–49b.

39. T 12.326.83a–b.

40. T 14.564.918c.

41. T 14.570.943b–c.

42. T 14.564.921b.

43. T 14.480.620b.

44. T 12.339.106b, 11.310(33)563b–c.

45. T 14.562.913b–14b.

46. T 12.334.76b–81c, 12.336.81c–83c.

47. T 11.310(30).547b–49b.

48. T 12.328.89b–97c.

49. T 12.337.88c.

50. Akira Hirakawa, *A Study of Primary Mahāyāna Buddhism (Shoki daijō bukkyō no kenkyū)* (Tokyo: Shunjūsha, Showa 43), pp. 276–77.

51. T 11.310(32).555b.

52. T12.337.88c.

53. This *sūtra* appears in two versions in Chinese translation: T 14.565.921c and T 14.566.930c.

54. T 14.474.528a–29b, 14.475.547a–48c.

55. T 12.353.217a, 11.310(48).672c.

The Tibetan Tradition

Janice D. Willis

7. Tibetan Buddhist Women Practitioners, Past and Present

A Garland to Delight Those Wishing Inspiration

The renowned teacher Kalu Rinpoche, who was one of the greatest meditation masters of this century, had this to say about women and the Dharma:

> Regardless of whether you are a man or a woman, regardless of your particular situation in this life, if you have faith, confidence, and diligence, if you have compassion and wisdom, you can become enlightened. If you are merely caught up in your emotional confusion and continue to let that dominate your life, no matter whether you are a man or a woman, enlightenment will be difficult to attain. But if you have the necessary qualities for Dharma practice, the kind of body you have makes no difference at all.[1]

Similar assessments have been voiced by other great Tibetan lamas, including my own precious guru, Lama Thubten Yeshe. Surya Das, in *The Snow Lion's Turquoise Mane,*[2] relates that "Namkhai Norbu Rinpoche says that women are more likely than men to attain, through Dzogchen practice, the Rainbow Light Body of perfect enlightenment; he claims to quote Garab Dorje, the first Dzogchen patriarch, in that vein."[3] And "Padma Sambhava, the second Buddha, said, 'Male, female: no great difference. But when she develops the aspiration for enlightenment, to be a woman is greater.' "[4] Still, when modern-day women look to the Tibetan tradition, they seem to find few examples of realized women practitioners.[5] Without such models, their faith and determination to practice remains hindered and dissatisfied.

I remember reading a book review written in 1987 by Anna Grimshaw, who several years ago spent four months at Julichang Nunnery in Ladakh and published a book about her stay there called, *Servants of the Buddha: Winter in a Himalayan Convent.*[6] Grimshaw's review was of the "coffeetable book," *The World of Buddhism*, by Heinz Bechert and Richard Gombrich. In her critique of the work, Grimshaw noted that "a serious weakness" of the book was that, although "the subtitle of the volume is: 'Buddhist monks and nuns in society and culture,' reference to, let alone discussion of, Buddhist nuns is almost nonexistent."[7] Happily, such is not the case today. Rather, today there is a persistent interest in, and a desire to learn more about, Buddhist women practitioners—both monastic or lay—of all traditions and of all historical periods and geographic spaces.

It seems to me that in the past five years or so, particularly since 1990, many new publications have sought at least to take notice of women practitioners. A few have even appeared that focus exclusively on exemplary women practitioners. Slowly, then, a library of works is appearing that addresses the issues of women's place, status, and importance within Buddhism. This development is to be applauded, I believe, and encouraged.

My suggestion is that we now begin to fashion for ourselves a "special lineage of renowned women practitioners." As a model for how this might be done, here I will: (1) fashion such a lineage of Tibetan Buddhist women practitioners who have been inspirational for me personally; and (2) briefly narrate some of the details of the life stories of a few of these women. In an important way, what a listing like this does is show us that such exemplary women have existed and do now live. This provides encouragement to women to practice as they did. In a sense, as stated above, this is like creating a "special lineage" of women practitioners—not women of one particular sect or school, not merely a listing of important nuns, but an enumeration of women practitioners who can inspire us, whether they be Buddhist *yoginīs* or tantrikas, nuns or laywomen.

When I first attempted to formulate such a list, I came up with only six or seven names. Having talked with friends, scanned my personal library, and reflected upon the matter, I came up with a few more. And soon, I could see that about thirty or so women, in my opinion, clearly belonged in such a "special women's lineage." Whom did I list, and whom should we list?

A special lineage of Tibetan Buddhist women practitioners—in addition to renowned women like Yeshe Tsogyal, Machig Labdron, and Dakmedma—ought to, it seems to me, extend back to India, since so many famed Tibetan women practitioners are said to be reincarnations of certain Indian women saints. It would include such inspirational women as Mahāmāyā, the Buddha's mother; Mahāprajāpatī, his aunt and the woman who became the first Buddha nun; many of the renowned early Indian teacher-nuns; as well as tantrikas like Niguma, wife and partner of Nāropa, herself the author (with Sukhasiddhi) of the practice tradition transmitted until today in the Shangpa Kargyudpa. The great practitioner, Gelongma Palmo, fashioner of the fasting ritual associated with the thousand-armed, eleven-headed form of Avalokiteśvara,[8] also belongs in such a lineage.

Such a "special women's lineage" would actually begin with the two chief female representatives of practice, namely, the great goddesses Vajrayoginī and Tārā. Added to this would be a listing of eminent women practitioners starting from India at the time of the Buddha, including Mahāmāyā, Mahāprajāpatī, the early *therīs* (female elders), Mandāravā, Niguma, along with Sukhasiddhi, and Gelongma Palmo. Crossing over into Tibet, we would certainly want to include such early exemplary practitioners as Yeshe Tsogyal, Machig Labdron (1055–1149), Dakmedma (consort of Marpa, 1012–96), Rechungma, along with Paldar Bum. The latter two were Milarepa's most renowned women disciples. Skipping through several centuries, the list might continue by noting the life and inspirational practice of Ahkon Lhamo. The latter was instrumental in maintaining a number of Nyingmapa practice lineages, as well as Mindoling Monastery itself, and a host of Nyingmapa nunneries.

The latter half of the nineteenth century and the early twentieth century saw a number of revered Tibetan women practitioners, such as the abbesses of Samding, the state nunnery of Tibet; Jetsun Ani Lochen (1852–1953); Delog Dawa Drolma; Drigung Khandro (the reincarnation of Achi Chokyi Drolma, also called "Grandmother Tārā");[9] Ayu Khandro;[10] Doljin Khandro Suren (the great Mongolian *chod* master);[11] Jetsun Kushog; Ani Pelu and Ani Rilu, the latter two being Sogyal Rinpoche's two great-aunts;[12] the Abbess of Chi-me Lung Gompa (of whom Lama Thubten Yeshe was the reincarnation); the mother of Lama Thubten Zopa Rinpoche; Khandro Chenmo Rinpoche;[13] Ani Tsen-la; other accomplished nuns in Tibet, many of whom suffer greatly under Chinese rule; and other female Tibetan Buddhist practitioners whom you find especially inspiring.

But not all inspirational Tibetan women were nuns or *tantrikas*. Many have made important contributions as lay devotees. Among these women, I would list Rinchen Dolma Taring,[14] Ama Adhe,[15] Ama Dolma,[16] and many, many others. In this way, I personally would fashion a lineage of more than thirty-two exemplary and inspirational women practitioners. In doing so, one can readily recognize the many Tibetan (as well as Indian and other) women Buddhist practitioners who are worthy of being included in a "special lineage of inspirational women practitioners." I see no reason why similar lineages of women practitioners cannot be created to serve as models for Buddhist women in other geographic areas or cultural traditions, and I encourage all women who desire such inspiration to do just that.

Lives of Exemplary Tibetan Buddhist Women Practitioners

In what follows, I will briefly discuss the lives of some of the women I have listed above. My comments will focus cursorily upon eight of these thirty-two, namely: Gelongma Palmo, Yeshe Tsogyal, Machig, Dakmedma, Ahkon Lhamo, Jetsun Ani Lochen, Delog Dawa Drolma, and Rinchen Taring.

Gelongma Palmo

Before the spread of Buddhism into Tibet, there lived a young princess in India. She was known for her intelligence and, of course, for her beauty. However, when she was a young woman, she contracted a dreaded disease, similar to leprosy, that was particularly virulent and contagious. Afflicted by this disease, she became ugly and disgusting to look at. For the sake of her parents' happiness, she decided to leave the kingdom, to go far away from home and become a nun. After being a nun for some time, she came upon a teacher who was deeply moved by her situation. He taught her the method of Avalokiteśvara, the Buddha of Compassion. For several years she made this her main practice. Even so, during this time her disease got worse and worse. Her body was covered with sores and it became very painful for her to sit or lie down. Still, she persisted with the practice.

After several years, she had a dream in which she saw a being dressed in brilliant white. That being came into her room holding a vase that was filled with a pure liquid. In her vision she saw this being pour this pure substance all over her body from head to toe, and in the dream she felt as though her body was completely liberated from the disease. The next morning when she awoke she found that her dream had been actualized: her body was completely renewed, as though nothing had ever been wrong with it. In that moment she was completely filled with intense devotion to Avalokiteśvara. When she saw her healed body, she thought first of this Buddha, and just then she had a completely clear vision of thousand-armed Avalokiteśvara, who approached and dissolved into her. From that time on, Gelongma Palmo not only made Avalokiteśvara meditation her chief practice, but she developed a complete system for doing so and she conjoined it with a ritual of fasting. The particular form of practice she developed has come down to us today as the practice method known as *nyung.nas.* In fact, the tradition of *nyung.nas,* which is so popular in all Tibetan nunneries today, is known as the "tradition of Gelongma Palmo."[17]

Yeshe Tsogyal

There are two fairly recent translations of the life story (Tib. *rnam.thar*) of Yeshe Tsogyal: one done by Tarthang Tulku entitled, *Mother of Knowledge: The Enlightenment of Ye-shes mTsho-rgyal,*[18] and one done by Keith Dowman called *Sky Dancer: The Secret Life and Songs of the Lady Yeshe Tsogyel.*[19] Rita Gross has produced a very thoughtful essay about Yeshe Tsogyal, based upon these two translations.[20]

In brief, Yeshe Tsogyal was Padmasambhava's chief female Tibetan disciple and his Tantric partner. (His other chief Tantric consort was the Indian disciple Mandāravā.) In addition to her many individual accomplishments, we owe our gratitude to Yeshe Tsogyal for preserving for us both the life story of Padmasambhava himself[21] and for preserving a number of his important works, such as *The Tibetan Book of the Dead.*[22]

Machig Labdron

The life story of Machig Labdron has been mentioned or partially translated by a number of Tibetologists. For example, she is mentioned in 'Gos Lo-tsa-wa's *The Blue Annals,*[23] and Allione's *Women of Wisdom,* which gives an abbreviated version of her life.[24] It is especially wonderful that a complete version of Machig's life history is now available in English translation.[25] A brief but succinct summation of Machig's life is given by Keith Dowman in his *The Power-Places of Central Tibet.*[26] It reads as follows:

> Machik Labchi Dronma (1055–1149) settled at Karmar late in her life. She was ordained by Drapa Ngonshe in her youth and became fluent in the *prajnaparamita sutras.* Later she met her root Guru, the Indian yogin Padampa Sangye, at Tingri, and received the entire transmission of the *choyul* tradition, becoming the principal exemplar of this practice. Through exposure to charnel-ground demons in *choyul,* this yoga is particularly efficacious in inducing awareness of the pure nature of all emotion and the empty essence of all kinds of mental obstruction, including disease, which is all reduced to psychosomatic functions. Machik then cohabited with the yogin Topa Bhadra, but scorned as a *samaya* breaker she left Tingri to begin an itinerant existence in eastern Tibet. She gave birth to three boys and two girls.

Then she came to Sangri alone, and re-ordained, she spent several years in retreat here.[27]

But Machig is really known in the Tibetan tradition for two other great accomplishments. Early on in her meditations, her chief practice had been Amitayus, the Buddha of Long Life, and this method reached Tibet because Machig taught it to Rechungpa, Milarepa's famous disciple. She accomplished the practice of Amitayus and thus was able to pass on that tradition to subsequent practitioners of the Kargyudpa sect of Tibetan Buddhism.

Her second great accomplishment was that she designed a completely new method of Tantric practice, which is known as *chod*. If you look at Western sources and get an abstract philosophical description of *chod* practice, namely, as a method of practice of cutting through or severing the clinging to ego, one might get the impression that it is a violent sort of meditative practice. But, in fact, when among those who practice *chod*, who are inside the practice, one learns that the method involves a great deal of singing, playing of musical instruments, dancing, and even specific gaits in walking. It is particularly significant that this meditative technique, which is so unusual and unique, was designed by a woman practitioner. No other tantric method I know of exhibits *chod's* unique features.

Dakmedma

Dakmedma, whose name means "nonself" or "selflessness" (Tib: *bdag.med.ma*; Skt: *anātman*) was wife and partner to the famed Tibetan translator, Marpa Lotsawa. In the life story of Milarepa, Tibet's most famous yogi and the renowned disciple of Marpa, Dakmedma is portrayed as the embodiment of compassion, acting as mother and comforter to Milarepa throughout his ordeals. But, like other women in that text, her motherliness is interpreted as a sign of attachment and therefore actually impedes Mila's obtaining the teachings and realizations he seeks. Quite another picture of Dakmedma emerges in other accounts, such as *The Life of Marpa*,[28] where she appears as an accomplished practitioner of Tantra in her own right, almost as advanced as Marpa himself. Indeed, in one important episode, it is only Dakmedma—and not Marpa—who can impart the necessary instructions to the couple's dying son. Marpa is shown as too overwhelmed with remorse. Dakmedma, on the other hand, is shown as having the necessary skills to instruct her son, and as having always been a guru to him.

Ahkon Lhamo

The present-day Nyingmapa Buddhist Center in Poolesville, Maryland (Kunzang Odsal Palyul Changchub Choling, KPC) is headed by the American-born former housewife Catharine Burroughs, who, in 1987, was recognized as being the reincarnation of Genyenma Ahkon Lhamo, a famed Tibetan yogini of the seventeenth century. In 1988 Penor Rinpoche formally enthroned Burroughs.[29] I wanted to learn more about the *yoginī* whom Burroughs reincarnates. To do so, I spoke with Rick Finney, a good friend and former member of KPC.[30] Rick reported that in late 1994, Terton Kusum Lingpa had visited KPC and had spoken at length about the many previous lives of Ahkon Lhamo. A complete transcript of his talks was made and plans are underway to have these stories printed.[31]

In brief, the story of Ahkon Lhamo's seventeenth-century life is as follows. She was born the sister of the founder of the Payul monastic tradition. She was recognized very early on as being the reincarnation of White Tārā, Niguma, and Mandāravā. Later it was said that she also embodied Vajravārahī and Queen Akara Tsaldrung, and that she was the spiritual "daughter of Machig." She spent her life in strict meditative retreats and became known as a great *yoginī*. Being a perpetual cave-dweller, she always appeared unkempt, yet people flocked to her various cave retreats to receive her blessings. She said nothing to them, but simply touched their heads. (The present-day reincarnation says she has "very strong *tactile* memories of touching hundreds and thousands of greasy heads!") At Ahkon Lhamo's cremation, it is said, her skull flew out of the fire and traveled in the air for about a mile, finally falling at the feet of her brother. The skull landed intact and bore the Tibetan letter *ah*. This relic has been preserved; it was brought to the United States by Penor Rinpoche and presented to the present incarnation.

Jetsun Ani Lochen Rinpoche

A brief presentation of the life story of Jetsun Ani Lochen appeared in my essay in *Feminine Ground*.[32] Tibetan authors have also written about her. These include Rinchen Taring in *Daughter of Tibet*[33] and Lobsang Lhalungpa, both in an interview about his own gurus published in *Parabola* magazine[34] and in his introductory "chronicle" to *Tibet—the Sacred Realm: Photographs 1880–1950*.[35] A few years ago a page-long recounting of Ani Lochen's life story appeared in a Snow Lion Publications newsletter;[36] in the special "Year of Tibet" edition of *Cho Yang*,[37] a more complete version of her life story appears, along with line drawings of key episodes.

The life stories of famed women practitioners tell us very clearly that it does not matter where we started or how many hardships we have faced, women can still become accomplished practitioners. Ani Lochen's story is particularly relevant in making this point. Lochen was born near Tsopadme. Both of her parents had been married formerly. Her father, Dondrup Namgyal, had been an alcoholic most of his life. He was also known as being a quarrelsome type. Later in life, he got a job with a Bhutanese lama named Kalwar Lama. That lama later died, leaving a young wife, Tsentsar Pemba Dolma, who had originally hailed from Nepal. The couple had had no children. Dolma then hired Dondrup (who was to become Lochen's father) as a companion to accompany her as she went on a religious pilgrimage. After some time spent like this, the couple decided to get married.

They both wanted to have a son. In order to bring this about, Dolma asked all the women in the villages through which they traveled for advice on how to have a son. They advised her to collect large stones from all the sacred sites they visited, and to carry them on her back until auspicious signs appeared. After some months of doing this, Dolma had a dream that she took to mean that she had conceived a male child. Dondrup was very pleased. But when the child was born, it was a little girl, and this made Dondrup furious. They named the child Lochen. Their home life was not happy; especially after Lochen's birth, Dondrup drank much more and was quite abusive to Dolma.

Once, when Lochen was about four years old, Dondrup came home drunk and told his wife he was leaving her. Then he proposed that since they had only one daughter, they should cut her in half and each take a half. Little Lochen overheard this and ran away. She hid under some thorny bushes. Before she knew it, a week had passed while the villagers searched for her. Even her father showed some concern. But Lochen had been experiencing visions of deities and had been feeling very light and blissful, so she was completely unaware of the time that had passed. When she finally emerged, she was greeted by some village children. On the spot, she asked them to sit down and began teaching them the mantra of Avalokiteśvara, *Om maṇi padme hum.* Many of the adults in the village had a hard time with this, calling the young girl arrogant. Some even said she was possessed by demons.

When Lochen was about six, she began to give teachings in public to crowds. Slowly her fame started to spread and people made offerings to her. She took a special liking to one such offering, a small goat, which she began to ride around throughout the western areas of Tibet, giving teachings. One day an aged male *mani.pa* (master storyteller) showed up in the area, and after questioning Lochen, he announced to the villagers that she was very knowledgeable in what she was teaching. The *mani.pa* gave Lochen further teachings and she continued to teach for some time.

When Lochen was thirteen, she met a lama named Pema Gyatso who was to become her root guru. Pema Gyatso was a Kadampa lama, and he told her that if she were willing to observe the ascetic precepts known as the "Ten Innermost Jewels of Kadam," he would accept her as his disciple. She decided right then and there that whatever this lama asked, she would do. If ever she failed to understand completely the lama's teaching, she cried and wailed; so great was her earnest desire to learn the Dharma. However, another monk at Pema Gyatso's monastery came to him complaining that the girl received more offerings than he or any of the other monks received. He also accused her of teaching things beyond her comprehension. When Lochen next saw her lama, the lama refused her entrance into the monastery and, instead, threw his shoes down on her. Thus, she was abused by her guru as well as the monks. Still, much like Milarepa's devotion for his guru Marpa, Lochen persisted with complete faith in her guru, Pema Gyatso. Even so, it was a long time before he agreed to give her any further teachings.

On one occasion, in an attempt to humiliate Lochen, Pema Gyatso asked her to strike a boulder with his walking stick. She did so and excrement poured forth from the boulder. Then he took the staff and struck the boulder in the same place. A natural image of Avalokiteśvara's mantra appeared. It is said that this is when she realized that her lama was clairvoyant. Some time later, Lochen entered a three-year retreat under his guidance. After that, for some time she, Pema Gyatso, and some of his other disciples went on extended pilgrimages throughout most of Tibet. For a while Lochen, Pema Gyatso, and the other stayed in Lhasa. One day during that time, Pema Gyatso became extremely ill, and although Lochen nursed him, he never recovered. Lochen remembers seeing many rainbows overhead when the lama died. After his death, Lochen stopped wandering and decided to take up residence in a cave called Sangye Drak. She stayed there during the winters, and in the summers moved to Shungseb. This is the place where Lochen's nunnery was later established.

Lochen performed a number of extended meditative retreats. During some of these, she "died" and traveled to other realms. Her fame as an accomplished meditator spread throughout all regions of Tibet. From her nunnery at Shungseb, she gave advanced meditation instructions to some of Tibet's highest lamas.[38]

Rinchen Dolma Taring's account says that Ani Lochen lived to be 130 years old. Lobsang Lhalungpa, who was proud to have studied with her, claimed that she lived to be 115. *Chö Yang* says that she lived to be 101, giving as her dates 1852–1953.[39] More important than the actual age at which she died is that this wondrous woman practitioner is recognized by all Tibetan Buddhist traditions as having been one of the most accomplished teachers of this century.

Delog Dawa Drolma

A wonderful book that appeared in 1995 narrates the life story of Delog Dawa Drolma, the renowned teacher and medium, who was the mother of Chagdud Rinpoche, now a well-known teacher in the United States. This book, called *Delog: Journey to Realms Beyond Death*,[40] contains Delog Dawa Drolma's five-day-long deathlike "journey," at age sixteen, to the various realms beyond death. No other narration of afterdeath experiences is comparable to Dawa Drolma's own richly detailed account, which deserves to be read in its entirety.

Rinchen Dolma Taring

Daughter of Tibet[41] is a familiar, truly classic autobiographical account written by Rinchen Dolma Taring, an aristocratic member of pre-1959 Tibetan society. Valuable firsthand information on the life of women in the society of that time is recounted there. Ms. Taring is still going strong, living in Rajpur, India, and, at the age of eighty-five, continues to carry on an energetic life of service and teaching, setting an inspiring example. Another book that recounts the stories of Tibetan women from various walks of life, including Taring, is *One Hundred Voices of Tara: A Spiritual Journey Among Tibetan Women*, which will appear in 1999. The author, Canyon Sam, met Ms. Taring in Rajpur in 1994, and stayed in her home for a week of extended discussions.

From the beginning, at the request of His Holiness the Dalai Lama, Taring was a tireless contributor to the well-being and education of the newly exiled Tibetan community. Abandoning her former sense of class superiority, she selflessly plunged in to help establish the Tibetan Homes project, to found the Tibetan Central Schools, and to spearhead several other desperately needed institutions. Having benefited from a European-style education as a young aristocrat, Taring became the consummate teacher. Even while still in Tibet prior to 1959, she had been recruited by the Chinese to teach Tibetan to more than seven hundred Chinese students. Her talent for teaching English was especially in demand following the Tibetans' flight from the

Chinese in 1959. One of Mrs. Taring's first tasks, after the exile, was to teach English to His Holiness's bodyguards.

Taring now lives with her grand- and great-grandchildren. Highly educated herself, she is very much concerned with proper elocution. One of her sons is married to a Muslim woman from Tibet, and during Canyon Sam's visit, Taring continued daily English lessons with the young wife. Although Taring sometimes complains of sore arms and legs, she remains a vigorous woman. Once after missing a bus, Taring suggested that the two of them *walk* into town, and Sam says that it was only with great difficulty that she managed to keep up!

Sam describes two brief, but inspiring encounters that occurred during their walk into town. She observed that whenever they passed people—whether business folk or beggars, at work or just sitting—all the town's people without exception stood and bowed as Taring passed. This reverence was shown because Taring had been so instrumental in helping each one of them according to their individual, specific needs. For one she had found an ophthamologist, for another she had arranged a child's higher education, and so forth. One man ran and addressed her in Hindi, repeatedly pointing in the direction of her house. As it turned out that even after thirty-five years of living in India and speaking Hindi daily, Taring continues to take Hindi lessons from the man one day each week. Thus she also remains the consummate student. This particular characteristic—of never ceasing to both teach and study—reminds me of my own precious guru, and so I find it especially inspiring. I would therefore definitely include Ms. Taring in my "special lineage of Tibetan women practitioners."

The stories of great women practitioners are endless. So I hope that others will be added to this lineage and that others will create their own special lineages of Buddhist women practitioners. Such special lineages, I believe, are truly "garlands to delight those wishing inspiration."

Notes

1. See Kalu Rinpoche, *The Dharma That Illuminates All Beings Impartially Like the Light of the Sun and the Moon* (Albany: State University of New York Press, 1986), pp. 91–92.

2. Surya Das, *The Snow Lion's Turquoise Mane: Wisdom Tales from Tibet* (New York: HarperCollins, 1992).

3. Ibid., p. 250.

4. Ibid., p. 250.

5. Resources on Tibetan Buddhism include Keith Dowman, *The Power-Places of Central Tibet: The Pilgrim's Guide* (London: Routledge & Kegan Paul, 1988); Lobsang P. Lhalungpa, trans., *The Life of Milarepa* (New York: E. P. Dutton, 1977); Nalanda Translation Committee, *The Life of Marpa the Translator* (Boulder: Prajna Press, 1982); Kalu Rinpoche, *The Dharma That Illuminates All Beings Impartially Like the Light of the Sun and the Moon* (Albany: State University of New York Press, 1986); Sogyal Rinpoche, *The Tibetan Book of Living and Dying* (San Francisco: HarperCollins, 1992); Zopa Rinpoche, Lama Thubten, and George Churinoff, trans., *The Seventh Dalai Lama, Nyung Na: The Means of Achievement of the Eleven-Headed Great Compassionate One, Avalokitesvara* (Boston: Wisdom Publications, 1995); and George Roerich, trans., *The Blue Annals* (Delhi: Motilal Banarsidass, 1979).

6. Anna Grimshaw, *Servants of the Buddha: Winter in a Himalayan Convent.* (London: Open Letters Press, 1992; rpt. Cleveland, Ohio: Pilgrim Press, 1994).

7. Grimshaw's review of *The World of Buddhism* entitled "Spiritual Corporations," *Times Literary Review*, February 15, 1985, p. 181.

8. Several authors have briefly alluded to Gelongma Palmo, who is perhaps better known by her Indian name, Bhikṣuṇī Laksmi. See, for example, Miranda Shaw, *Passionate Enlightenment: Women in Tantric Buddhism* (Princeton, N.J.: Princeton University Press, 1994), pp. 126–30; and Lama Zopa Rinopche and George Churinoff, trans., *The Seventh Dalai Lama, Nyung Na: The Means of Achievement of the Eleven-Faced Great Compassionate One, Avalokitesvara* (Boston: Wisdom Publications, 1995), pp. 193–96.

9. The suggestion that the current Drigung Khandro is a reincarnation of Achi Chokyi Drolma is made in Das, *The Snow Lion's Turquoise Mane*, p. 111.

10. For more on Ayu Khandro, see Rita Gross, *Buddhism after Patriarchy: A Feminist History, Analysis, and Reconstruction of Buddhism* (Albany: State University of New York Press, 1993), pp. 87–88, and Tsultrim Allione, *Women of Wisdom* (London: Routledge & Kegan Paul, 1984), pp. 236–57.

11. A video about this great *chod* practitioner has recently been produced, called *We Will Meet Again in the Land of the Dakini*, distributed by Mystic Fire Video.

12. Sogyal Rinpoche narrates a number of stories about his two aunts in *The Tibetan Book of Living and Dying* (New York: HarperCollins, 1994), pp. 225–27, 241, and 366.

13. A recent interview with Khandro Chenmo Rinpoche appears in *Cho Yang: The Voice of Tibetan Religion and Culture* 5 (1992): 61–64.

14. Rinchen Dolma Taring's life is narrated in her autobiography: *Daughter of Tibet* (New Delhi: Allied Publishers, 1970).

15. Ama Adhe is one of two Tibetans whose life and imprisonment in Tibet is chronicled in David Patt, *A Strange Liberation: Tibetan Lives in Chinese Hands* (Ithaca, N.Y.: Snow Lion Publications, 1992).

16. A video chronicling a day in the life of this amazing Tibetan woman doctor has been produced by Sheldon Rochlin and Mikki Maher: *Tibetan Medicine: A Buddhist Approach to Healing*, distributed by Mystic Fire Video.

17. Much of this account is taken from Kalu Rinpoche, *Dharma That Illuminates*, pp. 96–97.

18. See Tarthang Tulku, trans., *Mother of Knowledge: The Enlightenment of Ye-shes mTsho-rgyal* (Berkeley, Calif.: Dharma Publishing, 1983).

19. Keith Dowman, *Sky Dancer: The Secret Life and Songs of the Lady Yeshe Tsogyel* (London: Routledge & Kegan Paul, 1984).

20. See Gross, "Yeshe Tsogyel: Enlightened Consort, Great Teacher, Female Role Model," in *Feminine Ground: Essays on Women and Tibet*, ed. Janice D. Willis (Ithaca, N.Y.: Snow Lion Publications, 1989; rpt. 1995), pp. 11–32.

21. See Kennth Douglas and Gyendolyn Bays, trans., *The Life and Liberation of Padmasambhava*, 2 vols. (Emeryville, Calif.: Dharma Publishing, 1978).

22. Three English translations of *The Tibetan Book of the Dead* are now available. In order of publication, these are: W. E. Evans-Wentz's *The Tibetan Book of the Dead* (Oxford: Oxford University Press, 1957); Francesca Fremantle and Chogyam Trungpa's *The Tibetan Book of the Dead: The Great Liberation through Hearing in the Bardo* (Boulder: Shambhala, 1975); and Robert A. F. Thurman's *The Tibetan Book of the Dead: Liberation through Understanding in the Between* (New York: Bantam Books, 1994).

23. See George Roerich, trans., 'Gos Lo-tsa-wa's *The Blue Annals* (Calcutta: Asiatic Society of Bengal, 1949); rpt. Delhi: Motilal Banarsidass, 1979).

24. Tsultrim Allione, *Women of Wisdom* (London: Routledge & Kegan Paul, 1984), pp. 141–204.

25. Jerome Edou, trans., *Machig Labdron and the Foundations of Chod* (Ithaca, N.Y.: Snow Lion Publications, 1996).

26. Keith Dowman, *The Power-Places of Central Tibet: The Pilgrim's Guide* (London: Routledge & Kegan Paul, 1988).

27. Ibid., p. 248.

28. Chogyam Trungpa and Nalanda Translation Committee, trans., *The Life of Marpa the Translator* (Boulder: Prajna Press, 1982).

29. For an account of Catharine Burroughs' life, see Vicki Mackenzie, *Reborn in the West* (New York: Marlowe & Company, 1996).

30. Also the copyeditor of my book, *Enlightened Beings: Life Stories from the Ganden Oral Tradition* (Boston: Wisdom Publications, 1995).

31. So far these materials have not yet appeared in published form.

32. Willis (1989), pp. 105–9.

33. See Taring, *Daughter of Tibet*, pp. 165–67.

34. See *Parabola* 3.4 (November 1978): 49.

35. See *Tibet—the Sacred Realm: Photographs 1880–1950* (New York: Aperture, 1983), p. 33.

36. Publication data not available.

37. See *Chö Yang: The Voice of Tibetan Religion and Culture*, "Year of Tibet Edition" (Dharamsala, India: Council for Religious and Cultural Affairs, 1991), pp. 130–43.

38. Ibid., p. 142–43.

39. Ibid., p. 130.

40. Delog Dawa Drolma, *Delog: Journey to Realms Beyond Death* (Junction City, Calif.: Padma Publishing, 1995).

41. Taring, *Daughter of Tibet*.

Sarah Pinto

8. Pregnancy and Childbirth in Tibetan Culture

Attitudes toward childbirth are often polarized. In many circles, both political and spiritual, childbirth is seen to represent either the epitome of the feminine ideal or the source of women's oppression. It is also sometimes seen as a purely biological phenomenon. However, when viewed in some depth and without a medical agenda, childbirth can be understood to be the ritual enactment of shared cultural values. It is vital to recognize the symbolic potency of birth in all cultural systems and to understand it for what it reveals about a culture's views on women, the body, and generativity. In most world cultures, birth is women's domain. Because of this, childbirth rituals illuminate the myriad ways that women shape their world in contrast to the institutions that structure their place in society.

As women in almost any society will attest, childbirth is a deeply spiritual act. This is particularly the case in Tibetan culture, where Buddhism pervades all levels of life. To examine how Buddhism shapes childbirth practices and attitudes, I traveled to Dharamsala, India, to speak with members of the lay and monastic Tibetan communities. My research involved formal interviews with five women, ranging in age from 25 to approximately 60, and a number of informal conversations with Tibetan women and men. These people were of diverse geographic and socioeconomic backgrounds; all women who were formally interviewed were born in Tibet. I also spoke with two Rinpoches (reincarnate lamas) and a Western-trained medical practitioner from Delek Hospital. It is crucial to bear in mind the upheaval of traditional Tibetan culture in the wake of Chinese occupation. Refugee communities in Dharamsala and throughout India are concerned with both sustaining Tibetan culture and religious tradition, and integrating their practices with Indian and Western cultures. As it stands now, childbirth among Tibetans in Dharamsala is an amalgamation of traditional belief systems and the Western medical system.

In Buddhist Tantric texts, the womb symbolizes the field of emptiness (*śūnyatā*) in which all things arise and fall, the field in which the conventional and the ultimate are indistinguishable. Both emptiness, the philosophical ground of all phenomenal existence, and the wisdom of one who knows it are personified as "the Great Mother." *Śūnyatā* and generativity are in many ways intertwined, as phenomena are said to be "born" out of emptiness. Stephen Beyer has said of Tārā visualization practice:

> In a universe where all events dissolve ontologically into Emptiness, the touching of Emptiness in the ritual is the recreation of the world in actuality; where solid reality is but a fabric of consciousness, the deity's ritual gestation and birth are no mere imitation of her primal genesis, but the concrete formation of a symbolically potent reality.[1]

Like Buddhist thought, popular Tibetan beliefs about pregnancy and birth seem to operate on both the levels of the ultimate and the mundane. Just as the mundane and ultimate converge philosophically, so, too, these two levels are manifest in cultural treatments of women's bodies. This was made evident to me in the ways that women described their ritual practices and beliefs about childbirth. The female body, specifically the womb, is the place from which life becomes immanent and, like the field of emptiness that it symbolizes, is a locus for the Buddhist dialogue of ultimate and conventional.

This dynamic is particularly evident where two aspects of childbirth are concerned. The first revolves around the pervasive notion that childbirth is an intrinsically "dirty," impure process. In most parts of Asia, it is commonly believed that birth and other female reproductive processes, such as menstruation, are inherently impure, inherently polluted and polluting. It was made clear to me in conversation that birth in Tibetan cultural systems is considered to be a very "dirty" process. The question remains, however, as to what exactly is meant by "dirty."

At the conventional level, birth is felt to be dirty simply because it is "messy." Its impurity is akin to the impurity of any bodily fluid, male or female. At this level, dirtiness is described as a pragmatic rather than existential concern, as women describe the proper locations for birth and how one should prepare for the "mess" of birth and afterbirth.

On the ultimate level, the concept of "dirtiness" moves childbirth from the realm of the merely messy into the realm of the "impure," entailing a sense of inherent, existential foulness. Whereas conventional dirtiness is situational, ultimate dirtiness involves social and cosmic relationships. This concept involves characterizing certain people as impure in relation to others, the ranking of groups according to level of purity, and, most importantly, the ability of certain individuals to pollute others, to render them less pure and, thus, less spiritually sound. The fluids of childbirth, the placenta, and by association the womb, are considered to be highly offensive to extremely pure and powerful entities, human and nonhuman. It is the capacity to insult deities that makes such things most dangerous to inhabitants of the earthly realm. As Lobsang Dolma Khangkar has said,

> If [the placenta] is left open for the sky to see it, then there are certain kinds of deities who protect places, like earth protectors and some other kinds of beings, who would get very upset by seeing something so impure. Because they get so upset, then they could create some bad influences in the child that would manifest in the form of skin diseases and other kinds of problems.[2]

There seems to be a great deal of overlap between the conventional and ultimate understandings of the impurity of birth. The two views—first, that birth is normal but messy, and second, that it is existentially impure—often arose in the course of a single conversation or description. In general, the idea that birth is a fundamentally dirty process seems to come from voices of authority: Tibetan medicine, texts, monks, and lamas. Laywomen, on the other hand, emphasized the practical, "conventional" aspects of impurity. In many ways, it seems that the practical ways of dealing with this dirtiness are rooted in a conceptual understanding of the feminine and of the division of the world into categories of pure and impure, extending from the world of practice into a place of archetypal values.

These contrasting ways of understanding the impurity of birth became clear to me in a conversation with Chokyi Nyima Rinpoche, a lama teaching in Nepal. "We have no sense," he initially said, "of the pregnant woman being dirty or polluted. Pregnant women are not isolated or forbidden from touching people, like with the Hindus." However, he went on to say that for certain people, people of certain astrological signs, to be in the presence of either pregnant women or corpses is extremely dangerous to both health and general safety. Although this may not necessarily indicate that pregnant women are "like" corpses in every sense (a similitude that Chokyi Nyima was quick to downplay), it is certainly interesting to note their association in the same category of avoidance. Pregnant women and corpses, epitomizing the liminal moments of birth and death, hover at the doorways to earthly life. The liminality of birth renders pregnancy potentially threatening.

A similar kind of contradiction between birth as normal and as dangerous was evident in descriptions given by laywomen. On the one hand, many asserted that the dirtiness of birth means that it is a process that must be kept away from certain types of people and places, indicating a kind of dangerousness. On the other hand, they would often insist that it is only the physical "messiness" of birth that makes it dirty. A woman who gave birth fifteen years ago in her home in Lower Dharamsala noted that it is especially important that birth does not take place "near where you have the altar, near the gods," indicating an antagonistic relationship between the act of childbirth and the divine. However, when I asked why this is so, she answered:

> It is nothing like you are not allowed or something, but it is just that it is considered dirty. So on the floor they will have old clothes [under the birthing woman].

When I asked the same woman what it was about birth that makes it dirty, she said:

> It is just from the blood and all the dirt and mess. Otherwise it is nothing else. Just the whole mess.

The polluting nature of birth and the belief that it is something ideologically separate from everyday life also emerged in response to questions as to where the birth takes place and who is present. Traditionally, Tibetan women gave birth in a location apart from the space of day-to-day life, in an isolated room in the home or in the family's barn or cowshed. There were no midwives or persons with specialized training in delivery; births were assisted by servants or female family members. Except in situations of extreme danger, and sometimes not even then, there was little medical intervention. Nowadays, most births take place in hospitals or clinics, as Tibetans in India come to rely more and more on Western medicine for care during pregnancy, which is generally outside of the purview of Tibetan medicine. Currently, many women are attended by a nurse or nurse-midwife, and in problem deliveries, by a medical doctor. It is very difficult to get a precise percentage of births that take place in-hospital in Dharamsala, but estimates range from 85 to 95 percent.

According to informants, medical texts, and religious texts, in Tibet and in most exile situations until the last decade, births have traditionally taken place in a location other than where daily life and interactions occur. When she is about to deliver, a pregnant woman will move to "another" space, even if just another room in the house. The women I spoke with made it clear that this room is not "special," it is just a room in the house. According to Thubten Sangay, in the journal

Tibetan Medicine, "At an auspicious time the expectant mother should move to a quiet, clean room in which the child is to be born, gathering with her all the requisites for delivery."[3] Some women said that it is "bad luck" for a woman to give birth in the house of her brother (possibly indicating her natal home). The following three cases are all examples of places to which women are said to go to deliver:

> The baby was born in another room. . . . When they deliver a baby it is considered quite dirty, so they do it in a separate room.
>
> In [my] case [my] husband had a friend who used to work for [us]. He went somewhere, so this room was empty. The baby was born there, in this friend's house.
>
> If you have a big house then you could have another room for the baby, but since there were just two or three rooms [we] make sure it is not near where you have the altar, near the gods . . . and not near the kitchen.

In many parts of Tibet, women traditionally give birth in the family's barn or cowshed. According to the brother of His Holiness the Dalai Lama, it is Tibetan custom that a woman about to give birth go to the cowshed because "it makes a mess."[4] And as one woman told me,

> Back in Tibet, in Kham, where I am from, I haven't seen it, but I have heard tales, you know, that when a woman is pregnant, she delivers her baby in the cattle shed and she is there for almost seven days.

The cattle shed is specially prepared for the birthing woman. It is cleaned and a bed is brought in. It is interesting to note that in many descriptions of the place of birth, cleanliness and "softness" are emphasized, even if that place is a cowshed. This may indicate that birth is not only moved to a separate space to prevent the dirtying of normal living space, but that a woman's transition to such a place—to a "soft, quiet" atmosphere—is for her own benefit. Whether a woman moves to a cowshed or a room in a house, her change of location is only in part due to her impurity. This change of location is also woman-friendly, putting a birthing woman in a "special," privileged (even if just ideologically) space and removing her from the hubbub of daily life.

Before the mother and her new baby are permitted to return to the house, a purification ceremony is traditionally performed by female friends or relatives, as was described to me on several occasions:

> Q: What happens after the baby is born?
>
> A: She has the baby in the shed, and after that she has to have a proper bath and everything before she can come back in the house.

Q: What is a proper bath? What does that mean?

A: It is a ritual also. Like have you seen these juniper leaves? It is like incense, the way we do it [gestures the waving of incense wands]. They do that in front of her . . . then she changes her clothes and comes back in the house.

In cases where a child is born in the home, a similar ritual involving incense and bathing must be performed before visitors may come to call. According to Norbu Chopel,

> When a child is born a purification ceremony is performed. . . The ceremony is performed to free the baby from the impurity of the delivery. Until this has been performed, people avoid visiting the house. In any case, the family would not allow anyone in, as they believe that the entire atmosphere within the house has been polluted by the delivery.[5]

Not only is birth set apart spatially, it is also set apart socially. Only certain people are permitted to be present and to play an active role in the process of delivery. For most Tibetan women, traditionally, the presence of the husband at a birth is neither expected nor desired. As one woman laughingly said, "He was nowhere in sight—not even in the house." A nurse at Delek Hospital said to me, "We always ask the fathers if they want to stay in the room for the birth, but they always say, 'Oh no!' and wait outside."

As with the physical separation of the birthing woman, the exclusion of men from the scene of delivery was described to me in both conventional and ultimate terms. Conventionally speaking, Tibetan women consider it more practical to give birth among women. Keeping birth within the realm of women only is felt to be entirely logical behavior, as birth is believed to be something that concerns women alone, something "naturally" female. To include men in this process, it seems, would be both illogical and unnecessary. As one woman said, in response to my question of why her husband was not present at the birth of her child,

> There is no particular reason as such, but then, what's the point? [laughs] If he were there, he wouldn't be able to help at all. It makes him worried, you know. It's just better if he stays away.

However, many of the same women said that men avoid any association with birth because of its inherent dirtiness, which they consider to be a threat to them and their manhood. An informant from an aristocratic Lhasa family, who had given birth nearly forty years earlier in Tibet, first responded to my question about the presence of men at a delivery by saying, "Men are now allowed." After thinking for a few seconds, she went on to say, "There is a lot of blood and things. It is not good for him. It makes him not a good man."

Medical sources, including lectures by the esteemed "Lady Doctor," Lobsang Dolma Khangkar, are quite clear about the foulness of the womb, viewing it from the perspective of the developing fetus, rather than that of the pregnant woman. In the thirty-sixth week of gestation, the "child starts to experience the dirty environment which exists in the mother's womb" and "wishes to leave that environment."[6] At this moment, suddenly aware of the "uncleanliness, foul smell, experience of darkness, [and] a feeling of being imprisoned," the infant experiences suffering. According to other sources, not only does the baby experience the desire to leave the unclean environment of the womb, he or she is also endangered by the impure physical substances of birth. Toward the end of pregnancy, the mother and infant-in-utero are considered no longer in harmonious relationship with each other physically. The baby expresses its wish to be out of this "dirty place" by kicking and moving about.

There is a way of viewing the baby's aversion to the womb that does not center on female impurity. The infant's aversion to the womb can also be symbolic of an individual's transition through various stages of life. It can signify a culturally recognized *readiness* to move on to a new state of being. Such a view is surely not out of line with the Buddhist concept of impermanence. Without ignoring the profoundly negative representations of the female body related to impurity, we can also see the infant's desire to leave the womb in terms of impermanence. While these notions radically separate the mother and infant, indeed pitting them against one another, they also indicate that at a certain point in the pregnancy the mother and child are ready to become separate entities. The baby is ready to be born into the world of immanence as a discrete individual.

In a sense, pregnancy is a paradox. It is a radical and experiential challenge to the idea that "self" and "other" are separate. The mother and gestating fetus are neither one nor two, but are bound in a dance that defies the categories of self and other. The infant's aversion to the womb *at a certain stage* can be seen as a symbolic acknowledgment that this dance has been completed, and that the categories of self and other should be more firmly established through the act of birth. It acknowledges the gradual movement from one to two, and the space in-between where mother and child are neither one nor two. Importantly, this transition is reckoned according to potent cultural symbols, that is, to the symbols of dirtiness and impurity that are prevalent throughout Asia.

The other dimension of childbirth that is central to our discussion of the ultimate and the conventional, the sacred and the mundane, is the matter of religious ritual. Again, the conventional/ultimate dynamic arises in a way that is wholly Buddhist and is integrated in a way that is wholly Tibetan. There are two levels of religious practice in which a woman will generally participate while she is pregnant. One level of practice implies that pregnancy is entirely mundane. While birth is certainly a spiritual event on both the personal and social levels, Buddhism and its rituals pervade all aspects of Tibetan life. Thus, we should be hesitant to exaggerate the spirituality of birth based solely on an observation of its ritualization. Laywomen made it very clear to me, as I found myself wanting to romanticize, that birth is "nothing special," but is something most women will encounter at some time or another. At the mundane level, a pregnant woman will engage in daily practice, continuing with whatever spiritual practices she may have begun before her pregnancy or even before her marriage. These prayers were often described to me as "just our normal prayers" or "my regular practice." They may include circumambulation of the temple, or the repetition of familiar, oft-repeated mantras. Prayers are believed to both ensure a healthy child and, when practiced in conjunction with circumambulations, ensure that the infant is small and easy to deliver. Knowledge on this level is common to all and the practices that help ensure a healthy baby and an easy birth are self-prescribed. One woman summed up the "nothing special" level of practice nicely:

> [A pregnant woman] does whatever prayers she normally does. Mantra, chants, you know, with a *mala* [prayer beads], and some common prayers which we have in the books. I prayed to goddess Tārā. It helps in the sense that Tārā brings happiness and wards away evil, she makes a person be reborn as a human being, with nothing wrong with its organs. We normally do our prayers for everybody, so when the baby is there, of course, we do it for the baby also. It is just included.

The other level at which religious practice functions during pregnancy and birth elevates pregnancy to a "special" status, setting it apart ritually from daily life. At this level, a woman will seek the guidance of a lama or another member of the religious institution to determine what specific prayers need to be offered in her particular case. Lamas are consulted by the woman and her family from the time she first thinks she may have conceived up to and after the actual birth itself. The first visit involves a divination to know whether or not the child will be healthy, what location is best for the birth, and, occasionally, whether it is a boy or girl. Today, women not only ask a lama whether the child should be born in a hospital or at home, they also ask in which hospital the child should be born. Depending on the situation, the lama will then prescribe specific prayers. These prayers do not need to be repeated by the woman herself in order to be effective. Often, particularly in well-to-do families, it is the case that the family will hire a monk to perform the necessary prayers and offerings for them. A lama may also be called to the place of the birth in the case of difficulty, to offer prayers and give advice as to what religious practices should be done to facilitate the birth. A common ritual for a difficult birth is for a lama to offer a prayer into a pat of butter that the expectant mother then eats. This interesting description was shared in an interview with a laywoman:

> There are some cases where some high lamas do some kind of prayers on a piece of butter and the mother eats it. And this helps for a good delivery. And there are cases where, when the baby comes out, it has the butter either on its head or in its mouth. But this didn't happen to me.

Many reasons are given to explain why the prayers are effective. I was told by one woman that her easy delivery was "because the gods were with me." According to Chokyi Nyima Rinpoche, however, it is a woman's deep faith in the prayers that gives her the "confidence" necessary for an easy birth. A laywoman in her fifties told me,

> You believe it will be effective, so it is effective. Just like when you visit a doctor, if you think a medicine will work, then it does. It is just your belief. If you go to a doctor with a half-mind, then the medicine will not work.

Prayers are also felt to work on a physiological level. The repetition of mantras can nurture an altered spiritual state by balancing the "winds" that make up a person's psychophysical anatomical system. When out of balance, these winds result in what was described to me as "nervous energy," producing such negative emotions as anger and jealousy. I was told by one woman that reciting the mantra of Avalokiteśvara (*Om maṇi padme hum*) "deepens her heart," bringing her winds into balance and facilitating an easier, less painful delivery.

Through both faith and its complex medical system, Tibetan Buddhism promises women that adherence to its tenets will benefit them and their offspring. Likewise, many sources, both informants and texts, told me that a good practitioner is more likely to have a very easy, even painless, birth. According to Kamtrul Rinpoche, a lama of the Nyingma tradition, "If a woman happens to be a good practitioner or a realized being, most probably she will not have much of a problem. Like if she delivers today, then the next morning she is O.K."

We see in the rituals surrounding the time of pregnancy and birth the Buddhist dialectic of mundane and transcendent, or in laywoman's terms, the everyday and the "special." As in Tibetan ontology, in childbirth rituals the womb emerges as the locus for the convergence of these categories in the tangible world. A pregnant woman is simultaneously separated from society and embraced by it at the time of birth. She is separated by notions of dirtiness and impurity, and by the rituals that mark their identity as temporarily "special." And yet she is aligned with society by her normal daily practices and the idea that she is doing what is "natural" to women. The ritual and cultural symbolism of Tibetan childbirth practices are varied and multidimensional, further complicated by the political forces that have caused breakdown and realignment within the society. As a constellation of beliefs and values, childbirth in Tibetan culture is infused with Buddhism through and through. It provides a window onto some of the central dynamics of Tibetan Buddhism and allows us to view the rich integration of religious meaning into the everyday life of Tibetan women.

Notes

1. Stephen Beyer, *The Cult of Tara: Magic and Ritual in Tibet* (Berkeley: University of California Press, 1978), p. 68.

2. Lobsang Dolma Khangkar, *Lectures on Tibetan Medicine* (Dharamsala, India: Library of Tibetan Works and Archives, 1986), pp. 83–117.

3. Thub'ten Sangay, "Tibetan Traditions of Childbirth and Childcare" trans. Gavin Kilty, in *Tibetan Medicine,* 7 (1984), Library of Tibetan Works and Archives, Dharamsala, India.

4. From the film *Compassion in Exile,* Mickey Lemley.

5. Norbu Chopel, "Tibetan Superstitions Regarding Childbirth," in *Tibetan Medicine* 7 (1984), Library of Tibetan Works and Archives, Dharamsala, India.

6. Khangkar, *Lectures.*

Karma Lekshe Tsomo

9. Change in Consciousness

Women's Religious Identity in Himalayan Buddhist Cultures

For centuries, the Tibetan cultural diaspora has extended its influence, creating patterns of sociopolitical consonance and dissonance throughout the Himalayas and contingent geographical regions. From the former Soviet Buryat Republic in the west to the Kingdom of Bhutan in the east, from Siberia in the north to Nepal in the south, Tibetan Buddhist culture is a pervasive force in the everyday lives of millions of people today. Historically, dating back to the sixth century when the teachings were first brought to Tibet and evolving continuously until today, Buddhist philosophy and psychology have influenced the value systems of regional cultures throughout the Himalayan expanse and beyond, informing decision-making in every aspect of daily life. Among the geographically diverse areas of Buddhist cultural influence, there is hardly a place as remote and fascinating as the western reaches of the Himalayas, stretching from the Zangskar valley of Ladakh through Spiti to the region of Kinnaur, and into Nepal. Travel in these remote regions is treacherous and exhilarating, careening through a panorama of snowy peaks, golden valleys, moonscapes, avalanches, fantasy monasteries, hoary cliffs, army convoys, gaping chasms, and idyllic threading rivers. The high inhabited altitudes (between 10,000 and 17,000 feet), the rarified air, and the barren, mountainous terrain create a preternatural atmosphere, while the people's distinctive dress and way of life transport the visitor to another world of experience.[1]

In wintertime Kinnaur and parts of Ladakh may be reached at great risk, but motor roads into snow-covered Zangskar and Spiti are open for only three months a year. Access during the rest of the year is by foot over frozen river beds and commodities from outside are rare and expensive even during summer. Economic survival in the region has always been highly precarious, and even more so since the

Communist takeover of Tibet. The sealing of traditional borders and trade routes has forced many local men to abandon traditional occupations in favor of wage-paying jobs in Indian cities, leaving the women to eke out a living from subsistence agriculture and nomadic pasturalism. As a result of this social dislocation, a disproportionate number of households are headed by women, who bear the burdens of family and field alike. Unseasonal snowfall can deter potential trekkers, who have become a valuable source of livelihood since the region opened to foreign tourists in recent years.

The objective of this study is to understand how the Buddhist teachings are reflected in the lives of Himalayan Buddhist women, especially women in the Western Himalayan regions of Kinnaur, Spiti, and the Zangskar valley of Ladakh, with whom I have lived for many years. To what extent are these women's identities shaped by Buddhist thought? What do the Buddhist teachings tell them about their own nature and potentialities? How are they empowered or disempowered by it? This study is an investigation of the area between philosophy and cultural studies and attempts to bridge the two disciplines. It explores the relationship between "high philosophy" and folk wisdom, especially among women, who may have limited familiarity with the former. Who are the purveyors of culture in village societies and how does one acquire the elements of religious lore and belief? What is women's role in all of this and how is it changing?[2]

Obviously, it is important to clarify that there are forces other than Buddhism at work in Himalayan women's lives. Factors such as environment, biology, economics, and traditional social structures are interwoven with Buddhist traditions. The isolated, frozen environment in these mountainous regions dictates relentless hard work for mere survival. Traditional social structures emphasize the importance of marriage and fulfilling family relationships for women, biology ordinarily results in childbearing and childrearing, while economics typically spell hard work and a subsistence livelihood. Himalayan cultures are thoroughly infused with Buddhist values, but everyday mundane realities and social customs unrelated to Buddhist teachings also play a role in women's lives. Day in and day out, the people eat a diet of roasted barley flour mixed with butter tea, supplemented by flat bread, curd, or noodles, surviving from one short growing season to the next. Women's lives are a rhythm of carrying water, caring for children amidst huge drifts of snow, foraging for dung and twigs as far as a day's walk away, cooking over an open hearth, coping with illness and death unaided by medical care, laughing and praying with friends over a warm fire. How do Buddhists beliefs play out in the rhythm of these women's everyday experience?

Philosophical Foundations of Himalayan Life

Buddhist beliefs give meaning to the lives of Himalayan peoples in many ways. The theory of rebirth leads them to accept great hardships and sufferings with fortitude and a joyfulness that is obvious to even the casual visitor. Jovial humor provides a welcome diversion from the astonishing poverty and dangers of daily life. At least one prized photograph of His Holiness the Dalai Lama graces the altar of every home, giving solace and hope. People ceaselessly recite the *mantra* of compassion for all living beings, *Om maṇi padme hum,* and erect heaps of stones carved with the *mantra,* called *maṇi* walls, to be circumambulated all along the road. Children are taught to prostrate before they can walk and learn to make daily offerings to the Buddha, at their mother's side. Folk wisdom is thoroughly steeped with Buddhist content, guiding actions of body, speech, and mind. No opportunity to create merit is wasted and even the smallest nonvirtue is avoided—this is the ideal way of life.

The harsh and barren Himalayan environment, personal hardships, as well as good fortune, are all taken philosophically, being understood as the results of karma. The term karma, literally meaning "action," denotes the universal, impersonal law of cause and effect whereby an individual's actions, positive or negative, ripen as pleasant or unpleasant results. One's personal life experiences are shaped by causes and conditions, created both in this and previous lifetimes, and one's future is determined by one's present choice of actions. Whereas karma is deemed inexorable, in that every cause gives rise to a result and no result is experienced without cause, karma can be expiated through acts of purification and future happiness can be assured through the accumulation of wholesome deeds, or "merit." This belief explains the fervor with which Himalayan Buddhists engage in prayer, meditation, prostrations, circumambulation of holy shrines, and acts of generosity, especially to the Three Jewels—Buddha, Dharma, and Saṅgha. As people travel from place to place along mountain trails and valley floors, they circle holy objects clockwise, taking their children and animals with them. No opportunity to accumulate good karma is ignored, and circumambulation of the sacred *maṇi* walls is a natural way for nomadic peoples to create merit.

Teachings on the law of karma encourage ethical behavior and an optimistic view of life. Misfortunes are understood as the ripening of unwholesome actions and may even be a cause for rejoicing, since once the seed of an action has ripened, it is spent and will not ripen again. The sufferings of illness, for example, are the result of an individual's deeds in this or some previous life, the ripening of impressions imprinted upon the mind stream. Among even the humblest segments of society, an understanding of karma is assumed to engender an awareness of the quality of everyday actions. The most prevalent interpretation of karma is an active one that focuses on creating virtuous actions and avoiding nonvirtuous ones, day by day, moment to moment. This active interpretation of karma as operating over many lifetimes gives people an explanation as to why virtuous people may encounter misfortunes (as a result of unpurified negative deeds), while nonvirtuous people may enjoy the fruits of positive actions (as a result of meritorious deeds created in the past). Nevertheless, although this active interpretation reinforces an ethic of individual responsibility, a deterministic interpretation may still be subtly at play in some minds. This is reflected in an attitude of resignation to life circumstances, which may stifle initiatives to ameliorate problems and difficult situations.

The ramifications of such a misinterpretation of karma are especially significant for women who, if common wisdom be believed, have more sufferings than men and often feel powerless to change their situations.[3] A fatalistic misconception of karma can be remedied through education, yet formal religious education has been beyond the reach of most Buddhist women for centuries. Women have always had access to public teachings and empowerments, but their attendance at these religious events is curtailed by family responsibilities that are assumed to take priority for women. Moreover, without a grasp of the complex terminology involved, the teachings are usually beyond their comprehension, interpreted as a blessing or a seed of future understanding. It is only in the last ten years that women in Tibetan cultural areas have been afforded the tools of deeper understanding, gaining access to the Buddhist texts and the centuries of accumulated wisdom they contain.

In addition to teachings on the precious human rebirth, impermanence, suffering, and karma,[4] teachings on loving kindness and compassion inform personal and social interactions. These teachings are well honed by women, who care for infants, children, the ill, frail, elderly, and dying. Buddhist lore on the theme of compassion and its rewards is accessible to all through religious liturgies, opera, drama, and folk songs that are transmitted from generation by *manipas* (reciters), performers, and ordinary people. Each village has its skilled musicians, whose songs are full of Buddhist meaning.[5] Each village also has its storytellers whose expertise is valued round the fire at night. Due to long familiarity with these songs and stories, people young and old are able to recount moral tales and transmit them to remind one another to live a good life, even if the advice is frequently offered in the lapse. To generate "Dharma awareness" and a "pure heart" are injunctions, like slogans, heard often everyday.

Buddhist ethical ideals and cultural denominators pass uninterruptedly from generation to generation, transmitted mainly by women in the home. The practical application of these ideals is repeatedly stressed in every teaching and spate of advice. Laypeople are encouraged to refrain from the ten nonvirtuous actions (killing, stealing, sexual misconduct, lying, harsh speech, divisive speech, malice, covetousness, and wrong views) and to practice the ten virtues (the reverse of the nonvirtues) instead. From an early age, children learn to avoid taking the life of even the smallest of insects, who love life and suffer just as we do. Groups of little children can be seen crowded around a bug, enjoining one another not to harm it: "That's nonvirtuous, you know!"

Although both women and men enjoy a remarkable degree of sexual freedom in Tibetan cultural areas, adultery and "harming others through improper sexual conduct" are proscribed. The liberal sexual mores prevalent in Himalayan societies stand in sharp contrast to those of the conservative Hindus, who find the incidence of polygamy and polyandry repugnant. Divorce and remarriage are so widespread in these societies that one routinely inquires whether siblings have the same mother and father (*"Pa.chik ma.chik yin.bes?"*). Although there is a stigma against premarital sex, primarily because it can lead to pregnancy and impede arranged marriage plans, pregnancy before marriage is considered a mistake rather than an immoral act. The ideal of chastity for women remains, however, partly because extramarital liaisons are contrary to Buddhist precepts and partly because such liaisons jeopardize the harmony and integrity of the family. Lay Buddhist followers may formally receive the five lifelong precepts of a Buddhist layperson (*upāsaka* or *upāsikā*) to abstain from killing, stealing, lying, sexual misconduct, and intoxicants. In many areas, however, due to the extreme cold, the precept to refrain from drinking falls by the wayside. The monks and nuns remind the laity that alcohol consumption can lead to more serious moral lapses,[6] yet undisciplined monks have themselves been known to indulge.

Himalayan Women's Everyday Lives

Western feminist responses to patterns of gender discrimination are sometimes limited by a lack of understanding of the lives of women in non-Western cultures. In the process of gaining such an understanding, moreover, there is a danger of overlaying one's own cultural presumptions and expectations on a starkly different realm of experience. A practical approach to this dilemma is to self-consciously factor in one's own perceptual lens and be open to the possibility of a totally different reality. In this way, through practice, one comes to appreciate both those elements that accord with one's own experience and those that do not. In setting aside one's preconceptions, one's vision expands to include new realms of experience beyond ordinary, self-referential reality. Precision in this process of cultural understanding is a learned skill, a matter of balancing precariously between the known and unknown. Unavoidably, one's assumptions about identity and familiar judgments are challenged in the face of another actuality. Accustomed concepts of gender are starkly challenged in immediate experience.

In Himalayan cultures, for example, a female child is seen as a mixed blessing. In one sense she is a joy, but in another sense she is a liability. At birth, a girl is sometimes mourned as a futile investment, since she will eventually marry into another household. Being susceptible to pregnancy, she is a risk. At the same time, if able-bodied, she is an asset as a worker and caregiver in the home. When questioned, some parents evince equal regard for baby girls, but others forthrightly disavow them, saying, "Girls only grow up to get pregnant." Vulnerability to pregnancy is a liability for all women in pre-contraceptive societies, and entails great health risks due to inadequate medical facilities. The concept of planned pregnancy is novel in these remote regions.

The hazards associated with being a woman are even greater for the female religious practitioner. First, they are subject to social expectations that make marriage difficult to escape. A family will be willing and proud to have a son become a monk, but one monastic in the family fulfills their religious duty; a daughter is best off at home where she can help out. Women with strong religious inclinations feel disappointed, but obliged to abide by their parents' decisions. They are free to pursue religious practice at home, but social, marital, maternal, and household responsibilities leave little time and are potentially problematic. Even given the chance to do intensive practice, they feel vulnerable to sexual exploitation in solitary mountain retreats and finding teachings, facilities, and a suitable companion is not so easy.

Psychological factors are also at play. In Himalayan Buddhist cultures a woman should be serene and subdued, humble and not arrogant, calm rather than harried, patient rather than angry, kind rather than uncaring, other-centered rather than self-centered, content rather than greedy, subdued rather than unruly. Interestingly these are the same traits valued in a Buddhist practitioner, especially ordained Saṅgha members, meaning that nuns are expected to embody them all the more. The resignation with which women accept their subordinate status may be viewed as quiescence or apathy, but within these cultures equanimity is a virtue and seeking one's own advantage is not.

Himalayan societies are arranged hierarchically, encompassing gender, class, education, wealth, ordination status, and even caste, although Buddhism does not recognize caste. These societies make no pretense that its members are equal, but their social system is believed to be equitable, flexible, and efficacious, regardless of inequalities. Ancient legal conventions are still in place for resolving disputes, and the compelling principle is to provide fairly for all so as to prevent disputes from arising in the first place. A women may inherit land, but more often her share takes the form of hereditary jewelry and portable property that moves with her to her husband's home. Nevertheless, her place is defined as secondary to the males in her life.

There has always been considerable social mobility in Tibetan societies, both in the religious and political spheres, yet equality, as in total equity in the mundane sphere, was considered an unattainable ideal. Living beings simply do not have equal education, money, power, experience, capabilities, karmic affinities, and opportunities. From the moment of birth, beings are dealt different cards from the karmic deck—all of their own creation. Tibetans often tell the story of a king who redistributed property and wealth to all citizens equally, hoping to equalize the circumstances of his country's citizens. Within a short time, however, the original inequalities developed again until, after three attempts, he conceded it was futile and abandoned his plan.

Women in Tibetan cultural areas have always enjoyed greater social freedom than their Indian, Chinese, and Islamic neighbors, with rights, power, and freedom in greater measure than most women have had until modern times. They inherited property, divorced, remarried, had affairs, managed businesses, restaurants, and estates. Yet, due to custom, women in Tibetan cultures tend to accept a role subservient to men, particularly in the domestic sphere. At the same time, women are aware of gender inequalities, especially in religious life. When questioned, laywomen freely express their concerns, including a dissatisfaction with gendered social norms. Both laywomen and nuns regret their limited access to Buddhist teachings, and both groups express their appreciation for those who accept the hardship of monastic life in the pursuit of their spiritual goal.

It is on the spiritual plane that equal opportunity exists, at least theoretically, for it is here that all sentient beings are said to be endowed with the potential for enlightenment. This is significant for women because it establishes their spiritual equality and, moreover, points out the discrepancy between the religious ideal and women's limited access to the mundane tools for spiritual advancement. The Mahāyāna tradition teaches that all beings have Buddha nature, the capacity for complete awakening, yet the image of perfection—

Śākyamuni Buddha—is male. The Vajrayāna branch of Mahāyāna explicitly states that women have the potential to achieve awakening here and now, in this lifetime, in a woman's body. Yet how is a woman to proceed toward that goal without religious education, practice facilities, and the elements of sustenance? The problem is somewhat self-perpetuating, since the spiritual leaders of all four major traditions—Nyingma, Sakya, Kagyu, and Gelug—are male, and focus their energies primarily on furthering institutions for monks.

Thus, despite the lack of any theoretical bar to women's spiritual attainments, women are underrepresented in existing religious institutions. Buddhist literature contains references that can be used to justify male superiority, and even the works of such enlightened figures as Āryadeva and Shantideva describe a male rebirth as superior. Although denigrating women constitutes a breach of the tantric precepts, certain verses of the Tibetan spiritual exemplar Milarepa portray women in an unambiguously negative light.[7] Scriptual references such as these lead to lower expectations of women and cause women to doubt their own capabilities. It is common to hear even educated householders proclaim, "Nuns do not need to do studies. They are content to recite *Om maṇi padme hum.*" Such references may also be responsible for gender stereotyping, as in the common assertion that "Women are more emotional," implying that women have more emotional afflictions. It is distressing to hear people say that women are not interested in serious meditation or study and are happy cooking, cleaning, chanting, and donating to monks. Nuns and laywomen both tend to question their own abilities and lack the necessary self-confidence to engage in higher practices and philosophical studies. Lower societal expectations of women thus become a self-fulfilling prophecy.

Himalayan women largely fail to recognize the blatant inequalities that strongly affect their lives, particularly their lack of representation in government and religion. Even those who do, often lack the incentive to challenge male domination and, instead, tacitly support it. They accept men's authority unquestioningly and feel powerless to change their situation of subordination even in the face of great hardships.

Burden or Blessing? Women's Religious Potential

Women in Himalayan Buddhist cultures receive conflicting messages as to their nature, role, and ultimate potential. On the one hand, feminine energies are portrayed as something to be subdued. The oral histories of both Tibet and the Zangskar valley of Ladakh record legends of Guru Padmasambhava pinning down an indigenous demoness to facilitate the importation and ascendence of Buddhism. On the other hand, women are promised release from the sufferings of cyclic existence (*saṃsāra*) and are said to be capable of enlightenment in a female body.[8] In yet another context, male and female are depicted as energies within all beings to be balanced and enhanced. Wisdom is viewed as female and skillful means as male, with the two conjoined in the attainment of supreme enlightenment. This symbiosis is symbolized graphically by the union of deity and consort in Tibetan iconography and visualized in Buddhist Tantric practice.

Enlightened beings in female form are an integral part of the lives of both women and men from childhood on. In fact, some of the most popular bodhisattvas, protectors, and enlightened figures in the Tibetan tradition are female. Invocations to Tārā, the protectress in twenty-one aspects, sound from the monasteries in Tibet, Mongolia, Nepal, and throughout the Indian Himalayas each morning. The female deity Palden Lhamo is Tibet's national protector and a host of other dieties regularly speak through female mediums, healing, protecting, and proferring advice of a very practical nature. Vajrayoginī is the main object of meditation for thousands of Tantric practitioners, male and female, who aspire to a swift rebirth in her Khachö pure land. *Ḍākinīs*, enlightened beings in female form, populate practitioners' spiritual environment. Prajñāparamitā, as her name implies, embodies the perfection of wisdom and is regarded as the mother of all enlightened ones. These and myriad other enlightened women have a powerful impact within the Tantric Buddhist worldview. They exhibit strength, compassion, wisdom, and are an imminent presence in the lives of ordinary people.

On the mundane plane, Buddhist women face many challenges in religious life. However egalitarian Buddhist theory may be, in Buddhist societies rebirth as a woman is typically viewed as an inferior incarnation. The most common term for a woman in Tibetan, *skye.dman*, literally means "inferior birth." In the process of spiritual evolution, working one's way up in the seemingly endless cycle of successive rebirths, women are clearly at a disadvantage. Generally speaking, despite their efforts, women garner far less support than their male counterparts. Monks are ordinarily invited to perform household rituals, while nuns are not. Whether they perform services or not, monks are regarded as worthy of support, while nuns receive far less.

In the Himalayan region, this disparity is apparent not only in the account books of monasteries for women and for men, but in the expectations families place on daughters who have become nuns. Although nuns have "renounced" (*rab.byung*), meaning "left the household life," their status as nuns does not free them from obligations to their natal families. In the Tibetan cultural context, the idea of renunciation means renouncing cyclic existence (*saṃsāra*) and marriage, but not necessarily one's parents and kin. Marriage is understood as entailing many sufferings for women, including childbirth, hard work, and possible oppression by husband and in-laws. Although women may interpret the hardships of their lives as a blessing—a teaching on the unsatisfactory nature of cyclic existence—they also realize that their power is limited, abdicated in fact, in marriage. Societal norms have taught them that power is vested in males, both in the secular and religious spheres. Women's power of decision-making is curtailed by both custom and circumstance. For instance, Buddhism places no ban on contraception, but it simply is not available to most women in these remote areas and only those few who are educated would find the confidence to seek it. As a result, women's bodies become worn, ill, and aged through repeated childbearing and the duties of childrearing. An awareness of these problems prompts many girls, both the timid and the brave, to enter monastic life.

In Ladakh and Spiti, women renunciants are addressed as *jomo* ("revered woman"), a repectful term for a nun. Another term in currency, *ani jomo*, adds the common Tibetan term of address, "*ani*." This term, which can be glossed as "auntie," contrasts starkly with the respectful terms *gu.shab* ("reverend") and *bla.ma* ("guru," or "teacher") that are used for monks. As the status of nuns in the Tibetan tradition improves, this term is falling into disuse and being replaced among educated people by the more respectful Lhasa Tibetan term *chos.lags* ("one who practices Dharma"). The precise term for an ordained novice nun is *dge.tsul.ma* (Skt: *śrāmaṇerikā*), though this is rarely used as a term of address.

Because the quorum of twelve fully ordained nuns required in the Mūlasarvāstivādin tradition never reached Tibet from India, full ordination as a *dge.slong.ma* (Skt. *bhikṣuṇī*) is currently not available in the Tibetan tradition.[9] Novice nuns receive the thirty-six precepts[10] of a *dge.tsul.ma* and are regarded as members of the Saṅgha (*dge.dun.ba*), the "assembly" of ordained ones that constitute a field of merit. Their status is therefore technically equal to that of novice monks (*dge.tsul.ba*), but in actual fact, in the religious hierarchy as well as ordinary social interactions, they are expected to defer to the monks. Nuns in the Tibetan tradition are not discounted or classed with laywomen because they are not fully ordained, as is the case in Theravādin countries, but prostrations are rarely made to them, even by other women. The laity is less likely to request nuns to do rituals in the monastery and in many Himalayan areas nuns are never invited to perform funeral rites or other rituals in the home. Lack of support for women's practice has forced generations of female religious to remain at home, rather than join an established religious community, as do the monks. An unmarried woman may shave her head, don monastic robes, and engage in spiritual practice, but in exchange for her upkeep, she is expected to perform the duties of a household servant—looking after the stove, fields, animals, and children. Surrounded by the distractions of worldly life, these women find it difficult to create an environment for their spiritual practice. Without monasteries, they are marginalized physically and psychologically, often too humbled even to formally receive the precepts they in fact observe.

The value of monasticism is discussed in many Buddhist texts of both the Theravāda and Mahāyāna traditions. There is a prevalent belief that receiving the precepts of a renunciant creates imprints (*bag.chag*) on one's mind stream that are meritorious in themselves, and monastic life, free from family obligations, is seen as the ideal circumstance for Dharma practice. In the Tibetan tradition, both novice and full monastic precepts are viewed as a lifelong commitment. Indeed, some teachers claim that without such a feeling of commitment, the precepts are not properly received. A feeling of serious commitment to monastic life is no doubt thought to ensure adherence to the precepts, particularly to celibacy as a way of life. Although there is a certain stigma attached to disrobing, particularly for nuns,[11] it is permissible to "offer the precepts up" and it is acknowledged that ex-monastics often make positive contributions to society in lay life.

The benefits of monastic practice—freedom from the entanglements of family life—are more obvious for women, who generally bear primary responsibility for the care of the family. The monastery represents a safe space, free of worldly concerns, which allows for fulltime spiritual practice. Laywomen (and men) are welcome to attend prayers and ceremonies with the nuns, but rarely have the time to do so, except for special visits by Dharma teachers (*bla.ma*). Monasteries where nuns constantly gather for prayers are seen as a haven from marriage and many nuns feel grateful to find a place in them. Ordinarily nuns find monastery life satisfying, but after some years, many sense a need to learn more about the practices they are constantly engaged in, particularly the philosophical foundations for the practices. At this point, Himalayan nuns have few options. Unlike their male relatives who have access to study programs in Tibetan refugee institutions, the nuns often have nowhere to go.

Overall there is a history of neglect and of ambivalent attitudes toward nuns, but this is not only a failure of men. It is a curious fact that women as well as men, tend to support men's religious institutions far more than they support women's. Such patterns of support seem to indicate an underlying assumption that men's religious practice is intrinsically more valuable than women's. Only very recently, with increasing feminist awareness, is this pattern beginning to change. With encouragement from both Western and Tibetan women and men,[12] nuns are beginning to voice their concerns and gain greater confidence in their activities. In spite of their subordinate status and educational disadvantages, they are struggling to establish viable communities both in India and Nepal. Being marginal to established religious hierarchies may even work to their advantage. Excluded from positions of religious power and free of male domination, women are often able to introduce innovative measures, particularly in education, health, and the arts. Nuns are certainly not immune to controversy, particularly as their numbers increase; overall, public opinion tends to be more critical of the misbehavior of nuns than of monks. Although many monks are openly supportive and welcoming of the recent improvements for nuns, the increased attention and donations nuns are receiving, primarily from Western donors, is certain to arouse resentment in some quarters. There may be a reluctance to share power and resources. Nevertheless, as women demonstrate that they are capable of creating flourishing centers and monasteries of their own in service to the Dharma and the local people, they are gradually garnering support and proving themselves worthy of increased respect.

Among those in Tibetan Buddhist populations who choose to become nuns, some are orphans and semi-orphans, but most come from devout Buddhist families with both parents still living. It is not the case, as is often claimed, that women who become nuns are society's castoffs or misfits—too ugly to get a husband, victims of unrequited love, victims of tragedy, divorcees, widows, or somehow desperate or undesirable.[13] It is true that there are cases where a woman's choice to enter a monastery or her parents' decision to allow that choice has been influenced by astrology, particularly the popular notion that a person's character is shaped by one's birth year within the twelve-year animal cycle. For example, the marriage prospects of a woman born in a dragon year may be limited, since the power and potential dominance of the dragon are not seen as desirable traits in a wife. Rarely are nuns placed in monasteries by their parents, as is common with monks. This is primarily because girls are socialized to work in the home and are valued in this capacity, and second, because the status of nuns is lower than monks. Among women who enter monasteries in the Himalayan region, the majority express a desire to become a nun at an early age out of a sincere affinity for religious life. While many receive their parents' blessings, others do so against their parents' wishes.[14] Those who are orphaned often have an easier time getting permission from their families to become nuns, but may come under pressure to marry from elder siblings or other relations.

Most Himalayan nuns are ordinary village girls attracted to the spiritual life. Sometimes they gravitate to the monastery due to the sufferings they have witnessed: the death of a parent, a suicide, poverty, childbirth, domestic tensions, or the hardships of single women caring for children. Unlike many Western people, they come to Buddhist practice with a secure sense of their own identity and their place within a family, a community, and a web of complex, but comfortable human relationships. Families and communities are founded on close interrelationships involving families, villagers and monastics, insiders and outsiders, rather than radical disjunctions between insular individuals. Quarrels are apt to be prevented or patched up early on, since villagers are highly interdependent. In such harsh snowbound environments as these, creating and maintaining harmonious community relations can even be a survival issue. Buddhist ideals of selflessness and renunciation are institutionalized in ordinary aspects of life: caring for others, putting others' needs before one's own, patiently enduring pain, cheerfully ignoring deprivation. Religious practice gives meaning to life in many ways, informing ethical choices, guiding personal relationships, and holding forth the promise of liberation from suffering.

Despite the religious dedication of nuns, their situation has traditionally been quite pitiful. At the 1994 Sakyadhita conference in Leh, Ladakh, Tenzin Palmo, a Ladakhi nun and doctor trained in the traditional Tibetan medical system, related:

> Nuns in Ladakh, numbering about 340 and residing in 14 nunneries, constitute roughly one tenth of the total monastic population. In addition, there are approximately 180 nuns living in 9 nunneries in the remote valley of Zangskar, constituting about 20% of the monastic population there. . . . [By contrast] there are 13 major and more than 400 minor monasteries for monks who number more than 3,000. The monasteries have been holding big chunks of land for their maintenance, granted by the kings of Ladakh in olden times. This is not the case with the nunneries. The result has been the flourishing of the monkhood, and not the nunhood in Ladakh in the spheres of religious education, higher ordination, progress, and maintenance. Another strong factor militating against the progress and development of nuns in Ladakh is the lack of a tradition of stewardship by abbesses as the counterparts of incarnating head lamas of monasteries, who command tremendous social esteem and veneration.
>
> The pathetic conditions of the nuns is such that they are no more respected than are household maidservants and they have but a mere smattering of religious knowledge and practice. And, as nuns reli-

giously bound to live a celibate life with no family to look after, they are exploited fully by their parents, kith and kin, and villagers, and have little opportunity to attend to their studies and practices. They can be found washing clothes, roasting and grinding barley, at the water mills, in the fields, and in the kitchens of village houses, irrigating, weeding, harvesting, thrashing, winnowing and carrying the crops and chaff back to the grain store. In short, they will do nearly every task a village woman will do, with a single exception: in the Vinaya rules, nuns are forbidden from carrying the *zora* (scythe). Nuns are found side by side with their village sisters, in the hearths, the stables, the fields, and the high pasture camps where livestock are kept.

Presently in Buddhist Himalayan regions nuns play diverse roles in society, largely dependent on their different economic and educational backgrounds. Many of the old nuns are illiterate, but have all their prayers by memory and practice continuously, whether at home or in a monastery. Most are extremely poor and some are blind from the smoke from dung fires that provide their only heating in winter. Many of the brightest young nuns have traveled outside their native places in search of study opportunities, and a few have become qualified in traditional Tibetan medical lore. Bright young nuns from remote Himalayan areas are eager to study, but few have the opportunity since nunneries in India are overcrowded and study programs for women are few. There are high hopes on all sides that those nuns able to study outside will become "lamps of Dharma" and contribute actively to preservation and dissemination of their ancient cultural heritage once they have completed their education.

The karma of becoming a nun is regarded as better than that of a layperson, male or female, but inferior to that of a monk. Monks are respected for their ritual expertise and laypeople turn to them for leadership and advice. By contrast, nuns feel obligated to help their families and are expected to help them with whatever is needed, including menial tasks that would be below the dignity of monks. Nuns feel inclined and honored to serve monks for whom they feel great devotion. Unlike many lay-followers, nuns are consciously striving for the highest goal of Buddhahood for the sake of liberating sentient beings from suffering, rather than the goals of worldly happiness or higher rebirth. Their role is securely within the religious world, yet they maintain strong family connections that compromise their autonomy. Lacking any visible means of support, the nuns are dependent on the generosity of family relations for their survival. Despite years of devout practice on the part of laywomen and nuns, ritual authority is firmly in the hands of monks who are the chief officiants at religious events. Family connections, dependence on village support, and work obligations detract from religious practice. The symbiotic nature of the lay-monastic relationship is different for nuns than for monks.

Changing Perceptions of Gender and Cultural Identity

The role of cultural identity in a changing world is significant for women seeking to understand who they are and who they can become. In the case of Himalayan Buddhist women, personal identity is intimately linked with Buddhist cultural identity—the role and potential of women in the Buddhist worldview. It is ironic that feminist awareness is increasing at precisely a moment when traditional cultural identities are shifting. What will be the future of Buddhist minorities in a predominantly Moslem or Hindu society in an increasingly secular world? What is the future of Buddhist values under the onslaught of Western consumer culture? Who will protect the traditional cultures of Zangskar, Spiti, and Kinnaur when their ancient calm is disturbed?

Although the peoples of the Himalayan region are acutely aware of their poverty and the hardships of their lives, their attitudes toward life are remarkably hardy and thoughtful. Luxuries are not much known or coveted as yet. In the sparsely furnished houses, domestic equipment is usually limited to a wood-burning stove, a few cooking pots, a tea churn (*dong.mo*), some small tables, water containers, and perhaps a wool carpet or two. Families with some outside source of income may have a few modern conveniences such as a pressure cooker, a thermos, plastic jerricans for carrying water, and a kerosene lamp. Efforts are being made to find the delicate middle path to be steered between romanticizing these people's poverty and exploiting them through modern material culture. Every road that opens, every tourist season that arrives, represents a danger to an ancient culture. Central among the challenges facing Himalayan peoples is how to maintain their ancient way of life and yet also achieve a higher standard of living, how to adjust to the inevitable inroads of modern life without sacrificing traditional values.

Educational opportunities for a new generation of Himalayan women will definitely be transformative, but the changes will depend upon the type of education received. The same winds of change that promise to free women have equal potential to destroy them. Children attending government schools in Kinnaur and Spiti learn Hindi language, Indian history, Hindu culture, and many adopt Hindu names to gain acceptance; children in Zangskar learn Urdu. A situation similar to that of Native Americans exists when the only education opportunities available are in the hands of the majority culture. Children who are not interested in what these schools are teaching have virtually no educational alternatives. Gender is also a factor: many girls are kept at home to work and take care of younger siblings while their brothers are sent to school to develop the career skills for economic advancement in the modern Indian context. With this education come cultural values that are different from the Buddhist values learned at home. Young people interested in a Buddhist education have had to travel outside. Previously they went to the cultural heartland of Tibet, while more recently they have had to seek places in the already overcrowded Tibetan refugee monasteries in India. The critical need for traditional learning centers in Himalayan border areas to provide culturally appropriate Buddhist education and training for future generations of women and men cannot be overstressed.

Himalayan Buddhist communities are relatively homogeneous, yet as in most communities, they incorporate both conservative and more progressive elements. In addition, there is a serious generation gap that is widening between the often illiterate, religiously oriented older generation and the better-educated, secularly oriented younger generation. All of these factors are reflected in Himalayan Buddhist women's communities, which are relatively homogeneous, with the usual juxtapositions between conservative and progressive, old and young, religious and secular. These communities are unavoidably dependent on male religious figures to some extent—for ordination and instruction in philosophy, ritual, and monastic discipline. Things are beginning to change, however, influenced by movements for women's rights both in India and abroad. Now that the impetus for change has begun, both monks and laypeople, especially the educated ones, are generally quick to support efforts by the nuns to improve their living conditions and education.

Devout Buddhists, especially monks, respect the spiritual practice of all, whether female or male. Yet there are both conservative and progressive elements within the monks' communities, and there are certainly some monks who resist changes in the status quo, particularly moves that threaten their privileged position, such as equality for nuns. Since His Holiness the Dalai Lama, the undisputed spiritual leader of Himalayan Buddhists, speaks out forcefully and repeatedly for religious equality, personally endorsing women's right to full ordination, any resistance to the idea of improving conditions for nuns is ordinarily expressed in more subtle ways, such as neglecting to help.[15]

Interestingly, the only case of overt gender discrimination I have witnessed among Himalayan nuns in recent years concerns the educational advancement of nuns. A well-respected meditator and scholar named Tsering Tashi left his retreat cave in 1993 to teach the nuns of Yangchen Choling Monastery in Spiti. Teachings were progressing well when monks from his monastery arrived to forbid him to continue. As a member of that monastery, Tsering Tashi was compelled to leave Yangchen Choling in 1994, even though he was enjoying teaching the nuns. Two years later, Tsering Tashi's own teacher, a ninety-six-year-old lama named Kachen Drubgye who holds the highest scholastic degree offered by Tashi Lhunpo Monastery in Tibet, recommended that he resign from the monastery and resume teaching at Yangchen Choling, assuring him that the nuns would take care of him in his old age. In August of 1996, Tsering Tashi packed up the things in his cave and moved to a room newly constructed for him at Yangchen Choling, where he is now again instructing the nuns in Buddhist philosophy.

In the beginning nuns had to venture far from home to receive a religious education—to Dharamsala, Manali, or South India. But since 1988, there has been an effort to establish equivalent study programs for nuns in their Himalayan homelands. Most of the Tibetan refugee monasteries in India have admitted at least some nuns and monks from Himalayan areas. The multicultural nature of these monasteries, along with pilgrimages to sacred Buddhist sites, has broadened the experience of those who go "to India" to study. Their political awareness is raised as these monks and nuns lend their voices to the Tibetan independence struggle and their gender awareness is raised by seeing the valiant, visible role nuns have played in spearheading the Tibetan resistance movement, demonstrating women's capacity for self-sacrifice and leadership. Their exposure to Tibetan exile society has also raised their cultural awareness in the face of an ongoing effort to Indianize the border regions, and subsume within the Hindu fold all people and religions. Seeing young Tibetan refugee women receive equal educational opportunities in the Tibetan Central Schools has been consciousness-raising, encouraging Himalayan women to increase their educational expectations. Innovative programs in Tibetan refugee monasteries for women have also come to be held as a standard.

Once restrictions are lifted, women hasten to assert their rights, in politics, education, business, and religion. For example, in Spiti all village heads (*pradan*) are currently women and the Chief Minister for Home and Vigilance for the state of Himachal Pradesh from 1994-96 was a Kinnauri Buddhist woman, Bindhyeshwari Negi. Even if there is initial reluctance to admitting women to unaccustomed fields of endeavor and even if women must work harder to prove themselves, once women assume positions of power and fulfill their duties well, they earn society's respect and gain access to further advancement. The same pattern holds true for nuns. Before, when nuns were illiterate, poverty-stricken, and poorly disciplined, people did not seem to take them very seriously. Now that they are becoming educated, well-trained, multilingual, and confident, society in general is according them greater respect and offering them more support. Before 1988, for instance, there were no monasteries for women in Spiti, but as the nuns set about building two new monastic education centers, they received widespread village support. Now when the nuns arrive to solicit donations for their newly constructed monasteries, the villagers vie with one another to offer them tea, cookies, and whatever they can afford to donate. The nuns report that even the poorest who can only afford to donate Rs. 10 or a few kilos of *tsampa* (roasted barley flour, the staple diet) are anxious to support the nuns and their newly founded communities. Even if there is some resistance to nuns' increased numbers and advancement among conservative factions of the monk's community, the people are proud to see educated young nuns emerging on a par with nuns from other areas.

Recovering Women's Spiritual Heritage

Most Tibetan cultural heroes and Śākyamuni Buddha, the central prototype of an enlightened being, are male, but spiritual role models also appear in female form. Although fewer in number than men, highly realized women are an integral feature of Tibetan history and cosmology, widely recognized and greatly revered for their spiritual achievements. In Tantric practice, both women and men achieve realization and enlightenment by identifying with these enlightened female archetypes, actively visualizing themselves with female physical characteristics and positive qualities.

In the immense cycles of time traversed by an infinitude of sentient beings, concepts of gender are understood to be fluid; beings are male in some lives, female in others, possibly androgenous or hermaphrodous in others, all wandering aimlessly in the wheel of *saṃsāra* under the influence of karma and delusion. Clinging and aversion—to self and others, to species and gender, to ideas and phenomena—are sources of suffering that bind beings within the wheel of cyclic existence and prevent them from realizing their spiritual potential and ultimate happiness.

Theoretically, all beings are destined for enlightenment, but a strong tension between text and practice persists. The spiritual goal described in the texts seems very distant for ordinary Himalayan women, trapped in a woman's body and living an ordinary, and difficult, life. This tension is most poignant for nuns, who have dedicated their lives to the Dharma, but are hampered by gender in accomplishing their goals. Inadequately educated and untrained to serve as religious specialists in their own right, they may depreciate their own potentialities and remain content with simple repetitious religious practices. Accustomed to a marginal role in society and lacking other options, they may live at home with their families or become attendants to male teachers and wind up attending to worldly, especially household, tasks. Handicapped by limitations in every sphere, they may not fully realize the benefits of seeing images of human perfection in female form; the ideal may appear too remote.

Now that conditions for Himalayan Buddhist women are improving, and Buddhist studies programs for women are being inaugurated in several locations, prospects are good for redressing the neglect women have endured during previous centuries. With internal determination and international support, women feel encouraged to recover the lineage of their female spiritual predecessors. As equal heirs of the Buddhist treasures, they may now take full advantage of the riches of their own cultural heritage.

Notes

1. Resources on the western Himalayan region include J. Crook and H. Osmaston's encyclopedic *Himalayan Villages* (New Delhi: Motilal Barnassidas, 1994) and Harish Kapadia, *Spiti: Adventures in the Trans-Himalaya* (New Delhi: Indus Publishing, 1996).

2. Among the studies that inform this discussion are Barbara Niri Aziz's book, *Tibetan Frontier Families: Reflection of Three Generations from D'ing-ri* (New Delhi: Vikas Publishing House, 1978), and her articles, "Ani Chodon, Portrait of a Buddhist Nun," *Loka* 2:43–6, and "Buddhist Nuns," *Natural History* 3 (1989): 223–31; Hanna Havnevik's *Tibetan Buddhist Nuns* (Oslo: Norwegian University Press, 1990); Anne Klein's book, *Meeting the Great Bliss Queen: Buddhists, Feminists, and the Art of the Self* (Boston: Beacon Press, 1994), and her articles, "Primordial Purity and Everyday Life: Exalted Female Symbols and the Women of Tibet," in *Immaculate and Powerful: The Female in Sacred Image and Social Reality*, ed. Clarissa W. Atkinson et al., (Boston: Beacon Press, 1985), pp. 111–38 and "The Birthless Birthgivers: Reflections on the Liturgy of Yeshe Tsogyel, the Great Bliss Queen," *Tibet Journal* 12. 4 (1987) 19–37; Beatrice D. Miller's "View of Women's Roles in Buddhist Tibet," in *Studies in History of*

Buddhism (Delhi: B. R. Publishing, 1980), pp. 155–66; Sherry B. Ortner's book, *High Religion: A Cultural and Political History of Sherpa Buddhism* (Princeton, N.J.: Princeton University Press, 1989), and her article, "The Founding of the First Sherpa Nunnery, and the Problem of 'Women' as an Analytical Category," in *Feminist Re-Visions: What Has Been and Might Be*, ed. Vivian Patraka and Louise A. Tilly (Ann Arbor: Women's Studies Program, University of Michigan, 1983), pp. 93–134; and Janice D. Willis' *Feminine Ground: Essays of Women and Tibet* (Ithaca, N.Y.: Snow Lion Publications, 1989).

3. Traditionally, the five sufferings of women include menstruation, pregnancy, childbirth, separating from one's parents, and having to serve a husband. Although the Buddha's mother purportedly gave birth without pain, normally birth is counted one of the major human sufferings, for both mother and child.

4. Hearing, reflecting, and contemplating these "four thoughts that turn the mind to the Dharma" is essential for further understanding. A precious human rebirth, free from the eight nonleisure states and endowed with the ten opportunities, is the optimum, indeed the only realistic chance for spiritual evolution.

5. Musicians in the Himalayan region are considered "low caste," but are nonetheless respected as professionals and are essential at marriages and special events.

6. A well-known story tells of a monk confronted by a woman on a forest path. She threatens suicide unless the monk either drinks some wine, kills a goat, or sleeps with her. The monk, assuming that drinking wine would be the least serious transgression, eventually commits all three.

7. See June Campbell, *Traveller in Space: In Search of Female Identity in Tibetan Buddhism* (New York: George Braziller, 1996), p. 32.

8. See Tsultrim Allione, *Women of Wisdom* (London: Routledge & Kegan Paul, 1984); Keith Dowman, *Sky Dancer* (London: Routledge & Kegan Paul, 1984); Reginal Ray, "Accomplished Women in Tantric Buddhism of Medieval India and Tibet," in *Unspoken Worlds: Women's Religious Lives in Non-Western Cultures*, ed. Nancy Falk and Rita Gross (San Francisco: Harper & Row, 1979), pp. 227–42; Miranda Shaw, *Passionate Enlightenment: Women in Tantric Buddhism* (Princeton: Princeton University Press, 1994); Tarthang Tulku, trans., *Mother of Knowledge: The Enlightenment of Ye-shes mTsho-rgyal*, by Nam-mkha'i snying-po, ed. Jane Wilhelms (Berkeley: Dharma Publishing, 1983); Janice D. Willis, "Dakinī: Some Comments on its Nature and Meaning," *Feminine Ground: Essays on Women and Tibet* (Ithaca, N.Y.: Snow Lion Publications, 1989), pp. 57–75.

9. For details, see the chapter on "The *Bhikṣuṇī* Issue" in Karma Lekshe Tsomo, *Sakyadhita: Daughters of the Buddha* (Ithaca, N.Y.: Snow Lion Publications, 1989).

10. These include the ten precepts that novice nuns and monks receive in other Buddhist traditions, with some subdivided and some added.

11. In common parlance, men "give up [being a] monk" (*tra.wa lok.ba*), while women "get spoiled" (*tro.la dro.wa*).

12. Notable among male supporters is His Holiness the Dalai Lama, who repeatedly encourages nuns to excel in religious studies, particularly philosophical debate. In September 1995, his Private Office was instrumental in organizing a special intermural debate tournament in Dharamsala for nuns from five monasteries in India and Nepal. This was the first public debate tournament for nuns of the Tibetan tradition in recorded history. On the basis of this precedent, such debates are expected to become annual events. The second was held at Ganden Choeling, Dharamsala, in September 1996; the third at Dolma Ling near Dharamsala in October 1997; and the fourth at Jangchub Choeling in south India in 1998.

13. The exceptional case of a woman who joined monastic life as a result of her husband's infidelity is documented by Barbara Nimri Aziz in *Tibetan Frontier Families: Reflection of Three Generations from D'ing-ri* (New Delhi: Vikas Publishing House, 1978), pp. 184–85.

14. Technically aspirants are required to have the permission of their parents, but women are often forced to run away from home to become nuns because their parents oppose their decision. Barbara Nimri Aziz cites a typical case. Ch'ö-dzom, the only child of a farming family in D'ing-ri, escaped marriage by going on pilgrimage and then taking the *rab.byung* (vows of renunciation, generally eight in number) away from the watchful eyes of her parents. Ibid., p. 104.

15. His Holiness the Dalai Lama has said that he personally would like to see the institution of a *bhikṣuṇī* lineage in the Tibetan tradition, and spoke out in support of women's right to full ordination in a public statement at the first Sakaydhita conference in Bodhgaya in 1987. The Ministry of Religious and Cultural Affairs of the Tibetan Government-in-Exile has been hesitant to take a stand on what is perceived to be a controversial matter, obstensibly because of the difficulty of verifying that the extant *bhikṣuṇī* lineages in the Chinese, Korean, and Vietnamese traditions have been transmitted uninterruptedly from the time of the Buddha, but perhaps also for fear of offending *bhikṣus* in Theravādin countries. According to Saṅgha statutes, instituting a Bhikṣuṇī Saṅgha is not a matter to be decided by one person, even a Dalai Lama, but must be determined by consensus at a gathering of elders of the Bhikṣu Saṅgha. His Holiness has stated that more important than official government recognition is the acceptance of *bhikṣuṇīs* by society.

Part II

Contemporary Buddhist Women

Forging Identity

Cait Collins

10. Conception and the Entry of Consciousness

When Does a Life Begin?

For whatever reasons, many women will go to great lengths to avoid having babies. In 1991 it was estimated that one in five clinical pregnancies in the United Kingdom ended in abortion; one in three British women now has at least one termination before the age of thirty. Commonly used contraceptive methods include the Pill and other means of hormonal manipulation, the intrauterine device (IUD), and barrier methods, as well as "natural" ways such as fertility awareness. As a final solution, there is always surgical sterilization. Yet none of these methods, not even sterilization, either for men or for women, is 100 percent effective. The IUD and some of the lower dosages of progestogen-only Pills do not always even function as contraceptives, in the sense that they do not necessarily prevent conception as in sperm-meets-egg. Instead, they are thought to work by preventing implantation of the fertilized egg, or zygote, thus inducing what some would consider an early abortion. The emergency "morning-after pill" prevents implantation if a fertilized egg is present.

Although one of women's most immediate concerns, the issue of birth control (including both contraception and abortion) is relevant to all—not only to most noncelibate people but also to those celibates, such as monks and nuns, who are called upon to advise and counsel others. Opinions are varied as to the ethical implications of contraception, particularly postfertilizational contraception and abortion, and the more recently surfacing issues of fertility medicine and experimentation using human embryos. In making reproductive decisions, people may be influenced by many factors, including religious teachings, scientific views, personal compassion for either women or unborn children, and self-interest. Opinions are often polarized in the debates between pro-life and pro-choice, or life-begins-at-fertilization versus consciousness-is-an-emergent-property. In the midst of these debates, many people try to find some middle ground; for example, there are those who believe that abortion is morally wrong, but still support the right of an individual to choose to have one, while others condone it as an unfortunate but nevertheless necessary action under some circumstances, but not in others. Although proponents of these views may be equally compassionately motivated, the gulf between the religious or spiritually based viewpoints and the scientific or materially based viewpoints can be wide, and unfortunately there is a tendency for many in each mutually contending camp to be dismissive of other positions. Rarely are proponents of one view informed by another.

For anyone concerned with the ethical implications of these issues, however, the most basic questions must include these: Is the zygote, or embryo, or fetus, a being from the moment of fertilization? If not, when does it become one? What constitutes "being-ness" and "human being-ness?" Without considering these questions from many angles and from the broadest possible range of information, both scientific and philosophical, how is it possible to form ethical judgements, specific or general, on these crucial ethical issues?

Many of the world's religions have fairly well-defined positions on these questions; the Roman Catholic Church is especially unequivocal and directive, and Buddhism also addresses the subject. The present discussion is an attempt to look at some of the underlying assumptions and understandings that may contribute to a Buddhist approach to the ethical concerns surrounding these issues.[1]

Buddhism differs from Roman Catholicism on the issue of contraception, in that most Buddhists do not see the prevention of conception as being necessarily negative. Still, they concur with the catholic position in stating that any postfertilization method of birth control, however early, is an act of killing a human being. This is clearly indicated in the Vinaya, or rules of conduct for Buddhist monks and nuns, which includes a prohibition against killing a human, and expressly includes within this prohibition the killing of a developing human or fetus. Unlike Christianity, Buddhism is a nontheistic religion, and all schools of Buddhism refute the postulate of an independent, inherently existent, ultimate self or soul, or *ātman*. But implicit in the teachings on rebirth is the recognition of the existence of a relatively functioning continuum of an individual, albeit subtle, consciousness that is not limited to association with the gross physical body and physiological processes. Thus Buddhist definitions of self can be seen as at least somewhat analogous to the theistic religions' concept of the soul or spirit. In the Tibetan Buddhist presentation, it is explicitly taught that there is a subtle consciousness, accompanied by a subtle wind or energy, that passes from life to life in the cycle of rebirth.[2]

While the various Buddhist schools and traditions differ as to the details of conception and the exact nature of the subtle consciousness that passes from life to life,[3] there is general agreement that the moment of fertilization marks the start of a new life, whether as a human being or another life form. The traditional view of human conception as presented in Tibetan Buddhism is particularly elegant and has profound symbolic significance in the context of Tantric practice.

In Tibetan Buddhism, human conception is seen as involving the union of three factors: sperm, "blood" (or egg), and the very subtle consciousness of accompanying wind (or energy) of a *bardo* being, or a being in the intermediate state between lives. It is explained that the *bardo* being becomes aware of a man and woman engaged in sexual intercourse. Attracted to one partner and annoyed by the other, it finds itself drawn into the womb, at which point it loses awareness. Of great interest to followers of Freud, it is also stated that if the being is to be born a male, it is attracted toward the female of the pair, and if it is to be born as a female, it is attracted to the male. All three of the basic psychological afflictions identified in Buddhism are necessary for the being to enter its new birth as a human: desire, aversion, and ignorance, or lack of awareness.

According to this description of conception, the three factors of sperm, egg, and consciousness of a *bardo* being must be present simultaneously at the time of the parents' sexual intercourse; with the union of these three factors, the being experiences the death of the *bardo* state and its new life begins immediately. Tibetan Buddhist texts on embryology go into considerable detail explaining the development of the gross physical body and the parallel development of the subtle body composed of winds, drops, channels, and *chakras*. In this, there are remarkable similarities between the ancient texts and current medical embryological observations. Yet as aesthetically satisfying, poetic, richly symbolic, and profoundly significant as these schemes are, especially in relation to Tantric practices, they are at variance with empirical medical observations and cannot be taken as factual or literal descriptions.

Natural conception does not occur in an instant; it is a process occurring over a considerable period of time. Sperm may remain in the female reproductive tract for as long as forty-eight hours before reaching the ripe ovum in the upper third of the fallopian tube. When one sperm penetrates the egg, this instant of penetration might be taken as the moment of conception, except for the fact that it may then take a further twenty-two hours for the nuclei of the two haploid reproductive cells to fuse to form one complete diploid cell, the zygote, which contains the genetic material of each of the parent cells and so has a full complement of forty-six chromosomes. If the moment of nuclear fusion and mixing of the parents' genetic material constitutes conception, then the poor *bardo* being may have been left hanging for up to three days since it first perceived its prospective parents' sexual activity and was overcome by desire and aversion.

Conception can also occur in the parents' absence; in vitro fertilization allows the sperm and ovum to mingle in a laboratory petri dish; both may have been collected long before and literally kept on ice until needed. It is difficult to understand how a *bardo* being could be motivated by desire or aversion in this case, unless it is attracted toward the petri dish in which the procedure is being done.

Identical twins develop if the zygote, as it divides and doubles itself over and over again to form a cluster of undifferentiated cells, splits during the two weeks following fertilization to form two separate clusters of cells, before becoming implanted in the wall of the uterus.[4] An orthodox Buddhist interpretation would require two separate *bardo* beings entering at the time of fertilization, but this becomes problematic when we consider that identical, multiple animal siblings are routinely produced from the zygote of animals in laboratories by artificial means, and there is no scientific indication that this could not be done with mammals, including humans, as well. It stretches credulity to believe that in all such cases multiple *bardo* beings— two, four, or ever more—enter the pre-embryo at the time of fertilization in anticipation of a scientist's later intervention to split the developing zygote.

The natural or artificial splitting of a zygote to create identical siblings is a form of cloning—the production from the genetic material in one cell of another genetically identical individual being. This process involves a father, which is not the case in another type of cloning: when the nucleus of an unfertilized egg is removed and replaced by the nucleus from another of the mother's body cells with a full set of chromosomes. The "zygote" formed in this case develops into a being genetically identical to its mother, the donor of both the egg and the cell nucleus, without the need for a father. This has been done experimentally with rabbits and other mammals, and there is no reason to doubt that it will be possible with humans.[5] The fusion of animal embryos to create chimeras has also been done; geeps have been created from the fusion of sheep and goat embryos. If the beings had been present in each embryo from the time of fertilization, such an experiment could not have worked to produce one fully functional complete being combining the genetic characteristics of both embryos.

At this point, it would be useful to look at some definitions. Buddhism does not make the same extreme distinction between humans and animals that is made in some other religions; both humans and animals are sentient beings. The term "sentient" here does not mean "conscious," as in aware or awake; an anaesthetized person is unconscious, but continues to be a sentient being in the Buddhist sense. The Tibetan term *sems.can* (pronounced "*semchen*") means "possessor of consciousness," but does not imply the gross mind that is associated with the brain and gross physiological processes; it also refers to *bardo* beings and dwellers in other realms of existence, such as the form and formless realms where beings lack gross physical bodies. Instead, it refers to a very subtle mind or consciousness that is indestructible and that, associated with the very subtle wind or energy, continues from life to life.

While humans and animals are sentient beings, plants are generally not considered to be so, regardless of certain nebulous borderline cases. Although an embryo or very young fetus is presumably not sentient in terms of possessing awareness based on gross physiological functions, since it lacks the necessary sense organs and nervous system, even without gross awareness, it would still be a sentient being in the Buddhist sense of possessing the very subtle consciousness. In the Buddhist sense, very subtle mind and very subtle consciousness are synonymous, neither implying wakefulness or awareness, where the very subtle wind is synonymous with the very subtle energy that accompanies the very subtle mind.[6]

The term "living," as in "living being," is also difficult to define. Every cell in our bodies is living, including each individual sperm and ovum. Body cells and tissues, even entire organs, can be kept artificially alive separate from the body; the whole body can be kept physiologically functioning after a person has been declared brain dead, that is, after the spontaneous electrical activity of the brain has ceased. There seems to be no reason, therefore, why an embryo or even a young fetus could not be kept alive, plugged into the support system of the mother's body via the placenta, without requiring the presence of the very subtle mind and wind of a sentient being. Thus "a being" may refer to a discrete living entity that has the capacity for awareness, although that capacity may be temporarily dormant. A being could be said to be a human when the very subtle mind and wind become associated with human gross physical matter or genetic material, or a dog when associated with dog gross physical matter, and so on.

Western scientific thought generally considers consciousness to be an emergent property arising from and always associated with gross physiological processes and some sort of gross nervous system. This system of thought largely ignores and is skeptical about subtler levels of body or mind, despite the wealth of evidence provided by such phenomena as acupuncture, Qi Gong, out-of-body and far-memory experiences, spiritual concepts that are seldom even mentioned in discussions on medical ethics. Because the scientific view of consciousness, premised on a materialist metaphysics, is limited to the functioning of the gross nervous system, the general medical consensus is that there is no evidence of conscious awareness in the fetus before twenty-two weeks of gestation. Thus there is no room for the concept of a subtle consciousness (or, in Judeo-Christian terms, a soul); therefore early abortion constitutes merely a removal of biological constituents produced by conception. In the United Kingdom, ejection of the zygote before implantation is not legally considered abortion, since conception is regarded as a process entailing implantation some ten to fourteen days after fertilization. Scientific experimentation carried out during this period is termed research on "pre-embryos" and "conceptuses"; thousands of such pre-embryos are currently in deep-freeze storage, in a state of suspended development, awaiting thawing or destruction as part of fertility treatment programs worldwide.

According to a Buddhist understanding, consciousness can never be an emergent property of anything other than a previous moment of consciousness. Several levels of consciousness are identified, ranging from the gross level, which is associated with the gross physical body, through increasingly subtle levels to the most subtle level of consciousness, which is associated with the very subtle wind that is the basis of the energy body underlying the gross physical body. Each individual sentient being's mindstream has existed beginninglessly, manifesting different physical forms in the different realms of existence in accordance with its karma, or mental, verbal, and physical actions. A sentient being is not created anew; it only appears as a new physical manifestation in each successive life in a beginningless series, conjoining a gross mind with its current life form.[7]

When the Buddha was teaching two and a half thousand years ago, such medical developments as mentioned here were, of course, unknown. Until relatively recently there has been no evidence to indicate that the traditional description of conception was understood as other than literally true. The Buddha also taught cosmology in accordance with the prevailing beliefs of his time: this world system was described as consisting of a central mountain, Mount Meru, surrounded by an ocean containing four continents and eight subcontinents. In the absence of any evidence to the contrary, it served well as a description of the outer world. It also has a deep significance in the context of

Tantric practice, and its symbolic, spiritual value has not been undermined by having been proven factually untrue.

With this cosmological precedent in mind, perhaps the traditional Buddhist view of conception will be reconsidered in the light of current scientific observations. It may be hypothesized that a being enters a physical base compatible with its karma, say, in a developing human body, when that physiological base is sufficiently developed to serve as a suitable support. Perhaps death occurs when a being leaves a physiological base that has degenerated and no longer functions as a suitable support.

If such an hypothesis is thought worthy of pursuing, it is important to try to establish the moment of entry of a being into a developing fetus. The cut-off date for abortions in the United Kingdom is currently at twenty-four weeks—the earliest possible time at which a premature baby has a chance of surviving. Despite a widely accepted medical view that the fetus is not capable of conscious awareness before twenty-two weeks, recent research investigating fetal responses to sound and other stimuli indicate evidence of prenatal perception from around twenty weeks; some researchers report that responses to sound can be observed in fetuses as young as fourteen weeks. If such responses can be proven to be volitional rather than reflexive, this would suggest the presence of subtle consciousness at this stage. Provisionally, one might suggest that the subtle consciousness is absent before implantation, but has arrived by fourteen weeks. This still leaves wide scope for exploration, for example, of sudden leaps in development that might indicate the arrival of the subtle wind and mind. Such leaps need not be associated with apparently conscious awareness—as evinced by responsiveness to sound, for example—because such awareness is likely to be associated with grosser levels of mind beginning to operate on the sensory level. The subtle consciousness might have been present earlier, before the central nervous system developed to a degree permitting gross sensory perception. Given the possibility of an association between the body's electromagnetic energy and the *qi*, or *prāṇa*, described in Asian medical systems, a useful focus of inquiry might be changes in the electrical energy of the developing embryo or fetus during the gestation period between fourteen days and fourteen weeks. Such a measuring of electrical energy is already used as a determinant of death in cases of persons or bodies functioning on life-support systems.

The moral implications of such investigations are profound and far-reaching, not only for Buddhists, but all those concerned with issues of birth control (including contraception and abortion), fertility treatment, and fetal experimentation, including those who are not satisfied with prevailing views in medical ethics. Whether beingness or personhood is gradually emergent, inseparable from physiological development, or not, we may wish to investigate the question with access to as wide a range of information as possible, from both scientific and spiritual sources.

The Buddha himself exhorted his followers to test his words and not believe them merely out of blind faith. Mahāyāna Buddhism further teaches that some teachings are to be understood literally as definitive, while others are to be interpreted according to different levels of understanding. Religions, including Buddhism, are primary sources of ethical guidelines, and medical ethics is clearly an area calling for ethical guidelines, motivated not only by compassion, but informed also by wisdom.

Notes

1. Among the resources that inform the discussion here are: Thomas Blum, ed., *Prenatal Perception, Learning and Bonding* (Berlin: Leonardo Publishers, 1993); Craig Donnellan, *Matters of Life and Death: Issues for the Nineties*, vol. 4 (Cambridge: Independence Education Publishers, 1993); Susan Downie, *Babymaking* (London: Bodley Head, 1989); Anthony Dyson and John Harris, eds., *Experiments on Embryos* (London: Routledge, 1990); Phillippe Frossard, *The Lottery of Life* (New York: Bantam Press, 1991); John Guillebaud, *Contraception* (London: Churchill Livingstone, 1985, rev. 1993); John Harris, *The Value of Life* (London: Routledge and Kegan Paul, 1985); and Mary Warnock et al., *Report of the Committee of Inquiry into Human Fertilization and Embryology* (Department of Health and Social Security, 1984).

Relevant resources presenting Buddhist points of view include Jeremy Hayward and Francisco Varela, eds., *Gentle Bridges* (Boston: Shambhala, 1992); Lati Rinbochay and Jeffrey Hopkins, *Death, Intermediate State, and Rebirth in Tibetan Buddhism* (Ithaca, N.Y.: Snow Lion Publications, 1980); and Martin Willson, *Rebirth and the Western Buddhist* (Boston: Wisdom Publications, 1987).

2. See Lati Rinbochay and Jeffrey Hopkins, *Death, Intermediate State, and Rebirth in Tibetan Buddhism* (Ithaca, N.Y.: Snow Lion Publications, 1980) and the Dalai Lama, *Sleeping, Dreaming, and Dying: An Exploration of Consciousness* (Boston: Wisdom Publications, 1997).

3. See Philip Kapleau, *The Wheel of Life and Death: A Practical and Spiritual Guide* (Garden City, N.Y.: Doubleday, 1989).

4. Siamese twins can result if the split occurs later than two weeks after fertilization, after the ball of cells has become implanted in the uterine wall and the primitive streak has appeared that marks the onset of development of body organs in the embryo. Siamese twins may be joined either superficially, perhaps by part of the skin, or may share major organs, even to the extent of

sharing one brain. There is also the occurrence of *fetus-in-fetu*, where one twin is contained inside the other; in one such case recorded, "the engulfed twin had developed to the equivalent of four months gestation . . . the engulfment had occurred at about four weeks after fertilization."

5. It is currently routine medical practice to test human sperm for their ability to penetrate an egg by mixing them with hamster eggs in a laboratory dish; if the sperm can penetrate a hamster egg, they can penetrate a human egg. The hamster egg fertilized by a human sperm begins to develop, but does not survive beyond the stage of dividing into two cells.

6. This could cautiously, or partially, be considered an analogue of the *qi* energy described in Chinese and Tibetan medical systems.

7. This series of rebirths only ends when the "being" evolves through purifying its mental confusion and perfecting its wisdom to attain a state of either liberation from the round of rebirth, or full enlightenment, which is synonymous with Buddhahood.

Anne C. Klein

11. East, West, Women, and Self

The Buddhist traditions which began their way into European and North American consciousness over the last 150 years are not yet mainstream here, but have increasingly become a dialogue partner in issues of concern both to the academy and to social activists. These two areas are related, and I want here to consider some of the cultural premises that govern the Western side of this dialogue. Only then are we in a position to recognize that it is neither strictly a Buddhist nor a classic Western understanding of self that motivates debate in contemporary feminist circles.

We can begin by considering the often-unacknowledged premises associated with philosophy of religion studies in the West. These touch on three interwoven areas of contemporary postindustrial sensibility: namely, the rise of secularism through denial of a special arena exclusive to the divine, the instrumentality by which the newly valorized secular arena could be improved even further, and the consequent foregrounding of those forms of subjectivity that most lend themselves to secular instrumentality. It is important to consider how these affect our understanding of persons, and subjectivity, and how they might look different if certain Buddhist premises were to come into play. These premises also relate directly to the matter of "engaged Buddhism," a category that itself reflects, and also challenges, contemporary cultural norms. Throughout this discussion I am interested in how the norms and premises invoked relate to the questions that contemporary women are raising about the nature of personhood.

The Secular

By secularism I mean above all the rising affirmation of the ordinary requirements of everyday life. These were precisely what could not, for Aristotle and other ancestors of Western sensibilities, be sufficient for the good life. A life governed only by these was not fully human. How did we get from there to here? While we cannot survey all the complexities involved in such a move, for the purposes of our discussion it is meaningful to point to the European religious reform movement as a significant turning point in this direction. The reformers affirmed the ordinary insofar as they were intent on rejecting any need for meditation between the human and the divine.

To the extent that the reformers succeeded, their movement erased the notion that there are special places, times, or actions wherein or whereby God is more intensely present than others. The church as locus and vehicle of the sacred was rejected, along with its mediating role. The fullness of Christian existence was now to be found outside the Church, within the activities of an individual's life, in one's calling, and in marriage and family. In this way, as Charles Taylor has observed, the entire modern development of the affirmation of ordinary life was foreshadowed in the spirituality of the reformers.[1] Under their influence, cultural sensibilities came to value less the kind of abstract philosophical understanding prized by Aristotle, and to favor instead more ordinary forms of information that help achieve the ordinary good things of life, especially those that facilitate comfort in the face of mental and physical suffering.

Valuation of the secular also tends toward the democratic, for the most valued things in life are those in which everyone can participate.[2] Sober and disciplined production is given pride of place, displacing in cultural esteem the heroic search for honor and glory that is now seen as self-indulgent. A new model of civility emerges in the eighteenth century, such that the life of commerce and acquisition is seen in a positive light previously unknown. Concomitantly, contemplation of abstract truths becomes secondary to manifest productive contributions to the common good.

The valuing of ordinary life in the spirit of the reformers did not mean that God became unimportant, however. Rather, for humans to take their proper place in the godly order, it was necessary to live according to God's wishes; love for the order of the world would translate into love for the world's creator. Thus, ordinary life is hallowed not through sacramental connection with the church, but rather through how it is lived. Marriage and a calling are not optional extras—they are the substance of life and human beings should give themselves to them purposefully, through proper labor. With the birth of the industrial revolution and the division of ordinary life into public and private sectors with their very different set of rewards, it is women who have borne the injunction to labor diligently and to maintain faith in an order of things that seemed to pass them by. The domestic side of ordinary life became, by and large, the province of women, and the public sector, the area that "mattered" in terms of politics and economics, became the province of men.

The valuation of ordinary life signifies in another direction as well, one that is at the root of the Judeo-Christian values that form us today. Secular life—which is to say, our life—is of unsurpassed value. The time in which the joys of secular life are available is also very short. Hence time is seen as a limited commodity and the sacrificing or volunteering of time, whether to certain larger causes or to particular individuals, is seen as a valuable gift.

With Sir Francis Bacon, the importance of instrumentality and the focus on ordinary life takes a further turn. The goal of life, says Bacon, is to relieve the human condition. Bacon's view of science remains influential today: science is to serve mankind even as it peers into the universe in search of God's purpose. Such service requires effective action, especially the production of concrete methods and materials for such action. The lowly tinkering artisan turns out to contribute more to the advance of science, and thus to the good life, than the leisured philosopher valued by Aristotle. Because service emphasizes the instrumental agency in the face of suffering, it comes to imperil the care and nurturance that, though welcome to the sufferer, are not deemed crucial to the scientific and medical training given to physicians and researchers, those persons credited with being the chief instruments of alleviating physical suffering. At the same time, these devalorized elements of human behavior are associated with women, often considered part of their "essential" nature. Though this view is currently under serious review in both the medical establishment and in gender studies, there has been a powerful cultural perception during at least the last century that it is men who are instrumental in curing disease and other ordinary maladies. Moreover, the instrumental stance implicit in this Baconian project, as my colleague Gerald McKenny terms it,[3] remains a critical element of contemporary life. It means, among other things, that as a culture we place particular value on the efficacious control of those objectively measurable things by which ordinary life is preserved and enhanced.

Locke is an important figure in furthering the Baconian project. It was he who most effectively proposed that God's intention for our happiness—which turns out to be nothing other than the satisfaction of our ordinary desires—is accessible to reason.[4] Reasoned understanding thereby becomes a collaborator in God's purpose, which suggests that God's purposes become more and more scrutable. The instrumental stance toward the world takes on its own spiritual meaning, and as a result, in Taylor's words, "The place of mystery in this religion shrinks to the vanishing point." In this form of deism, information, rather than ineffable spiritual states, is key, and the information-bearing aspect of subjectivity is emphasized over other aspects.

Another form of deism in the wake of Locke focuses on the way in which natural goodness, rather than reason, brings us to participation in God's plan.[5] With Rousseau and the Romantics, the debate between the two kinds of deism—with their respective emphases on the rational and on feelings—flares up into what Taylor calls "one of the deepest oppositions of our culture." It also becomes one of the primary oppositions of gender identity as popularly understood: the rational man and the emotional woman. The Lockeans have by and large held sway over the Romantics, if not in the literary sphere, at least in the manner in which worldly agency is gauged and valorized. Hence, agency means above all rationally expressed and visibly instrumental agency, which has historically been largely the province of men.

The split between reason and emotion is reflected not only in gender associations, but also in discussions of subjectivity in general. Such discussions are framed primarily in terms of the reasons or feelings that characterize a particular subjective condition. And when these contents of the mind seem in contradiction with each other, woe is me. As Rousseau, that great foreshadower of contemporary reflexivity, said in his *Confessions*, "There are times when I am so unlike myself that I might be taken for someone else of an entirely opposite character."[6] Indeed, despite our best efforts, the ordinary things of life, especially one's responses to them, often do not add up. Hence we feel a need to control, manage, or otherwise construct meaning.

Such tremendous emphasis on instrumentality and associated forms of information, whether emotional or reasoned, has left us overwhelmed. "We are now in an age in which a publicly accessible cosmic order of meaning is an impossibility," writes Charles Taylor.[7] Similarly, Fredric Jameson observes that because the view of society's workings as a whole is lost to us, all effort goes into characterizing one's own particular location within that social formation.[8] This contributes, in Jameson's view, to certain important trends in postmodern reflection. It also contributes, in my view, to the current impasse in feminist debates between the so-called essentialist and constructionist or postmodern understandings of personhood. These are not simply academic positions, though they are also that; more significantly, they suggest radically different ways of understanding the meaning of human subjectivity. More on this shortly.

In a world of instrumentally driven information, what is a philosophical rationalist to do? Who will pay attention besides other rational philosophers? Faced with this impotence, Jane Flax, in *Thinking Fragments*, suggests several choices, including:

1. Relinquishing the material world to the scientist, which is tantamount to conceding that the only order that matters is that which can be measured by the instruments of reason;
2. Denying the material world's existence, which is tantamount to the same thing, with the added concession that adequate reasoning is unavailable; or
3. Reclaiming the world by "textualizing" it, a predominant strategy of the moment in which there is no world outside the text and everything is interpretation.

This renewed but differently skewed emphasis on the instrumental and the linguistic drives the philosophy of religion in the direction of textualizing the subject—understanding subjectivity solely in terms of language, insofar as this is the chief instrument of cultural, historical, and other subjective conditioning. In that case, the subject either fractures into multiple levels of meaning and positionality, or the search is on to find an essence—as in some feminist circles in recent decades—that will not be so vulnerable to fracturing.

My point is that such textualizing, certainly in postmodern hands, reveals that it is often a great challenge to construct a story that makes sense and takes account of all the details. Even the most ordinary objects of the senses can never be fully known. Likewise, a person's narrative is never complete, since it can always be expanded, and it is rarely, if ever, entirely coherent, since it inevitably includes conflicting plots and perspectives. Does this make narrative coherence impossible? If so, are we motivated to discover some other type of personal coherence, one that is compatible with, but not in service to, the instrumental and linguistic models of coherence, which are partially a legacy from early turns to the secular?

I would like to suggest that this question looks very different if posed within certain traditional Buddhist understandings of subjectivity.[9] Though some Buddhist discussions of subjectivity recognize elements analogous to the categories of reason and emotion, there are other equally significant positions that see mind as possessing a different sort of coherence than the narrative cohesion despaired of above. I refer to a cluster of categories widely discussed in Buddhist epistemological literature, as well as in basic (non-esoteric) meditation manuals: the subjective attributes of concentration, stability, clarity, and intensity. These are states governed by neither reason nor feeling. Mindfulness and concentration are not merely sources of new ideas about the self, but comprise a new sensibility about subjectivity.

As I have observed elsewhere, perhaps only a tradition that takes seriously the possibility of a nonverbal subjective state of silent concentration can feature its objective analogue, the unconditioned, as part of a path to liberation. This does not mean that the subject *is* silent— incapable of expressing herself—but that she deliberately *has* silence as a possibility. Such silence must be strongly distinguished from the hushed voices of Asians viewed through the lens of Orientalism, or of women and minorities.

Because "silence" is such a dangerous issue for women, it is very important to note that there are radically different forms of silence, whose significance is also radically different—neither an avoidance of speech nor an inexpressibility of the subject matter nor a silence of the senses, for indeed sensory objects are keenly observed. The silence of mindfulness is not an inability to speak;[10] it is a chosen state with its own purpose, and comes from a capacity of mind, not a failure of speech. In this it is radically distinguished from the Orientalist's silencing of *his* subject—the other, not the self—by the implicit claim that the Orient cannot speak for herself.

This type of sensibility is not what is being drawn upon in treatments of subjectivity or of Buddhism in the academy, however. By and large it has been those aspects of Buddhist traditions that seem to reflect contemporary values, rather than those that challenge them, that have been studied most closely. Buddhist philosophy has attracted great interest because its rigorous reflections on ontology and epistemology are readily valued by institutions dedicated to better understanding these foundational elements of ordinary life. Yet, for all their rich epistemological, ontological, and theoretical discourse, the Buddhist traditions have never been dominated exclusively by intellectual concerns. They have readily incorporated nonconceptual subjective states, as well as a variety of rituals, including meditative performances of intense visualization and the descent of oracular wisdom into the body of a chief counselor of the Tibetan government.

There is no reason why this dimension of subjectivity cannot have its place in a secularized philosophy of religion; states such as trance, hypnosis, and relaxation response have already achieved prominence in popular secular culture. However, to take these categories of subjectivity seriously is to shift the terrain of contemporary Western ways of understanding religion, which might bring the unlanguaged subject out of the dim and shrouded realm of the mystical (a realm all the more mysterious because it is absent in predominant cultural understandings of "ordinary life") and into daily life where it more properly belongs. Attention and concentration are everyday facts of life, after all, but they are overlooked partly because their instrumental value is not always apparent. Although they themselves do not "do" anything, they provide a locus or basis for doing, as well as for productive nondoing. What difference might it make to more clearly recognize attention and concentration as part of the range of subjective possibilities?

Recognizing such a dimension of subjectivity could go a considerable way toward alleviating the impasse between essentialist and constructionist or postmodern descriptions of personhood. Mindfulness bequeathes precisely the kind of centeredness and coherence associated with more positive aspects of essentialism, while at the same time revealing the constructed, momentary nature of world and self. Mindfulness as a valued category can also reshape our sense of the arena in which "instrumentality" takes its place. Once we recognize the value of such subjective states—that they are conducive to new forms of self-understanding and to ethical behavior—then sitting still or otherwise cultivating attentiveness can be included among instrumentally useful endeavors. However, the coherence associated with mindfulness has nothing to do with the narrative coherence that postmodern perspectives eschew. Rather, it suggests the possibility of a type of coherence that does not depend on a well-ordered narrative arc; simply being in the moment means that the dynamic of attention itself provides coherence.

Ritual Instrumentality and Social Engagement

Serious consideration of the existence and unique efficacy of mental states ungoverned by language might well change how we understand and analyze those types of behaviors that both scholars and practitioners of religion understand as "ritual." This, however, would require a shift in our understanding of instrumentality. Catherine Bell has elegantly discussed how Western theories of ritual are based on a hierarchical bifurcation between thought (only secondarily instrumental) and action (a primary form of instrumentality). Just as Western theories of mind tend not to invite curiosity about possible noninstrumental states not governed by language, Western ritual theory does not make a clear space for this dimension either.[11]

Jonathan Smith has described ritual as "a means of performing the way things ought to be in conscious tension to the way things are."[12] He discusses a hunting ritual wherein the hunter enacts a far more gracious encounter with the bear who will be his victim than can possibly be emulated in the rough and tumble of an actual hunt.[13] In these and other ways of ritual analysis, the central axis of doing and not doing remains unchallenged. For the Buddhist practitioner, however, especially of the Tantric rituals common in Tibet and much of Asia, rituals often explore the way things *are*, at least by Buddhist lights, and the way they ought to be *understood*. Unlike hunting rituals, and unlike most of the rituals important in Western Jewish and Christian traditions, these meditative rituals do not re-enact or celebrate a particular communal, personal, or historical event.[14] For this and other reasons it is insufficient to understand such ritual as, in Smith's terms, a performance of how things ought to be (though it is partly that), just as it is insufficient to understand its performers as unthinking actors. But from the perspective of many Buddhist traditions, particularly the Indian and Tibetan forms, to leave it at that is to miss the point. The most common rituals, which involve inviting and identifying with a particular figure of enlightenment, such as Tārā, Yeshey Tsogyal the Great Bliss Queen, The Queen of Existence, Vajrayoginī, Kālacakra, Cakrasaṃvara, or Dorje Phurba, are neither a commemoration of nor a preparation for an actual event of doing; they are best understood emically as practices that transform subjectivity and understandings of self in a palpable way that can be maintained outside the ritual circle. Concentration, intense focus, and clarity of vision are critical aspects of such ritual behavior. The locus of "instrumental" efficacy is in the subjective dimension.

How likely is it that Western philosophers of religion will find it meaningful to incorporate this or other categories or premises of Buddhist perspectives? We have noted that the great imperative of the Baconian project, and one that still governs much of our thinking today, is to relieve the human condition. But the Buddhist purpose is to leave the human condition. This requires a different kind of agency, in which focused and mindful observation is valued, not only for what it reveals about the world and its objects, but for what it reveals about the possibility intrinsic to the subject itself. These claims suggest criteria for meaningful subjective "presence" that are different from those that govern postmodern/essentialist debates in and out of feminism. In speaking of attention, the quality of "presence" refers not to how much of an object one knows—not how successfully one captures the object, for this is regarded as impossible by Buddhists and postmodernists alike—but rather how focused, intense, and clear the knowing mind itself is. If ritual enhances this kind of presence, it is instrumental in ways that may improve the human condition, but not in the sense that Bacon and subsequent adherents of his position generally intend.

The horizons of efficacy are culturally determined in ways not widely recognized. This becomes particularly clear if we consider the recent development known as "engaged Buddhism." Here we must note that, just as Buddhist sensibilities have begun to seep into the North American cultural consciousness, so American sensibilities are increasingly a part of Buddhism in the West, especially when it comes to matters like engagement—social or personal. For this reason there is a natural impetus to try to establish that Buddhist practitioners are engaged in acceptable social, political, and personal enterprises in ways equal, or perhaps even superior, to others in our realm.

I would not undermine the good citizenship of Buddhist practitioners. But it is also important to acknowledge that we are currently inventing much of what it means to be personally engaged as a Buddhist and that we often judge such "engagement" on the basis of a secularized, privatized value system that had little or no place in traditional Buddhist cultures. To what extent might it be possible to learn something *new*, culturally or personally, from Buddhist traditions? Are we always bound to assimilate Buddhist teachings, categories, ideas, and practices, to ideas with which we are already familiar? The modern West already possesses powerful ideas about the nature of social, political, and personal engagement. Is the emphasis on engaged Buddhism simply another avenue for impulses already in place? Are we simply using Buddhist images to bolster and perhaps enhance what we already believe to be important?

For example, we have noted that with the advent of Locke and rational deism, the mystery of the world and of religious experience lost emphasis. To follow this mold, Buddhist sensibilities would have to relinquish elements of wonder and gratitude, the relativizing of the importance of the goals of ordinary life, and the reasoning that supports them, based on a view of the larger scheme of things. Therefore, I want to ask whether Buddhist engagement, even in the twentieth-century West, need not still access its own version of grace, wonder, and mystery.

From this point of view the matter of "engaged Buddhism" raises an important question: In establishing Buddhist credentials in terms easily assimilable by the contemporary status quo, is something uniquely Buddhist being lost? Who determines what constitutes "engagement"? By what definition are praying monks more or less engaged than political protesters, or are Tantric practitioners who protect crops from hail more or less engaged than those who distribute food to the needy?

Cultural negotiation is a delicate matter. This is not an either/or proposition; it is possible that we both learn something new, and also that we assimilate some of what is learned to what is already familiar. In understanding this, we must face squarely two conflicting tendencies in Western interpretations of Buddhism—the tendency to see

Buddhism as world renouncing and quietistic, and the tendency to see it as a prime resource for the liberal agenda already familiar to us.

The Enlightenment, in whose light or shadow we still carry on our secular lives, is an individualistic culture that prizes autonomy and places high importance on self-exploration, especially of feeling. Its vision of the good life is democratic and usually involves personal commitment. Thus, we help others partly because it is their right to receive such help. And to a large extent social engagement means that we help others in ways that are explicit, material, and quantifiable.

Social engagement raises the further question of the role of suffering in human life, since such engagement is often directed at alleviating it, whether by distributing food, medical technology, or the education by which these and other goods can be attained. Buddhism, whose classic first principle is the ubiquitousness of pain, might seem to lend itself very nicely to a liberal agenda of social engagement. Still, the worldview that governs how modern secular Western culture deals with suffering and its causes is quite different from the worldview that traditional Buddhists bring to the matter. The issues of social and interpersonal engagement are an important link here, yet due in large measure to their valuation of the secular, contemporary women and men mean something different by the "suffering" or "the unsatisfactory" than is meant in traditional Buddhist cultures.

Another complicating factor is that although in many Buddhist traditions both the rhetoric and deep meditative experience override division into sacred and profane, institutionally this is not the case. Monasteries and nunneries, or remote caves and hermitages, housed those whose lives were dedicated to the greatest good recognized in Buddhism—practices that would alleviate the suffering of all sentient beings. For them, the unsatisfactoriness of life was not a temporary obstacle to ordinary enjoyment, but an inalienable condition of life itself.

We must also briefly note the way in which these same factors contribute, along with others, to reshaping our understanding of personhood. Once the sanctity of church and its mediation is rejected, and each person stands alone in relation to God, his or her fate is separately decided. In this way, a deepening appreciation for ordinary life has gone hand in hand with a heightened valuation of the personal tastes of the individual.

England and America in the seventeenth century produced the novel ideal of the companionate marriage, which bequeaths to us our whole contemporary understanding of marriage, sexual love, and personal fulfillment through relationships.[15] Marriage now is valued, not only because it produces legal children and inhibits widespread fornication, but because it provides "mutual society, help and comfort."[16] Starting among the wealthier classes in Anglo-Saxon countries and in France in the late seventeenth century, we find a growing idealization of marriage based on affection, true companionship between husband and wife, and devoted concern for children.[17] These changes are linked also to the rising importance of sentiment—not the actual existence of affection, but a changing sense of its importance.[18] We now find love, family, or at least relationships, central to human fulfillment. Companionate marriage and a demand for private space—virtually unavailable to anyone before the end of the seventeenth century—arose together. Families born of affection required or deserved an intimacy that could not flourish in the fishbowl world of traditional society.

Thus we see the family withdrawing from the control of wider society. No longer can fellow villagers interfere in what we today consider intimate family affairs. Henpecked, abusive, or cuckolded husbands once were targets of public collective ridicule, presumably due to their role in breaking down the proper patriarchal order. Such deviance could not be regarded as just a matter between a man and his wife because order was shared—something in which everyone participated.[19] And as the family retreats, the public character of religion grows.

In the prerevolutionary period, American Protestantism produced three kinds of religious temperaments: evangelical, moderate, and genteel, the latter prominent among social elites of the colonies.[20] Unlike the evangelical and moderate temperaments, which were largely committed to an inward route of religiosity, the genteel spirituality was inseparable from solidarity with established institutions and participation in their rituals. Piety was directed outwardly and so, in the words of Philip Greven in *The Protestant Temperament*, "The piety of the genteel became a public act, not an inner preoccupation." The implicit need to "prove" or "validate" one's spiritual dedication by external deeds fosters competition in the area of social engagement.

In contemporary understanding social engagement is meant to enhance ordinary life, because that is where meaning is found. Moreover, those persons who are socially engaged construe both themselves and those whom they help as unique individuals with particular needs, feelings, destinies. The leadership of social or intellectual movements largely falls to individuals who are charismatic or brilliant or both. Although the morally engaged may not be motivated by personal recognition, identification with a known leader is a tremendous boost for a righteous cause. Where would Tibetans be without the Dalai Lama, Afro-Americans without Martin Luther King Jr., and so on? But the penchant for singular leaders also masks a deeper truth—the dependent arising of unidentifiable doers and doings or, in social terms, of cooperation. Moreover, the cult of individual accomplishment survives despite evidence of the obvious importance of collective achievement.

Melissa Franklin, a Harvard physicist, gave a brief but wonderful National Public Radio disquisition on the eve of the Nobel Physics Prize awards in 1995. These prizes, she noted, are given only to one, two, or three persons. They celebrate the birth of a great idea and the individual who had it. There is good reason in this. Scientists, and science, get celebrated as a result. The theoretically incomprehensible gets tamed: Einstein was a genius, Einstein had a great idea (whatever it was), and Einstein got the Nobel Prize. It's a story we can handle, that we can all celebrate together. It makes us a community of celebrators, but it tears apart the community of scientists.

Melissa Franklin was one of 450 scientists who discovered the top quark, the final quark, the lost horizon of physics. None of these 450 expect ever to get the Nobel Prize. It would terribly crowd the royal Norwegian dinner table. It would be messy in other ways as well, for there would be too many people to be celebrated as individuals. Yet, says Dr. Franklin, she and the others do not believe there are any one, two, or three of them that can be singled out above the rest. And yet, of course, the discovery of the top quark is a major spark, an inspiration to the credo of cooperation. Prizes do not facilitate cooperation, though they may encourage individuals who sometimes inspire, coerce, or otherwise construct collaborative efforts. Yet a community can support only so many chiefs. How do the rest of us experience our individuality? In other words, where does this leave us as engaged persons? Can we benefit others anonymously and still be both effective and the sort of individual this culture prepares us to be? Are we, as Western Buddhists and as engaged Buddhist persons, consciously or unconsciously sustaining the cultural assumptions of personhood at the same time as we try to change the culture in other ways?

This question may be the key to our engagement. For engagement to be Buddhist, it should engage not only instrumentally effective acts, but also stem from a deep understanding of what it is we are doing with our lives and the struggle we survive in gaining our goal. It is not entirely new for Buddhists to engage in secular activities, but it is new for Buddhist practitioners to be engaged in secular causes in a culture that primarily validates the secular over, or at least equal to, the sacred realm of traditional religion, any traditional religion. We must examine the possibility of engaging Buddhist sensibilities in daily life without wholly entering into the modern absorption in the secular.

Attitudes toward Suffering: Buddhism and the Baconian Project

The contrast between the Baconian determination to relieve the human condition and the traditional Buddhist determination to leave it cannot be overlooked. Corollaries of the Baconian position, as it accompanies the modern era, are that all suffering is meaningless, morally, psychologically, and socially. In Buddhism, however, suffering signifies in two quite different ways. It is, as the discussion of the four truths tells us, something to be abandoned. Compassion, in numerous Tibetan prayers and practices, is defined as the intention to overcome others' suffering and its causes. But, for all the emphasis on overcoming it, the experience of suffering does have meaning. It is understood not as punishment—as in some Jewish or Christian contexts—but as the inevitable outcome of past deeds and, even more significantly, as the actual expiation or purification of those very deeds. At the same time, it is inconceivable in a traditional Buddhist context to attempt to relieve human beings of all suffering whatsoever, without also relieving them of distinctly human being. Pain and suffering are intrinsically part of the human condition. As much as they seek to alleviate it, Buddhists do not forget its inevitability. This distinguishes Buddhism from New Age optimism and associated forms of denial. We do what we can, but we never expect to mop up the infamous infinity of our past actions. For Buddhists, only liberation can truly put suffering behind us. The recognition of living beings' intimate and irrevocable association with suffering is a central and crucial Buddhist position that may have much to contribute to current debates—debates based in part on overblown expectations encouraged by the new choices and possibilities for control offered by modern science, technology, and medicine.

In view of this, what constitutes engaged service? The activities of the bodhisattvas, those vowed to compassionate connection with all beings, are often described in terms of the six activities of giving, ethics, patience, joyful effort, contemplation, and wisdom. Only three of the six—giving, ethics, patience, and perhaps effort—are directly related to interpersonal relationships. Even if we say that activities matter, what sorts of activities do we mean?

In the modern age, distributing food, medicine, education, jobs, and income are manifestations of social activism. The Dalai Lama regularly commissions groups of practitioners to come together to pray for the well-being of the world. Is this not also social engagement? But it does not fit contemporary models of social or personal engagement, for many reasons. Many Buddhist traditions consider that persons benefit not only from material substances, but also from "waves of splendor," a literal translation of the Tibetan term *spyin bslabs*, often rendered as "blessings." Engaging with deities through prayer is a form of social activism if we consider the forces they embody to be related to our human condition. Most traditional Buddhists do, whereas secular, instrumental perspectives do not.

What about being an example to others, an inspiring person? Consider the testimony of Palden Gyatso, tortured in Chinese prisons for three decades, expressing his forgiveness even as he exhibits the tools of his torture, which he purchased from his guards to display to the world. Is this not engaged Buddhism? Can such a powerful example of generosity of the human spirit fit into an instrumental secular worldview?

Like the post-Lockeans, and unknowingly influenced by that very tradition, engaged Buddhists say that the life of the laity is precisely the place to find, experience, and honor the sacred. I want to propose that we carefully appreciate the different routes to personal and social engagement that Buddhisms offer. Their emphasis does not depend primarily on either God or reason. These differences are worth preserving because they suggest moral sources different from the ones that have come down to us in Western religious or secular traditions. Above all, there is an emphasis on the intimate human wish to experience our own deepest nature. This is not only an intellectual predilection, or even a psychological one, but a fundamental delight in experiencing the radiant unconditioned nature of the mind's potential or enlightened state. Affirmation of such a state is the most embarrassing aspect of Buddhist tradition vis-à-vis modern sensibilities, and for that very reason, possibly the most vital and valuable. The question is whether such a principle can have real meaning in the contemporary secularized world of engaged participants.

Notes

1. Charles Taylor, *Sources of the Self* (Cambridge: Harvard University Press, 1989), p. 218.

2. Ibid., p. 214.

3. Gerald McKenny, *To Relieve the Human Condition* (Albany: State University of New York Press), 1997. My comments on Bacon are much influenced by discussions with Dr. McKenny.

4. Taylor, *Sources of the Self*, p. 328.

5. Ibid., p. 265.

6. *Confessions*, p. 126. Quoted by Barbara Johnson in *The Critical Difference*, p. 4.

7. Taylor, *Sources of the Self*, p. 512.

8. See Fredric Jameson, *The Ideologies of Theory: Essays 1971--1986, Volume 2: The Syntax of History* (Minneapolis: University of Minnesota Press, 1988), pp. 145–47.

9. For further elaboration of this point see Klein, "Presence with a Difference: Buddhism and Feminism on Subjectivity," *Hypatia, Journal of Women and Philosophy*, special edition on Women and Religion (Fall 1994). Some parts of this section are summaries of this article and of sections from my *Meeting the Great Bliss Queen: Buddhists, Feminists, and the Art of the Self* (Boston: Beacon Press, 1994).

10. See Gayatri Chakravorty Spivak, "Can the Subaltern Speak," *Marxism and the Interpretation of Culture*, ed. Cary Nelson and Lawrence Grossberg (Urbana: University of Illinois Press, 1988), especially p. 293ff.

11. Condensed from *Meeting the Great Bliss Queen.*

12. "The Bare Facts of Ritual," in Jonathan Z. Smith, *Imagining Religion: From Babylon to Jonestown* (Chicago: University of Chicago Press, 1982), p. 63. These points are elaborated further in Klein, *Meeting the Great Bliss Queen*, chapter 7.

13. *Imagining Religion*, p. 63.

14, This important observation was made by Paula Saunders in a seminar sponsored by the Rice Center for Cultural Studies, Fall 1991.

15. Taylor, *Sources of the Self*, p. 227.

16. Ibid.

17. Ibid., p. 289.

18. Ibid., p. 202.

19. Ibid., p. 291.

20. Ibid., p. 312.

Sara Shneiderman

12. Appropriate Treasure?

Reflections on Women, Buddhism, and Cross-Cultural Exchange

As Buddhism solidifies its foothold both in the West and in myself, both my own and the Western world's initial wide-eyed fascination with Buddhist philosophies and cultures so different from our own has quieted. Now, many of Buddhism's age-old values have begun to penetrate and grate gently against the Western cultural identity that both I, and my society as a whole, have grown up with. One of the most provocative, promising, and precarious areas of discussion within this larger cross-cultural dialogue between Eastern and Western philosophies and cultural values arises when we turn our attention to questions about women in Buddhism. For young Western women such as myself, who have come of age in a cultural environment generated by feminism's third wave—one that emphasizes individualistic self-development and an unassailable right to choose our own destinies—Buddhism's cultural trappings and practices that work toward deconstructing subjectivity may challenge the very basis of our feminist self-understanding and development. At the same time, however, they may offer an enticingly different path to positive self-realization.[1]

Over the last few years, a number of works have been published that discuss Western women's encounters with Buddhism from a variety of theoretical and personal angles. Among these are Anne Klein's *Meeting the Great Bliss Queen,* which juxtaposes Buddhism, feminism, and the author's personal experience to discuss the "art of the self"; Miranda Shaw's *Passionate Enlightenment: Women in Tantric Buddhism,* an historiographic review of women's roles in newly reinterpreted Tantric texts; and *Pure Heart, Enlightened Mind: The Zen Journal and Letters of Maura "Soshin" O'Halloran,* the posthumously published personal journal of a contemporary Irish American woman's years of Zen training in Japan.

The intensity of connection that I feel with these women and their work is encouraging, as it offers a realm of positive approaches to Buddhism for me as a Western woman. However, I cannot help but feeling that, as much as these discussions have opened up exciting new ways of examining and experiencing female identity within Buddhism from Western perspectives, they seem to have neglected a crucial set of actors in the East meets West/feminism meets Buddhism equation: our non-Western Buddhist sisters.[2] Although Klein, Shaw, and O'Halloran all give voice to others or act themselves as female exemplars for Western Buddhist women, in all of these writers' accounts, contemporary Asian Buddhist women remain mute, or at best anomalous participants in what, from one perspective, can be seen as primarily male-dominated religious power structures.

As we shall see here, advancing a moralistic brand of Western feminism that criticizes traditional Buddhist institutions as monolithically oppressive to women is only one of many possible viewpoints, and it can be highly problematic. However, as the construct upon which much of both younger Western women's self-understanding and much of contemporary academic discourse is premised, Western-centered feminism cannot be dismissed without comment. Instead, it must be reevaluated and perhaps refashioned to give expression to voices, both Eastern and Western, that may have not been heard previously within the feminist discussion.

Along these lines, Anne Klein repeatedly states that her work is oriented toward reworking Western feminism and Western women's relationships to Buddhism. But for many legitimate reasons, her current agenda consciously excludes an exploration of Eastern women's potentially divergent experiences:

> The conversation between Buddhist and feminist voices necessarily takes place across several crucial divides, all of which are formidable. It moves not only between East and West but between secular and religious, male and female, traditional and modern. Though difficult to negotiate, these divides are well worth exploring, for they reveal the diverse perspectives at play in the *identities of many contemporary Western women*.[3]

Shaw's subjects, although spiritually potent Indian and Tibetan women, are removed from the flow of cultural time and exalted as examples for Western women; Shaw does not offer an explicit examination of these historical figures' relationship to the lives of their indigenous female descendants. As a personal account, O'Halloran's journals necessarily focus on her own spiritual development as a Western woman in a Japanese environment, and not on Japanese women's engagement with Buddhism.

These observations are not intended as criticisms of any of these women's works in themselves. All of these books have been published in the last few years; it is clearly a privilege to have any access at all to women's descriptions of their personal and academic experiences within Buddhist traditions. Each author mentioned delineates a specific niche for herself and explores it eloquently; none of them fails to achieve her objectives, since none of them claims to articulate the position of contemporary Asian Buddhist women. Because these authors are at the forefront of a highly charged cross-cultural discussion, it may, in fact, be essential that they begin with discussions of their own subjective experiences (explicit in O'Halloran's journal, implicit in Klein's and Shaw's approaches and commitment to their theoretical and historical material) in order to claim some authority. Perhaps it is presumptuous to suggest that Klein, Shaw, O'Halloran, or I, could even begin to address the diverse situations of modern Tibetan, Indian, Japanese, and other Asian Buddhist women, much less constructively engage them with our own.

However, I cannot ignore the curious internal emptiness that I feel at the silence from sisters on the other side of Klein's cultural divide; I cannot see how we, as Western Buddhist women, can compassionately cross it only for ourselves, without exploring indigenous Buddhist women's often very different, culturally constructed subjective experiences within our shared tradition. I would like to redefine the divide that Klein so elegantly navigates so that the pass can be crossed from both directions; if Asian Buddhist women so desire, they may be able to gain as much from our Western feminist history as we do from their Buddhist tradition. Even if they are not interested in explicitly feminist ideas, Buddhist women from diverse cultures should be able to meet and share respect, understanding, and spiritual and cultural goals.

Over many trips to Nepal and India, I have had the opportunity to meet and work with many communities of both indigenous and Western Buddhist women. At times, I have engaged with both groups of women in my capacity as an anthropologist conducting fieldwork. At other times, we interacted as fellow Buddhist practitioners without any explicitly defined academic roles governing our relationships. Drawing from my experiences with both roles, the ideas outlined here are inherently an encounter between Self and Other, East and West, since I, as observer and writer, was and continue to be a Western woman traveling in foreign, traditionally Buddhist cultures. Each concrete, momentary encounter between Asia and Western women that I shall describe alludes to more enduring theoretical questions about these cross-cultural relationships. By retroactively placing my own observations and perceptions within the discursive context broadly defined by the three works that have been introduced, I can create three different, yet interconnected narratives: First, I can trace my own spiritual and personal growth as a young Western woman shaped from a young age by feminist thought and practice and now interested in Buddhist thought and practice; second, I can broaden the conversation begun by Klein, Shaw, and O'Halloran by offering perspectives on the interaction between contemporary Asian and Western Buddhist women in Nepal; and third, I can analytically apply what I have learned from these three authors to the collage of Himalayan experiences that I describe.

Interconnected Narratives

All too often, Westerners who have been studying Buddhism in their own countries travel to Kathmandu or Dharamsala expecting to see the form of their personal practice replicated in the monasteries or nunneries that they visit or live in. Coming from all points along the spectrum of Buddhist experience, such Westerners may experience a cultural discordance that leads them to denigrate what may be more traditional structures of Buddhist learning and living than those that have been adopted and adapted in the West. Similarly, among Western scholars of Buddhism and Western Buddhist practitioners, one finds an emphasis upon textually based, institutionally oriented forms of Buddhism as the most fully "developed"—and therefore acceptable—ones. Anthropologist Charles Ramble, who has worked extensively in Nepal's Buddhist Himalayas, explains that visiting Western scholars of Buddhism or Tibetan culture often ask, "Why do you want to go to the mountains? Tibetan culture is dead. It exists only in their books."[4] Perhaps not coincidentally, the textually embedded, institutional aspects of Buddhism respected as primary by scholars such as the one Ramble quotes are the aspects (of Mahāyāna Buddhism in particular) that have been most effectively transmitted to the often highly literate West. This preference for the textually preserved aspects of Buddhist traditions tends to exclude those who participate in Buddhism from nontextual or noninstitutional perspectives. Often, these people are indigenous Asian women.[5]

The characterization of certain indigenous Buddhist lifestyles as somehow less appropriate than those familiar in the West was reflected in encounters I had with Western practitioners residing at monasteries in Kathmandu. For example, from a Western perspective, the local toilets and other facilities were unacceptable because they were different and not up to their own hygienic standards. For this and other reasons, they maintained their own separate residences and spent most of their time among the resident Western community without interacting in depth with the ethnically Tibetan monastics. From this trivial example, we can gain some initial insight into the difficulties at hand in creating the most basic conditions for cross-cultural communication and shared understanding between Western and Asian Buddhists.

Speaking more specifically about differences among Asian and Western Buddhist women, I recall the subtle but potent cultural and gender dynamics that functioned in the relationship between a small community of Western nuns and a far larger community of ethnically Tibetan nuns affiliated with the same monastery. In the course of many conversations with Western and ethnically Tibetan nuns in residence there, I pieced together a general understanding of the ever-evolving relationship between the two groups of women. Although these examples are taken from one specific monastic community, these observations on the divergences and points of connection between Asian and Western women may prove relevant in other, increasingly multicultural communities throughout the ethnically Tibetan diasporic belt.

In general, the Western nuns and female lay practitioners in residence live in special quarters at the main monastery, which is also inhabited by about two hundred monks. All the lamas (teachers) and other dignitaries also stay in these quarters when in residence or visiting the monastery. The ethnically Tibetan nuns live in separate quarters that have recently been constructed about ten minutes' walk away from the monastic center of activity. These nuns do not have their own teachers in residence, but trek up and down the hill between their rooms and the monastery every day to receive teachings.

Although the monks and nuns ostensibly have equal accommodations and education, most of the nuns are far behind their male counterparts in their academic accomplishments. There are twenty-two-year-old monks who have finished their course of study, whereas many twenty-eight- and thirty-year-old nuns still lag far behind. This disparity is apparently due to historical inequalities that are now being rectified; in the past, nuns had been used for maintenance purposes, left illiterate, and otherwise neglected, but now there is a new movement afoot to bring their living and educational standards up to par with the monks'. Unlike most monks, who begin memorizing Tibetan Buddhist texts as children, many of the women join the nunnery at a much older age and being, for the most part, unable to read, have much catching up to do.

As one Western nun put it, "They can't do the fancy things [like sand mandalas and lama dances] yet—they're still learning their ABCs." She clearly did not consider herself one of "them," despite her shared identity with them as a Buddhist nun. Western nuns seem to be in a strange meditating position—they are often as educated and proficient in their practice as many Tibetan monks, or more so, yet they are still women who theoretically belong in the nunnery, where nuns generally receive fewer privileges than monks. The nun quoted above, like other female Western practitioners, both monastic and lay, lives in the monastery compound instead of with the nuns. She seems to feel compassion for the Tibetan nuns and is pleased that their conditions are improving, but seems to consider herself at a very different level of Buddhist practice and achievement.

Initially, I was disturbed by the lack of connection and shared community between this nun and the ethnically Tibetan nuns. In my naiveté, I expected a greater sense of solidarity between Western and ethnically Tibetan Buddhist women. But, although she appreciated and deeply supported the ethnically Tibetan nuns' efforts, this nun seemed concerned that I distinguish her from the ethnically Tibetan women who were, in her perception, on a different spiritual plane. At the time, I was disturbed by the sense that this nun, and others like her, had appropriated traditions that should have been, but were not, equally accessible to the ethnically Tibetan women themselves. It seemed that they had extracted these traditions to fit their own educated, Western context, without fully considering the implications that this appropriation might have for their indigenous ethnically Tibetan counterparts.

"Appropriation" is the key word here. By my definition, the word suggests lifting a treasure out of one cultural context and inserting it into another without attending to the well-being and needs of its original keepers.[6] While setting out her book's objectives, Klein hints at the unbalanced power dynamic that may be represented by such attitudes of Western women as just described:

> By understanding the different ways in which North American and Tibetan cultures construct persons as connected or separate, we can better understand what a Western woman can appropriate from Buddhist traditions, how she might change or contribute to those traditions, and what limitations there might be in using them as a resource.[7]

Klein is aware of the process of appropriation occurring as Western women adopt Buddhist traditions, aware that in order to be used effectively in tandem with Western women's uniquely independent notions of selfhood, Buddhist concepts must be distinguished from their traditional contexts and recalibrated to link up with our already constructed systems of cultural identity. Klein does not see this process as an inherently problematic one, nor do I. Western women have been attracted to Buddhist traditions, have begun to pick and choose from among these traditions using criteria different than those indigenous Buddhist women and men might employ, and have initiated anew in the West the process of syncretic adaptation that Buddhism has historically undergone during each of its geographic transitions. There is nothing in this current process of change that differentiates it fundamentally from the others that Buddhism has weathered, and in that sense, it should not bother me that Western women are able to alter Buddhist traditions to their own taste.

But the matter may not be so simple. As Western women of my generation begin to participate in this process of appropriation, it may be precisely our independence and self-confidence, inculcated in many from a young age, that allow us to adopt Buddhist traditions as positive, empowering ones. In part, Western women are able to thrive and cultivate themselves within Buddhist religious traditions that are at some level hierarchically structured, male-dominated, and that often exclude their own women, precisely because we have learned to ignore such institutional barriers and to see our individualistic desires as ultimately attainable. Coming from cultures that do not encourage such values, young women such as the ethnically Tibetan nuns at the Himalayan monastery and the Japanese women that, as we shall see, Maura O'Halloran has trouble identifying with, may not have the same freedom and ease of access from which to build a relationship with Buddhist traditions on their own terms. This is not to suggest that Western individualistic or feminist ideals are necessarily better than the complex cultural webs that create Asian women's lives. In fact, it can be argued that the concept of patriarchy and its associated power structures are inherently Western constructions—that women from other cultures have vastly different, but essentially positive worldviews and roles within the systems to which they belong. Nevertheless, Western women possess a different set of internalized cultural resources, which may allow them more individual and institutional agency to effect change within the Buddhist traditions that they have adopted.

Both Shaw and Klein highlight these cultural differences in self-conception as crucial components in our understanding of the relationships between Buddhism and feminism. Shaw refutes more traditional Western scholars' claims that women in Tantric relationships were only objectified tools for men by offering a different interpretation of Tantric Buddhist women's concepts of selfhood:

> A situation is postulated in which women are depersonalized and exploited. The postulated depersonalization of the women is predicated upon their possession of an individual self as it is constructed in the mainstream of Western thought. . . . This commodified self is at variance with traditional Indian and Buddhist understandings of personhood.[8]

Laying out the key differences in Western and Tibetan conceptions of the self as she illuminates experiences unique to Western women engaged in Buddhism, Klein makes a related point:

> To sum up, in the West, "individuation" has by and large meant the emergence of consciously chosen activities and attitudes. . . . The road to adulthood and personhood is marked by a range of choices unknown in traditional societies, and the individual's responsibility for those choices is great. . . . The challenges and definitions of Tibetan personhood are very different, and yet they also suggest a dialogue between separation and connectedness. The personal boundaries that result from Tibet's cultural dialogue are formed through an amalgamation of its people's attitudes regarding their relationship to society, natural environment, and the cosmos, and to the privileged authority of the past.[9]

Both scholars argue that Western culture tends to focus on the development of the individual self, praising separation and "special," "unique" qualities as legitimating personhood, while Tibetan Buddhist thought posits the self as a fluid, only tentatively boundaried component of a larger, cosmically interconnected reality.

The implications that these different notions of selfhood have for contemporary Asian and Western Buddhist women are great. The formative emphasis placed on individual self-development for Western women may be precisely what draws us to Buddhist practice, as a means of deconstructing our painfully "independent" Western selves and cultivating a compassionate connectedness within ourselves and with others that our culture does not encourage. However, it is precisely the independence and separateness that we so desperately want to transcend that enables us to engage with Buddhism on the level that we desire. We may gain access to male-dominated enclaves of spiritual authority precisely *because* we are perceived to have a sense of individual authority, self-confidence, and societal power generally associated with men, rather than the immanent, undefined, and potentially impotent "self" often assigned to women in both our own and other cultures.

In a sense, we become honorary men in these Buddhist cultures. O'Halloran takes pride in feeling like "one of the lads,"[10] although she is initially aware of being "the only woman and only foreigner studying here."[11] As we have seen, Western nuns in the Tibetan tradition often choose to live and practice with the resident monks rather than their Asian monastic sisters. In terms of spiritual and intellectual achievement, they may feel far more comfortable with men who have pursued similar studies and practices than with women who lag far behind. For women like Maura and the Western Tibetan Buddhist nun mentioned above, the identities of "foreigner" and "female" become conflated into something altogether Other. Their status as "foreigner" overrides that of "female," allowing them to dissociate themselves from both the internal and external restrictions encountered by indigenous women attempting to practice at the same level. As Klein says of her own experience, "I studied in much the same way as the [male] Tibetans themselves did . . . owing to my 'importance' as a Westerner and the irrelevance in that context of my being a woman."[12]

O'Halloran is painfully aware of the cultural distinctions between herself and the Japanese women with whom she comes in contact:

> Women are really repressed here, forced into the mold of a giggling innocent. At first I rather enjoyed the surprise and admiration with which I was treated. Now I feel its oppressiveness, for it's only because I'm female. My heart went out to Kobai-san. She wished she could sit as freely and naturally as I, but couldn't. Such a simple thing. Always raised to sit like a lady, she was too self-conscious to be merely comfortable.[13]

O'Halloran's status as a woman does factor into others' perceptions of her and win her the mixed blessing of extra attention, but as a Western woman, confidently grounded in herself, she is able to rise above these petty sexisms and legitimize herself beyond all expectations through her remarkably deep practice. Many Japanese women, like Kobai-san, however, are not. As O'Halloran explains, her Japanese counterpart is unable to break either the internal or external bonds of her culture's sexism. She cannot practice freely because she is too self-conscious of both the immediate "unlady-like" act of sitting quietly with herself in a roomful of intimidating male practitioners and of the more general "unlady-like" connotations that serious Buddhist practice has in her culture. O'Halloran is compassionate toward women like Kobai-san because she, in her own way, has experienced the hardship of being a woman in a predominantly male religious community, but her compassion can only go so far. Ultimately, she accepts the honorary male privilege that being a foreigner confers, and practices as such, leaving her Japanese sisters to work with their own cultural limitations.

Of course, not all Japanese women appear as weak characters in O'Halloran's journals; she greatly admires the enlightenment she recognizes as immanent in many older women's daily lives:

> Then I saw her—skinny, 70, down on the floor vigorously scrubbing the already gleaming wood with such earnestness she didn't even hear my call. I felt ashamed. She trundled into the garden and dug me up *kiku* from the ends of the rows she'd already neatly trimmed, thinned, and transplanted. . . . She was off about her work. Ashamed, thoroughly ashamed, I bought an ice-cream and pushed my barrow past the rice fields with the radios, the many bent bodies at their jobs. I wondered what they thought about, if they thought at all. Were they all like so many Zen masters, living their koans—digging and digging and only digging?[14]

and:

> The woman twinkled, dimpled, wiping her hands on her apron, smoothing it across her sparse hips. She made *mat-cha* [tea] for us, a long ritual of wiping and whirling the universe into a bowl. She knelt by the fire, dipping water from the soot-encrusted cauldron. Slowly, almost caressing her utensils, she poured. Her features were dim in the soft light of the room, but one side glowed colours thrown up by the fire. I was drawn into her every movement.[15]

These women demonstrate their commitment to the Dharma though the minute movements of their daily lives, within the constraints of traditional Japanese women's roles. As far as we know, they have not undergone formal Zen training in the way that O'Halloran has; they are not Zen masters in any institutionally defined sense. However, as O'Halloran describes, they have mastered the small slice of reality in which they so mindfully live. The institutionalized Zen practice that O'Halloran undertakes is not the only means of working toward enlightenment—these laywomen, too, have attained a deep awareness and clarity through the intricacies of their lives as they are.

In this way, it is clear that although hierarchical exclusion from monastic institutions may unfairly limit Asian women's modes of spiritual praxis, these women may possess their own modes of practice. Often unnoticed by Western women, rich daily rituals such as those O'Halloran describes may be equally valid ways of working toward enlightenment. The women that appear in O'Halloran's journals, like many women with a minimum of formal education throughout the ethnically Tibetan cultural world and other parts of Asia, have cultivated themselves within the confines of their social roles as laywomen, rather than within the male-dominated monastic mainstream. This is not to suggest that the male mainstream is intrinsically a superior mode of practice; nevertheless, it is from this monastic tradition that most Western practitioners, male and female, learn. Although there are many forms of *upāya*, or skillful means, very few Western women or men would willingly take on the role of an uneducated housewife as their Dharma practice; instead, they would probably prefer to use their privileged foreign identity to enter traditionally male enclaves of institutional religious practice.

But perhaps this is simply a culturally constructed projection of the roles that Asian women play. Independently of the academic works by Western Buddhist women that I have been discussing, there is also a large and growing body of literature in which Asian female practitioners discuss their experiences within various Buddhist traditions.[16] A thorough comparison of these works with those like Klein's and O'Halloran's and further interpersonal dialogue would be valuable for illuminating Buddhist women's experiences on both sides of the fence.

Creating this kind of dialogue between Asian and Western Buddhist women will be a delicate process, as was evident during and after the Fourth International Conference on Buddhist Women in Ladakh. Asking whether Western Buddhist women should feel an especially compassionate bond with Asian Buddhist women due to their shared status as women opens up a heated theoretical debate from both feminist and Buddhist perspectives. In the context of feminist discourse, arguing that they should connect with each other as "women," regardless of their other life circumstances, suggests an essentialist position in which, regardless of cultural, religious, racial, economic, and other differences, *all* women share a universal understanding based on their membership in the category of "women." Poststructuralists and others criticize this view as a white, Western, middle-class construction that does not adequately acknowledge the diverse experiences and needs that constitute the varied realities women around the world are living; from this point of view, Western women must acknowledge that we cannot necessarily know how any other women feel and that we cannot claim any kind of privileged connection to Tibetan, Japanese, or other women simply because we share the same gender characteristics and the same religious tradition. It may be necessary instead to construct our individual identities and operate without any particular allegiance to other women.

From an essentialist perspective, women like O'Halloran and Western nuns living in Asia would be expected to attach themselves to the women in the cultures they encounter, either taking on the characteristics assigned to the category of "woman" in their host cultures or attempting to alter indigenous women's religious status to bring it closer to their own. Either way, it is somehow inappropriate for them to accept privileges denied to their indigenous sisters simply by emphasizing the "Western" component of their identity over the "female" component. If, however, their desire to engage in Buddhist practice has nothing to do with their gender or any other distinguishing feature of their identities, then the treatment of other women, Asian or Western, is largely irrelevant to their individual pursuit of enlightenment.

Bringing this debate into a Buddhist context, Klein argues for a middle way between these two theoretical extremes, which I also find most appropriate:

> The central dilemma is clear: how can we suggest a female sense of self that is neither overly essentialized nor so contingently constructed that its existence is in question? It is in reframing this oppositional relationship that Buddhist perspectives seem most useful for contemporary feminist debates and women's lives.[17]

The concept that women can connect with each other simply on the basis of their femininity is attractive, but at the same time, it is important to respect our own and others' unique cultural, religious, and personal identities, comprised of our individual narrative histories. Klein suggests that Buddhist philosophy can help mediate between these two approaches: Buddhism questions the construction of individual selves, emphasizing an understanding of universal selflessness, and simultaneously emphasizes the realization of this truth through cultivating the individual self.

The constructivist argument parallels one that is often offered as a typically Buddhist one in answer to questions about women's status in traditional Buddhist cultures. It defers to Buddhism's metaphysical concepts of nonduality, claiming that dualistic distinctions like male and female, Eastern and Western are simply descriptive categories that we use to make sense of the phenomenal world, but that are empty in the absolute. Through Buddhist practice, all selves can ultimately be deconstructed and thus move beyond phenomenal gender and culture distinctions. In some sense, Maura O'Halloran exemplifies this ideal, transcending sexism and other social boundaries to achieve the luminescent enlightenment that speaks so clearly from her journal's pages. As already noted, the troubling thing is that, in part, Maura is able to become a successful, full-fledged practitioner because she has begun with a different set of cultural assumptions than her Japanese companions.

Asserting that gender and other distinctions are irrelevant in light of Buddhism's egalitarian philosophy does not acknowledge the cultural realities that often prohibit or deter women from practicing in the first place. Quoting Klein, "We cannot say precisely where and how religious egalitarianism fails to translate into social egalitarianism, but clearly the amalgamation of social, political, and economic power is an obstacle."[18] Although Buddhism's religious egalitarianism is a large part of its drawing power for many Western practitioners, we must not allow ourselves, whether women or men, to use it as a smokescreen to hide social realities around us that do not parse. Nonduality and nondiscrimination are ideals to work toward, both internally and externally, not manifest realities that allow us to excuse or ignore difficult phenomenal truths. As Klein says, we cannot know why or how our philosophical expectations of Buddhism do not match up with the lived realities that we observe. Sadly, it appears that very few Western Buddhist women want to describe what they see in contemporary Asian women's realities because, ironically, fully acknowledging women's different and often unequal roles in Asian Buddhist traditions may appear to challenge Buddhism's egalitarian potential in the West.

Tranformative Encounters, Intangible Bonds

I felt that there was a very strong and positive sense of self within the communities of ethnically Tibetan women, both monastic and lay, with whom I engaged in Nepal. My bonds with both nuns and laywomen were generally very different—warmer and friendlier—than the relations I was able to forge with monks. Although most of the textual and philosophical Buddhist teachings I received came from men, simply being with Buddhist women brought me into the indigenous tradition in a uniquely immanent and embodied way. I often felt an intangible common bond with these women, perhaps because I was looking for it, but more likely because the atmosphere they created and warmly invited me into was premised on a different mode of relationship than that I experienced with monks. The contrast between the male and female monastic communities seems embedded in the different histories of their respective members: monks often join the monastery or are placed in it by their parents for the highly valued purpose of textual study and practice, while nuns often join seeking an alternative to the marriage and family commitments otherwise compulsory for ethnically Tibetan women. The religious life may serve more as a source of positive communal relationship than as a path toward individual enlightenment or intellectual development. In a society that possesses strong gender divisions and few empowering options for women beyond marriage and motherhood, becoming a nun may allow a woman to develop herself personally, forge relationships with other women, create a self-defined community, and fulfill a unique social role in traditional Tibetan societies.[19]

Because these more concrete objectives may often be ethnically Tibetan nuns' primary focus, rather than philosophically motivated enlightenment, Western nuns' choices to practice and study with monks rather than nuns may appear justified. Western women may choose to focus on their own practice in the potentially more "serious" spiritual environment that a monks' monastery offers and be ambivalent about constructing a community based only on an ostensibly shared understanding of womanhood. Instead, they may wish to further their own meditative development in the most rigorous setting, regardless of whether they live and work with women or men, indigenous or not.

However, it seems that these two goals—maintaining Buddhist practice and establishing sisterhood—should be complementary, rather than mutually exclusive. Both Western and Asian women should find ways to practice fully that do not require becoming honorary men. Ideally, we should be able to integrate both halves of our dual identities as both women and Buddhist practitioners, rather than feeling compelled to disavow one in favor of the other. Of course, the missing piece in this identity configuration for Western Buddhist women is our identity as Westerners. Western women may assume that they can create equal relationships with indigenous Buddhist women based on their common identity as "women," transcending perceptions of cultural difference and identifying themselves in an essentialist fashion as simply "women."

However, this manipulation of identity may not be concretely feasible, for each individual lives as a complete whole. Aspects of a complex identity—gender, nationality, class—cannot be easily erased, so, cognizant of them, each must practice her own humanness as honestly as possible. However, no individual will be free until all sentient beings are free to do this; we cannot rest completely in our own practice while we know that there are women, born into the very tradition we have appropriated, who are unable to explore their own inner landscape due to gender distinctions. Buddhist practice itself may be our primary means of effecting change in both the internal and external worlds, but since the forms of our practice are located in the hierarchical entity we wish to alter, it may be necessary to either remove our practice from that framework or work to alter the framework itself through creative, nontraditional means.

Miranda Shaw's historical examination of women in Tantric Buddhism presents an alternative model for a vital, Buddhist women's spiritual community. Shaw also attempts to transform modern Western Buddhism's attitudes toward women through her academic discovery and promotion of a hitherto hidden history of spiritually potent Buddhist women. The Tantric *yoginīs* that Shaw describes are generally not nuns, but wandering, wild women who come together to hold all-female forest revels:

> One Tantric practitioner . . . reported how he fortuitously discovered a yogini assembly. . . . At nightfall he saw many women enter the temple courtyard bearing flowers and preparations for a feast. Their nocturnal ritual preparations and their crowns, elaborate jewelry, and rainbow-colored dresses signaled to him that they were yoginis.[20]
>
> Instead of practices to which women might on occasion hope to be omitted, the feast in its classical form appears to be a ritual performed either exclusively by women or communally by men and women, as a matter of course. Women gathering in circles to feast, perform rituals, teach, and inspire one another constitutes a practice that also appears in the secular literature of the period.[21]

This suggests a vastly different model for Buddhist women's spirituality than the traditional monastic environment. These divergent structures (lay and monastic) and images are conjoined only by the fact that they involve Buddhist women, without any other necessary connection. This discontinuity is disturbing, especially as it relates to the disparities between contemporary Eastern and Western Buddhist women outlined above. Although Shaw presents an exciting picture of independently potent, spiritually liberated medieval Tantric women who are free of hierarchical constraints, this historically constructed image diverges greatly from the realities that most indigenous Buddhist women live today, whether in monastic or lay environments.

Shaw's work may appeal to Western women because it presents an ideal we may wish to emulate—an ideal that may influence the ways in which we adapt Buddhism in the West. Western Buddhists have the unique chance to influence a religion in its transformative stages—to constructively assimilate Buddhist cultural and philosophical traditions with Western feminism—especially when scholars like Shaw demonstrate the basis for that integration in traditional Buddhist texts. However, the problem remains that although Shaw and other Western women can appropriate a lost historical equality by reconstituting Buddhist traditions around feminist and other Western values, indigenous Buddhist women may not be privy to these images and texts that have such liberating and transformative potency or to the feminist self-understanding that makes these images of women so potent for Westerners.

Once again, the frustrating concept of appropriation comes into play. After reading Shaw's work, I had the sense of handling a treasure that had fallen by chance into my hands, one that should be returned to its rightful owners. Shaw has begun this process by unearthing these texts and distilling them into a coherent set of positive images reflecting women's spiritual potentiality. However, creating the circumstances on our side of the cultural divide that would encourage modern ethnically Tibetan women to rediscover these texts and continue their spiritual foremothers' legacy needs to be done in ways that avoid culturally imperialistic power dynamics.

In order to avoid such dynamics, perhaps Western women simply need to develop their own interpretation of Buddhist philosophy and practice along their own unique cultural lines and leave others' experiences of it alone. But that answer is not satisfactory either, since both Western and Eastern women are very much engaged with Buddhism as a historical and cultural entity that does not always offer women the same spiritual opportunities as men. There are as yet no concrete solutions for this dilemma, but it is crucial that the matter be placed on the table as this nascent cross-cultural discussion develops between practitioners East and West, female and male.

Another challenge in the process of adapting Buddhism to the West lies in diffusing the sexisms inherent in our own societies. Western feminism developed in response to the abuses of a largely patriarchal religious and cultural system, and it is inappropriate to assume that these inequalities have already been completely erased. An experience at a Dharma teaching in Kathmandu demonstrates how insidious Western sexism can be, especially when coupled with assumptions that Buddhist teachings spring from a pure and unchallengeable source.

Reading the dedication of merit after a Dharma teaching, an entire Western congregation read lines from a chant book that referred to "the Buddha and his sons." A number of Western women and I were disturbed about this and approached the lama to ask about its source. Attention drawn to the incriminating line, the lama chuckled and told us that "sons" was a mistaken translation, that the original Tibetan term—"children" of the Buddha—was nongendered. The lama was happy to change the translation for future sessions but his Western male translator, surprisingly, was not. He was not immediately convinced that the inclusive translation was appropriate and, even if it were, he was very reluctant to use it. Hence, we see that the problem goes both ways. We may construct Buddhism as we see fit in the West, but no matter how much we may think that we are exempt from the embedded sexist realities that exist for Tibetan and other indigenous women, sexism is also part and parcel of our own cultural tradition.

The questions discussed here are enormous and all-encompassing, and even after many months of working with ethnically Tibetan Buddhist women in Nepal and several years of serious consideration, I feel no closer to the resolutions that I seek. Even as my understanding of the issues has become more subtle, the questions themselves continue to expand as I delve more deeply into them. Advancing concrete answers at this stage might stifle potentially fruitful discussion; instead, I seek to generate conversation by offering these open-ended thoughts for consideration.

Notes

1. Extensive thanks to Mark Unno, Karma Lekshe Tsomo, and all of the participants of the 1995 Sakyadhita Conference on Women and Buddhism for helping me think, rethink, and revise the ideas contained within this paper.

2. Some may question the use of the word "sister" as one that assumes an essential relationship between Western and Eastern women that may not genuinely exist. Here I use the term in the sense that it is used throughout Asia as an identifying title; among both friends and strangers, both men and women may address a women as "sister."

3. Anne C. Klein, *Meeting the Great Bliss Queen: Buddhism, Feminism and the Art of the Self* (Boston: Beacon Press, 1995), p. xviii. Italics mine.

4. Charles Ramble, "The Founding of a Tibetan Village: The Popular Transformation of History," *Kailash* 10.1 (1983): 267–90, at p. 267.

5. This is not to suggest that all Asian Buddhist women are nonliterate; such an assertion would be inaccurate and offensive. However, in my area of experience—the Nepali Buddhist Himalayas—the majority of Tibetan Buddhist women are not literate in Tibetan, the language in which their Buddhist philosophy and history is encoded. Ironically, as more and more women in this region gain literacy in Nepali (which serves as a trade and business language), fewer and fewer women become literate in the traditional Tibetan liturgical language. I am currently conducting research on this trend.

6. Donald Lopez uses a similar metaphor to discuss Western scholars' appropriation of Buddhist texts: "These were texts that were seen as cultural artifacts of modern Asian societies, but from an earlier time, a classical period, that modern Asians had long forgotten and thereby forfeited any rights to: those responsible for the decay could not be trusted with the treasures." From "Foreigner at the Lama's Feet," *Curators of the Buddha* (Chicago: University of Chicago, 1995), p. 284.

7. Klein, *Great Bliss Queen*, p. 12.

8. Miranda Shaw, *Passionate Enlightenment: Women in Tantric Buddhism* (Princeton: Princeton University, 1994), p. 10.

9. Klein, *Great Bliss Queen*, p. 37.

10. Maura, O'Halloran, *Pure Heart, Enlightened Mind: The Zen Journal and Letters of Maura "Soshin" O'Halloran* (Boston: Charles E. Tuttle, 1994), p. 17.

11. Ibid., p. 23.

12. Klein, *Great Bliss Queen*, p. xiv.

13. O'Halloran, *Pure Heart*, p. 108.

14. Ibid., p. 197.

15. Ibid., p. 222.

16. See, for example, the stories told by Songgyong Sunim, Aoyama Sensei, Maechee Pathomwan, Hiuwan Fashih, and others in Martine Batchelor's *Walking on Lotus Flowers: Buddhist Women Living, Loving and Meditating* (London: Thorsons, 1996); also Jamyang Sakya and Julie Emery, *Princess in the Land of Snows: The Life of Jamyang Sakya in Tibet* (Boston: Shambhala, 1988).

17. Klein, *Great Bliss Queen*, pp. 9–10.

18. Ibid., p. 53.

19. See Hanna Havnevik, *Tibetan Buddhist Nuns* (Oslo: Norwegian University, 1989), or Anna Grimshaw, *Servants of the Buddha* (Cleveland: Pilgrim Press, 1994).

20. Shaw, *Passionate Enlightenment*, p. 82.

21. Ibid., p. 83.

Shaping New Traditions: Unity and Diversity

Karma Lekshe Tsomo

13. Comparing Buddhist and Christian Women's Experiences

The First International Conference on Buddhist Women in Bodhgaya, India, in 1987, was a tremendous stimulus to research on issues that concern Buddhist women and nuns. According to their individual interests, women have increasingly been exchanging information on the history, education, ordination, and present living conditions of women in the various Buddhist traditions: translating texts, writing articles, establishing learning and practice centers, and meeting together to delve into issues of psychology, philosophy, ethics, and family that are of special concern to women. Now, as women discuss these issues in greater depth and seek new directions for future inquiry, it would be very constructive to look at the experiences of spiritually oriented women of other religious traditions and to learn more about women from a comparative standpoint. It is my contention that Christian women have much to learn from the Buddhist tradition with respect to meditation and that Buddhist women have much to learn from Christian women with respect to service to society. From their special vantage point as women, spiritual practitioners of these traditions have much to contribute toward interreligious understanding and world peace.

Discovering Spiritual Common Denominators

Some years ago, when I was studying at the Institute of Buddhist Dialectics in Dharamsala, I was invited to participate in a program of interfaith dialogue. This was the third segment of an ongoing program of exchanges between American Benedictine and Tibetan Buddhist monastics for the purpose of furthering interreligious understanding. In this program Benedictine monks and nuns travel to India and stay for months at a time in Tibetan monasteries, engaging in dialogue with their Buddhist counterparts. In exchange, Tibetan monks and nuns travel to the United States and stay for up to six months in Christian monasteries, engaging in dialogue with their counterparts there. Over the years, participants have developed insight into and a genuine appreciation for each other's views and way of life. The program has continued for over seven years now, with great benefit on both sides.

As the only nun at the Institute of Buddhist Dialectics at the time of the third exchange, I was asked to welcome the nuns. After introductions, the first question asked concerned ordination opportunities for Buddhist women. I was happy to report that the future looked very bright for nuns of the Tibetan tradition, at least, since His Holiness the Dalai Lama had just spoken at our first Sakyadhita conference in Bodhgaya and given his approval for nuns to travel to Taiwan, Hong Kong, or Korea to receive full ordination. When I asked the nuns about their prospects regarding ordination, they sighed and replied that the situation looked quite hopeless under the present pope.[1] I was amazed to discover the extent of our common concerns as we continued our conversation and exchanged views on meditation, India, monasticism in the modern world, women's role in male-dominated religions, the relationship between scholarship and contemplation, and other topics.

No topic was too mundane or too lofty for investigation. I learned, for example, that to avoid the problems entailed in admitting emotionally unbalanced individuals to their monasteries, their order has been giving psychological testing to prospective novices for many years. I also learned that vast differences of interpretation of doctrine exist even among the members of a particular Christian monastic order, depending on their historical knowledge, present experience, openness, and insight. When the monks of the institute gathered to engage the Christians in dialogue, inevitably their first question was: "What is God?" A senior Christian monk's conventional definition from the catechism, "God is the creator of heaven and earth," drew blank expressions from the Tibetan monks, since this is a view they regularly debate and refute. Just then, however, a junior Christian monk skillfully rescued the situation by saying, "That is one definition, but we can also understand God as love and the fullness of life." The Buddhist monks were able to comprehend this concept of God much more readily. The exchange continued in this vein over a period of many days. Monks and nuns on both sides cited striking parallels between the traditions, while not shying away from noting the differences. The

Christians had definitely done their homework—they knew more about Buddhism than many Buddhists. While displaying the sincerity of their own convictions, they were remarkably open-minded and also acutely aware of social issues. When a Tibetan monk asked if the abbots of Christian nunneries were men, his Christian counterpart replied "Never!" to the merriment of all.

With this experience as an introduction into the world of interfaith dialogue, I have continued to meet and discuss issues of mutual interest with Christian nuns and laywomen over the years. In 1990, I traveled to Oklahoma and stayed for four days at Osage Monastery with some of the nuns I had met in Dharamsala. The women of this community practice Zen meditation morning and evening, incorporating spiritual teachings from all the world's major religious traditions. Inspired by Buddhist meditation traditions, they had begun searching for meditation techniques within their own tradition. Pulling out a fourth-century meditation text called the *Philokelia* and dusting it off, they found a breathing meditation technique very similar to the Buddhist practice of *satipaṭṭhāna*. Thus, their genuine appreciation for other paths was helping them discover the essence of their own tradition. In the company of these openhearted contemplatives, I had the good fortune to explore common elements in Buddhist and Christian women's experiences.

There are a number of interesting angles from which to observe and compare these experiences. One approach is to investigate women's role in the two traditions from an historical point of view, discussing renowned female religious practitioners and their contributions to their respective traditions, bringing it up to date by citing examples of contemporary paradigms. Another approach is to document the development of feminist awareness in recent years in the two traditions, comparing the challenges confronted by each and the changes that have been inspired by increased awareness of women's issues. Yet another approach is to discuss the philosophical assumptions underlying each tradition and their implications for women's spiritual development. The purpose of the present study is to open the discussion by pointing out certain common models, problems, and potential solutions. A greater understanding of women in variant religious traditions will help strengthen women as they encounter daunting social changes.

Empty Promises: Rhetoric versus Reality

Overall, women's movements around the world have been more concerned with secular issues—legal, economic, and political equality—than with the spiritual dimensions of women's experience. Nevertheless, secular issues are integrally linked with the patriarchal nature of the world's major religions and the influence these religions have had upon women and their personal development. Frequently in the course of history, as is well known, women have been unable to articulate their spirituality without risk of ridicule or worse, as in the witch hunts of the Middle Ages. Since women's spiritual potential and religious experience have largely been ignored or devalued by organized religions, they have often been pushed to the fringes or out of mainstream religious traditions. Consequently, we find women active in heterodox offshoots of established religious traditions and in spiritualist movements, nature worship, exorcism, witchcraft, and theosophy. It is easy to understand why women, feeling marginalized and bereft of a meaningful place within established traditions, have consciously and creatively sought alternatives or developed their own. This approach is fraught with difficulties, however, because contravening social expectations and going against the religious grain have made women vulnerable to criticism, denigration, and persecution.

Even a superficial study of the histories of Buddhism and Christianity reveals that, although women have emerged as saints and visionaries in their religious traditions, their part in the institutions and power structures of these traditions has been extremely limited. Both Buddhist and Christian institutions are characterized by highly visible male clerics who maintain control of administrative, scholarly, and formal religious functions, while women generally serve in supportive roles. Even though women are generally more numerous and more committed in ordinary religious activities, in both traditions they have historically occupied subordinate posts. The question of whether women have consciously rejected administrative roles and positions of prominence in favor of service and contemplation or whether they have been neglected, excluded, or oppressed by religious institutions has been discussed in both formal and informal forums. Many people feel that women have not had a choice in the matter, and have generally been denied access to the upper echelons of religious hierarchies irrespective of qualifications. In many cases, the problem for Buddhist women is quite fundamental: they have not had access to the religious education that would qualify them to hold such positions. This cannot explain the situation of Christian women, however, who may be as well educated or, as in the case of the Catholic orders, better educated than the men.

Monastic life is perhaps the most obvious common ground for comparing Buddhist and Christian women's experiences.[2] Nuns in both faiths formally take lifelong vows of celibacy and consciously reject household life to concentrate on religious practice, even though marriage is ordinarily the socially acceptable role for women in both Asia and the West. Until recently marriage, childbearing, parenting, and domestic labor have been the primary activities that defined women's lives. In both East and West, monastic life has been one of the few socially acceptable alternatives to these intrinsically gendered expectations. In societies with few other career opportunities for women, the monastic option, at once confining and freeing, has provided opportunities for learning, spiritual enrichment, and independent personal development. Although cloisters and nunneries have occasionally been shelters for castaways and orphans, women of contemplative inclination have found in them the opportunity to concentrate on inner transformation with companions similarly intent on spiritual practice. Contemplative life often symbolized freedom from the sexual and psychological domination of men, obligatory reproduction, and domestic chores. Only in the present century has remaining single become an acceptable option for women in some societies, opening up many possibilities, including a life of intensive spiritual practice outside the monastic environment.

Scriptural portrayals of women in Buddhism and Christianity are mixed; the texts contain some very positive images and also some very unflattering ones. Although we find stories of spiritually accomplished women, they are far fewer in number than the stories of men. This can be at least partially explained by the fact that both textual traditions have been compiled and edited almost exclusively by men. Hence, there is a distinct possibility that gender bias and misogyny have slipped into the scriptures over the years at the hands of male scribes. Regardless, these scriptures are presented as the revealed word of God or the authentic speech of the Buddha. When gender bias is given scriptural authentication and scriptures are regarded as beyond question, women are left helpless to negotiate their status within the tradition. Over millennia, then, women have learned that remaining pious and silent is the safest mode of spiritual expression.

The religious lives of women—Buddhist and Christian—are fraught with contradictions: they may serve the Church or temple as volunteers—unpaid—for as long as they like, and contribute materially as much as they like, yet they are barred from the more visible, audible, and highly rewarded positions of responsibility. From a feminist standpoint, whether or not the traditional religions are salvageable is still an open question. Let us take a closer look at these two traditions through women's eyes and attempt to draw some comparisons between them.

Buddhist Women's Journey

In both early and later traditions, Buddhism's position on gender issues, as recorded in the texts, is quite ambivalent. On the one hand, we find the Buddha's affirmation of women's capacity to attain the highest goal of liberation (*nibbāna*) and ample evidence that the goal was accomplished by thousands in his lifetime. On the other hand, we find numerous derogatory references to women's supposed limitations. The most damning evidence of gender discrimination found in the texts is the Buddha's alleged hesitation to admit women to the Order and his formulation of the eight special rules (*gurudharmas*) stipulating the subordination of the nuns (*bhikṣuṇīs*) to the monks (*bhikṣus*).

According to scholars, the authenticity of this account is highly dubious and it is indeed difficult to accept the theory that the Buddha, a spiritually realized person, could hold such a jaundiced view of half the human race. The traditional explanation, among those who assume the account to be authentic, is that the Buddha was making allowances for the (sexist) configuration of prevailing social conventions, and formulated these rules to shield the newly founded order of women renunciants from public condemnation. In this view, allowing women to wander unprotected through the forests and towns, vulnerable to abuse and assault, was a revolutionary act. Still, the Buddha's hesitation to ordain women rests uneasily in the contemporary mind. Could the Enlightened One have been so concerned about public opinion and so lacking in the courage of his convictions?

The conjecture that the Buddha formulated the *gurudharmas* to provide physical protection for the *bhikṣuṇīs* does not withstand the test of logical analysis. How does bowing to junior monks afford one protection? In actual fact, only one of the eight *gurudharmas* can possibly be construed as protective—the one that requires nuns to do the rainy season retreat in a place where there is a monk. The other seven *gurudharmas* seem to serve no other purpose than ensuring that women will rank second in the monastic hierarchy. Considering these logical inconsistencies, along with linguistic evidence indicating that these passages were written considerably later than the texts in which they are found, it is not difficult to see why scholars question the legitimacy of those scriptural excerpts that are most damaging to women.

From earliest Buddhist times, women, though assured of equal opportunity on the theoretical level, have labored under unequal conditions in their pursuit of liberation. Alms have rarely been allocated equally to nuns and to monks; ordinarily, the merit accumulated by offering to nuns is assessed as less than offering to monks. Scholars even surmise that the Bhikṣuṇī Saṅgha in Sri Lanka died out due to the starvation of the nuns. Alms were scarce in times of famine and the nuns were last in line. Even now in Taiwan, where conditions for Buddhist women are probably the best they have ever been, monks are given priority over nuns in all respects. The ideal image of a renunciant is still masculine in gender and passages from the scriptures that are disdainful of women are quoted even today.

The major critiques of Buddhism's position on women have come from Western women who have unflinchingly drawn attention to instances of gender bias found in the scriptures.[3] Sexist passages in the texts have been highlighted in their evaluations and often seem to overshadow the many positive references to women in Buddhist literature. Derogatory references to women in the texts have surely affected both attitudes toward women and traditional interpretations of Buddhist doctrine overall. It is not only the texts that are problematic, however. If charges of gender discrimination were based simply upon demeaning literary references, these passages might be discounted as remnants of a bygone era or interpolations of male scribes. Unfortunately, however, women encounter discrimination within Buddhist societies even today in the modern world. Despite assurances of equal opportunity in the practice of Buddhism, women confront continual hindrances in the pursuit of their spiritual birthright.

The serious discrepancy between theoretical gender equality and de facto bias demands explanation. When the texts themselves assert women's equal capacity for the attainment of enlightenment, how can the injustices suffered by Buddhist women be excused? This paradox reflects a serious, traditionally unacknowledged flaw in the interpretation and implementation of the Buddha's teachings. Since sexual discrimination had no place in the teachings of Śākyamuni Buddha, it has no place in Buddhist societies.

Were we to ignore the discriminatory passages in the texts and allow women equal opportunities for ordination, study, and practice, what would be the result? Why is there so much resistance in some quarters to the equitable inclusion of women in the tradition? Perhaps (as is whispered) there are fears in some quarters that nuns would become so numerous as to encroach upon the financial support of the monks or so well respected as to threaten the undisputed power and prestige of the monks. The high standards of women's meditation practice and moral discipline may bring embarrassment to monks whose practice has become lax. Perhaps women will become so respected that the public will prefer them as teachers. These fears may justified. Even so, there are also many benefits that may result from recognizing the equality of women, including greater support for the

Saṅgha that would naturally accrue to the monks. Women can help revitalize the tradition through conscientious practice in ways that will rekindle piety, contribute to a general resurgence of Buddhist scholarship, and help educate a new generation of Buddhist followers who will broaden the base of spiritual and material support. Giving women an equal chance and wholeheartedly encouraging them in the study of the teachings and the practice of meditation, can have many beneficial consequences. A population rich in spiritually nourished women capable to counsel families, mediate disputes, create safe communities, set public policies, and help restructure splintered societies through implementing Buddhist values of tolerance and compassion can make a powerful contribution to a healthy future for our endangered planet.

Christian Women Awake

Despite many positive models in scripture and in history, women in the Christian tradition have also had to deal with discrimination, in the texts and in everyday life. Women dismayed by this situation have responded in different ways. Feeling that the church is oblivious to their needs, many Christian feminists have left their churches in recent years. Others bear their frustration and alienation in silence. Still others, critical of the patriarchal model of religious authority, attempt to achieve equality by struggling to transform the church from within.[4]

Because the commitment of Christian women to their churches has traditionally been strong, the process of feminist awakening has often been uncomfortable: it unmasks certain deficiencies in the church. With the dawning of feminist awareness, women have become discouraged with cooking, cleaning, serving, and raising money for a church that does not serve their interests. Catholic women frequently express the pain they feel when they discover that the church, the thing they love best, has rejected them. Yet those who turn away from the patriarchal church often feel a wrenching sense of loss and may be unable to find anything to replace the spiritual void in their lives.

Some Christian women feel that the problem is not simply a matter of outdated patriarchal administrative structures, but a deeper philosophical problem related to the male symbology of the Christian religious ideal. Not only is the visible church leadership predominantly male, but God is identified as a male and so is his son Jesus, the savior of "mankind." This raises a legitimate question: If humanity is created in the image of God and God is a male, what is the place of women? On the other hand, if God is beyond gender, indeed beyond conceptualization, why the masculine imagery? It is argued that a parental metaphor for God as creator could as easily be mother as father, yet the language of God has, until recently, been exclusively male. Why did traditional doctrine not simply use the word "Creator" and allow the worshipper her own vision of the Almighty?

Questions such as these are leading to a reevaluation of traditional assumptions. Despite an increased awareness of women's issues in society, many traditional church leaders feel uncomfortable with the changing gender climate because it demands changes in their patriarchal behavior and the way they administer their parishes. While these leaders value women's participation in church functions, many feel threatened by the mandate to transform the structure of traditional institutions to include women on equal terms. Only recently have some begun to address the imbalance between women and men in the church and the lack of leadership opportunities for women there. In certain parishes, church leaders are beginning to value women's religious experience and to redress a long tradition of patriarchy. Changing attitudes are partially a reflection of changing social circumstances. Since half of the women in the United States are employed, they no longer have as much time to devote to volunteer church work. Religious activities still afford women a valuable social outlet but, for the church to remain a priority in their hearts into the next century, it must become more responsive to their spiritual needs and relevant to their modern lives.

There are, especially within the Roman Catholic tradition, a number of gentle and heroic female saints to serve as powerful role models for women, including the saintly and inspiring figure of Mary, the mother of Jesus, revered by many as "the mother of God." Despite these examples, sensitive women with a knowledge of the texts find it difficult to come to terms with derogatory allusions to women. Some of these women solve the problem by dismissing it altogether, claiming that it is irrelevant to the spiritual goal. Others, however, find it impossible to dismiss the disdain for women evident in some passages in the scriptures, a problem more serious than gender-exclusive language.

Christian women have formulated some creative responses to negative images of women found in the texts. One such response is a reinterpretation of early church history that brings to light the highly visible role that women played in the tradition's formative years, a significant role that has largely been ignored. Another approach has been active engagement in solving the problems of the world, emulating the concern of Jesus for the downtrodden. Some women, denied the opportunity for ordination within the Roman Catholic fold, have taken ordination in the more liberal Anglican or Protestant denominations. Others, feeling a call to the priesthood, have chosen to celebrate the sacraments in nontraditional settings, serving in the role of priest without formal recognition and despite official opposition.

Among the Christian women most active in education and social service have been the sisters of the Roman Catholic orders. Especially after World War II, sisters gradually moved beyond the cloister. Increasing opportunities for higher education brought heightened awareness of social injustices and active involvement in the women's movement. In the early 1960s, for example, twenty thousand American sisters volunteered to work among the poor in South America in "service to God through service to others," constituting a vanguard in the movement that has come to be known as "liberation theology." Working among the poor and oppressed in their own countries and abroad, Catholic sisters have come to understand and to articulate the social injustices experienced by women, including themselves. In just thirty years, as a direct consequence of living the tenets of their faith, Catholic sisters have become outspoken participants in the women's movement and have begun applying feminist analysis to their own situations and community structures.

Naturally, one of the first issues to be confronted was the ordination issue. By 1970 most Protestant denominations had begun to admit women to the ministry and the Anglican bishops followed suit soon thereafter, but the Roman Catholic Church continues to bar women from the priesthood even today. Forbidding women to administer the Eucharist prevents women from celebrating the most ancient sacrament of the Christian Church without the assistance of men, and hence forces them into a position of gender-related spiritual dependency. In legislating women's dependency upon men in a crucial religious act, this prohibition parallels the requirement of dual ordination for Buddhist nuns. As an unequivocal expression of sexism, this prohibition has served to rally Catholic women to the feminist persuasion and compelled them to gather their collective strength. Although the problem of ordination for women appears unresolvable at present, at least under the current Vatican leadership, ironically the ordination issue has served a significant function in forcing women to recognize their subordinate position. Moreover, the controlling position of men within the religious hierarchy has led many women to question not only the dominance of men, but the value of hierarchy altogether, and has inspired them to advocate sweeping structural changes within the church.

Reassessing Women's Religious Histories

With rare exceptions, the contributions of women have generally been ignored in traditional religions, and Buddhism and Christianity are no exception. Women have not been credited with playing a major part in the founding and shaping of these religions, yet the texts that record their histories have been penned almost exclusively by men. Often unacknowledged, women have played an indispensable role in defining and upholding standards of ethics, and in transmitting them to future generations. Observing the numbers of women actively engaged in religious practice today, we become aware that women must have played similarly major roles in centuries past. It therefore becomes essential that religious history be carefully reread to determine the valuable roles women have played. Women's strengths have been in ensuring domestic harmony, inculcating religious values in the home, and shaping the character of future generations, but Christian women such as St. Teresa of Avila, St. Catherine of Sienna, and St. Elizabeth Seton, have also played valuable political and administrative roles.

To their credit, except for certain specialized rituals, Buddhism and Christianity allow women the freedom to participate equally in the religious practices of their respective traditions. Women have not been excluded from religious rites as they have been in later Vedic tradition in India or excluded from places of worship as in certain Muslim countries, nor have Buddhist and Christian societies given women an inferior status under the law. Religious practices for women do not differ in character from practices for men and the highest stage of religious attainment (rebirth in heaven for Christians and enlightenment for Buddhists) is the same for both genders. In each, women are and always have been highly visible and enthusiastic in their religious devotion, even attaining the highest levels of saintliness.

Women in the two traditions have been given opportunities, if limited, to learn the tenets of their faith, but have generally been absent from positions of religious leadership and power. Since time immemorial, there have been women who have recognized that they are capable of receiving spiritual nourishment without dependence on men, yet religious structures, education, ritual, and ordination have all been dominated by men. Although women have had access to the popular, pedestrian aspects of their traditions, rarely have they gained admission to the higher echelons of scholarship and authority. Preferential access to education has always been given to men. As a result, the great teachers in both traditions have typically been male, whereas women's public religious role has been largely suppressed. Buddhist and Christian women, both lay and monastic, are alike in that the outward forms of their religious lives have been directed by men, while inwardly they attend to their own spiritual needs. Only recently have certain segments of these populations begun to question male authority and become more independent in articulating the landscape of their spiritual paths.

The Buddhist and Christian traditions are alike in that strong cases may be made for both the presence and the absence of positive female role models, depending upon one's point of view and denominational affiliation. In both, women have frequently been blamed for the lust of men and have been expected to observe higher standards of moral conduct than men. Unlike many other religious traditions, Buddhism and Christianity offer women both lay and monastic models for spiritual practice. Both have produced female exemplars of human character development; both offer women models for intensive contemplation and for effectively integrating spiritual practice into daily life. Both traditions give women explanations for their sufferings and methods for coping with them; both have also been criticized by feminists as instrumental in teaching women to tolerate oppression rather than to struggle against it. Both have been faulted for perpetuating gender stereotypes and for creating an imbalance of power between women and men. In all of these respects, we may conclude that there is a remarkable commonality in the experiences of Buddhist and Christian women.

Another similarity within both traditions is the wide range of attitudes, from conservative to radical, that exist toward women's issues. The feminist movement, a comparatively recent social development, has had an impact primarily upon the better-educated segments of the population. A sizeable number of women in both traditions feels that religious practice is a matter of inner experience rather than a matter of power, position, or gender, and have therefore either avoided looking at or decided to ignore the inequalities they themselves experience. These women form the bedrock of both traditions, sincerely maintaining pure moral principles, quietly pursuing the contemplative life, and actively putting compassion into practice. The women who genuinely embody religious ideals, and unobtrusively integrate the teachings into their daily lives, are role models that deserve our wholehearted support and admiration. Although they may not play an active political role in improving the status of women, they demonstrate women's capacity to realize their spiritual potential, by conscientiously striving for spiritual fulfillment within their respective traditions. At the other end of the spectrum are the women who find sexism within the tradition intolerable and hypocritical and thus deny the usefulness of the tradition for women altogether; these women seek spiritual fulfillment elsewhere. However, the majority of women still find meaning in the ancient scriptures and spiritual practices. Not surprisingly, the mainstream leadership within both Buddhism and Christianity has generally promoted a conservative response among women, thus discouraging the development of feminist awareness and maintaining the status quo as befits a privileged elite.

The Buddhist and Christian paths rest on very similar ethical foundations, enjoining their followers to observe ten major moral principles (the ten virtuous actions of the Buddhist tradition and the ten commandments of the Christian tradition) and to live with loving kindness and compassion toward other living beings. Both traditions stress almsgiving, inner peace, personal honesty, and purity of mind. Both have strong contemplative traditions and emphasize the power of prayer, or positive aspirations. There are even similarities in some ritual practices, making prostrations, offering candles, and so on. While there are some women, within both the Buddhist and Christian traditions, who have rejected organized religion altogether and have chosen to create their own religious symbols, liturgies, and communities, the majority still find meaning in the ancient scriptures and spiritual practices.

As similar as Buddhist and Christian women's experiences are, there are also differences. For example, Christians commonly believe that a male intermediary is necessary to communicate with God, such as a priest interceding to request forgiveness of Jesus for effecting salvation, whereas no such intermediary exists for Buddhists. For most Christians spirituality is a "relationship with divinity," but for Buddhists it is the individual's quest for human perfection and enlightenment. Women in Christianity have been barred from ordination, but women in Buddhism have had access to full ordination since earliest times and still do today in China, Korea, and Vietnam. Thousands of women in these countries are ordained as *bhikṣuṇīs* and perform all the functions that *bhikṣus* do, although this does not translate to equal ecclesiastical power.

In terms of effecting change within the tradition, however, Christian women have been far more active than Buddhists. Christian women have been discovering and revealing the structural flaws in patriarchal religious institutions for years, aware that these structures both reflect and reinforce women's unequal status in society, while women in the Buddhist tradition are only just beginning to become aware of the inequalities they suffer. While many Christian women have become estranged from their churches due to their awareness of these problems, only a small number of Buddhists have rejected Buddhism on the basis of sexist discrimination. While Christian feminists have been dissenters standing squarely within the tradition, most Buddhist feminists are Westerners new to Buddhism who, for reasons of ethnicity and geography, stand outside the mainstream of the tradition.

In recent decades Christian women, including nuns, have gained renown in socially constructive roles as nurses, doctors, teachers, administrators, and social activists, but ordinarily neither the Buddhist nor the Christian establishment has cast women in the public role of specialist in ritual. For hundreds of years women in both traditions have served as spiritual mentors for others and yet have failed to achieve positions of highest religious authority. In spite of strong egalitarian ideals in Western minds, women in positions of religious leadership are rare in both Asia and the West. In neither environment have women achieved parity with men or gained recognition as leaders in the religious sphere.

Some argue that the oppression of women has philosophical roots: that it is directly linked to the identification of God, or the human ideal, as male, and, that as long as the ultimate is represented in male form, women will be defined as secondary. This critique deserves serious consideration from both philosophical and psychological points of view. Establishing a paradigm of male superiority at the ultimate level justifies male domination on the mundane level.

The philosophical concept of human equality has important ramifications for women. The concept prevalent in Judeo-Christian societies, that each being has an equal right to life and self-determination, has no precise equivalent within the Buddhist teachings. There are two reasons why the claim that "God created all men [sic] equal," possibly stemming from the biblical tenet that "All are equal in the sight of God," has no exact counterpart in Buddhist thought, first, because there is no creator god, and second, because each being takes birth in accordance with karma, the law of cause and effect.

The theory of karma is equivalent to the biblical tenet, "As ye sow, so shall ye reap," carried over many lifetimes. One's present experience is the result of one's past action and one's future will be the result of one's present deeds. The law of karma entails individual responsibility and intention, extending beyond the simply mechanical to the psychological sphere.

A deterministic interpretation of karma is particularly harmful for women, given their subordinate status; it is a common belief that women face more hardships as a result of their negative karma. A fatalistic interpretation of karma is not only dangerous for women, but may also be used to justify other social inequalities and discriminations based on race, caste, and social class. From a Buddhist point of view, the Christian concept of equality fails to account for the differences in human beings' circumstances; children born in poverty simply do not have the same chances of success as children born to affluent parents.

In Buddhism there is a parallel to the Christian concept of equality, and that is the notion that human beings have equal potential to achieve liberation from suffering, as did the Buddha, the exemplar of human perfection. The Mahāyāna tradition in general asserts that Buddhahood is attainable by all sentient beings, human and nonhuman, since each possesses Buddha nature, or the seed of enlightenment, within. Among the multitude of different Buddhist traditions, some claim that beings are enlightened already, but do not realize it, and that the task of spiritual practice is simply to realize one's already perfectly enlightened nature. Pure Land Buddhists believe that beings with faith in Amitabha Buddha are all equally capable of salvation. All of these claims pertain to spiritual equality—the theoretically equal potential of both women and men for liberation and enlightenment—but do not necessarily imply social equality in the everyday world. These claims are similar to Christian claims of equality in the sight of God that do not necessarily translate to social parity.

Despite the many parallels that may be drawn between Buddhist and Christian women's experiences, it must be recognized that women around the world are affected by radically different philosophical, social, and cultural perspectives from childhood on, including perspectives on gender. For instance, although Christian parents may have a preference for either a boy or a girl, once born, the child is presumed to have roughly equal opportunities in the world. By contrast, in Buddhist societies, a girl child is generally presumed to have taken an inferior rebirth on the basis of deficient merit. In such cultures a girl is socialized to expect and to accept more hardships in life. She may be given less and inferior food, made to work harder than her male siblings, and kept at home to work rather than being sent to school like they are. At a young age, she may even be told that she is useless, since she will be married into another family, or troublesome because she is vulnerable to pregnancy. When society's evaluation of the female gender is so biased and deprecating, it is not surprising to find parents selling their daughters into prostitution and marrying them off to the highest bidder. What is surprising is the glaring contrast between the perpetuation of gender bias and the Buddhist ideals of compassion and enlightenment for all.

One of the most significant differences between Buddhist and Christian women's experiences concerns educational opportunities. These days, as secular education is becoming more universally available, countries that are predominately Christian usually provide men and women with equal opportunities for religious education. Such education is accessible through parochial schools, Sunday schools, seminaries, universities, public library resources, grants, and scholarships. By contrast, in many parts of the Buddhist world, women have few opportunities to master the tenets of their faith and must struggle to gain even a rudimentary understanding. Without opportunities for comprehensive religious training, Buddhist women are largely confined to supportive roles in the sphere of religion. The lack of religious education, in addition to the lack of adequate secular education, explains the shortage of Buddhist women teachers today. The education gap that currently exists between Buddhist women and men makes parity in other areas of endeavor impossible.

The conventions of culture and tradition tend to support a status quo that men dominate, at least publicly. Women have been a powerful force in the creation of culture, but the amorphous entity "tradition" has also frequently been the matrix within which women are silenced and oppressed. For example, we are told that there are no fully ordained nuns in Sri Lanka (or Burma or Thailand) because, "There is no tradition of *bhikṣuṇīs* in Theravāda." We are told that women do not speak out against domestic violence because, "It is the tradition in our culture for women to be humble." Without employing logical reasoning or historical analysis, tradition can be invoked to justify the oppression of women.

It may be argued that religion has not been particularly oppressive to women, but has only reflected the gender bias of society as a whole. If this is the case, if follows that a general improvement in women's status in society will lead to improved status and opportunities for women in religion. As in other fields, the tendency to devaluate women's spiritual potential can be reversed through consciously validating women's accomplishments. Whether the negative portrayals of women in religious texts reflect gender biases that already existed in the society or are intrinsic to the traditions, they are nevertheless self-perpetuating and detrimental to women's spiritual growth. Before repudiating traditional religions as a whole, these texts need to be reread and reinterpreted with a new awareness of women's possibilities.

The present era of rapid social change presents women today with new risks as well as new opportunities. If, attracted by the glitter of modern culture, women abandon spiritual values and devote their energy entirely to worldly pursuits, it will be a great loss for humanity. If, instead, women use their new-found freedom for spiritual growth, their power to triumph over the stresses of modern living and effect positive changes in society is unlimited.

One constructive result of a conscious spiritual orientation among women will be an expanded role in the sphere of organized religion for women of all traditions. As little as ten years ago in the Tibetan tradition, for example, it would have been as foreign to imagine a woman as a Buddhist scholar as to picture a man as a mother. In the space of only ten years, education for women has advanced so quickly that the notion of higher Buddhist studies for women is now becoming commonplace. For centuries men have dominated the field of philosophy, but Tibetan Buddhists now take for granted that ten years from now, there will be women scholars of equal competence. Once equivalent facilities are available and women exert themselves conscientiously, only delusions of incapability can prevent women from achieving the heights of spiritual attainment.

The single most striking evidence of inequality in a male-dominated tradition is its refusal to ordain women. In an era that values freedom of speech and freedom of religion, how can it be possible that women are denied their religious rights? The implication that women are intellectually or spiritually inferior to men has no place in either Buddhism or Christianity. The fact that there are forces within these traditions that would silence the legitimate aspirations of women to receive higher ordination reveals that traditional institutions are not yet confronting realistically certain anachronistic elements that are preventing these religious traditions from becoming a real force for the liberation of humanity.

Drawing from Spiritual Springs

This study presents only a brief comparison of women's unique experiences in the Buddhist and Christian traditions. The sphere of monastic life, where the parallels between Buddhist and Christian women become most evident, deserves a separate study. Although this presentation is inadequate both in detail and depth, I have attempted to give an overview of the experiences and aspirations common to women in these two respected religious traditions and to point out certain divergences in terms of philosophical foundations, institutional structures, ordination opportunities, and the growth of feminist awareness. While pointing out the common problems Buddhist and Christian women face, I have tried to emphasize the opportunities they enjoy for sustained spiritual growth within their respective cultural heritages, rather than dwelling on the obstacles they have encountered. What becomes clear is that Buddhist and Christian women draw from analogous spiritual springs, experience similar problems related to gender bias within their respective traditions, and would have greater power to effect positive changes in the world if they were to achieve equal opportunity. It is not necessary to accept all aspects of a tradition in order to benefit from it, nor is it necessary to reject a tradition in its entirety because of particular unacceptable aspects. Rather than relinquish their religious convictions, some women are playing crucial roles in critiquing, reinterpreting, restructuring, and revitalizing these traditions.

Buddhist and Christian women have much to share and much to learn from one another, especially in terms of meditation and social action. The important role women play in community development, though sometimes overlooked, is well documented and will grow as women develop greater confidence in their abilities to move forward. By networking in their local communities, women spiritual practitioners can provide each other with encouragement and support for the spiritual values they share and learn to appreciate their differences. By developing solidarity on an international level, women can effect great benefit in the world through a sharing and mutual infusion of spiritual values directed at personal and social change. By bridging religious differences, women set an example for the people of the world to emulate in overcoming strife and discovering commonalities in the human heritage on the deepest spiritual level.

Notes

1. Daphne Hampson discusses this in, "Women, Ordination and the Christian Church," in *Speaking of Faith: Global Perspectives on Women, Religion and Social Change*, ed. Diana L. Eck and Devaki Jain (Philadelphia: New Society Publishers, 1987).

2. Studies on monastic women include Thubten Chodron, *Spiritual Sisters* (Seattle: Dharma Friendship Foundation, no date); Suzanne Malard, *Religious Orders of Women* (New York: Hawthorne Books, 1964); and Karma Lekshe Tsomo, *Sisters in Solitude: Two Traditions of Monastic Ethics for Women* (Albany: State University of New York Press, 1996).

3. See, for example, Rita Gross, *Buddhism After Patriarchy: A Feminist History, Analysis, and Reconstruction of Buddhism* (Albany: State University of New York Press, 1993); Diana Paul, *Women in Buddhism: Images of the Feminine in Mahāyāna Tradition* (Berkeley, Calif.: Asian Humanities Press, 1979); and Chatsumarn Kabilsingh, *Thai Women in Buddhism* (Berkeley, Calif.: Parallax Press, 1991).

4. Two studies documenting Catholic women's responses to these challenges are Sandra Marie Schneiders, *New Wineskins: Re-Imagining Religious Life Today* (New York: Paulist Press, 1986) and Mary Jo Weaver, *New Catholic Women: A Contemporary Challenge in Traditional Religious Authority* (San Francisco: Harper & Row, 1985).

Theja Gunawardhana

14. Aung San Suu Kyi

A Woman of Conscience in Burma

Aung San Suu Kyi is the Buddhist leader of Burma's National Democratic League.[1] She is also the daughter of Burma's national hero, Aung San, who was assassinated just before Burma gained the independence to which he had dedicated his life.[2] Aung San Suu Kyi is struggling to restore the lost democratic rights of a nation which has been laboring under a military dictatorship for more than thirty years. Her party won the 1990 elections, but the ruling junta refused to concede its power.[3]

On July 20, 1989, Aung San Suu Kyi was placed under house arrest in her family home in Rangoon. On that day, the Burmese government placed eleven truckloads of armed troops in front of her house, who cut her phone lines and blocked her from leaving. For six years, she was detained without due process of law. She was never once permitted to leave her family home—a prisoner of the government of Burma, held in isolation from the outside world. Finally, in February 1994, she was allowed to receive outside visitors for the first time: U.S. Congressman Bill Richardson, a representative of the UN, and a reporter from the *New York Times*. Aside from this first visit and other infrequent visits from members of her immediate family, her only other human contact was visits from her attendant and the military officer who served as her contact with the Burmese government.

The philosophy of the Buddha is particularly relevant to the contemporary scene in Burma. The Buddha was a keen, sensitive observer of the social and political developments that were rapidly transforming the Indian states during his lifetime. He taught the ten duties of kingship (*daśa-rāja-dharma*), which include liberality, morality, self-sacrifice, integrity, loving kindness, austerity, nonanger, and nonviolence. The *Pada Mānaya Kusala Jātaka* (a past-life story of the Buddha) implies the right of citizens to wage a struggle against political rulers who abuse these principles of good government. Aung San Suu Kyi is an ardent student of the Buddhist methodology for solving the problems of violence and cruelty through nonviolence and loving kindness.

In 1988, Aung San Suu Kyi entered the revolt of her people to give leadership to the uprising. An intellectual deeply immersed in the Buddhist *sūtras*, and daughter of the great national hero Aung San, Suu Kyi has all the qualities of a superior being: generosity, truthfulness, patience, compassion, virtue, selflessness, and freedom from anger, hatred, and ill will. She is completely free of the craving for power. The dictatorship tries in vain to break her indomitable spirit.

Suu Kyi, has found her own inner liberation through deep study of her country's Buddhist heritage. Born in Burma, she tended this heritage carefully while living in India, England, Japan, and Bhutan. In spite of the long years outside her homeland, she never lost her Burmese identity or her love for the Burmese people and she never forgot the father she lost when she was only two years old.

The Father

In the book *Freedom from Fear*, compiled by Dr. Michael Aris of Oxford University, Suu Kyi's husband, Aung San Suu Kyi presents a careful and sensitive reconstruction of her father's life.

> Aung San's family had a reputation for intelligence and learning, but while his three brothers started their education early, he refused to go to school "unless mother went too." The strong-minded Daw Su was indulgent with her youngest and allowed him to remain at home until he was nearly eight, when he himself decided that he was ready for school. The decision was prompted by the occasion of an elder brother entering the local monastery for the short period of novitiate customary for all Burmese Buddhist boys. Whether it was the attractions of monastic life or of the white "dancing pony" on which candidates for the novitiate were paraded around the town as part of the ordination ceremonies, Aung San expressed a strong desire to become a novice. His astute mother was quick to seize the opportunity to point out that first he would have to read and write.[4]

Aung San, a brilliant student, was always intensely interested in discovering the means to free his country from foreign rule. At the age of fifteen, he won a scholarship and a prize for standing first in the national examinations. At the National School, he began to take an interest in the speeches of political personalities and to participate in debates. In 1932, he graduated with distinction in Burmese and Pāli and then went to study at Rangoon University, one year after a major uprising had been suppressed and its leaders executed by the British.

As in other occupied Southeast Asian countries, the early nationalist organizations were devoted to the preservation and purification of the Buddhist religion and traditional culture. In Burma, the Young Men's Buddhist Association, founded in 1906, was the first body to respond to British oppression. In 1920, this organization became the General Council of Buddhist Associations, which was the first national alliance in Burma. Burmese nationalism was incited by U Ottama, a learned Buddhist monk who roused the patriotic impulse of the nation with his spirited agitations for the freedom of Burma. It is worth noting here, however, that one of Aung San's lasting convictions was that monks should not participate in politics. He believed that to mix religion with politics was to go against the spirit of religion itself. He appealed to the Saṅgha to purify Buddhism and to "broadcast it to all the world so that all mankind might be able to listen to its timeless message of love and brotherhood till eternity.... This is the highest politics which you can do for your country and people." Aung San maintained a deep and abiding interest in Buddhism, which often found expression in his political life.

In 1935, Aung San's involvement in student politics rapidly accelerated. He participated in many strikes and demonstrations, and gradually rose into the leadership of the revolt against the British. In February 1941, he returned to Burma disguised as a Chinese seaman after negotiating an offer from the Japanese to support the Burmese with arms and money.

In March 1943, Aung San was promoted to the rank of major general and invited to Japan to be decorated by the emperor. On August 1, Burma was declared a sovereign and independent nation. Aung San knew, however, that the Japanese had infiltrated the Burmese government and military, and would eventually have to be thrown out. After many complex and difficult maneuvers, the Burmese troops finally rose up against the Japanese on March 27, 1945. On May 15, Aung San won the support of the re-invading Allies. On June 15, there was a victory parade in Rangoon and the Burmese army marched in victory alongside units representing the British Empire and the Allied forces. Aung San successfully negotiated for final independence with Clement Atlee's Labor government. It was, in the words of Aung San Suu Kyi, "the finest hour of the Burmese nationalists, when ideological differences and personal considerations had been put aside for a common cause."

For two years after this victory, Aung San plunged into efforts to build a nation. Factions reappeared, power struggles abounded, accusations and treachery festered everywhere, but the young leader tirelessly negotiated with the powerful and tried to educate and unify the powerless. Then, tragically, on July 19th, 1947, only six months before the final transfer of power from the British government to the Burmese, he was assassinated along with six other members of the executive council, including his eldest brother, Ba Win. On January 4, 1948, the independent Union of Burma was born.

The Daughter: Destiny Intertwined

Aung San Suu Kyi was born on June 19, 1945. For the first fifteen years of her life, she was schooled in Burma, and then went on to India and Great Britain to continue her education. In 1967 she earned a degree in politics, philosophy, and economics at Oxford. She later learned Japanese and was a visiting scholar at Kyoto University in 1985–86. In 1987, she was a fellow at the Indian Institute of Advanced Studies in New Delhi. At the time of her return to Burma in 1988, she was enrolled in the School of Oriental and African Studies at London University, where she was working for an advanced degree.

Fate, in the guise of her mother who had suffered a severe stroke, brought her back to Burma in March 1988. She left her husband Michael and her two sons at home in Oxford, and flew thousands of miles to be at her mother's side in a Rangoon hospital. After three months it became apparent that her mother was not improving, so Aung San Suu Kyi decided to bring her mother to the family home.

At exactly this same moment in time, Burmese students had begun to take to the streets calling for radical change in the government. Ne Win, the man who had ruled Burma since he led a military coup in 1962, made the shocking announcement that he was resigning. He called for a referendum on Burma's political future. Suu Kyi, like the rest of Burma, was electrified. It was at this significant juncture that she made up her mind to step forward, both blessed and burdened with her unique status as the daughter of the national hero.

Nationwide turbulence followed Ne Win's resignation on July 23, 1988, because of the immediate refusal by his party to agree to a referendum on Burma's future. Suu Kyi's house quickly became the main center of political activity in the country, and every conceivable type of activist poured in to visit her. She addressed a colossal rally at Shwedagon Pagoda on August 26. By the time her mother died on December 27, the mass demonstrations had resulted in bloodshed as the authorities tried to stem the tide of revolt sweeping the country. In response to the violence inflicted on the Burmese people by the military officers, Suu Kyi and her close associates formed the National League for Democracy. Her mother's mass funeral in January 2, 1989, rallied the nation behind her. The newly formed party posed a grave threat to all that the army had come to represent.

During the next seven months Aung San Suu Kyi toured Burma, and consolidated her party's strength. At all times, she insisted that the movement should be based on a nonviolent struggle for human rights. She spoke to the common people of Burma in a way they had not heard for so long—addressing them as individuals worthy of love and respect.

In April 1989, as Suu Kyi was campaigning in a small village, six soldiers under the command of a captain jumped down from a jeep and took aim at her. She sent her followers to the side of the road and approached the soldiers, saying that it was "better to have a single target than bring everyone else in." A major intervened and revoked the order for her assassination.

Suu Kyi had put into practice her belief that those who struggle for democracy must be prepared for any sacrifice. She also believed that since fear (*bhaya*) corrupted the military junta, fearlessness (*abhaya*), the strength of the principle of nonharm (*ahiṃsa*), was the best weapon against it. The six soldiers apparently felt too ashamed to shoot a single defenseless woman.

In the days leading up to Martyr's Day, July 19, 1989, matters came to a head. On this day, when the death of her father and his cabinet is traditionally commemorated, Suu Kyi planned to lead the march and ceremony in Rangoon. During the preparations, she decided to voice the belief, shared by many but never spoken in public, that the army was still being controlled by the retired general Ne Win. She expressed doubt that the ruling junta ever intended to keep their promise of transferring power to a civilian government. On the day of the march, the authorities moved quickly to fill the streets with troops. Faced with the prospect of terrible bloodshed, Suu Kyi called off the march.

Many of Aung San Suu Kyi's supporters were arrested on Martyr's Day. In response to this, she announced a hunger strike, but was arrested the evening before, on July 20, 1989, the day after the forty-second anniversary of her father's assassination. On September 2, her husband and two sons, Alexander and Kim, who had come to Burma to be with her, left for England. Her sons' passports were invalidated and their Burmese citizenship revoked. It was the last time the boys were allowed to see their mother for several years. On the following Christmas, Michael Aris described the last time he saw his wife:

> The days I spent alone with her that last time, completely isolated from the world, are among my happiest memories of our many years of marriage. It was wonderfully peaceful. Suu had established a strict regime of exercise, study, and piano which I managed to disrupt. She was memorizing a number of Buddhist *sutras*.[5]

Until very recently, Suu Kyi was confined to her home, continuing to study the *sūtras*. Her house arrest extended until 1995, a violation of international law. During this time, in repeated written appeals, she invited her persecutors to enter into a dialogue with her, but to no avail. There is great power in her writings, which grow in compassion and clarity. Suu Kyi's oppressors offered her freedom to leave Burma on the condition that she never return. On principle, out of compassion (*karuṇa*) for her people, she has chosen to remain in her homeland as a prisoner. In doing so, she is practicing the highest expression of the perfection of giving (*dāna pāramitā*), the gift of life itself.

To commemorate the European Parliament's awarding her the 1990 Sakharov Prize for Freedom of Thought, Aung San Suu Kyi wrote:

> It is not power that corrupts, but fear. Fear of losing power corrupts those who wield it, and fear of the scourge of power corrupts those who are subject to it. Most Burmese are familiar with the four *a-gati*, the four kinds of corruption. *Chanda-a-gati*, corruption induced by desire, is deviation from the right path in pursuit of bribes or for the sake of those one loves. *Dosa-gati* is taking the wrong path to spite those against whom one bears ill-will, and *moha-gati* is aberration due to ignorance. But perhaps the worst of the four is *bhaya-gati*, for not only does *bhaya*, fear, stifle and slowly destroy all sense of right and wrong, it so often lies at the root of the other three kinds of corruption.

Suu Kyi took the struggle in Burma to a higher dimension when she wrote,

> The quintessential revolution is that of *the spirit*, born of an intellectual conviction of the need for change in mental attitudes and values, which shape the course of a nation's development. . . . Without a revolution of the spirit, other forces that produced the iniquities of the old order, would continue to be operative, posing a constant threat to the process of reform and regeneration.

She stresses what the Buddha taught—the inner revolution first.

Suu Kyi bears no hatred toward her oppressors. Her *ahiṃsa* is based on her observance of the first of the five precepts, which recognizes the sacredness of life, and hence, the unity of all sentient beings. Nonviolence, *ahiṃsa*, and *karuṇa* are three names for the same principle, and there are limitless ways of applying it. Her meticulous application of this principle has resulted in the gathering of many forces outside of Burma in support of her struggle. Hopefully, the world will take a closer look at her work and her suffering. Suu Kyi's Dhamma practice gives her the inner strength to work for her country's freedom in a true "revolution of the spirit."

Editor's Note: Despite Aung San Suu Kyi's release from house arrest in 1995, little has changed since that time for the people of Burma under State Law and Order Restoration Council (SLORC) rule: Bravely standing up to the miliary junta, Suu Kyi and her colleagues convened a National League for Democracy (NLD) convention to begin drafting an alternative national constitution, leading to the arrest of two hundred seventy-three NLD officials.[6] Blatant attempts to silence prodemocracy forces have included threats of annihilation and the arrest and disappearance of many NLD supporters. Despite some economic liberalization, elected NLD representatives are prevented from playing any meaningful role in the government. Visitors and news reportage both to and from Burma is still severely restricted, and the people are prevented from peacefully exercising their basic human rights. Appeals for reconciliation have come from many quarters, but SLORC refuses all attempts at dialogue and shows no sign of relinquishing its dictatorial powers.

Suu Kyi continues to live a life of monastic simplicity at her family home in Rangoon. She maintains a disciplined daily meditation practice, as during her years of house arrest,[7] and frequently mentions Buddhist principles in conversations with colleagues and interviewers. Convinced that "armed struggle would only perpetuate the cycle of violence,"[8] she envisions a nonviolent mode of politics infused with spiritual values. She has said that her highest ambition is purity of mind.

Notes

1. See Kanbawza Win, *Daw Aung San Suu Kyi, the Nobel Laureate: A Burmese Perspective* (Bangkok: CPDSK Publications, 1992).

2. Aung San Suu Kyi tells the story of her father in *Aung San of Burma* (Edinburgh: Kiscadale, 1991). Her other publications include *Aung San* (St. Lucia: University of Queensland, 1984), *Burma and India: Some Aspects of Intellectual Life under Colonialism* (New Delhi: Indian Institute of Advanced Study, Shimla, in association with Allied Publishers, 1990), *Freedom from Fear* (London: Viking, 1991), and *The Voice of Hope* (New York: Seven Stories Press, 1997). The story of her father's assassination is told in Kin Oung's *Who Killed Aung San?* (Bangkok: White Lotus, 1993) and Josef Silverstein, *The Political Legacy of Aung San* (Ithaca, N.Y.: Cornell University, Southeast Asian Program, 1972).

3. See Alan Clements, *Burma: The Next Killing Fields?* (Berkeley, Calif.: Odonian Press, 1992).

4. *Freedom from Fear*, p. 4.

5. Ibid., p. xxiii.

6. Barbara Victor, *Aung San Suu Kyi: Nobel Laureate and Burma's Prisoner* (Boston: Faber & Faber, 1998), p. 187.

7. Aung San Suu Kyi, *Letters from Burma* (London: Penguin Books, 1997), p. 160.

8. Aung San Suu Kyi, *The Voice of Hope: Conversations with Alan Clements* (New York: Seven Stories Press, 1997), p. 26.

Dharmacharini Sanghadevi

15. A Model for Laywomen in Buddhism

The Western Buddhist Order

It is still very early in the introduction and establishment of Buddhism in Western societies. The seven different socioreligious classes of persons comprising the Buddhist community—monks (*bhikṣus*), nuns (*bhikṣuṇīs*), female probationers (*śikṣamānās*), male novices (*śrāmaṇeras*), female novices (*śrāmaṇerikās*), male lay devotees (*upāsakas*), and female lay devotees (*upāsikās*)—do not yet exist. Even the word "Buddhism" is an imprecise term of Western coinage covering a range of meanings, including the teachings on the path to enlightenment, the institutions of Buddhism as an organized religion, and the cultures in which Buddhism is historically imbedded.

The structures and institutions of Buddhism should, strictly speaking, grow out of the needs of the growing body of individuals who are beginning to practice the teachings, rather than the other way around. It follows, then, that the term "laywomen" cannot be applied to women practicing Dharma in Western countries, because we cannot assume at this stage that it is necessarily desirable to have the seven socioreligious classes of persons in the West. Although some Western women *do* think of themselves as laywomen, they may have been influenced by Asian male teachers who are, or have been, *bhikṣus*. They do not fit the role that has come to be expected of their Dharma sisters in the East.

When we explore the role of laywomen in Buddhism as it has developed in Asia since the time of the Buddha we find that, broadly speaking, laywomen have tended to play a supportive rather than leading role in the development of Buddhism as an organized religion. Their main contribution has been giving material sustenance of various kinds to the *bhikṣus*. Where *bhikṣuṇīs* have existed, they have also benefitted from this kind of support, although it seems that over time they received less material support than the *bhikṣus*.

Over the course of centuries, at least in some parts of the Buddhist Asia, the spiritual life became increasingly identified with the life of the *bhikṣu*, particularly in countries where Theravāda Buddhism is practiced. In the Theravādin countries, such as Burma, Cambodia, Sri Lanka, and Thailand, where the *bhikṣuṇī* ordination either died out or never became established, the spiritual aspirations of laywomen became increasingly centered on earning merit to gain a good rebirth. At the time of the Buddha, however, this was not the only role that laywomen played. Laywomen also reflected and meditated on the Dharma as taught by the Buddha, and many attained to "stream entry" (*sotāpanna*, the first level of transcendental experience) and beyond.[1] Being active in their own right as "farers of the way," they were keen to help spread the Dharma and to share what they had learned from the Buddha or his disciples with others within their own sphere of influence.

In those countries where the Mahāyāna form of Buddhism is practiced and the division between monastic and lay is less distinct, a number of married individuals have been great teachers. Although the majority of these teachers were men, there were also a number of well-known *yoginīs* who became important teachers in their own right. For example, in Tibet we have the records of Niguma, Machik Labdron, and Yeshe Tsogyal. There are also women teachers who lived a celibate life, but were not nuns in the technical sense.

The survival and spread of the Buddhadharma in the modern world depends on spiritually vital practitioners who go for refuge to the Three Jewels, as was the case at the time of the Buddha. Again and again in the Buddhism scriptures, we find stories of meetings between the Buddha and a woman or a man who expresses heartfelt appreciation of the Buddha and his Dharma, saying, "I, revered sir, go to the Lord for refuge, and to Dharma, and to the Saṅgha. May the Lord accept me as a lay follower going for refuge from this day forth for as long as life lasts." At the time of the Buddha, the going for refuge was what distinguished the Buddha's disciples from the followers of other teachers and sects, and indicated that these disciples wished to take the Three Jewels as the guiding principles of their lives. If an individual wished to join the order of *bhikṣus* or *bhikṣuṇīs*, that individual would go for refuge in a manner similar to those wishing to practice as lay disciples, then ask the Buddha to receive ordination—the "going forth." It is significant that the individual's statement of going for refuge to the Three Jewels came first, then the statement of wishing to work out the going for refuge either as a lay disciple or as a *bhikṣu* or *bhikṣuṇī*.

According to Buddhist tradition, there are three levels of Saṅgha:[2] the *ārya-saṅgha*, the *bhikṣu* or *bhikṣuṇī saṅgha*, and the *mahāsaṅgha*. It is clear in the *Ratana Sutta* of the *Sutta-nipāta* that it is primarily in the *ārya-saṅgha* that one takes refuge. The *ārya-saṅgha* comprises all those who have entered the Transcendental Path, namely, stream enterers and beyond. From references in a number of *sūtras*, it is clear that there were householders, both women and men, as well as *bhikṣus* and *bhikṣuṇīs*, who had entered the Transcendental Path. It is incorrect to translate the third phrase of the refuge formula—*saṅghaṃ śaraṇaṃ gacchāmi*—as "I go for refuge to the order of monks." The order of *bhikṣus* and *bhikṣuṇīs* is not equivalent to the *ārya-saṅgha*, because the *bhikṣu* and *bhikṣuṇī* communities also contained many people who were not yet on the Transcendental Path.

The fact that householders also entered the Transcendental Path illustrates that the motivation to practice is a major factor in spiritual life. If an interview given some years ago, Dilgo Khyentse Rinpoche said he thought it was rare for Dharma students these days to put even twenty percent of their energy into practice, their distractions and habits being much stronger than their diligence. Hence, spiritual progress is slow.[3] Presumably at the time of the Buddha, householders who entered the Transcendental Path were able to apply themselves to practice with sufficient diligence and singlemindedness that, although living "in the world," they were not unduly distracted from their main purpose.

The spiritual life requires conscious and persistent effort toward transformation, but is seen as more reliable than worldly life, since all worldly wealth and comforts are left behind at the time of death. Spiritual success rests on going for refuge to the Three Jewels, developing faith in that which transcends the vicissitudes of the mundane world, and steadily training the mind to focus on the Three Jewels until gradually consciousness becomes transformed, mind states become increasingly positive, and eventually reality itself is experienced. The fruits of spiritual practice are not lost at death, because consciousness modified through practice bears traces of the fruits of practice from life to life.

There are degrees of "going for refuge" and Buddhists make their first contact with the Three Jewels in a variety of ways. For some, the first introduction may have been as a young child hearing an elderly grandmother saying her prayers in front of a small shrine which may have been nothing more than a faded picture of the Buddha, with a small candle and some incense or flowers resting on a shelf in the same room where the family ate, slept, or worked. For others, the first introduction may have been through reading a book on Buddhism given by a friend or casually selected from a shelf in a local library. Others may have attended a meditation class in hopes of learning to relax or as a result of seeing a figure in robes walking down the road. Responding with interest at that first moment of connection, even if it is devoid of any rational understanding, is the first step in going for refuge.

If this first contact makes a sufficiently deep impression, it is usually just a question of time before one consciously seeks more information, whether through books on Buddhism or walking through the doors of a Buddhist center. If, after learning what it means to go for refuge in the Buddha, Dharma, and Saṅgha, one begins to more consciously apply the teachings, one has begun to move at least provisionally in the direction of those early disciples of the Buddha who went for refuge "for as long as life lasts." Interest in Buddhist practice may be expressed in observing precepts, meditation, or study and reflection upon the teachings. At first efforts may fluctuate, but with sufficient confidence and commitment, the act of going for refuge becomes effective. Eventually, on the basis of these conditions, one may experience the arising of insight, thus "entering the stream." It is said that the survival of the Buddhadharma depends on the existence of individuals who have reached the stage of stream entry and beyond.

A stream-enterer is an individual in whom the three fetters—a fixed view of self, doubt, and dependence on rites and rituals as ends in themselves—have been broken. Such an individual is said to course ever more deeply and fully in the transcendental. In more modern terms, these three fetters may be described as habit, vagueness, and superficiality. The positive counterparts that are cultivated to break through these fetters are creativity, clarity, and commitment.[4]

In Mahāyāna the key concept is the arising of *bodhicitta*, the will or thought of enlightenment. *Bodhicitta* is like an eruption of the transcendental within the mundane, radically altering the landscape of human consciousness and pouring out boundless compassion. The arising of *bodhicitta* represents the altruistic dimension of going for refuge. For the survival and spread of Buddhadharma in the modern world, beings need to work intensively on themselves and work intensively with and for others, to break through the three fetters and become *bodhisattvas*. A selfish Buddhist is a contradiction in terms.

In the Western Buddhist Order, to which I belong (known as Trailokya Bauddha Mahasangha in India), a great deal of importance is placed on teamwork and on sharing the Dharma with others, whether directly or indirectly. This may involve setting up and running a Dharma center in London, a social welfare project in India, or a retreat in Spain. Working in teams with other like-minded individuals mutually enhances one another's going for refuge—encouraging, inspiring and, when necessary, offering and receiving constructive criticism. As a team, Buddhists learn to share and cooperate, breaking down barriers between self and others.

The survival and spread of the Dharma requires spiritually committed individuals working together in close cooperation to effect the transformation of themselves and the world. Given the right kind of encouragement and guidance, all women Dharma practitioners are capable of reaching the level of effective going for refuge and beyond; they can play as great a part as they wish in ensuring that Dharma flourishes in the modern world.

Women coming into contact with the Dharma via the Western Buddhist Order are encouraged to take their spiritual aspirations seriously. They have opportunities to learn meditation, study the Dharma, attend retreats, get to know members of the order, and so on. "Ordination" takes place when an individual is recognized, by those order members who know her well, as effectively going for refuge. A recommendation is made to the woman Public Preceptor responsible for conducting the public ordination of women that year. Providing she is satisfied with the recommendation and the other Public Preceptors she works with are happy to give their blessing, too, arrangements are made for the woman to be ordained. There is a private and a public ordination ceremony, where she takes the Three Refuges and the ten precepts from her preceptor. The ten precepts (*kuśala-karma-pathas*, "ways of skilful action," or *kuśala- dharmas*)—embracing actions of body, speech, and mind—are a broad and far-reaching traditional set of precepts which make clear the key principles one must practice to effect the transformation necessary to become enlightened.[5]

The Western Buddhist Order has only one set of precepts for both women and men, and therefore only one ordination, called Dharmacharini for women and Dharmachari for men. In the Western Buddhist Order one is ordained simply as a full practicing member of the order, not as a laywoman or layman, nun or monk, or any of the other three classes in the Eastern socioreligious hierarchy. The order embraces those who live in family situations, those who are single parents, those who are single, and those who are celibate. In doing so, if offers a new model to the rest of the Buddhist world. At present, there are some 168 Dharmacharinis in the order and several hundred more have requested ordination.

Women who join the order are committed not only to their own personal spiritual practice, meditation, dharma study, devotional practice, and observance of the precepts, but are also committed to the life of the order itself. They meet regularly—on a weekly, monthly, and annual basis—to meditate, communicate, and discuss matters of mutual spiritual interest. A monthly order journal contains reports on the practice of Dharmacharinis and Dharmacharis worldwide. Friendships, and living and working relationships, are cultivated wherever possible. These may be temporary, such as evening Dharma study groups or weekend retreats in the countryside, or more permanent, such as running a residential retreat center.

Women teach the Dharma, run centers, manage and work in team-based "right livelihood businesses," found communities, write articles on various aspects of practice, and foster spiritual friendships with those who wish to join the order. In fact, women are free to take as much responsibility for the development of the Western Buddhist Order as they wish.

In recent years Sangharakshita, the founder and head of the Western Buddhist Order, has handed over full responsibility for ordinations to a small team of women and men Public Preceptors. This is a very significant development.

The Western Buddhist Order has both men's and women's wings, reflecting an important aspect of how the order has evolved over time. When Sangharakshita first founded the Friends of the Western Buddhist Order in 1967, he assumed that all our activities would be mixed, for men and women together. Within a few years we began to experiment with holding single-sex events; both men and women found definite benefit in spending time solely in the company of their own sex. Apart from reducing distractions, it also helped break down conditioned patterns of behavior that run very deep, patterns that are continually reinforced with members of the opposite sex.

Now all new Friends of the Western Buddhist Order centers aim to offer single-sex study groups, retreats, and eventually communities and work situations to those becoming more deeply involved. Although some people in the West find this unusual at first, most come to appreciate and value these opportunities. For women, it is an opportunity to explore and discover their potential apart from men, to find their own way of doing things, rather than automatically taking men's lead. From a Dharma perspective, it is not helpful for women to fight against male leadership either; instead, it is helpful to cultivate receptivity to those we can genuinely learn from, whether women or men. In single-sex situations, women can concentrate on their own spiritual, intellectual, and practical affairs without conflict or tension stemming from male/female reactions and issues.

The single-sex element in order activities helps women to develop their own individual initiative. Although the women's wing of the order has grown more slowly than the men's, the numbers of women being ordained has increased considerably in recent years.

In principle, women can play as big a part as they wish in ensuring that the Dharma flourishes in the modern world, based on effectively going for refuge. For personal development, it may be sufficient to know one essential Dharma teaching, such as "all conditioned things are impermanent," focusing the mind single-pointedly on this phrase. But to share the Dharma with others and help create facilities where others can practice meditation, it is necessary to be articulate, practical, and well versed in the teachings. We may also need to be able to converse with bank managers and property dealers, and other practical matters. In Mahāyāna terms, we need to cultivate *upāya-kauśalya*, or skill in means. Otherwise, although we may be able to transform ourselves, we can do very little to help transform the world.

In many parts of the world, women are still heavily conditioned by society to think of themselves primarily as mothers and caregivers of families. Women and children must be educated to believe that many things are possible for them. A special responsibility falls on Western and Eastern Dharma sisters and brothers to help Dharma sisters in need of greater education, both secular and religious.

The Friends of the Western Buddhist Order (FWBO, or Trailokya Bauddha Mahasangha Gana) is very active in India, particulary among the formerly "Untouchable" community who converted to Buddhism under the guidance and inspiration of Dr. Ambedkar.[6] The background of these people is one of great poverty and deprivation and education of any kind has been very hard to get. The order is running both social and Dharma projects, for the scope of the work is endless.[7]

The fact that hundreds of women arrive for retreats—having gained permission from their husbands and the support to leave their families for even a few days—represents a profound breakthrough. Some of these women also attend literacy and sewing classes, put their children in one of our *balwadis* (kindergartens), or have children in one of our hostels, so they can attend a city school and gain more education. Tens of thousands of women benefit from these programs and there are now twelve Indian Dharmacharinis, with many more women requesting ordination.

In addition to addressing possible deficiencies in secular education, those who think of themselves as "laywomen" must be on the lookout for any unhelpful elements in their social conditioning if they are to become effective in working for the Dharma. Possibly one of the greatest contributions laywomen can make to the survival and spread of the Buddhadharma is to cease blind support of the Bhikṣu Saṅgha. There is nothing to be gained spiritually in venerating someone who is not worthy of veneration, and unfortunately not all *bhikṣus* are so worthy. The danger is that we end up respecting people because of their lifestyle or the color of their clothes, rather than because of the quality of their going for refuge. This can lead to passivity on the part of the woman and complacency on the part of the *bhikṣus*, perpetuating the misunderstanding that monastic ordination is equivalent to spiritual commitment.

In truth, going for refuge is primary, as it was at the time of the Buddha. Lifestyle is secondary, in the sense that it is an expression of our going for refuge. There is no doubt that living a simple, celibate life can certainly be very conducive to deepening our going for refuge. But let us not be blind to the actual situation in many parts of the Buddhist East, where we can find *bhikṣus* who are more interested in politics than the Dharma and materially more comfortable than many of those who support their temples, and who, despite appearances to the contrary, may be enjoying certain sensual and even sexual pleasures, which the Vinaya does not permit.

If being a laywoman in Asia means feeling dutybound to serve and venerate the Bhikṣu Saṅgha under any circumstances, then it may be better to give up thinking of oneself as a laywoman and to think more in terms of being a woman in Dharma who goes for refuge in the Buddha, Dharma, and Saṅgha "for as long as life lasts." If one thinks of oneself as spiritually incapable of achieving more than a good rebirth because of one's position in the socioreligious hierarchy, then it may be better to step outside this framework. One would be better off joining forces with other like-minded women (and men) to encourage and support one another's going for refuge and to share the fruits of one's practice with others.

Efforts are currently being made in some quarters to establish or reestablish *bhikṣuṇī* ordination. The thinking behind these efforts needs to be examined very carefully to see whether this is the best way to further women's spiritual progress. Is it certain that men are in a better position spiritually because they can so easily become *bhikṣus*? Undoubtedly many social benefits come one's way by being an officially recognized member of the Saṅgha, but is that good enough reason for women to want to be part of the "official" Saṅgha, too? Surely *bhikṣuṇī* ordination in the technical sense is not necessary for living a simple, celibate lifestyle as a committed Dharma practitioner.

Most women fall outside the various Buddhist ecclesiastical systems as they presently exist. This needs to be recognized as an advantage, rather than as a disadvantage. It is necessary to recognize that most of these systems need a radical overhaul, and until that overhaul has taken place, spiritually committed women would be better off not being part of them. Not being part of them means that women are, in a sense, freer than the men who participate in those systems. It means that women are freer to think and grow along different lines, which takes courage, imagination, and a willingness to stand alone.

Notes

1. See I. B. Horner, "Greater Discourse to Vacchagotta," *The Middle Length Sayings*, Vol. II (Oxford: The Pali Text Society, 1989), p. 11.

2. Sangharakshita, *A Guide to the Buddhist Path* (Glasgow: Windhorse, 1990), p. 105.

3. "Invisible Realities," *Tricycle: Buddhist Review*, Spring 92, pp. 37–43.

4. Sangharakshita, *The Taste of Freedom* (Glasgow, Scotland: Windhorse, 1990), pp. 16–36.

5. Sangharakshita, *The Ten Pillars of Buddhism* (Glasgow, Scotland: Windhorse, 1984).

6. Sangharakshita, *Ambedkar and Buddhism* (Glasgow, Scotland: Windhorse Publications, 1986), pp. 78–79.

7. See Hilary Blakiston, *But Little Dust* (Cambridge: Allborough Press, 1990); *The Karuna Report* (Oxford: The Karuna Trust, 1995); and Terry Pilchick, *Jai Bhim* (Glasgow: Windhorse Publications, 1988).

Rita M. Gross

16. Feminism, Lay Buddhism, and the Future of Buddhism

About half of the converts to Buddhism in the West are laywomen who take their Buddhist practice very seriously. Their method of combining life in the modern world with serious Buddhist practice will be, in my opinion, significant for the future of Buddhism worldwide and for Buddhist women in every Buddhist country. I believe that the future of Buddhism will increasingly depend on lay, rather than monastic, practitioners and that many of the most interesting and creative developments in Buddhism will initially come from lay Buddhists. Furthermore, I believe that feminist reconstructions of Buddhist life will be an important component of this new lay Buddhism.

Two major areas of concern need to be addressed. The first is that Buddhism offers very weak models for meaningful lay Buddhist life and must forge new paths in the West and in the modern world. The second set of issues concerns creating styles of lay Buddhist life that accord with a feminist vision of androgyny rather than the unsatisfactory mutual incompleteness fostered by patriarchal gender roles.

Classical Buddhism was in many ways the religion and lifestyle of its monastic elite. Monastics not only kept the simple ethical code of Buddhism, but also pursued its philosophical and meditational disciplines, thought to be essential to attaining enlightenment. The laity, by contrast, were taught and observed the lay version of the ethical precepts, but were not expected to have the time, interest, or will power to pursue Buddhist meditation and philosophy seriously. Therefore, Buddhism, as a lay tradition, is faced with serious structural problems. Since Buddhism values neither pious devotion to deities, nor unquestioning adherence to doctrines, nor faithful performance of ritual as effective means to release, one is left with a very serous question: *What is Buddhist observance for the non-monastic householder in a tradition that regards the deep personal transformation that results from protracted meditation and study as the only means to release?*

Classical Buddhism worked out an answer to this question that promoted a deeply symbiotic relationship between the lay and monastic communities and that provided a means for lay Buddhists to work toward their own eventual enlightenment. Called the "two accumulations," this solution thought of the whole process of spiritual attainment as quite long and occurring in different stages. To be free, one needed to accumulate sufficient merit and sufficient wisdom. Merit was earned mainly through generosity, and brought one to a life situation in which the accumulation of wisdom, which actually fosters enlightenment, would be possible through study and meditation. The most effective method of accumulating merit was generosity to those who are engaged full-time in the accumulation of wisdom. Thus, lay Buddhists could participate meaningfully in the perpetuation of the tradition, while at the same time promoting their own future spiritual well-being through the practice of generosity.

In this system, laywomen, if they controlled their own resources, were not at any disadvantage to laymen. Buddhist literature contains accounts of highly admired generous laywomen, such as Viśākhā, who sometimes were more committed to Buddhism than were their husbands. In cases in which the household as a whole was committed to the support of monks, the laywomen, who managed food and other household resources, were the actual donors who, day by day, ladled out the food supplies into the monks' begging bowls. Women were at a disadvantage only in situations in which they did not control resources and their husbands or fathers disapproved of the monks. Such stories also occur in Buddhist literature.

However, this system also presumes the existence of a large body of Buddhists who have both the financial resources to support monastics and the wish to delay their own intensive involvement in Buddhist study and practice. As such, it is a highly unlikely model for Western Buddhists to adopt. Not too many wealthy Westerners are adopting Buddhism. Furthermore, most people who take on Buddhism as their religion of choice, whether wealthy or not, are primarily interested in it as a full-scale discipline of study, practice, and ethics for themselves; most of them do not want to become monks or nuns in the process of taking on commitments to serious Buddhist study and practice. If they could support someone in monastic practice, they would, but very, very few have such resources available. Virtually everyone contributes to the maintenance of meditation centers, but they also use these centers extensively themselves and a large portion of their financial support to the institutions is in the form of fees they pay to attend programs.

Thus a very different model of non-monastic lay Buddhism is being created among Western Buddhists. In this model, for lay as well as for monastic practitioners of the religion, the heart of their involvement in Buddhism is a commitment to the practice of meditation and the study of Buddhist teachings. They may not engage in such disciplines as intensively as do monks and nuns, but they do them frequently and, at intermittent intervals, quite intensively. Many Western Buddhist laywomen, using this method of combining worldly life with serious Buddhist practice, have actually been able to pursue more advanced meditation practices and philosophical studies than do Buddhist nuns in many Asian contexts.

This non-monastic model is largely dependent on the needs of Western Buddhists, who do not have the economic basis to be monastics or to support monks or nuns, but I think it is also much more suitable for them than the classic symbiotic model. When lay meditators are at the heart of the Buddhist community, a much more complete version of Buddhism is followed by the average Buddhist. For, while generosity is central to Buddhist values, no one would claim that it is sufficient for the full practice of Buddhism. For that, study and practice are also required, in all versions of Buddhism, with the exception of East Asian Pure Land Buddhism. A model of Buddhism that centers on lay meditators may also accord with the needs of contemporary people in general, since lay meditation has also become quite important in Buddhist revivals in several Asian countries.

However, this non-monastic model of lay Buddhist life also brings up certain issues that intersect with central feminist concerns. The young Westerners first attracted to Buddhism in the '60s and '70s were childless and marginally employed, for the most part. Ten years later they had both careers and children. Meditation centers, probably for the first time in Buddhist history, were struggling to provide child care for meditators attending intensive meditation sessions. The Western women who became Buddhists became *Buddhists*, not enablers of Buddhist men. When the women insist on practicing Buddhism as fully as do the men, and when lay Buddhists with families and careers insist that the heart of their involvement in Buddhism is meditation and study, not just donating to others who meditate and study, vast changes are required. Fortunately, feminist thought had already considered related problems in great depth.

Much of the most practical feminist thought deals with an evaluation of patriarchal gender roles and with proposals for more attractive, equitable, and humane alternatives. Both the critique and the proposed alternative are summarized quite well in the suggestion that it is desirable to avoid *mutual incompleteness*, that is, extremely strong, rigid, and fixed gender roles that always result in caricatures, half-humans who are emotionally stunted and inept at many essential life tasks. With the extreme of male specialization in production and economic activities and female specialization in reproduction and care-taking that were the stereotypical ideal, a state of rather advanced mutual incompleteness has been achieved in all patriarchal religions and societies.

The alternative is not to banish all specialization, for people do have special abilities that warrant fostering. But specializations should not be expected to follow gender, as they do under patriarchy, since the results of psychological tests show overlapping curves for women and men in all areas. This fact is simply ignored by those who demand conformity to gender stereotypes, citing averages garnered from test results as their justification.

To avoid the mutual incompleteness fostered by rigid gender roles, some basic competencies should be expected of all human beings, rather than being assigned along gender lines. All people should be able and willing to take some responsibility for livelihood, rather than being dependent on others completely, as some women have believed is their right. And all people should be able and willing to nurture themselves and others emotionally and psychologically, rather than remaining "relational retards," to quote a friend's characterization of some men. These expectations beyond mutual incompleteness should not be viewed as merely unwelcome obligations thrust upon unwilling victims by social reformers. They are integral to becoming fully human, to realizing one's innate potential to be both competent and nurturing, which is the only way to live up to the opportunities that come with the "precious human birth."

More explicitly, of course, the well-known feminist suggestion that women share in the burdens and joys of livelihood and that men share in the burdens and joys of housework and child care is the agenda for going beyond mutual incompleteness toward androgyny. The prevailing patriarchal ways of constructing both production and reproduction and linking them with gender have already become obsolete and dysfunctional. But, to date, in moving from mutual incompleteness toward androgyny, women have made considerably more progress than have men. Both women and men seem to be more eager for, and comfortable with, women moving into male roles and specializations than vice versa. Women have taken on the responsibilities for livelihood and self-sufficiency to a considerably greater degree than men have taken on responsibility for housework and child care or for emotional maturity and communication skills. Once again, the shame associated with femaleness in patriarchal culture makes many people, of both sexes, reluctant to encourage men to become more womanly, though encouraging women to be more manly is frequently regarded as good advice.

In the Buddhist world, this was brought home to me very clearly in a small, but indicative example. Once, when I taught a course on Buddhism and feminism to a mainly Japanese-American Buddhist congregation, the men became quite enthusiastic at a certain point. They eagerly told me that they had decided they wanted to pass a rule that the presidency of the congregation should alternate between a woman and a man. At the time we were feasting on a wonderful meal that the women had prepared in the temple kitchen. I suggested that this was a wonderful idea, which should be balanced by the men doing some of the work in the temple kitchen, so that the women could, indeed, sit on the board without becoming overworked. The men's faces fell dramatically and drastically!

In the context of lay Buddhist practice, responsibilities for both livelihood and reproduction, the stereotypical male and female specializations must be structured in a way that is compatible with, and that fosters serious lay Buddhist practice. For lay Buddhists to be seriously involved with the accumulation of wisdom, not only the accumulation of merit, means that the priority is on one's Buddhist practice, whatever that comes to mean, not on one's livelihood or domestic involvements. The feminist critique of conventional ways of handling both livelihood and domestic life meshes well with Buddhist concerns to balance and limit these activities sufficiently to be able to engage in serious Buddhist practice. In the remainder of this paper, I will suggest lay feminist Buddhist methods of dealing with livelihood and reproduction.

To some, the primary feminist approach to the workplace is its demand for equal opportunity at all levels of employment and its advocacy that women be economically competent, rather than continuing to rely on men for their maintenance. Indeed, these are important concerns, the former in the interests of promoting justice and the latter in the interests of promoting human wholeness and psychological well-being. These dimensions of the feminist assessment of livelihood recognize that it is dangerous for women when they are discriminated against in the workplace, because they are then vulnerable economically and psychologically, and that most human beings develop a sense of vocation beyond their own domestic nest if they are not sequestered in their immediate environment. Though less clearly recognized, this agenda also frees men from the unfair and unreasonable expectations sometimes placed upon them to provide others with economic support.

However, that is only the first agenda in the feminist discussion of livelihood and the workplace. Congruent with the more radical feminist insight that women ultimately want not just to play the men's game using their rules, but to help write more humane and sane rules, feminists want not only access to the workplace, but a better working environment once there. Though there are many facets to this desire for a more humane, less alienating work environment, one of the most important concerns (and most relevant to Buddhists) is the unreasonable demand, in terms of time, called for in many professions. One constantly hears of the difficulties of working mothers trying to balance demanding, time-intensive careers with their desire to spend time with their children. This visible and often-discussed problem is only the tip of the iceberg, however. Work is scheduled and structured in a way to make it almost inimical to self-development, psychological growth, and long-term well-being. This generalization is more, rather than less true, in more rewarding, creative, and prestigious livelihoods. Parents wanting to spend more time with children, and finding it difficult due to work demands only highlights the dilemma faced by those who want both to contribute meaningfully through livelihood and to lead a meaningful and balanced life. When workdays readily creep up to twelve hours in length, insufficient time is left for becoming fully human through friendship, family time, artistic endeavors, exercise, and spiritual discipline. This is a doubly insane situation, for not only are people with careers prohibited from developing their full humanity; many other people are shunted into work situations in which their potential is underutilized, while others are unemployed.

For the lay Buddhist meditator, this situation presents serious obstacles. Traditionally, one of the reasons laypeople were not usually expected to practice meditation very seriously was precisely because of overwhelming time demands thought to be unavoidable in their domestic and economic lives. Being a lay Buddhist meditator is unquestionably much more demanding and time-intensive than being a lay member of most other religions. The model of lay Buddhist meditators being developed in both Western and Asian forms of Buddhism seeks to find a middle path between the traditional choices of being either a monastic with plenty of time for spiritual discipline or a layperson with very little time for it. The encouragement to become a workaholic that is so pervasive in contemporary society is certainly a major negative factor operating against the development of this new model. To deal with this situation, one could imagine a new dimension to the guidance on "right livelihood" that is important in traditional Buddhism. Not only does right livelihood involve having a job, rather than trying to con the system into providing some support, it should include a sense of balance and proportion that integrates work into the rest of life and avoids workaholism.

For lay Buddhist meditators, it is also important to spread the concern for livelihood between the sexes, rather than to link gender with responsibility for livelihood. The positive dimension of livelihood, its satisfaction and relevance, can be an important dimension of lay Buddhist practice. As such, female as well as male meditators need the opportunity for a positive relationship with livelihood. Insofar as livelihood can become all-consuming and burdensome, it is even more important for the sexes to share livelihood responsibility. Job sharing, or at least sharing the task of earning sufficient income, is a reasonable solution so that each has a livelihood and major blocks of time away from it. Feminists often advocate such arrangements, which many employers try to avoid making available. For Buddhists, who want to be able to spend significant amounts of time in spiritual discipline, such an option should also be appealing. Otherwise, the person who takes responsibility for livelihood is likely to end up with insufficient time for self-development and spiritual discipline, while the stay-at-home partner will not be so burdened and, in many cases, finds it much easier to blend spiritual discipline into the daily routine.

The other major human occupation that has been assigned following gender lines and that has been considered too distracting and time-consuming to be combined with serious meditation practice is, of course, the round of domestic, nurturing, and reproductive responsibilities. Since women have been so completely defined by and limited to their reproductive roles, and since an extreme level of conflict between methods of securing livelihood and ability to give childcare has been achieved in the contemporary world, restructuring this occupation is an extremely high priority. To do so, it is helpful to survey both Buddhist and feminist perspectives on parenthood and motherhood. Then we will be in a better position to suggest some restructuring of domestic and parenting activities that will avoid both mutual incompleteness and the overburdening that makes serious lay Buddhist practice so difficult.

Buddhist attitudes toward mothers (who were almost solely responsible for childcare in the contexts in which the classic texts were written) are complex and differ with the context. The literal mother was not a spiritually valued model; if anything, she is regarded as someone whose spiritual development is likely to be minimal. Motherhood is not idealized, as in some religious traditions. On the contrary, the sufferings attendant on motherhood are one of the things that makes female rebirth undesirable. Motherhood as a symbol is more highly regarded. This ambiguity regarding motherhood is typical of androcentric evaluations of motherhood. On the other hand, at least Buddhists do not idealize the self-sacrificing, overburdened mother as the woman who is fulfilling her true potential, a paragon of female virtue, to be emulated by all women—the mother to whom every son and husband is entitled by rights of masculine privilege.

A widespread Buddhist assessment of motherhood is that motherhood inevitably brings attachment, which, of course, always brings grief quickly behind it, and which is the emotion that traps one in endless *saṃsāra*. A mother cannot avoid attachment, but attachment is a negative, unproductive, pain-filled attitude, to be replaced by detached joy and equanimity. In the *Therīgāthā*, mothers frequently became nuns after being grief-striken by the death of children. In so doing, they make the transition from attachment to detachment, from motherhood to the spiritual life, from suffering to joy and equanimity.

The quality of attachment is the negative aspect of motherhood, not the care and concern for another, for such concern, when detached rather than attached, is highly prized, especially in Mahāyāna Buddhism. Diana Paul has very clearly delineated the difference:

> In similar ways the Bodhisattva strongly and intensely identifies with all living beings as a mother identifies with her child. Yet the Bodhisattva, unlike the mother, remains free and detached from living beings through the wisdom of Emptiness. The mother does not view the world as empty. She is in a never-ending cycle of attachment. The conflict between the mother's role and the spiritually free and detached individual is resolved by the Bodhisattva.[1]

Mothers are models in classical Buddhism only when they are embodiments of the feminine principle of wisdom, which gives birth to Buddhahood. This valorization is doubled-edged. On the one hand, it recognizes the utter primacy of birth-giving and nurturing as the foundation of life. To have positive maternal symbols at some level in a religious symbol system can help valorize parenthood and provide models for humans. A person can, for example, recognize that one does not have to be a literal mother to mother both projects and people. And perhaps literal parents could model themselves more upon the principle of even-minded wisdom that gives birth to Buddhahood, and less upon the model of attached samsaric styles of parenthood. On the other hand, embodiments of feminine wisdom give birth to Buddhahood, not to screaming infants who try one's patience, disrupt one's meditation practice, and produce dirty diapers. Not much has yet been said about handling that result of birth-giving in the context of being a lay Buddhist meditator!

Feminist considerations of motherhood have been quite different and are highly varied, ranging from Shulamith Firestone's early call for artificial wombs to endorsements of maternity as the most noble human enterprise. Of these, the discussions by Nancy Chodorow and Dorothy Dinnerstein of the dynamic that occurs when women are given sole responsibility for early childcare are most relevant for a reconstruction of androgynous parenthood for lay Buddhist meditators. According to both of them, "Much of what is wrong with men and women as individuals (and us as a society) . . . is traceable to the fact that women do all the mothering."[2] They both are convinced that "the oppression of women originates in the female monopoly on mothering."[3] Both of them also see dual parenting as the way to end the oppression of women as well as to raise saner, more whole people who are not caught up in the dysfunctionalities of gender roles.

In postpatriarchal Buddhism, parenthood will need to be constructed quite differently than it has been in conventional society, Buddhist or non-Buddhist. Building parenthood on the foundation of serious lay meditation practice means that parenthood should be undertaken much more deliberately, mindfully, and seriously than has usually been the case previously. Then there may be some possibility for parents to become at least somewhat detached in their parenting. Dual parenting, in both literal and extended meanings, should be chosen for many reasons, and Buddhist meditation centers would routinely offer childcare in conjunction with meditation training.

When lay Buddhists take the accumulation of wisdom through meditation practice as a central expression of their Buddhist identity, then significant changes in how reproduction is structured are required. First, and most important, having children at all should become a mature choice, not a product of chance. For people whose foundation of mental and spiritual discipline is the development of mindfulness and awareness, to slide into reproduction mindlessly could easily be construed as a violation of the major precept to avoid sexual misconduct. Rather, being aware of one's likely behaviors ahead of time and being prepared with birth control, should be routine practice for lay Buddhist meditators, a refreshing change from practices commonly advocated in some religious traditions.

Furthermore, introducing some real egolessness and detachment into the childrearing process would greatly improve the experience of both parents and children. The percentage of children conceived and raised primarily as an extension of their parents' ego and the emotional abuse inherent in such a situation are astounding. Egoless parents would not conceive children out of habitual responses to societal pressure and then regard the children as extensions of themselves whose purpose is to fulfil the parents' needs and expectations. Some ability to regard children as beings whose karmic potentialities bring them temporarily into close relationships with oneself, rather than as possessions or objects to be shaped into the desired result, would cut some of the painful attachment. This attachment leads to grief, which is usually associated with motherhood in classical Buddhist texts.

Though this call for a more detached, egoless style of parenting applies to both men and women to some extent, I believe it would seriously and positively undercut one of the most unattractive aspects of femininity as constructed in patriarchy. This is the tendency, socialized into all women and believed by many, that they can always flee to maternity to find something to do with their lives. Because men do not have this easy biological exit from the quest for meaning and relevance in life, deep resentments between the sexes are fostered. Women who find in maternity the meaning they cannot find in their own lives, often fall into an extreme of attached parenting, living through their children.

The burdens placed on children when they are extensions of parents' egos are immense and can require many years of spiritual discipline to overcome. That such burdens were inflicted and carried in classical Buddhist cultures, not just in non-Buddhist societies, is demonstrated by the repeated theme in Buddhist biographical literature, of parents, especially parents of daughters, but also of sons to some extent, who objected strenuously to the child's desire not to marry and continue the family line, but to take up the religious life. But such Buddhist parents were undoubtedly not the lay Buddhist meditators being developed in contemporary forms of Buddhism—a further point in favor of developing an entirely new model of lay Buddhism.

Egoless and mindful decisions to take on parenthood should also have profoundly positive effects on several other issues. In the context of egolessness and the bodhisattva vow, the primary issue surrounding children should become a concern for the quality of life available to the children that are reborn, rather than the mindless pro-natalism that fuels so many public policies and private prejudices. Adoption should be a widely favored option of egoless detached parents who have taken the bodhisattva vow, whether or not they can conceive their own children. Especially for those who do not readily conceive, adoption, rather than medical extremes, should be a routine option. There are already plenty of children in the world—too many for the safety of the Earth, in all likelihood. Recognizing this, mindful and detached, egoless parents would also limit their reproduction. Recognizing the hazards of overpopulation, reproductive choices are not made solely on the basis of private ability to support another child or desires for one. Limiting one's own reproduction to care, properly and fully, for children already born could well be considered part of the most basic precept of nonharming. Everyone loses from excessive reproduction—from the planet, to crowded, undernourished, poverty-stricken people, to children who do not receive sufficient attention from their parents, to parents who are too consumed with childcare to take care of themselves emotionally and spiritually.

Parents who are Buddhist lay meditators need to structure their parenting in a manner that is not in conflict with their own disciplines of meditation and study. This means that dual parenting, extended parenting, and communal care networks are essential. Formal institutions in the Buddhist world must be involved in this extended childcare. First generation Western Buddhists are struggling with questions of how to educate their children about Buddhism and how to raise Buddhist children in a non-Buddhist environment. This is not an issue that can be dealt with family by family. As "monasteries," that is, places dedicated to spiritual discipline, become replaced at least in part by meditation centers frequented by lay Buddhists, childcare and children's education become the concern of Buddhist centers in a way that has probably not happened previously. Buddhist lay meditator parents usually do not want to break their spiritual discipline entirely during the years that they have young children. The old solution of having women deal with the children until they are old enough to be able to manage at Buddhist ceremonies and meditation sessions is not appropriate in the feminist perspective, which insists that women be accorded the privileges and responsibilities that go with the "precious human birth," rather than being treated as a servant class. Therefore, in Western Buddhist institutions currently there is considerable experimentation in how best to meet the needs of lay Buddhist meditators with children.

Concerning routine, daily childcare, arguments for extended networks, including significant primary involvement from fathers, can be made on two levels. First, one should recognize considerations of fairness and of promoting human wholeness beyond mutual incompleteness. Childcare is rather time-intensive and absorbing. Parents routinely complain of the difficulty of getting anything else done that involves concentration and withdrawal for a period of time, such as meditation practice or study. Mothers who are lay Buddhist meditators need and deserve time for their own spiritual discipline. In situations in which mothers commonly have employment outside the home, fairness would dictate that they receive significant help from their partners in parenting—the stereotypical female specialization—just as they are providing help with the stereotypical male specialization—providing economic support. Such arrangements would ease one of the greatest sources of frustration among contemporary women. From the other side, those who argue that childcare is so rewarding and satisfying that women are foolish to want to do anything else cannot, in good conscience, make it difficult for men to participate in such a rewarding and renewing experience. That would be another form of gender privilege, something that is consistently undermined by Buddhist doctrine and humane social arrangement.

Additionally, the post-Freudian feminist psychoanalytic analysis of Dorothy Dinnerstein[4] has great relevance in the Buddhist context. As she and many others reconstruct it, infancy and early childhood are not especially easy experiences for the infant. It is a time of discovering limits and frustrations and experiencing the beginning of long-lasting resentments against those conditions. In Buddhist terms, the infant or young child is discovering and being introduced to the inevitably samsaric character of human existence. *Nothing* a parent does, no quality of care, no matter how appropriate and loving, can alter or change this basic fact, which is very disturbing to both parent and child. Some parents, like Siddhārtha Gautama's father, struggle to keep their children from experiencing *saṃsāra*, seeming to believe that if they are loving and available enough, unlike their own parents, their children will avoid finitude and limitation. Some grown children have a hard time disentangling what their parents did to them that may have been abusive, from their own inevitable childhood introduction to limitation and finitude, frustration and dissatisfaction.

In this drama of blame and guilt, mothers often come in for more resentment than fathers. I believe Dinnerstein is right when she postulates that this is because, in a culture that places women alone in primary responsibility for childcare, women preside over the incidents of frustration and limitation that initiate us into the human condition. Women are, therefore, subconsciously blamed for those inevitabilities.[5] Succinctly, in Buddhist terms, she is arguing that in conventional patriarchal culture, women, more than men, introduce us to *saṃsāra*, and are, on some level, blamed for it in a way that men are not, even if the child later learns that such suffering is inevitable and results from karma accrued in past lives.

For Buddhism, unlike Dinnerstein, the introduction to *saṃsāra* is not the only message there is. Only the first two of the Four Noble Truths talk about *saṃsāra*. The last two talk about release, freedom, and spiritual discipline. But the gurus and religious teachers who introduce us to those disciplines and to the possibility of *nirvāṇa* are almost always men. This male monopoly on spiritual teaching is as damaging as is the female monopoly on childrearing. Furthermore, there may be links between these two monopolies. Because women are informally, but rather systematically excluded from religious leadership and from teaching roles in Buddhism, they are left with the task of introducing their children to *saṃsāra*, while men are freed both to pursue *nirvāṇa* for themselves and to teach the methods promoting freedom to others. Perhaps, subconsciously, women have been excluded from teaching roles *because* of their conventional associations with our initiation into limited and frustrating samsaric human existence. This is a rather unpleasant and vicious circle!

For Buddhism a great deal is at stake in breaking this vicious circle. The point at which many links can be severed is with the large-scale involvement of laywomen in Buddhist meditation, and a massive reform of monastic institutions regarding the education and training of nuns. With these changes in place, reconstruction can occur in two directions: Women will take on teaching roles in Buddhism, whether inside or outside the recognized structures of authority, thereby breaking the male monopoly on the introduction of spiritual discipline and *nirvāṇa*; and men take on their share in childcare, thus breaking the female monopoly on the introduction of the next generation to *saṃsāra*. Breaking these two monopolies will begin to undo all the extra and unnecessary negativity and pain brought to *saṃsāra* by those monopolies.

Notes

1. Diana Paul, *Women in Buddhism: Images of the Feminine in Mahāyāna Tradition* (Berkeley, Calif.: Asian Humanities Press, 1979), p. 66.

2. Rosemany Tong, *Feminist Thought: A Comprehensive Introduction* (Boulder, Colo.: Westview, 1989), p. 149.

3. Ibid., p. 156.

4. Dorothy Dinnerstein, *The Mermaid and the Minotaur: Sexual Arrangements and Human Malaise* (New York: Harper & Row, 1963), pp. 28–34.

5. Ibid., pp. 76–78, 111–12.

Karma Lekshe Tsomo

Epilogue

Religion in modern times is moving in many directions. For some, it is moving away from the spiritual to the dogmatic, while for others it is manifesting as the magical. For some, the spiritual has been replaced by psychotherapy and self-help, while for others it is being expressed in social service. The authentic spiritual richness of many religious traditions is being recovered, revealing itself in ritual, contemplation, nature, and the ordinariness of daily life, while elsewhere the spiritual is being obscured by secular concerns.

Life for many in the West, and increasingly in the East, has become a series of unfulfilling relationships, consumer binges, mortgage payments, and gastronomic indiscretions. People easily become trapped in a vicious cycle of desires and ambitions, and in protecting what they have acquired. Covertly, many intuit the unsatisfactory and ephemeral nature of material pleasures, superficial relationships, and emotional dependencies, and the more courageous begin to seek alternatives. Few rush to cast off wealth and security, but since the '60s many people have sought a simpler lifestyle, without "all that stuff," and the spiritual dimension of human experience has mainstreamed, becoming an acceptable topic of public discourse.

When the spiritual impulse dawns, there are innumerable offerings from which to choose. The United States especially has become the archetypal spiritual marketplace. Among the spiritual traditions that have taken root on Western soil, Asian religious systems are prominent. Because transplantation often involves a radically different cultural landscape, new caretakers, and new influences, the traditions mutate in fascinating ways, and fulfill important needs for many people in their new environment. Among these Asian transplants, the various Buddhist traditions have become the focus of much attention.

How can Buddhism's global popularity in recent years be explained? For some, the adoption of Buddhism is a social statement—a rejection of consumerism, materialism, egotism, militarism, and a host of other social ills. For some, it is a response to the spiritual vacuum created by ideological dogmatism—whether religious, political, or scientific. Viewed through its multiple cultural expressions, there is a sense that Buddhism is fluid and negotiable. From among the varieties available, one can select a teacher or tradition that appeals to one's particular sensibilities: artistic, psychological, philosophical, personal, and environmental. Often it is a chance encounter with a friend, a teacher, or a book that strikes a cord that resonates deeply and induces one to check out a particular center or tradition. And if one does not feel comfortable in one, there are others to explore.

The future of Buddhism in the West will be shaped to some extent by a distrust of organized religion and an aversion to established doctrine and hierarchy. Western people rarely have an instinctive faith in Buddhism like those who are raised in devout Buddhist families, but many find the pragmatic methods of Buddhist psychology helpful for dealing with the stresses of modern society, and it is cheaper than psychotherapy. Many are attracted to Buddhism because of its flexibility and the range of philosophical possibilities it presents. There are schools that specialize in logical analysis and others that reject logic altogether, those that utilize colorful ritual and others that "just sit," those that are pragmatic and others that are devotional, those that are meditative and others that are socially engaged, those that provide solitude and others that provide community. All Buddhist schools accept the concept of enlightened mind, however they define that, and regard it as an actual human probability, verifiable through empirical investigation. The selection of a particular school of practice is left to the individual.

From a Buddhist perspective, the spheres of religion, philosophy, psychology, and ordinary life need not constitute separate categories. The term "Dharma" includes them all and much more. In one sense, the term can be applied to all religious and most philosophical traditions that lead to liberation and enlightenment. Although Buddhists make a distinction is between "true Dharma," or traditions that teach methods for achieving liberation from *saṃsāra*, and "worldly Dharma," meaning traditions concerned with achieving other benefits, and also distinguish between the Dharma of "insiders," meaning Buddhist schools of tenets, and the Dharma of "outsiders," or non-Buddhist schools, a liberal interpretation of the term Dharma would include all paths that lead to the achievement of enlightenment, whether it be defined as liberation from the sufferings of *saṃsāra* or the state of perfect Buddhahood.

All Buddhist philosophical traditions and varieties of religious practice provide tools for transforming one's mind and one's life. The various cultural and religious traditions represent the perpetually changing patterns of human meaning, expressed through art, literature, and actions in everyday life. It is often difficult to disentangle the techniques for mental cultivation from the cultures within which they are embedded. But whether in Asia or the West, these practical techniques need to be understood on their own terms, apart from the cultural accoutrements, even if these elements are the initial attraction. Buddhism utilizes both reason and inner experience, and assumes that the two are compatible—a key point for a feminist analysis of Buddhism.

Buddhism Journeys West

As Buddhism traveled from India to other lands over the course of 2,600 years, it continuously adapted, assimilated, and reconciled itself to new cultural environs, absorbing local deities and ideas along the way. The process of acculturation—a dynamic interactive process weaving together a multiplicity of cultural, social, and personal strands—is a complex confluence. Although the current cultural encounter between Buddhism and the West may be its greatest challenge yet, the ancient cultures of China, Japan, and Tibet may have appeared equally as exotic in their time. As Anne Klein, Sara Schneidermann, and others have suggested, the introduction of Buddhism in its traditional guises is only the beginning of an unpredictable process in which culturally constructed concepts as basic as mind, personhood, gender, freedom, and equality, not to mention matters of ultimate spiritual concern, must be reconsidered from the ground up. All perceived congruences are tentative. Moreover, embedded social and economic factors strongly influence the current transmission of Buddhist cultures and their reception in the West. For example, awed by the practical usefulness of Buddhist spiritual technology, a vertiable emporium of tools for mental transformation, many students assume that all purveyors of the tradition are fully realized, and therefore certain sexual and financial improprieties may be overlooked. Fascinated by the exoticism, beginners in Buddhist circles often put their good judgment on hold, failing to check the qualifications of the teacher, misreading advances, enjoying flirtations, and overextending themselves personally and financially. There is a tendency to want to do the longest retreats and get closest to the most famous masters, to strive for the highest teachings, the highest practices, the highest empowerments, from the highest lamas—and to get totally burnt out, confused, or disillusioned in a very short time. Buddhist demographics are both random and predictable: the members of ethnic (Chinese, Korean, Thai, and so on) Buddhist temples are predominantly immigrant Asians and the members of nonethnic centers are predominantly educated, upper-middle-class Caucasians. In all these centers, women play a major, if often subordinate, role. All these factors will influence the Western acculturation of Buddhism.

The Buddhist Encounter with Feminist Ideas

Feminists look at the role of women in Buddhist cultures and blink. If Buddhism is to have global relevance, it must begin to address some pointed questions about gender issues, not only for Western women but for Asian women as well. Buddhists look at the variety of feminist positions and feel bewildered. How can these perspectives inform one another?

To be relevant for today, Buddhism must speak about liberation as not only a distant goal, but also as an immanent, accessible social and intellectual freedom. Modern Buddhism needs to incorporate many kinds of people—women, children, and men of all social, cultural, and economic backgrounds—and their concerns, fully and immediately. It must recognize that feminist thinking is a strong stream in the cultural consciousness of Western people today.

The importation of Buddhist cultures to the West has occasioned a ripening of feminist awareness among many. It has brought certain traditional patriarchal patterns of Asian cultures to the attention of women and men alike, and stirred them to question sexist attitudes within both Buddhism and their own cultures. To the thoughtful observer the fact that almost all ethnic Buddhist teachers, of all traditions, are male brings the discrepancy between theoretical equality and the empirical negligibility of women into stark relief. Once this discrepancy enters the American Buddhist's field of awareness, even peripherally, other issues integral to both Buddhist and feminist transformation also come to light.

Before Buddhism can be wholeheartedly embraced by Western women, a number of core questions need to be asked, even if they are not easily answered: If Buddhism purports to effect the welfare of all, why has it not been a more active force in righting wrongs against women? If Buddhism is egalitarian, why does the myth of male superiority continue to operate in Buddhist societies? If Buddhist saints were enlightened, why did they not challenge the assertion that good karma leads to a male rebirth and bad karma leads to a female rebirth? Historically, have fewer women than men achieved enlightenment, and why? Some questions are of immediate concern: Can women come to terms with sexist elements in the tradition, adopting the useful elements and ignoring the discrepancies between rhetoric and reality? Can they transform the tradition, exposing and expunging the unsavory sexist elements? And how is a transformation going to happen when the leaders of the various Buddhist traditions are predominantly male, especially if women continue to abdicate authority in favor of men?

Experiences in a Buddhist culture or a Western Buddhist center may help crystallize incipient feminist awareness. In personal practice, gender issues may not be discernible, but in institutions they are inescapable. Meditation practices may be nongendered, but teachers, teachings, practice styles, and administrative structures are often tarnished with gender bias. Although women's equal potential for enlightenment is verbally affirmed in most Western Buddhist settings today, one may also hear it said that women are more emotional than men, or have more problems or delusions. This ambivalence toward women is unsettling, and unmasks a serious tension between theory and real life.

Visibly contributing to this tension is the fact that, in both Asian and Western Buddhist settings, teachers and religious specialists are overwhelmingly male, even when most of the supporters are female. The same may be true in Western religions, but the contradiction is more jarring in Buddhist settings because women theoretically have equal access to the ultimate goal. In the West, the contradiction is compounded by the fact most Asian Buddhist teachers have been raised with traditional notions of gender identity and gender relations. Many male Buddhist teachers have acquired their attitudes toward gender in exclusively male monastic environments and have little experience dealing with women on an equitable basis. This can lead to the exploitation of women students, an inability to acknowledge women's capabilities, and an unwillingness to share power. Students with feminist sensibilities who are intrigued by Buddhist philosophy cannot fail to notice these incongruencies.

Feminist thinking has already affected the development of certain Western Buddhist centers—in the liturgy and leadership, for example—but its influence could be greater. A feminism that is relevant for Buddhists must be broad enough to encompass the views and collective experience of people of diverse social, cultural, and philosophical backgrounds and lifestyles. An exclusivistic stance is hard to justify because of Buddhism's emphasis on loving kindness and compassion for all living beings. A feminism that is relevant for Buddhists must speak a language that all women can understand. It must be inclusive enough to reach the majority of women, who are poor, educationally disadvantaged, and concerned with survival issues, such as feeding their families, more than intellectual questions. Inclusive language means much more than simply "s/he"; the world's women need to be included in people's thinking.

Discrimination against women does not occur in a vacuum; it is linked with racism, environmental destruction, consumerism, health, nutrition, and social and economic exploitation. Gender studies thus encompasses cultural studies, political science, religious studies, psychology, and economics, synthesizing and reconfiguring these disciplines in new ways. Although traditionally women have been excluded from the higher echelons of the public forum, they have always been central to the formation, transformation, and continuity of cultural and religious identity, because they are the dominant transmitters of ideas and cultural denominators to successive generations. Therefore, there is great irony in the fact that women's place in religious and cultural institutions has been conspicuously peripheral. Acknowledging this gap can lead to a new vision of personal and cultural possibilities.

Buddhist Feminist Strategies

The meeting of Buddhist and feminist perspectives is thus fertile ground for innovation and mutual enrichment on many levels. As Buddhists and feminists explore more fully the spiritual dimensions of women's experience, they are developing more effective strategies for addressing the social injustices women face. Simultaneously, they are gaining new insights on personhood, subjectivity, family, sexuality, and ethics, informed by women's unique experiences in Buddhist cultures.

A heightened awareness of women's issues is gradually bringing changes in Buddhist societies and in Western Buddhist centers, despite a backlog of inequalities. The Buddhist teachings on compassion and universal liberation make it imperative that social realities be brought closer to philosophical ideals. One practical means of eradicating gender discrimination is to subtly and persistently raise women's issues with teachers of all traditions. This strategy has already caused a shift in perceptions. Because sexist behaviors and innuendos immediately raise questions, rebuttals, and shackles, many male teachers, especially those living or visiting in the West, have already softened their positions. In the course of time, some have even become outspoken defenders of women's rights. As delicate or controversial as it may be to question male privilege within the tradition, many feel that it is a duty that must be shared by all who care for women and for Buddhism. Through their highly visible presence in Western centers and their constant attempts at dialogue on gender issues with teachers and students, women have become catalysts for change in all the Buddhist traditions. They are forcing teachers and practitioners everywhere to take a new look at old attitudes toward women's roles.

Buddhist teachers living and traveling abroad have been influenced by feminist perspectives and have developed more liberal attitudes on many social issues. These teachers are then in a position to influence the opinions of other, more conservative teachers and practitioners in their countries. This is helping to turn the tide at a rapid speed. For example, the question "Where are the lady lamas?" asked repeatedly by Western practitioners has led to many improvements for women in the Tibetan tradition in just one decade, including new study programs, practice centers, and other opportunities. Although many more improvements are needed, significant reforms have been made by repeatedly articulating women's concerns. More extensive international alliances and more effective, culturally appropriate strategies for direct action will help Buddhist women reach their goals.

The encounter between Buddhist and feminist ideas has spawned a Buddhist women's movement that embraces individuals of many cultures united by their Buddhist values and feminist commitments. With shared values of compassion and loving kindness, a sense of immediacy, faith in women's potentialities, and a willingness to step out of familiar conceptual frames, Buddhist women around the world have initiated intercultural dialogue on a deeply personal, deeply spiritual level. Women are proving the immense value of listening to different voices and learning from the wisdom of each. They are ready to explore a new mode of spirituality that is openhearted, inclusive, wise, and genuinely kind—what His Holiness the Dalai Lama calls "a true spirituality that is beyond religions."

Bibliography

Allione, Tsultrim. *Women of Wisdom*. London: Routledge & Kegan Paul, 1984.

Aoyama, Shundo. *Zen Seeds: Reflections of a Female Priest*. Tokyo: Kosei Publishing Co., 1990.

Arai, Paula. "Sōtō Zen Nuns in Modern Japan: Keeping and Creating Tradition." *Bulletin of the Nanzan Institute for Religion & Culture* 14 (Summer 1990), 38–51.

Arai, Paula. *Women Living Zen: Japanese Sōtō Buddhist Nuns*. New York: Oxford University Press, 1999.

Aziz, Barbara Nimri. "Buddhist Nuns." *Natural History* 98. 3 (1989), 41–48.

———. *Tibetan Frontier Families: Reflections on Three Generations from D'ing-ri*. New Delhi: Vikas Publishing House, 1978.

Barnes, Nancy Schuster. "The Bodhisattva Figure in the *Ugraparipṛcchā*." In A. K. Warder, ed., *New Paths in Buddhist Research*. Durham, N.C.: Acorn Press.

———. "Buddhism." In Arvind Sharma, *Women in World Religions*. Albany: State University of New York Press, 1987, 105–33.

———. "Buddhist Women and the Nuns' Order in Asia." In Christopher S. Queen and Sallie B. King, eds., *Engaged Buddhism: Buddhist Liberation Movements in Asia*. Albany: State University of New York Press, 1996.

———. "Striking a Balance: Women and Images of Women in Early Chinese Buddhism." In Yvonne Y. Haddad and Ellison B. Findly, eds., *Women, Religion, and Social Change*. Albany: State University of New York Press, 1985.

———. "Women in Buddhism." In Arvind Sharma, ed., *Today's Woman in World Religions*. Albany: State University of New York Press, 1994, 137–69.

Bartholomeusz, Tessa. "The Female Mendicant in Buddhist Sri Lanka." In José Ignacio Cabezón, ed., *Buddhism, Sexuality, and Gender*. Albany: State University of New York Press, 1992, 37–61.

———. *Women under the Bō Tree*. New York, N.Y.: Cambridge University Press, 1994.

Batchelor, Martine. *Walking on Lotus Flowers: Buddhist Women Living, Loving and Meditating*. London: Thorsons, 1996.

Beyer, Stephan. *The Cult of Tara: Magic and Ritual in Tibet*. Berkeley: University of California Press, 1973.

Blackstone, Kathryn R. *Women in the Footsteps of the Buddha: Struggle for Liberation in the Therīgāthā*. Richmond Surrey: Curzon Press, 1998.

Blakiston, Hilary. *But Little Dust*. Cambridge, U.K.: Allborough Press, 1990.

Bloss, Lowell W. "The Female Renunciants of Sri Lanka: The *Dasasil mattawa*." *Journal of the International Association of Buddhist Studies* 10.1 (1987): 7–32.

———. "Attitudes toward Women and the Feminine in Early Buddhism." In José Ignacio Cabezón, ed., *Buddhism, Sexuality and Gender*. Albany: State University of New York Press, 1992.

———. "Theravada 'Nuns' of Sri Lanka: Themes of the Dasailmattawa Movement." Unpublished monograph, 1984.

Boucher, Sandy. *Opening the Lotus: A Woman's Guide to Buddhism*. New York: Ballantine Books, 1997.

———. *Turning the Wheel: American Women Creating the New Buddhism*. Boston: Beacon Press, 1993.

Buswell, Robert E. "Is Celibacy Anachronistic? Korean Debates over the Secularization of Buddhism during the Japanese Occupation Period." Unpublished monograph, 1990.

Byles, Marie B. *Journey into Burmese Silence*. George Allen & Unwin, London, 1962.

Campbell, June. *Traveller in Space: In Search of Female Identity in Tibetan Buddhism*. New York: George Braziller, 1996.

Chang, Pao. *Biographies of Buddhist Nuns*. Trans. Li Jung-hsi. Osaka: Tohokai, 1981.

Cissell, Kathryn. "The Pi-ch'iu-ni Chuan: Biographies of Famous Chinese Nuns from 317–516 C.E." Ph.D. diss., University of Wisconsin. Ann Arbor University Microfilms International, 1972.

Devendra, Kusuma. "The Dasasil Nun: A Study of Women's Buddhist Religious Movement in Sri Lanka." Unpublished manuscript. Colombo: Department of Pali and Buddhist Studies, 1987.

Devine, Carol. *Determination: Tibetan Women and the Struggle for an Independent Tibet*. Toronto: Vauve Press, 1991.

Drolma, Delog Dawa. *Delog: Journey to Realms beyond Death*. Junction City, Calif.: Padma Publishing, 1995.

Dowman, Keith. *Sky Dancer: The Secret Life and Songs of the Lady Yeshe Tsogyel*. London: Routledge & Kegan Paul, 1984.

Dresser, Marianne. *Buddhist Women on the Edge: Contemporary Perspectives from the Western Frontier*. Berkeley: North Atlantic Books, 1996.

Edou, Jerome. *Machig Labdron and the Foundations of Chod*. Ithaca, N.Y.: Snow Lion Publications, 1995.

Falk, Nancy. "The Case of the Vanishing Nuns: The Fruits of Ambivalence in Ancient Indian Buddhism." In Nancy Falk and Rita Gross, eds., *Unspoken Worlds: Women's Religious Lives in Non-Western Cultures*. San Francisco: Harper & Row, 1979, 207–24.

———. "An Image of Women in Old Buddhist Literature: The Daughters of Māra." In Judith Plaskow and June Arnold, eds., *Women and Religion*. Missoula, Mont.: Scholars Press, 1974, 105–12.

Friedman, Lenore. *Meetings with Remarkable Women: Buddhist Teachers in America*. Boston: Shambhala, 1987.

———. and Susan Moon. *Being Bodies: Buddhist Women on the Paradox of Embodiment*. Boston: Shambhala, 1997.

Fronsdal, Gil. "The Transition from Monastic to Priest in Japanese Buddhism." Unpublished monograph, 1990.

Gombrich, Richard, and Gananath Obeyesekere. *Buddhism Transformed: Religious Change in Sri Lanka*. Princeton: Princeton University Press, 1988.

Grimshaw, Anna. *Servants of the Buddha: Winter in a Himalayan Convent*. Cleveland: Pilgrim Press, 1994.

Groner, Paul. "Vicissitudes in the Ordination of Japanese 'Nuns' During the Late Nara and Early Heian Periods." Unpublished monograph, 1990.

Gross, Rita M. "Buddhism." *Women in Religion*. London: Pinter Publishers, 1994, 1–29.

———. *Buddhism after Patriarchy: A Feminist History, Analysis, and Reconstruction of Buddhism*. Albany: State University of New York Press, 1993.

———. "Buddhism and Feminism: Toward Their Mutual Transformation." *The Eastern Buddhist* 19.2 (Autumn 1986): 62–74.

———. "Buddhism from the Perspective of Women's Bodies." *Buddhist-Christian Studies* 1 (1981): 72–82.

———. "Yeshe Tsogyel: Enlightened Consort, Great Teacher, Female Role Model." In Janice D. Willis, ed. *Feminine Ground: Essays on Women and Tibet*. Ithaca, N.Y.: Snow Lion Publications, 1989.

Gunawardena, R. A. L. H. "Subtile Silks of Ferreous Firmness: Buddhist Nuns in Ancient and Early Medieval Sri Lanka and Their Role in the Propagation of Buddhism." *The Sri Lankan Journal of the Humanities* 14.1 and 2 (1988): 1–59.

Hanh, Thich Nhat. *Vietnam: Lotus in a Sea of Fire*. New York: Hill and Wang, 1967.

Havnevik, Hanna. *Tibetan Buddhist Nuns*. Oslo: Norwegian University Press, 1990.

Hirakawa, Akira. "History of Nuns in Japan." *Buddhist Christian Studies* 12 (1992): 143–58.

———. *Monastic Discipline for the Buddhist Nuns: An English Translation of the Chinese Text of the Mahāsāṃghika-Bhikṣuṇī-Vinaya*. Patna: K. P. Jayaswal Research Institute, 1982.

Horner, I. B. *The Book of Discipline*, 6 vols. London: Routledge & Kegan Paul, 1982.

———. *Women under Primitive Buddhism: Laywomen and Almswomen*. Delhi: Motilal Banarsidass, 1930.

Huang, Chien-yu Julia and Robert P. Wellner. "Merit and Mothering: Women and Social Welfare in Taiwanese Buddhism," *Journal of Asian Studies* 57, no. 2 (May 1998): 379–96.

Ingram, Paul O. "Reflections on Buddhist-Christian Dialogue and the Liberation of Women." *Buddhist Christian Studies* 17 (1997): 49–60.

Kabilsingh, Chatsumarn. *The Bhikkunī Pātimokkha of the Six Schools*. Bangkok: Thammasat University Press, 1991.

———. *A Comparative Study of Bhikkhunī Pātimokkha*. Varanasi: Chaukhambha Orientalia, 1984.

———. "The Future of the Bhikkhunī Saṅgha in Thailand." In Diana Eck and Devaki Jain, eds., *Speaking of Faith: Global Perspectives on Women, Religion, and Social Change*. Philadelphia: New Society Publishers, 1987.

———. *Thai Women in Buddhism*. Berkeley, Calif.: Parallax Press, 1991.

Kajiyama, Yuichi. "Women in Buddhism." *Eastern Buddhist*, new series, 15.2 (1982): 53–70.

Kamens, E., trans. *The Buddhist Poetry of the Great Kamo Priestess: Daisaiin Senshi and Hosshin Wakashū*. Ann Arbor: University of Michigan Center for Japanese Studies, 1990.

Kawanami, Hiroko. "The Religious Standing of Burmese Buddhist Nuns (thilashin): The Ten Precepts and Religious Respect Words." *Journal of the International Association of Buddhist Studies* 13.1 (1990): 19.

Keyes, Charles F. "Mother or Mistress but Never a Monk: Buddhist Notions of Female Gender in Rural Thailand." *American Ethnologist* 11.2 (May 1984): 223–35.

Khiang, Mi Mi. *The World of Burmese Women*. London: Zed Books, 1984.

King, Sallie B. "Egalitarian Philosophies in Sexist Institutions: The Life of Satomi-san, Shinto Miko and Zen Buddhist Nun." *Journal of Feminist Studies in Religion*, 4.1 (Spring 1988).

Kirsch, Thomas. "Buddhism, Sex Roles, and the Thai Economy." In Penny Van Esterik, ed., *Women of Southeast Asia.* DeKalb, Ill.: Northern Illinois University, Center for Southeast Asian Studies, 1982, 13–32.

Klein, Anne C. "The Birthless Birthgivers; Reflections on the Liturgy of Yeshe Tsogyel, the Great Bliss Queen." *Tibet Journal* 12.4 (1987): 19–37.

———. "Finding a Self: Buddhist and Feminist Perspectives." In Clarissa W. Atkinson et al., *Sharing New Vision: Gender and Values in American Culture.* Ann Arbor: UMI Research Press, 1987, 191–218.

———. *Meeting the Great Bliss Queen: Buddhists, Feminists, and the Art of the Self.* Boston: Beacon Press, 1994.

———. "Presence with a Difference: Buddhists and Feminists on Subjectivity." *Hypatia,* 9.4 (Fall 1994).

———. "Nondualism and the Great Bliss Queen: A Study in Tibetan Buddhist Ontology and Symbolism." *Journal of Feminist Studies in Religion* 1.1 (1985): 73–98.

———. "Primordial Purity and Everyday Life: Exalted Female Symbols and the Women of Tibet." In Clarissa W. Atkinson et al., *Immaculate and Powerful: The Female in Sacred Image and Social Reality*. Boston: Beacon Press, 1985, 111–38.

Komatsu, Chikō. *The Way to Peace: The Life and Teachings of the Buddha*. Kyoto: Hōzōkan Publishing Company, 1989.

Kyi, Aung San Suu. *Freedom from Fear*. London: Viking, 1991.

———. *Letters from Burma*. London: Penguin Book, 1997.

———. *The Voice of Hope*. New York: Seven Stories Press, 1997.

Law, Bimala Churn. *Women in Buddhist Literature*. Varanasi: Indological Book House, 1981.

Levering, Miriam. "Contemporary Discussion of the Eight Gurudharmas, with Some Observations Concerning Their Observance and Effects among Bhiksunis in Taiwan." Unpublished monograph, 1990.

———. "The Dragon Girl and the Abbess of Mo-Shan: Gender and Status in Ch'an Buddhist Tradition." *Journal of the International Association of Buddhist Studies* 5.1 (1982): 19–35.

Li, Jung-hsi, trans. *Biographies of Buddhist Nuns*. Osaka: Tohokan, 1981.

Mackenzie, Vicki. *Reborn in the West*. New York: Marlowe & Company, 1996.

Murcott, Susan. *The First Buddhist Women: Translations and Commentaries on the Therīgatha*. Berkeley, Calif.: Parallax Press, 1991.

Norman, K. R., trans. *The Elders' Verses II: Therīgatha*. London: Luzac and Co., 1966.

O'Halloran, Maura. *Pure Heart, Enlightened Mind: The Zen Journal and Letters of Maura "Soshin" O'Halloran*. Boston: Charles E. Tuttle, 1994.

Padmashuri, Dharmacharini. "The Breath of Liberty." *Golden Drum*, November 1989–January 1990.

Patt, David. *A Strange Liberation: Tibetan Lives in Chinese Hands*. Ithaca, N.Y.: Snow Lion Publications, 1992.

Paul, Diana. "Buddhist Attitudes Toward Women's Bodies." *Buddhist-Christian Studies* 1 (1981): 63–71.

———. *The Buddhist Feminine Ideal: Queen Śrīmālā and the Tathāgatagarbha*. Missoula, Mont.: Scholars Press, 1980.

———. "Empress Wu and the Historians: A Tyrant and Saint of Classical China." In Nancy Falk and Rita Gross, eds., *Unspoken Worlds: Women's Religious Lives in Non-Western Cultures*. San Francisco: Harper & Row, 1979, 191–206.

———. *Women in Buddhism: Images of the Feminine in Mahāyāna Tradition*. Berkeley: Asian Humanities Press, 1979; (rpt. Berkeley: University of California Press, 1985).

Phuong, Cao Ngog. "Days and Months." In Fred Eppsteiner, ed. *The Path of Compassion: Writings on Socially Engaged Buddhism*. Berkeley, Calif.: Parallax Press, 1988, 155–69.

Ray, Reginald. "Accomplished Women in Tantric Buddhism of Medieval India and Tibet." in Nancy Falk and Rita Gross, eds., *Unspoken Worlds: Women's Religious Lives in Non-Western Cultures*. San Francisco: Harper & Row, 1979, 227–42.

Rhys-Davids, Caroline, trans. *Psalms of the Sisters*. London: Oxford University Press Warehouse, 1909. (Reprinted as *Poems of Early Buddhist Nuns (Therīgāthā)*, eds. C. A. F. Rhys-Davids and K. R. Norman, [Oxford: Pali Text Society, 1989]).

Robinson, Phyllis. "A Feasibility Study of the Potential Role of the Khmer Nun as Mental Health Counselor." Unpublished monograph, 1990.

Rodd, Laurel Rasplica. "Nichiren's Teachings to Women." *Selected Papers in Asian Studies*, new series, 5. (1979).

Sakya, Jamyang and Julie Emery. *Princess in the Land of Snows: The Life of Jamyang Sakya in Tibet*. Boston: Shambhala, 1988.

Schuster [Barnes], Nancy. "Changing the Female Body: Wise Women and the Bodhisattva Career in Some *Mahāratna-kūṭasūtras*." *Journal of the International Association of Buddhist Studies* 4.1 (1981): 33–46.

Shakya, Min Bahadur. *The Life and Contribution of the Nepalese Princess Bhrikuti Devi to Tibetan History*. Delhi: Book Faith India, 1997.

Shaw, Miranda. *Passionate Enlightenment: Women in Tantric Buddhism*. Princeton: Princeton University Press, 1994.

Silmāthā, Pānadure Vajirā. *The Enlightened Nuns of the Buddha Era*. Colombo: National Book Development Council of Sri Lanka, 1994.

Spiro, Melford. *Buddhism and Society: A Great Tradition and Its Burmese Vicissitudes*. New York: Harper & Row, 1970.

Sunim, Samu. "Eunyeong Sunim and the Founding of Pomun-Jong, the First Independent Bhikshuni Order." *Women & Buddhism*. Toronto: Zen Lotus Society, 1986.

Talim, T. V. "Buddhist Nuns and Disciplinary Rules." *Journal of the University of Bombay*, 34.2 (1965): 98–137.

Taring, Rinchen Dolma. *Daughter of Tibet*. New Delhi: Allied Publishers, 1970.

Tsai, Kathryn A. "Biographies of Buddhist Nuns." *Cahiers d'Extrême-Asie* (Revue de l'École Française d'Extrême-Orient), 1985.

———. "The Chinese Buddhist Monastic Order for Women: The First Two Centuries." *Historical Reflections/Réflexions Historiques* 8.3 (Fall 1981): 1–20.

———. *Lives of the Nuns: Biographies of Chinese Buddhist Nuns from the Fourth to Sixth Centuries*. Honolulu: University of Hawaii Press, 1994.

Tsomo, Karma Lekshe. *Buddhism through American Women's Eyes*. Ithaca, N.Y.: Snow Lion Publications, 1995.

———. *Sakyadhita: Daughters of the Buddha*. Ithaca, N.Y.: Snow Lion Publications, 1988.

———. *Sisters in Solitude: Two Traditions of Buddhist Monastic Ethics for Women, A Comparative Analysis of the Dharmagupta and Mūlasarvāstivāda Bhikṣuṇī Prātimokṣa Sūtras*. Albany: State University of New York Press, 1996.

———. "Tibetan Nuns and Nunneries." In Janice D. Willis, ed., *Feminine Ground: Essays on Women and Tibet*. Ithaca, N.Y.: Snow Lion Publications, 1989, 118–34.

Tulku, Tarthang. *Mother of Knowledge: The Enlightenment of Ye-shes mTsho-rgyal*, ed. Jane Wilhelms, Berkeley, Calif.: Dharma Publishing, 1983.

Uchino, Kumiko. "The Status Elevation Process of Sōtō Sect Nuns in Modern Japan." In Diana Eck and Devaki Jain, eds., *Speaking of Faith: Global Perspectives on Women, Religion and Social Change.* Philadelphia: New Society Publishers, 1987, 159–73.

Van Esterik, John. "Women Meditation Teachers in Thailand." In Penny Van Esterik, ed., *Women of Southeast Asia.* DeKalb, Ill.: Northern Illinois University, Center for Southeast Asian Studies, 1982, 33–41.

Van Esterik, Penny. "Laywomen in Theravāda Buddhism." In Penny Van Esterik, ed., *Women of Southeast Asia.* DeKalb, Ill.: Northern Illinois University, Center for Southeast Asian Studies, 1982, 55–78.

Waldschmidt, Ernst. *Bruchstücke des Bhikṣuṇī-Prātimokṣa der Sarvāstivādins.* Leipzig: Deutsche Morgenlandische Gesellschaft, 1926.

Watkins, Joanne C. *Spirited Women: Gender, Religion, and Cultural Identity in the Nepal Himalaya.* New York: Columbia University Press, 1996.

Wawrytko, Sandra A. "Sexism in the Early Sangha: Its Social Basis and Philosophical Dissolution." In Charles Wei-hsun Fu and Sandra A. Wawrytko, eds., *Buddhist Behavioral Codes and the Modern World.* Westport, Conn.: Greenwood Press, 1994, 277–96.

Wayman, Alex and Hideko. *The Lion's Roar of Queen Srīmālā.* Delhi: Motilal Banarsidass, 1974.

Willis, Janice D. *Feminine Ground: Essays on Women and Tibet.* Ithaca, N.Y.: Snow Lion Publications, 1989.

———. "Nuns and Benefactresses: The Role of Women in the Development of Buddhism." In Yvonne Haddad and Ellison Findlay, eds., *Women, Religion and Social Change.* Albany: State University of New York Press, 1985, 59–85.

Willson, Martin. *In Praise of Tara: Songs to the Saviouress.* London: Wisdom Publications, 1986.

Win, Kanbawza. *Daw Aung San Suu Kyi, the Nobel Laureate: A Burmese Perspective.* Bangkok: CPDSK Publications, 1992.

Contributors

Paula K. R. Arai is currently Assistant Professor of Religious Studies and East Asian Studies at Vanderbilt University. She received her Ph.D. from Harvard University and is the author of *Women Living Zen: Japanese Buddhist Nuns.*

Cait Collins holds degrees in Religious Studies and Tibetan Language from the School of Oriental and African Studies, London University. She is trained in traditional Chinese medicine.

Lorna Dewaraja is retired Associate Professor of History at the University of Peradeniya. She is currently Director of the Bandaranaike International Diplomatic Training Institute in Colombo. Her books include *Sri Lanka Through French Eyes* and *The Political Administration and Social Structure of The Kandyan Kingdom of Sri Lanka.*

Beata Grant is Associate Professor of Chinese Language and Literature at Washington University in St. Louis. She is the author of *Mount Lu Revisited: Buddhism in the Life and Writings of Su Shih* and several articles on women and religion in pre-modern China.

Rita M. Gross, professor of Philosophy and Religious Studies at the University of Wisconsin-Eau Claire, is a longtime Buddhist practitioner and senior teacher with Shambhala Meditation Centers. She is author of *Buddhism After Patriarchy: A Feminist History, Analysis, and Reconstruction of Buddhism; Feminism and Religion—An Introduction;* and *Sorting and Settling: Buddhist Perspectives on Contemporary Social and Religious Issues.*

Theja Gunawardhana, late poet and founding member of the Sri Lanka Women's Institute (Mahila Samithi), served as Sri Lankan ambassador to Pakistan and Iran from 1974–79. She has written books as diverse as *China's Cultural Revolution, Mystic and Occult Christianity, Theosophy and Islam,* and *Ravana Dynasty in Sri Lanka's Dance Drama.*

Elizabeth J. Harris is Executive Secretary for Inter-Faith Relations of the Methodist Church, U.K. She completed her doctorate on the British encounter with Buddhism in fourteenth-century Sri Lanka at the Postgraduate Institute of Pāli and Buddhist Studies, University of Kelaniya. She wrote and presented the series, "The Way of the Buddha," for the BBC World Service.

Anne C. Klein is Professor of Religious Studies at Rice University and founding director of Dawn Mountain, a Tibetan temple, community center, and research institute in Houston. Her books include *Knowledge and Liberation; Knowing, Naming and Negation; Path to the Middle;* and *Meeting the Great Bliss Queen: Buddhists, Feminists, and the Art of the Self.* She is currently working on a Dzogchen text from the Bon tradition.

Sarah Pinto is a doctoral candidate in Antropology at Princeton University. Her research focus is traditional childbirth practices among the women of South Asia. She is currently conducting field research on midwifery in Bihar, India.

Sanghadevi, nee Christine Seymour, was ordained into the Western Buddhist Order in 1977. In 1993, she was responsible for ordaining other women into the WBO. She presently lives in Birmingham, U.K., as part of the Preceptor's college, a group of close disciples of Sangharakshita (founder of WBO) who now guide the movement.

Sara Shneiderman is an anthropologist, writer, and educator based in Nepal. She coordinates experiential education programs for American students and conducts research on women's religious experience in the Himalayas. She hold degrees in anthropology and religious studies from Brown University.

Hae-ju Sunim (Ho-Ryeon Jeon) is Associate Professor of Buddhist Studies at Dongguk University in Seoul. She was a visiting lecturer at Harvard University from 1996–97 and is a member of the eleventh Central Committee of the Chogyre Order of Korean Buddhism.

Karma Lekshe Tsomo teaches at Chaminade University and is an Affiliate at the East-West Center, Honolulu. Her books include *Sakyadhita: Daughters of the Buddha; Buddhist Through American Women's Eyes; Sisters in Solitude: Two Traditions of Monastic Ethics for Women;* and *Living and Dying in Buddhist Cultures.*

Senarat Wijayasundara teaches philosophy at Kelaniya University, specializing in the field of Buddhism and international relations. He is currently a visiting lecturer at the Buddhist and Pāli College in Singapore.

Janice D. Willis is Professor of Religious Studies at Wesleyan University. Her publications include *Enlightened Beings: Life Stories of the Ganden Oral Tradition; Feminine Ground: Essays on Women and Tibet*; and numerous articles on Buddhist philosophy and women in Buddhism. She is currently writing a spiritual autobiography.

Index